A Harmony of the Spirits

A

Translation and the

HARMONY

Language of Community

of the

in Early Pennsylvania

SPIRITS

Patrick M. Erben

Published for the
Omohundro Institute of Early American History and Culture,
Williamsburg, Virginia, by the
University of North Carolina Press, Chapel Hill

The Omohundro Institute of Early American History and Culture is sponsored jointly by the College of William and Mary and the Colonial Williamsburg Foundation. On November 15, 1996, the Institute adopted the present name in honor of a bequest from Malvern H. Omohundro, Jr.

Library of Congress Cataloging-in-Publication Data
Erben, Patrick M. (Patrick Michael)
A harmony of the spirits : translation and the language of community
in early Pennsylvania / Patrick M. Erben.
p. cm.
Includes bibliographical references and index.
ISBN 978-0-8078-3557-9 (cloth : alk. paper)
1. Language and languages—Variation. 2. Pennsylvania—History. 3. Pennsylvania—
Languages. 4. Language and culture—United States. I. Title.
P120.V37.E73 2012
409.748′09033—dc23
2011050214

Parts of this book draw on previously published work: "Book of Suffering, Suffering Book: The Mennonite Martyrs' Mirror and the Translation of Martyrdom in Colonial America," in Linda Gregerson and Susan Juster, eds., *Empires of God: Religious Encounters in the Early Modern World* (Philadelphia, 2011); "Promoting Pennsylvania: Penn, Pastorius, and the Creation of a Transnational Community," *Resources for American Literary Study*, XXIX (2005), 25–65; "'Honey Combs' and 'Paper Hives': Positioning Francis Daniel Pastorius's Manuscript Writings in Early Pennsylvania," *Early American Literature*, XXXVII (2002), 157–194.

The paper in this book meets the guidelines for permanence and durability of the Committee on Production Guidelines for Book Longevity of the Council on Library Resources. The University of North Carolina Press has been a member of the Green Press Initiative since 2003.

Frontispiece: Cover Page from Christoph Saur, *Der Hoch-deutsch americanische Calender . . .* (Germantown, Pa., 1761). Courtesy, American Antiquarian Society

16 15 14 13 12   5 4 3 2 1

For my wife, Rebecca — with love

Für meine Eltern, Manfred und Brunhilde —
in Dankbarkeit

Acknowledgments

The many individuals and institutions that have contributed to the completion of this book are linked through the one essential gift they have given
me—time. I offer them this volume as my heartfelt thank you.

As I am writing this, more and more funding for the humanities is being
cut, and scholarship has come under criticism bent on replacing careful
research and balanced discourse with divisive language based on stultify-
ing clichés. Even inside academia, the pursuit of knowledge and deeper
inquiry is being eroded by calls for measuring "performance." I hope this
book pays tribute and gives credence to the tangible and intangible bene-
fits of humanities scholarship and the insights into humanity and civilization it strives to provide. I thus thank the institutions that invested time
and money in my project. Most important, the National Endowment for
the Humanities and the Omohundro Institute of Early American History
and Culture furnished two years of postdoctoral funding—at the Institute
in Williamsburg—during which I had the opportunity to think, converse
with colleagues, hone my project, research, and write. These two years have
been among the happiest and most productive of my life. Other fellowships
and grants have provided crucial funding for travel and research during
key stages of this project: the Richard P. Morgan Fellowship in the History of the Book from the Library Company of Philadelphia and Historical
Society of Pennsylvania, the Franklin Research Grant from the American
Philosophical Society, and several Faculty Research Grants as well as a Seed
Grant from the University of West Georgia.

At the Omohundro Institute, I was privileged to enjoy a structure entirely
built to give scholars the place and time to work. As director of the Institute,
Ron Hoffman has created an environment like no other. He has graciously
and generously supported my project from my first colloquium through all
of its many stages. Publishing my book with the Institute is a great honor.
Fredrika Teute, editor of publications, has fostered a model of excellence in
scholarly publishing that many admire but few are able or willing to emulate. Her support of my project—commenting on many versions from dissertation to book manuscript, attending my conference presentations, and
informally talking over tea and coffee—has been unwavering and inspiring.
I don't think anyone else understands this book as well as she does. Simi-

larly, Karin Wulf and Chris Grasso are stellar scholars who have generously given me their time and expertise. Ginny Montijo has copyedited the book with patience, skill, and assiduity. Assistant editors Mendy Gladden and Nadine Zimmerli have answered endless questions and helped me with every detail of the publication process. Sally Mason, Beverly Smith, and Melody Smith made the Institute like my extended family, especially when much of my own was thousands of miles away. I tremendously enjoyed the time I spent with the other fellows at the Institute, talking about our work or eating dinner with our families: Wendy Bellion, Brett Rushforth, Sarah Knott, Alec Haskell, and Lisa Voigt.

At the University of North Carolina Press, I would like to thank everyone for their confidence in my project and for shepherding it through to the final product. They have produced a beautiful book of which I am truly proud.

One of the chief pleasures of researching this book has been getting lost in the archives. Vast worlds are still waiting to be explored, and I am excited about returning to archives and to the archivists who have helped me find what I needed and pointed out what I did not expect or know how to ask for: John Pollack at the University of Pennsylvania Rare Book and Manuscript Library, Paul Peucker and Lanie Graf at the Moravian Archives in Bethlehem, Jim Green and Cornelia King at the Library Company of Philadelphia, Don Rolph and Max Moeller at the Historical Society of Pennsylvania, Roy Goodman at the American Philosophical Society, Hunt Schenkel at the Schwenkfelder Library, Joel Alderfer at the Mennonite Heritage Center, Stephen Ness at the Lancaster Mennonite Historical Society, Diana Franzusoff Peterson at the Haverford College Quaker Collection, Amos Hoover at the Muddy Creek Farm Library, and Michael Showalter at Ephrata. I also thank the helpful archivists and librarians at the Houghton Library at Harvard, the Free Library of Philadelphia, the German Society of Pennsylvania, the Franckesche Stiftungen in Halle, and the Ingram Library at the University of West Georgia, especially Carol Goodson, who has always been willing to buy the books I requested.

The people who read my book manuscript invested much time and energy into my project when it was still in a rough and unwieldy state. In particular, I am grateful to Mark Peterson and Lisa Gordis for their insightful and supportive readings of my original manuscript; their comments are largely responsible for making the book readable. I have also profited tremendously from questions and comments I received at the conferences and colloquia of the Society of Early Americanists, the Omohundro Institute, the McNeil Center for Early American Studies, the Georgia Workshop in

Early American History and Culture, the American Literature Association, the Modern Language Association, the American Society for Eighteenth-Century Studies, and other academic meetings. Among these professional societies and organizations, the Society of Early Americanists is an especially amicable and nurturing group. Attending their biannual meetings is always like a homecoming for me, and I consider many of the colleagues there my dear friends. Especially supportive of my work through the years have been Ralph Bauer, Martin Brückner, Philip Gould, Rosemary Guruswamy, Carla Mulford, Tom Shields, and the late Jeff Richards, who is sorely missed by everyone.

Among the early Americanists, some have mentored me from the very beginning. David Shields once wrote the name "Francis Daniel Pastorius" on a note, commenting that someone who knows some German ought to work on this early American polymath. I received this note through my friend and mentor Reiner Smolinski when I was first looking for a master's thesis topic. Both Reiner and David have been among the most formative influences in my scholarly career. I would also like to thank once more my dissertation advisors Cris Levenduski and Michael Elliott at Emory University, without whose encouragement and expertise this project would never have moved forward. Winfried Herget at Johannes Gutenberg University in Mainz gladly directed my master's thesis on a topic that seemed rather arcane at the time. More recently, I have come to value deeply the professional and personal friendship of Oliver Scheiding and Jan Stievermann in Germany. I have received much inspiration from many outstanding scholars working on German radical Protestants and Quakers in early Pennsylvania, particularly Craig Atwood, Jeff Bach, and Aaron Fogleman.

At the University of West Georgia, I thank Jane Hill, Randy Hendricks, and David Newton, who, in their role as chairs, helped me balance my scholarship with my teaching and service obligations. Graduate director Josh Masters and the Department of English and Philosophy especially supported my work by regularly assigning me research assistants. Phil Purser, Ben Brown, Matt Sherling, and Lisa Cunningham provided invaluable support at various stages of the project. Among my students stand out the members of the most challenging and exciting course I have taught, a graduate seminar on utopian experiments in early America. I especially thank Jade Kierbow, Amy Ellison, and April Oglesbee, who were excited to work on radical German mystics.

My family, above all, has given me love, time, and encouragement unconditionally and most generously. My parents, Manfred and Brunhilde Erben, have been supporters of my intellectual and professional growth throughout my life, even though they cannot read most of what I write in English. They simply find joy in the stories I tell about the subjects of my book. They have always supported my decision to follow the many people from my native Westerwald area who decided to pack up everything and move to America more than three hundred years ago. I am grateful to my sister, Marion, because I know that my parents are always in good hands. I am also proud of her for going back to university. In recent years, I have received the most joy from the people one might consider the greatest distraction from one's professional life — my beautiful children, Samuel and Ruby. I love that they have no idea what the book their Papa has been working on for so long is really about. For them, I matter on an entirely different level, and the time spent with them has been infinitely more important than any book could ever be.

The person most affected by my working on this book has been my wife, Rebecca. From taking time away from her own academic career to support me, to moving to Williamsburg, to running the family during my many research trips, to taking the kids to the park on the weekends so I could write — her generosity in giving me time and support has been boundless. Yet, ultimately, she also did me the greatest service in telling me when it was time to stop working on the project. Our beings are intertwined professionally and spiritually in this book. Her support and dedication mean everything to me. Because of her, the conclusion of a project that has claimed such a large part of my life does not fill me with trepidation. My feelings for her and our marriage are best summed up in the words of Margaret Fuller: "Two persons love in one another the future good which they aid one another to unfold."

Contents

Illustrations

Editorial Note

Unless otherwise noted, translations are by the author. Usually, German and other non-English quotations are supplied in the footnotes. Occasionally, I provide short portions of the original in parentheses in the main text when the analysis directly concerns semantic differences. In my translations, I strove to represent as much as possible the meaning of the original, even if that sometimes meant changing the wording slightly. Like the translators I study in this book, my method of translation stresses felicity to the spirit rather than to the letter.

My transcription of original source material (in manuscript and print) generally follows the approach laid out in Mary-Jo Kline and Susan Holbrook Perdue, *A Guide to Documentary Editing*, 3d ed. (Charlottesville, Va., 2008); thus, I have kept editorial changes and intrusions to a minimum and retained most spelling errors or idiosyncrasies of early modern German and English orthography, except in cases where they would have confused the meaning. I have made several changes to adapt the original material to modern typography and to create greater ease of reading. I always changed the long *s* common in both English and German to the modern *s*.

The differences between the German handwriting and Fraktur printing (also known as Gothic type) and modern roman handwriting and type (used in both English and German) are significant and required several changes in the transcription process. In some fonts, the umlaut is represented by a small *e* printed above the vowel; this is changed to the modern way of representing the umlaut (which was already used by many printers in the early modern period). In German print and handwriting, double consonants were sometimes designated by a straight line above one consonant; this was used to save space (especially in manuscript) and is changed here to the double consonant. German variant spellings of English proper names and terms are retained in the footnotes, for example, "Pensilvania" or "Pennsilvania" for "Pennsylvania." I also changed some punctuation to adhere more to present conventions and thus avoid potential misunderstandings. For example, the virgule (/) was frequently used in the place where modern German punctuation uses a comma (especially in titles); I replaced all with commas (and occasionally semicolons or periods). Also, I changed all double hyphens (=) to single hyphens (-).

Early modern German handwriting is notoriously difficult to decipher for current readers. Whenever I was in doubt about the particular spelling but could decipher the word, I abided by modern conventions or made the spelling consistent with usages by the same author elsewhere in the manuscript source. In the footnotes, German and other foreign-language titles follow modern bibliographical conventions.

"Unter der Leitung seines Geistes"

SPIRITUAL TRANSLATION IN EARLY AMERICA

n a manuscript report written in 1819, Moravian missionary John Heckewelder (1743–1823) outlined a controversy among Moravian missionaries about which translation of the passion story from the Gospel of John should be used in the field: the translation by the late David Zeisberger (1721–1808) or a more recent one by Christian Frederick Dencke (1775–1838), who had criticized Zeisberger's translations for inaccuracies in the Delaware language. Heckewelder had sent a circular letter to all missionaries and then summarized the responses. Heckewelder and his respondents credited Zeisberger with nothing less than the discovery of spiritual correspondences between the German and Delaware languages. Missionary Johannes Renatus Schmidt (1784–1852), for instance, argued that Zeisberger's work was created "with much prayer and pleading to God, and under the guidance of his spirit." Much like the ancient translators of the Septuagint claimed divine inspiration in translating the Old Testament from Hebrew to Greek, Zeisberger's followers asserted a similar rationale for a linguist they termed "the first, the best translator." These and other responses harked back to seventeenth-century linguistic projects such as Jan Amos Comenius's attempts to create a universal language *(panglottia)* and the Rosicrucian claim to have discovered a new language. Heckewelder and other missionaries believed that Zeisberger had tapped into or even created a pure, spiritual language. In a new nation increasingly seeking to remove native Americans west of the Mississippi, Moravian missionaries such as Zeisberger and Heckewelder pursued a utopian program of linguistic and religious community building with and among Indian groups like the Delawares; crucially, their vision relied on early modern theories of linguistic and spiritual correspondences facilitated through translation.[1]

1. John Heckewelder, "Pro memoria; an Br. Seidel gerichtet, nach belieben zu gebrauchen [Comments on translation of passion story from Gospel of John by Zeisberger and Dencke], May 9, 1819,"

Esoteric, mystical, and utopian visions of reestablishing unity and peace for humankind have enjoyed renewed currency throughout history, especially in moments of conflict and war. The Neoplatonist idealism that informed seventeenth-century religious and linguistic reformers, as well as the Moravians' dream of building spiritual community among the North American Indians, reemerged during periods otherwise marked by utilitarian, empiricist, or even relativistic approaches to language and the relationship between culturally and ethnically different groups. In the turbulent environment of post–World War I Germany, the philosopher, sociologist, literary critic, and translator Walter Benjamin (1892–1940) pursued a similarly utopian vision of language and translation. In his 1923 essay "The Task of the Translator," Benjamin formulated his concept of pure language, grounded in Jewish mysticism and the Kabbalah. Kabbalist language theory sought to uncover mystical connections between all languages and an original, holy tongue. For Benjamin, this relatedness or kinship resided in "the intention underlying each language as a whole—an intention, however, which no single language can attain by itself but which is realized only by the totality of their intentions supplementing each other: pure language." The task of the translator was to integrate multiple tongues into one true language. Benjamin found this pure language "concealed in concentrated fashion in translations." Although translation theory usually distinguishes between original and translation, Benjamin compared *both* sides to "fragments [that] are part of a vessel"—equally significant pieces of a broken and scattered whole. Just as the goal of mystical union is a losing of the self through oneness with God, Benjamin saw as the goal of translation the collapse of signifier and signified and thus the end of language itself.[2]

Although seemingly out of step with twentieth-century linguistics, Benjamin's mystical concept of translation has been reapplied by translation theorist Lawrence Venuti. Short of using Benjamin's concept of pure

box 333, folder 7, Moravian Archives, Bethlehem ("mit Gebet u. Flehen zu Gott, und unter der Leitung seines Geistes"; "der erste [der beste] Übersezer *[sic]*"). On the relationship between linguistics, ethnography, and Indian policy in the early Republic, see Sean P. Harvey, "American Languages: Indians, Ethnology, and the Empire for Liberty" (Ph.D. diss., College of William and Mary, 2009).

2. Walter Benjamin, "The Task of the Translator: An Introduction to the Translation of Baudelaire's *Tableaux Parisiens*," trans. Harry Zohn, in Lawrence Venuti, ed., *The Translation Studies Reader* (London, 2000), 15–23 (quotations on 15, 20, 21); Willis Barnstone, *The Poetics of Translation: History, Theory, Practice* (New Haven, Conn., 1993), 236–237; George Steiner, *After Babel: Aspects of Language and Translation*, 2d ed. (Oxford, 1992), 63.

language, Venuti ascribes to translation the utopian agency of creating "intelligibilities" or understandings between foreign and domestic texts and readers, thus imagining community between both: "The domestic inscription is made with the very intention to communicate the foreign text, and so it is filled with the anticipation that a community will be created around that text—although in translation. . . . In supplying an ideological resolution, a translation projects a utopian community that is not yet realized." Whether, like Benjamin, one alleges an a priori bond between languages or, like Venuti, hopes to establish such kinship, the goal of translation might be a utopian harmony between languages, cultures, and peoples—the creation of a spiritual language engendering community.[3]

Benjamin's and Venuti's concepts closely reflect the efficacy that many early Americans ascribed to the practice of translation and the work of the translator in creating actual and spiritual communities from the fragmented cultural, ethnic, religious, and linguistic groups gathering in the New World, specifically during the founding and settlement of colonial Pennsylvania. For his own context—the moral and political confusion of Europe between World Wars I and II—Benjamin deployed mystical, early modern concepts of translation in the hope of knitting a web of kinship between hostile peoples. Similarly, early Americans harnessed seventeenth-century ideas about language, translation, and community to confront seemingly insurmountable differences among races, ethnicities, languages, religions, and cultures. This desire to wield translation as a utopian tool is nowhere more evident than in the writings of Moravian missionaries to the Lenni Lenape or Delaware Indians, who had been dispersed and decimated by imperial and early national removal policies, land grabbing, and racial vilification. The ability of translators to rediscover and build a common, spiritual language for Euro-American and native American people alike reveals a persistent impulse in early America: the utopian desire to use translation and multilingual communication as potent tools for distilling a common spiritual idiom from the multiplicities of languages, faiths, and cultures.

Such utopian notions of translation, of course, gloss over the parallel process of colonizing native American spirituality and language with Euro-Christian signifiers. Moravian missionaries used translation in preaching

3. Lawrence Venuti, "Translation, Community, Utopia," in Venuti, ed., *The Translation Studies Reader*, 485. Also see Venuti, *The Scandals of Translation: Towards an Ethics of Difference* (London, 1998); Venuti, *The Translator's Invisibility: A History of Translation* (London, 1995).

and hymn singing to shape a spiritual and communal reality among native American communities and, in doing so, altered indigenous thought patterns and cosmologies. Although this interpretation is more in line with postcolonial theory, early modern people such as the Moravians were far from sharing a postmodern constructivist notion of language. Instead, many early Americans held a persistent belief in the correspondence between linguistic and spiritual systems built upon a language of a higher order, which might then be harnessed to create shared understanding between disparate groups and individuals on a concrete social and communal level.[4]

Heckewelder's report, for example, described in painstaking detail not only other missionaries' observations of Zeisberger's process of translation but also the functions of his translations in the personal and communal lives of Moravian Indians. According to Heckewelder's summary of Schmidt's response, the Indian helper Jacob (a bilingual Moravian Indian assisting missionaries and translators) explained the difference between understanding the words and the sense of a translation. Citing Jacob's words verbatim (albeit with parenthetical insertions presumably clarifying his meaning), Heckewelder wrote in his report:

> When an Indian says: *I don't understand it* (such as something that was read or preached, etc.), it is not to be understood as if he meant the *Words*, but the true *Sense*—(the *Spiritual Sense*)—for he [Jacob] said the following about Br. David's translations: "that the mistakes that occur in them only consist of endings in some words, otherwise everything was in *good Indian*, and is mostly being understood, even if not everything."

Although Schmidt's and Heckewelder's mediation complicates the interpretation of Jacob's words, Indian converts seemed to appreciate and comprehend Zeisberger's emphasis on building spiritual and cultural bridges through his translations, thus dispensing with excessive literalism or perfect grammatical equivalence. According to Jacob, Zeisberger's translations looked beyond mere words and grammatical structures to conveying spiritual meanings. Although Jacob and other native American converts had encountered the Christian gospel for the first time through Zeisberger's translations and thus equated their verbal quality with the Word of God, Jacob's bilingual abilities and his claim that Zeisberger had written everything in *"good Indian"* supports the idea that translation rediscovered hidden spiri-

4. Lawrence Venuti, "Introduction," in Venuti, ed., *The Translation Studies Reader*, 6.

tual correspondences and thus forged a unified language from previously scattered fragments.[5]

Even more telling is the reaction of Indian converts to attempts at improving Zeisberger's hymn translations, known to many Indians by heart. In a meeting, Heckewelder reported, the Indian Johannes Papunhank exclaimed: "'Brothers! Do not ruin our beautiful verses! Let us quit doing this! Whenever I sing, pray, or just quietly think about these verses, I feel close to the savior in my heart! Yeah, I even yearn for this when I am *feeding the cows* in my barn.'" Papunhank's pious expression was certainly domesticated to a degree that made him almost indistinguishable from a Pennsylvania German farmer whose faith, ideally, pervaded his most mundane activities. For eighteenth-century Pietists such as the Moravians, the homely image evoked in Papunhank's description confirmed their belief that true faith could only be found through a religion of the heart and a personal relationship to Christ.[6]

Moravian Christianity and its peculiar language appealed to Delaware Indians like Papunhank because it resembled a native American spirituality that did not confine religious experience to standardized, institutionalized, and abstract moments of worship but located the numinous in daily activities and even interactions with the animal world. Heckewelder's underscore of *"feeding the cows"* demonstrates that he considered this connection

5. Heckewelder, "Pro memoria," box 333, folder 7, Moravian Archives. In this passage, Heckewelder quotes Schmidt quoting Jacob; nevertheless, Jacob's presumed words are interspersed with Schmidt's third-person perspective and commentary, mostly in parentheses: "Wenn ein Indianer sagt: *ich verstehe es nicht* (neml. dasjenige was vorgelesen, — geprediget, u.s.w. worden,) so ist es gar nicht *so* zu verstehen, als meynete er darunter die *Worte*, sondern den wahren *Sinn* — (den *Geistlichen Sinn*) — denn äußerte er [Jacob] sich über br. David seine Übersetzungen also: 'daß die fehler die in denselben vorkämen, blos in Endungen mancher Wörter bestünden, sonst sey alles *gut Indianisch*, und wird mehrentheils verstanden, wenn auch nicht alles.'"

6. Ibid.: "Brüder! verderbt uns unsere *schönen* Verse nicht! Lasset uns aufhören *damit!* Allemal wenn ich diese Verse *singe — bete*, oder nur in der stille *betrachte*, so fühle ich die Nähe des Heylandes in meinem Herzen! Ja so gar ersehne ich dieses wenn ich in meinem Stall ans *Kühe füttern* bin!" On Pietism in general and radical Pietism in particular, see Erich Beyreuther, *Geschichte des Pietismus* (Stuttgart, 1978); Hans Schneider, "Der radikale Pietismus im 17. Jahrhundert," in Martin Brecht, ed., *Der Pietismus vom siebzehnten bis zum frühen achtzehnten Jahrhundert*, vol. I of *Geschichte des Pietismus* (Göttingen, 1993), 391-437; Schneider, "Der radikale Pietismus im 18. Jahrhundert," Brecht and Klaus Deppermann, ed., *Der Pietismus im achtzehnten Jahrhundert*, vol. II of *Geschichte des Pietismus* (Göttingen, 1995), 107-197; Johannes Wallmann, *Der Pietismus*, Die Kirche in ihrer Geschichte: ein Handbuch, ed. Bernd Moeller, IV (Göttingen, 1990). On Pietist immigration to Pennsylvania, see Klaus Deppermann, "Pennsylvanien als Asyl des frühen deutschen Pietismus," *Pietismus und Neuzeit*, X (1984), 190-226; A. Gregg Roeber, "Der Pietismus in Nordamerika im 18. Jahrhundert," in Brecht and Deppermann, eds., *Der Pietismus*, 666-699.

between daily reality and spirituality convincing evidence of Papunhank's sincerity. The closeness to the savior Papunhank allegedly felt in singing Zeisberger's hymns was for Heckewelder indicative of a spiritual language that reunited signifier and signified in a mystical union and ultimately dispensed with the need for human language altogether. Thus, Zeisberger's verses — a union of Delaware Indian words and Moravian Christian ideas — had the same effect when Papunhank thought of them silently and quietly completed his chores. Translation served as the catalyst of Papunhank's brand of heart religion and was thus elevated to the status of pure language. The spirit Zeisberger invoked during the translation process and apparently inculcated in the product was believed to move readers or singers closer to God.

The mystical enthusiasm in Heckewelder's report does not discredit this type of evidence; rather, it provides a window into the personal and communal meanings of translation in a religious context. Such moments of language mysticism allow current readers to glimpse a widespread faith in spiritual translation in the writings of German and English radical Protestants in colonial Pennsylvania. Like linguistic, religious, and educational reformers in seventeenth-century Europe, radical Protestants in early America believed that linguistic differences were largely the result of a breech between God and mankind; translation was thus the process of either rediscovering hidden links or establishing new ones between the divine logos and human language and between speakers of different languages, ultimately resulting in the creation of a spiritual language. Early Americans and European observers often employed the metaphor of America as a new Babel to express their exasperation over the confusing multiplicity of languages, religions, cultures, ethnicities, and races; behind the metaphor lay frequent investments in the construction of communities as antidotes to the heritage of Babel.[7]

English Quaker and German radical Pietist immigrants, in particular, regarded translation as one of the most potent tools for rediscovering under-

7. With the exception of Edward G. Gray's *New World Babel: Languages and Nations in Early America* (Princeton, N.J., 1999), most scholars who use the Babel trope, including Randall Balmer, James Axtell, and Marc Shell, neglect to explore what linguistic difference and the Babel story in particular meant to European immigrants, especially in religious terms. See Balmer, *A Perfect Babel of Confusion: Dutch Religion and English Culture in the Middle Colonies* (New York, 1989); Axtell, "Babel of Tongues: Communicating with the Indians in Eastern North America," in Gray and Norman Fiering, eds., *The Language Encounter in the Americas, 1492–1800* (New York, 2000); Shell, *American Babel: Literature of the United States from Abnaki to Zuni* (Cambridge, Mass., 2002).

lying connections between different languages and faiths. Instead of a liability, religious and linguistic difference in early America constituted the perfect mission field for a utopian project of reconnecting the divine Word of God and the fallen word of human language. Throughout the colonial period, many European immigrants and settlers believed in hidden and unseen links between human beings, between the Bible and the book of nature, between human languages purportedly confused at Babel, and between human language and the divine logos. These beliefs had a profound impact on the textual construction of Pennsylvania in promotional literature and on debates about communal cohesion and conflict throughout the colonial period. Seventeenth- and eighteenth-century discourses of community in colonial America were thus shaped by a range of Neoplatonist, esoteric ideas and questions: the relationship between human language and inspired speech, alchemical experiments and mystical notions of divine signatures, and a variety of secretive, hermetic, pansophist, and utopian experiments in early modern Europe.[8]

In fact, esoteric speculations and utopian visions for a universal reformation of human affairs—especially of human language, communication, and knowledge—prospered precisely in those places where the most press-

8. A growing body of work traces the transatlantic or circum-Atlantic transmission of mystical and esoteric, alchemical, and pansophist theories and ideas and examines their impact on early American sensibilities, intellectual movements, and social experiments. As Phillippe Rosenberg has shown with regard to the late-seventeenth-century Quaker antislavery movement, seemingly retrospective intellectual forces could yield surprisingly progressive social results; see Rosenberg, "Thomas Tryon and the Seventeenth-Century Dimensions of Antislavery," *William and Mary Quarterly*, 3d Ser., LXI (2004), 609–642. Specifically, I share with Rosenberg an interest in the influence of early-seventeenth-century German mystic Jacob Boehme on German and English radical Protestantism and, by extension, New World communal experiments. For other work uncovering the impact of early modern mysticism, esotericism, alchemy, pansophism, and early modern science on Atlantic world ideas and discourses, see Catherine L. Albanese, *A Republic of Mind and Spirit: A Cultural History of American Metaphysical Religion* (New Haven, Conn., 2007); Ralph Bauer, "A New World of Secrets: Occult Philosophy and Local Knowledge in the Sixteenth-Century Atlantic World," in James Delbourgo and Nicholas Dew, eds., *Science and Empire in the Atlantic World* (London, 2007), 99–126; Bauer, "The Snake in the Garden: The Esoteric Hermeneutics of Discovery in the Early Modern Atlantic World" (work in progress); John L. Brooke, *The Refiner's Fire: The Making of Mormon Cosmology, 1644–1844* (Cambridge, 1996); Neil Kamil, *Fortress of the Soul: Violence, Metaphysics, and Material Life in the Huguenots' New World, 1517–1751* (Baltimore, 2005); Sarah Rivett, *The Science of the Soul in Colonial New England* (Chapel Hill, N.C., 2011); Walter W. Woodward, *Prospero's America: John Winthrop, Jr., Alchemy, and the Creation of New England Culture, 1606–1676* (Chapel Hill, N.C., 2010). Much work is being done by historians of science, religion, and medicine in early modern Europe, but I am here primarily concerned with scholarship that has a specifically transatlantic and early American dimension as well as a focus on language.

ing issues of early Euro-American society were being debated, such as the heterogeneous religious, ethnic, and linguistic environment of colonial Pennsylvania. Seventeenth-century European theories about the origin and designs for the reform of human language flowered among individuals and groups who attempted to reconcile a continued belief in mystically inspired language with an Augustinian desire to create community among different Christian denominations and among "heathen" converts in native American missions. Common to these impulses was the attempt to counter the effects of Babel by gaining access to a spiritually fulfilled language and by teasing out convergences among different languages and beliefs. This spiritual language, however, was not identical with the universal, new, perfect, or original languages sought after by early modern linguists in Europe. Rather, in the multilingual and heterodox environment of early America, radical Protestants such as English Quakers and German Pietists sought a common spiritual language in the interstices of mystical experiences of the divine and their human expressions. Translation, therefore, became the search for correspondences between spiritual ideals rather than perfect linguistic or doctrinal agreement.

At the center of this search lay similar notions about a commensurability of language, meaning, and interpretation. For many early modern Europeans and early Americans, language was both fallible and at the same time able to convey divine essences. As all existing human languages seemed equally flawed in communicating divine knowledge and experiences, linguistic diversity presented no exacerbation or exceptionally severe case. In fact, translation and multilingualism offered solutions for the problem per se. Translators or multilingual individuals understood the fallacy of equating human language with divine truth. Translation asked readers to confront the fallibility of the linguistic signifier and to search for the permanence of the divine referent or signified. Whereas translators were intimately acquainted with this task, others needed to learn it. Communication about spiritual things always depended on the spiritual state of both writers and readers.

During religious and political disputes such as the Keithian controversy in Pennsylvania during the 1690s and the debates over war and defense during the 1740s–1760s, a common pursuit of divine essences, however, seemed to yield to a Babel-like confusion. Yet, the desire to find spiritual unity in the face of seemingly insurmountable differences inspired translators and other multilingual individuals or groups. In the writings of the diverse people of early Pennsylvania, moments emerge when difference did not disappear but rather became normal, acceptable, or even useful. Indeed, translation in Pennsylvania was so pervasive that people promoted it and took it for granted. Most definitely, it was not the exception. Between undeniable periods of conflict and confusion, Pennsylvanians (or early Americans more broadly speaking) experienced moments when a constant state of being in translation resulted in the gift of community. Such subjective moments did not exist among all Pennsylvanians or become the rule. Often, only textual expressions of the hope to reach such a state remain. This book invites current readers to imagine—as many early Pennsylvanians did—that from the multiplicity of voices in translation or communal singing rose a common language of the spirit.

INVESTIGATING EARLY MODERN pursuits of spiritual and linguistic harmony requires several theoretical and methodological adjustments. Most important, the visions of the radical Protestants who established colonial Pennsylvania in the late seventeenth and early eighteenth centuries contradict commonplace assumptions about the advent and spread of Enlightenment ideologies in the Atlantic world. Rather than constituting a waning, exclusively Old World mentality, mystical, radical Protestant, and Neoplatonist concepts of language and community formation in America prospered and thus existed in dynamic tension with Enlightenment empiricism. English and German radical Protestants transferred to the New World pervasive early modern beliefs in the impact of hidden and invisible correspondences (between people, languages, substances, and so forth) on visible and concrete social, political, and religious formations—such as the founding of Pennsylvania as a "holy experiment." A dominant historiographic focus on the transmission of Lockean liberalism and its flowering in the American Revolution has subordinated the great diversity of linguistic, religious, and intellectual exchanges in the colonial period to the seemingly inevitable ascendency of British language, culture, and imperialism. Recentering the translation and multilingual dissemination of utopian, esoteric, and other Neoplatonist visions of linguistic and communal reform dislodges this prevailing Anglocentrism and shifts attention away from empire studies as a hegemonic lens for understanding the early modern Atlantic world. An inquiry into linguistic and religious utopianism recovers the movement and textual communication of seemingly marginal groups such as German radical Pietists and appreciates their visions as formative for discourses and models of community. Esoteric and utopian notions of linguistic and spiritual community served as alternative approaches to specifically eighteenth-century challenges such as the spread of imperial rivalry and warfare, which threatened earlier visions of a Philadelphian experiment.[9]

This book takes seriously the manifold expressions of a desire for mystical union among early modern people who pinned their hopes for reform or transcendence self-consciously onto esoteric planes of understanding. Historicity, in this case, means carefully reconstructing the seemingly foreign epistemologies of those immigrants who carried with them from Europe ideas of the correspondence, transformation, and perfection of human beings, languages, substances, and even communities. Their visions were deeply rooted in ancient and medieval cosmologies that had been adapted by widely popular thinkers like Jan Amos Comenius and Jacob Boehme to seventeenth-century challenges such as warfare, the alleged sterility of institutionalized religion, and the rise of secular epistemologies. Granted, many people in early America thought of linguistic multiplicity as an obstacle and used translation as a means to a practical end. Yet the archival record is brimming with the utopian desire that translation — not unlike the process of metallurgic purification pursued by alchemy — could transform the multiplicity of voices in America into a single, purer language and into a more coherent and peaceful society. Iconic translations or moments of translingual and interdenominational exchange exemplified the hope that a common spiritual language could once again unite disparate human communities and humanity with God. For these groups, visions of spiritual and linguistic unity facilitated through translation offered the solution to conflict and division.

Early Americans deployed *visible* tools of textual and oral commu-

9. For scholarship privileging a master narrative of the unfolding of Enlightenment, Lockean liberalism, and Whig political theory from the late seventeenth century to the American Revolution and the rise of the U.S. nation-state, see Bernard Bailyn, *The Ideological Origins of the American Revolution*, enl. ed. (Cambridge, Mass., 1992); Robert A. Ferguson, *The American Enlightenment, 1750–1820* (Cambridge, Mass., 1997); Gordon S. Wood, *The Radicalism of the American Revolution* (New York, 1992). In American literary studies, even the revisionist criticism of the 1990s and 2000s has largely retained an emphasis on English cultural origins. See, for example, Myra Jehlen and Michael Warner, eds., *The English Literatures of America, 1500–1800* (New York, 1997); William C. Spengemann, *A New World of Words: Redefining Early American Literature* (New Haven, Conn., 1994); Leonard Tennenhouse, *The Importance of Feeling British: American Literature and the British Diaspora, 1750–1850* (Princeton, N.J., 2007). For examples of Atlantic world history as imperial history, see David Armitage, *The Ideological Origins of the British Empire* (Cambridge, 2000); Armitage and Michael J. Braddick, eds., *The British Atlantic World, 1500–1800* (New York, 2002); Bernard Bailyn, *Atlantic History: Concepts and Contours* (Cambridge, Mass., 2005); J. H. Elliott, *Empires of the Atlantic World: Britain and Spain in America, 1492–1830* (New Haven, Conn., 2007); Jack P. Greene and Philip D. Morgan, eds., *Atlantic History: A Critical Appraisal* (Oxford, 2009).

nication to create or discover *invisible* communal bonds. Literary strategies—especially translation, manuscript exchange, and multilingual singing—were believed to reveal underlying spiritual connections between individuals and disparate groups, thus serving as textual coagulants for actual communities. Writers, editors, and translators used prefaces, letters, inscriptions in printed matter, and other types of framing devices to shape the meanings of the production, circulation, and reception of translation among writers and readers in early Pennsylvania. Translating divine truths or ideals from one language into another, done right, could reveal and even create a common spiritual language. Done wrong, it might plunge communities deeper into a Babylonian abyss.

In disciplinary terms, this book stands between literary and historical methodologies and assumptions. Texts are not just referents to a nontextual world of ideas or social forces but are also powerful projections of an unseen reality. In a world concerned with the efficacy of language in forging spiritual bonds, texts were of primary importance. My methodology thus necessitates longer quotations as well as more extensive interpretive passages or close readings. German-language quotations have been placed in the footnotes for the convenience of an Anglophone readership, although I remain ambivalent about the implications of such a submersion. I invite readers to peruse these selections and compare them to my translations, searching for alternate interpretations. I hope my own interaction with my readers will thus mimic the continual practice of translation, scrutiny, and debate across linguistic and spiritual differences practiced by the people and texts I study.[10]

Pennsylvania, more than any other province, reveals the ideas about linguistic and spiritual multiplicity and convergence that radical Protestant immigrants brought across the Atlantic and adapted to conditions found in the New World. In seventeenth- and eighteenth-century Germany and England, ideas about linguistic and religious renewal developed interdependently. The translation and circulation of Neoplatonist thought concerning the effects of Babel and the rediscovery of a divinely inspired language engendered a broad enthusiasm to create Pennsylvania as a Philadelphian community characterized by translingual and interdenominational unity. From this impulse arose a promotional literature that described Pennsylvania (circa 1680–1700) as a translingual and Philadelphian projection of the

---

10. On the intersections between literary interpretation and historicism, see Nigel Smith, *Perfection Proclaimed: Language and Literature in English Radical Religion, 1640–1660* (Oxford, 1989), vii.

social, communal, and linguistic reordering of human affairs in the New World. Promoters cast the new province as an antidote to the moral degeneration of Europe. The Keithian controversy and its aftermath (circa 1690s–1700s) constituted a crisis of trust in the capacity to establish a harmonious society from disparate parts. Both sides in the controversy accused one another of suppressing the testimony and conscience of the opposing party, thus highlighting the attempt to unify both individual and communal expressions of faith in a single, yet normative and even oppressive language. The multilingual manuscript writings of German immigrant leader and polymath Francis Daniel Pastorius (1651–1719), on the other hand, demonstrated that a common spiritual language could be forged only by reconciling—rather than suppressing—disparate languages of the divine as well as different human voices. Specific strategies—such as multilingual hymnody and translingual manuscript exchange—amplified personal affection as well as individual visions of divine unity to a larger level.

By midcentury, external pressures of war and calls for defense threatened to dislodge earlier alliances between radical Protestant groups. Suddenly, imperialist and Anglocentric languages of communal construction eroded previously held concepts of translingual and ecumenical unity. At the same time, such pressures reinvigorated a common sense of persecution and a stance of spiritual—even physical—martyrdom among the various "peace sects" who had constituted the first groups to immigrate to Pennsylvania, including Quakers, radical Pietists, Mennonites, Dunkers, Schwenkfelders, and Moravians. A radical Pietist group arriving in Pennsylvania from the 1740s onward, the Moravians (or Renewed Unitas Fratrum) were compelled primarily by a universalist missionary agenda that sought to generate a global, Christocentric community through the translation of scripture, hymns, and other key texts into a multiplicity of indigenous languages. Throughout the eighteenth century, Moravian missionaries and linguists applied the Neoplatonist and Augustinian search for a common spiritual idiom popularized in the seventeenth century by Jan Amos Comenius (last bishop of the former Unitas Fratrum or United Brethren) to their linguistic work, especially to the translation of hymnody and the compilation of vocabularies and grammars for native American mission congregations. Similar to Quakers and German peace sects during the French and Indian War, Moravians continued to oppose war and the linguistic and racial exclusiveness of the rising American nation through a persistent search for a pure, spiritual language.

The translingual readings in this book open access to a larger movement in early America and across the Atlantic: the formation of spiritually coherent communities through translation and other cross-cultural forms of communication. Transatlantic communication networks — specifically situated in the international migration of German Pietist groups such as the Moravians and the mission activities sponsored by the "Franckesche Stiftungen" (August Hermann Francke's center of learning and social welfare in Halle) — facilitated personal relationships, promoted shared religious sensibilities, and even sponsored common practical pursuits (such as the trade in medicine), thus transcending cultural and geographical divisions.[11]

This book's focus on translation proffers a radically different image of early American history, culture, and social experience. In particular, an analysis of pervasive translingual relationships, communication, and communal discourses dispels the simplistic dialectic between assimilation and ethnic isolationism that has dominated immigration history. Scholarship as well as popular opinion about the history and impact of polyphonic and multiethnic immigration has perpetuated the xenophobic fears and assumptions underlying Benjamin Franklin's warnings against German settlers and German cultural influence in the 1750s and 1760s. Only recently, historians

11. For scholarship focusing on transatlantic communication networks, see Rosalind J. Beiler, "Bridging the Gap: Cultural Mediators and the Structure of Transatlantic Communication," in Norbert Finzsch and Ursula Lehmkuhl, eds., *Atlantic Communications: The Media in American and German History from the Seventeenth to the Twentieth Century* (Oxford, 2004), 45–64; Beiler, "Distributing Aid to Believers in Need: The Religious Foundations of Transatlantic Migration," *Empire, Society, Labor: Essays in Honor of Richard S. Dunn*, special issue, *Pennsylvania History*, LXIV (1997), 73–87; Beiler, "From the Rhine to the Delaware Valley: The Eighteenth-Century Transatlantic Trading Channels of Caspar Wistar," in Hartmut Lehmann, Herrmann Wellenreuther, and Renate Wilson, eds., *In Search of Peace and Prosperity: New German Settlements in Eighteenth-Century Europe and America* (University Park, Pa., 2000), 172–188; Beiler, "German-Speaking Immigrants in the British Atlantic World, 1680–1730," *OAH Magazine of History*, XVIII, no. 3 (April 2004), 19–22; Beiler, *Immigrant and Entrepreneur: The Atlantic World of Caspar Wistar, 1650–1750* (University Park, Pa., 2008); Michele Gillespie and Robert Beachy, *Pious Pursuits: German Moravians in the Atlantic World* (Oxford, 2007); Mark Häberlein, *The Practice of Pluralism: Congregational Life and Religious Diversity in Lancaster, Pennsylvania, 1730–1820* (University Park, Pa., 2009); Sabine Heerwart and Claudia Schnurmann, eds., *Atlantic Migrations: Regions and Movements in Germany and North America/USA during the 18th and 19th Century* (Hamburg, 2007); Schnurmann, *Atlantische Welten: Engländer und Niederländer im amerikanisch-atlantischen Raum, 1648–1713* (Cologne, 1998); Schnurmann and Lehmann, eds., *Atlantic Understandings: Essays on European and American History in Honor of Hermann Wellenreuther* (Hamburg, 2006); Wilson, *Pious Traders in Medicine: A German Pharmaceutical Network in Eighteenth-Century North America* (University Park, Pa., 2000); Wellenreuther, "Continental-European Scholarship on Early Modern North American and North Atlantic World: A Report," *Early American Studies*, II (2004), 452–478; Finzsch and Wellenreuther, eds., *Visions of the Future in Germany and America* (Oxford, 2001).

have begun to examine a variety of modulations in the interaction between different European settler communities—English and non-English—as well as native Americans in the North American colonies. By attending to the role of translation in creating communal ideals in early America, this book interferes with the cultural and political myth that language diversity poses a fundamental threat to communal coherence—both in colonial America and today. Translation assumed a central role in early American society because it reflected the daily interaction with difference while simultaneously providing a potent trope for the highest-order goal of repairing human divisions by discovering a common spiritual language.[12]

A harmony of the spirits emerged whenever early Americans abandoned a normative or exclusive language, position, or idea and began to explore correspondences between seemingly irreconcilable positions. This book un-

12. For Franklin's infamous characterization of German immigrants as "Palatine Boors," see his 1751 essay "Observations concerning the Increase of Mankind," in Leonard W. Labaree et al., eds., *The Papers of Benjamin Franklin*, IV (New Haven, Conn., 1961), 225–234. His May 9, 1753, letter to Peter Collinson in London was widely circulated among English luminaries and politicians; the letter specifically created the chimera of a German realm impervious to English cultural and linguistic influence: "Few of their children in the Country learn English; they import many Books from Germany; and of the six printing houses in the Province, two are entirely German, two half German half English, and but two entirely English; They have one German News-paper, and one half German. Advertisements intended to be general are now printed in Dutch and English; the Signs in our Streets have inscriptions in both languages, and in some places only German." The Germans' insistence on their language and the power of their printing presses thus made it "almost impossible to remove any prejudices they once entertain" (477–486 [quotation on 484]). On Franklin's attitude toward the Germans and the Charity School movement, see Patrick M. Erben, "Educating Germans in Colonial Pennsylvania," in John Pollack, ed., *"The Good Education of Youth": Worlds of Learning in the Age of Franklin* (Newcastle, Del., 2009), 122–149. For scholarship perpetuating Franklin's notions of German immigrant isolationism in early Pennsylvania, see Ralph Frasca, " 'To Rescue the Germans Out of Sauer's Hands': Benjamin Franklin's German-Language Printing Partnerships," *Pennsylvania Magazine of History and Biography*, CXXI (1997), 350; and Sally Schwartz, *"A Mixed Multitude": The Struggle for Toleration in Colonial Pennsylvania* (New York, 1987), 10.

For more recent scholarship on cross-cultural group contact, especially in colonial Pennsylvania, see Kevin Kenny, *Peaceable Kingdom Lost: The Paxton Boys and the Destruction of William Penn's Holy Experiment* (Oxford, 2009); William A. Pencak and Daniel K. Richter, eds., *Friends and Enemies in Penn's Woods: Indians, Colonists, and the Racial Construction of Pennsylvania* (University Park, Pa., 2004); A. G. Roeber, *Ethnographies and Exchanges: Native Americans, Moravians, and Catholics in Early North America* (University Park, Pa., 2008); Peter Silver, *Our Savage Neighbors: How Indian War Transformed Early America* (New York, 2008); John Smolenski, *Friends and Strangers: The Making of a Creole Culture in Colonial Pennsylvania* (Philadelphia, 2010). Excellent examples of scholarship focusing on the work of linguistic mediators and translingual contact are James H. Merrell, *Into the American Woods: Negotiations on the Pennsylvania Frontier* (New York, 1999); Jane T. Merritt, *At the Crossroads: Indians and Empires on a Mid-Atlantic Frontier, 1700–1763* (Chapel Hill, N.C., 2003).

covers a web of translingual and intercultural exchanges—both as utopian ideal and as concrete reality—among German, English, and native American residents that was spurred by the explicit desire to construct communities based on common ideals rather than linguistic and cultural exclusiveness. The individuals and groups depicted in the following chapters faced and sometimes overcame their fear of difference by continually translating between languages, sensibilities, and ideas in the hope of speaking like one another and thus speaking the language of God. Above all, readers, writers, and translators did not think of linguistic multiplicity as a curse but rather as an opportunity for overcoming spiritual divisions. Although theirs was not a proto-multicultural ideology that considered difference intrinsically valuable, they nevertheless believed that unity could be achieved by finding hidden, underlying congruencies between a diversity of human expressions, faiths, and languages. I invite current readers to retrain their vision and read like the many radical visionaries who hoped to realize in America their hope for a linguistically and spiritually unified society: with an eye for the unseen links tying together a multiplicity of human languages and expressions.[13]

13. For an innovative approach that considers translation as a "prism" revealing the multiplicity of meanings, especially as applied to the Moravian translations into native American languages, see Julie Tomberlin Weber, "Translation as a Prism: Broadening the Spectrum of Eighteenth-Century Identity," in Roeber, ed., *Ethnographies and Exchanges*, 195–207.

Reversing the Heritage of Babel

VISIONS OF RELIGIOUS AND LINGUISTIC RENEWAL IN

SEVENTEENTH-CENTURY EUROPE

he early modern age was marked by an intense occupation with a variety of linguistic reform movements, such as the search for a perfect, universal, or original tongue. Most endeavors to change the religious and spiritual disposition of European society during this period were tied to designs to reform human communication, especially the problems of linguistic multiplicity and the declivity between human languages and divine truth. Ranging from the universal language championed by Jan Amos Comenius to the Quaker insistence on plain speech, religious reformers perceived human language as a corruption from a divinely inspired tongue. The division of human languages—purportedly caused by the events at Babel—appeared to be one of the foremost impediments to the reformation of religious and social affairs. Facing the upheavals of the Thirty Years' War (1618–1648) on the Continent and the Civil War in England (1642–1651), religious visionaries across Europe hoped that unifying human languages with the divine Word and with one another would bring peace and social harmony.[1]

The Spiritual and Linguistic Meanings of Babel

Even before this early modern fascination, linguists, philosophers, and theologians had probed the relationship between thought, language, and reality as well as the ability of humanity to communicate spiritual or divine ideas. They asked to what extent human language represented the language of the soul and, in turn, the workings of God's spirit. Did the constituent parts of language—words, grammar, inflection—have any essential connection to the world, or were they merely arbitrary constructs? Seventeenth-century

---

1. Wolfgang Kayser, "Boehmes Natursprachenlehre und ihre Grundlagen," *Euphorion*, XXXI (1930), 545.

philosophical and theological positions on the origin of human language can be roughly divided into two camps that follow either the Aristotelian or Platonic traditions. In the Aristotelian line of thought, "language was a distinctively social creation that found no correspondent echo in the world of things; human speech was a conventional and arbitrary construct, differentiated by an unbridgeable gulf from the world it represented." Platonic linguists held to a "necessary or 'motivated' (usually magical) connection between words and the things they signified." These two theories of the relationship between human language and the world are often known as the conventionalist and the naturalist approaches.[2]

Most Neoplatonist thinkers tempered a purely naturalist position by distinguishing between inner and outer speech. The Hellenic philosopher Plotinus traced a gradation from the unified and ineffable divine Being, to the internal speech of the soul, to the outward, inadequate human word; true communication only existed directly from soul to soul. Building on Plotinus, the so-called church father Augustine formulated a distinction between inner and outer speech. According to Augustine's *De Trinitate,* human speech is anticipated by words uttered inside ourselves. This *locutio cordis* (inner speech or language of the heart) contains notions acquired through human culture, but it also retains vestiges of divine meanings. This inner speech allows humans to see the Word of God as "through a glass," revealed in the mental images accompanying our thoughts in any language. For Augustine, silently reciting poems, rhythms, and melodies was particularly conducive to unifying the inner, human language with the Word of God.[3]

Augustine also believed that the linguistic miracle of Pentecost practically continued within the Christian church. Preached to in their own languages, the "heathens" would unite with Christians not necessarily in one idiom but rather in a single faith. No language should be rejected as "barbarian"; that epithet applied only to human beings who could or would not praise God. The linguistic unity at Pentecost thus reflects one of the most persistent dreams of Western culture: to unify humankind in language

2. Hugh Ormsby-Lennon, "Rosicrucian Linguistics: Twilight of a Renaissance Tradition," in Ingrid Merkel and Allen G. Debus, eds., *Hermeticism and the Renaissance: Intellectual History and the Occult in Early Modern Europe* (Washington, D.C., 1988), 312. Also see Lia Formigari, *A History of Language Philosophies,* trans. Gabriel Poole (Amsterdam and Philadelphia, 2004), 15–38 (quotation on 38).

3. Formigari, *A History,* trans. Poole, 37–38; Augustine, *The Trinity,* in John Burnaby, ed., *Augustine: Later Works* (Philadelphia, 1955), 17–181.

and spirit. Within this intellectual and religious tradition, Augustine represents a crucial transition from a philosophical occupation with the origin of human languages in antiquity to an ethical motivation for the unification of all people. According to Umberto Eco, the story of the *confusio linguarum* evolved from an allegorical account of linguistic multiplicity into "the story of how a real wound had been inflicted on humanity, a wound that might, in some way, be healed once more."[4]

For seventeenth-century Neoplatonists such as the popular German mystic Jacob Boehme, the account of the Tower of Babel and the confusion of languages primarily designated a *spiritual* event and only secondarily a change in the linguistic makeup of humankind. At Babel, God had disrupted the original unity between human language and the divine essence of all things as a punishment for human pride. Most concepts of the original language—whether favoring Hebrew or some type of *Ur*-language—claimed an original isomorphism of the Adamic tongue (that is, the language spoken in Eden) with the created world. This original language purportedly contained an iconic link between referents or signifiers and concrete things or objects in the physical world. Adam, in other words, spoke a divinely inspired language that perfectly expressed the divine essence of all things. With language and the world of things unified, communication between God and humanity as well as among humans was inspired to the same degree. Adam's linguistic act of naming all living creatures mirrored God's original act of creation. Mingled with human pride, this unified language, however, enabled people to challenge God's sovereignty. God thus *created* linguistic differences in order to confuse this "iconic bond" between language and creation. The idea that the events at Babel marked the separation of human language from its divine origins usually tied the linguistic fall to the first fall into sin: both were caused by human wickedness. Accordingly, the Babel of Genesis (a place of linguistic confusion) was already the Babylon of Revelation (a place of moral aberration). Linguistic and spiritual confusion were of one piece; both resulted from the inability of human beings to comprehend and communicate divine truth.[5]

4. Augustine, *Concerning the City of God against the Pagans,* trans. Henry Bettenson (New York, 1984), 861; Arno Borst, *Der Turmbau von Babel: Geschichte der Meinungen über Urpsrung und Vielfalt der Sprachen und Völker,* 6 vols. (Stuttgart, 1957-1963), II, 395-396; Formigari, *A History,* trans. Poole, 43; Umberto Eco, *The Search for the Perfect Language,* trans. James Fentress (Oxford, 1995), 17.

5. Eco, *Search,* trans. Fentress, 17; Borst, *Der Turmbau von Babel,* II, esp. part 1 ("Ausbau"), 168-169, 210-211, 220-237, 385-404. Also see Russell Fraser, *The Language of Adam: On the Limits and Systems of Discourse* (New York, 1977); George Steiner, *After Babel: Aspects of Language and Transla-*

The presumed disjunction between human languages and the divine logos also constituted the central problem in debates over Bible translation. Discussions about the translation of scriptures reverberated with fears of linguistic and spiritual corruption because the books of the Bible were regarded as the unmediated Word of God. The most iconic moment of biblical translation was the production of the Septuagint, the first Greek translation of the Hebrew Old Testament. The circumstances of the Septuagint's creation are captured in two different accounts that highlight competing traditions in the history of biblical translation. One account emphasizes that diligent biblical and philological scholarship provided the best humanly possible approximation of the divinely inspired original, whereas the other account alleges that divine inspiration continued to occur during the translation process. In the first account, six Jewish elders and scholars in Hebrew law were gathered by the Egyptian king Ptolemy Philadelphus in the third century BC to translate the Jewish books; impressed with the results, the elders of Israel "ordered that 'it should remain in its present form and that no revision of any sort take place.'" Accuracy, therefore, was ensured by the supreme knowledge of these scholars, and consequently further changes were barred, resulting in a veritable original in the Greek language. In the second and more widely acknowledged account, seventy-two translators gathered in seclusion and were guided by divine raptures or prophetic spirit to endow the translation with the very same divine essence presumably contained in the Hebrew. The Septuagint represented a translation of the Hebrew into the *koiné*, the Greek lingua franca spread by the conquests of Alexander the Great throughout the entire Mediterranean. Thus, the Septuagint mythically and practically fulfilled *both* approaches to reversing Babel: reuniting human language with the logos of the divine and uniting human languages with one another.[6]

Yet the distinction between scholarly accuracy and divine inspiration misses a crucial connection between both approaches: in both versions, translation was the product of a *communal* effort. Similar to the Pennsylvanian translation of the Dutch *Martyrs' Mirror* discussed below in Chapter 6, the Septuagint was produced with the cooperation of a number of

---

tion, 2d ed. (Oxford, 1992); Andrew Large, *The Artificial Language Movement* (Oxford, 1985), 19–42; Rhodri Lewis, *Language, Mind, and Nature: Artificial Languages in England from Bacon to Locke* (Cambridge, 2007), 112.

6. Jonathan Sheehan, *The Enlightenment Bible: Translation, Scholarship, Culture* (Princeton, N.J., 2005), esp. 1–25 (quotation on 5).

experts and elders who endowed the translation with both scholarly and spiritual authority. Importantly, tradition holds that seventy-two translators assembled the Septuagint (seventy being the closest round number) in seventy-two days. Why the emphasis on the number seventy-two? Here, the translation of the Hebrew Bible into Greek symbolically provides a remedy against Babel, where, according to most traditions, a single human tongue was divided into seventy-two languages.[7]

The symbolism of seventy-two scholars reversing the heritage of Babel thus emphasizes an important dialectic in the history and practice of Bible translation and, more generally, in the translation of religious or spiritual writings—between division and wholeness, individual and community. Translations dealing with communal transplantation and formation in colonial Pennsylvania registered that the process of translation forever struggled with the division of meaning resulting from the separation of human language from the divine Word. For religious translations to carry spiritual essences from one language to another, it was not enough to grasp an *individual* vision. Rather, translation always had to unite the community with the divine spirit. This expectation placed a special burden on translators as well as community builders: translation needed to carry the spirit of one community into a language accessible to the spirit of another; community builders, in turn, needed to find a language that could unite the spiritual foundations of its disparate parts. Bible translation in the radical Protestant traditions that shaped early Pennsylvania was an emblem for spiritual communication overall.

Linguistic Enthusiasm in Seventeenth-Century Europe

In the early seventeenth century, Neoplatonic and mystical occupations with language culminated in the work of the German shoemaker, mystic, and philosopher Jacob Boehme (1575–1624). Boehme's emphasis on the practice of piety, personal renewal, and the individual experience of and union with the divine became one of the driving forces of the Pietist movement in Germany and profoundly influenced radical Protestants in seventeenth-century England. Scholars have traced Boehme's intellectual roots among earlier mystics, especially Paracelsus (1493–1541), yet Boehme avowed direct revelation as the source of all knowledge of the divine. His

---

7. Willis Barnstone, *The Poetics of Translation: History, Theory, Practice* (New Haven, Conn., 1993), 165–174.

first biographer, Abraham von Franckenberg (1593–1652), initiated the story that Boehme's first revelation occurred in the form of sunlight reflected off a pewter dish, opening in him a vision of the divine and triggering his voluminous writings. Boehme's work stood at the center of speculations on language, especially the nature and possible restitution of the Adamic tongue.[8]

Boehme distinguished between two original uses of language. Following John 1:1 and Genesis 1, the divine Word created the world, and Adam's act of naming all animals and plants (Genesis 2:19–20) mirrored this linguistic act of creation. Boehme called this first *human* use of language *Natursprache* (language of nature), assuming that Adam recognized the divine essence of each part of creation and expressed this essence in language. The letters and syllables constituting this Natursprache were not chosen randomly, but they expressed through their sound the original quality and harmony of creation. To put it differently, Boehme believed that in paradise all language was musical because it resonated with the divine essence of things.[9]

Boehme considered the linguistic confusion of Babel responsible for man's loss of the Natursprache. Like Plotinus, he regarded linguistic diversity as a secondary outcome of the loss of man's implicit knowledge of the divine essences of language. Rather than the multiplicity of languages, Boehme considered as the most painful effect of Babel the continuous arguing over "dead letters" or doctrine, which he identified as the hallmark of all institutionalized churches. In *Mysterium Magnum,* he writes: "Dear Brothers, if you did not wear the cloak of the language of contention, one might show you much more in this place; but you are all still caught in

8. On Jacob Boehme, see Martin Brecht, "Die deutschen Spiritualisten des 17. Jahrhunderts," in Brecht, ed., *Der Pietismus vom siebzehnten bis zum frühen achtzehnten Jahrhundert,* vol. I of *Geschichte des Pietismus* (Göttingen, 1993), 205–240; Peter Erb, "Introduction," in Jacob Boehme, *The Way to Christ,* trans. Erb (New York, 1978), 1–26; Rufus M. Jones, *Spiritual Reformers in the Sixteenth and Seventeenth Centuries* (Boston, 1914), 151–234; Hans Lassen Martensen, *Jacob Boehme: His Life and Teaching; or, Studies in Theosophy,* trans. T. Rhys Evans (London, 1885); Andrew Weeks, *Boehme: An Intellectual Biography of the Seventeenth-Century Philosopher and Mystic* (Albany, N.Y., 1991); Weeks, "The Part and the Whole: Jacob Boehme and the Baroque Synthesis," *German Mysticism from Hildegard of Bingen to Ludwig Wittgenstein: A Literary and Intellectual History* (Albany, N.Y., 1993), 169–192. On the notion of "signatures" or "Signaturbegriff" in Paracelsus and its influence on Boehme, see Ormsby-Lennon, "Rosicrucian Linguistics," in Merkel and Debus, eds., *Hermeticism and the Renaissance,* 318; Kayser, "Boehmes Natursprachenlehre," *Euphorion,* XXXI (1930), 541–543; Erb, "Introduction," in Boehme, *The Way to Christ,* trans. Erb, 6.

9. Ernst Benz, "Zur metaphysischen Begründung der Sprache bei Jacob Boehme," *Dichtung und Volkstum,* XXXVII (1936), 340–357; Jan Stryz, "The Alchemy of the Voice at Ephrata Cloister," *Esoterica,* I (1999), 142, www. Esoteric.msu.edu/Alchemy.html.

BABEL, and you are quarrelers over the spirit of the letters." Boehme thus fueled the period's widespread Babel criticism among radical Pietism in Germany and the Philadelphian Society in England. Drawing heavily from Boehme's ideals, the notion of "Philadelphia" promised an apocalyptic end to the rule of the orthodox churches and an "unpartisan brotherly love that vanquishes all denominational doctrines and characterizes the conduct of true Christians." Resting on Boehme's theories, the Babel criticism of the seventeenth century pursued the tandem reform of human faith and language.[10]

Boehme's influence on linguistic theory and radical Protestant projects of religious reform was threefold. At their first publication, Boehme's writings were widely received among religious visionaries such as Jan Amos Comenius, the Czech linguist, educator, and last bishop of the Old Unitas Fratrum (the precursor of the Moravian Church, or Renewed Unitas Fratrum), as well as the mystic and theologian Johann Valentin Andreae, the probable author of the "Rosicrucian Manifestos." Boehme's work spread in various English translations during the Interregnum (1649–1660), when it became particularly influential among so-called Behemenists and the Philadelphians. Johann Georg Gichtel's first comprehensive German edition of Boehme's works (1682) exerted a tremendous influence on radical German Pietism in the late seventeenth and early eighteenth centuries.[11]

Almost simultaneously with Boehme's first publications appeared in Germany several anonymous writings known as the Rosicrucian Manifestos—*Fama* (1614), *Confessio* (1615), and *Chymische Hochzeit* (1616)—

10. Hans Schneider, "Der radikale Pietismus im 17. Jahrhundert," in Brecht, ed., *Der Pietismus*, 405; Jacob Boehme, *Sämtliche Schriften* (1730), ed. Will-Erich Peuckert, 11 vols. (Stuttgart, 1955–1960), VII, 261 ("[Ihr] Lieben Brüder, so ihr nicht das Röcklein der Streit-Sprachen an euch hättet, so dürfte man euch alhie ein mehrers weisen; aber ihr seyd noch alle in BABEL gefangen, und seyd Zäncker um den Geist der Buchstaben"). Also see Boehme, *The Way to Christ*, trans. Erb, 165. On Boehme's ideas about Babel, see Benz, "Zur metaphysischen Begründung," *Dichtung und Volkstum*, XXXVII (1936), 348; Kayser, "Boehmes Natursprachenlehre," *Euphorion*, XXXI (1930), 527.

11. Jacob Boehme, *Des gottseeligen hocherleuchteten Jacob Böhmens teutonici Philosophi alle theosophische Wercken . . . Theils aus des Authoris eigenen Originalen*, ed. Johann Georg Gichtel, 11 vols. (Amsterdam, 1682). For Boehme's influence on radical Pietism through Gichtel's edition, see Jeff Bach, *Voices of the Turtledoves: The Sacred World of Ephrata* (University Park, Pa., 2003). On Boehme's influence on Comenius, see Craig D. Atwood, *The Theology of the Czech Brethren from Hus to Comenius* (University Park, Pa., 2009). On Andreae, see Martin Brecht, "Das Aufkommen der neuen Frömmigkeitsbewegung in Deutschland," in Brecht, ed., *Der Pietismus*, 151–165; Brecht, "Johann Valentin Andreae: Weg und Programm eines Reformers zwischen Reformation und Moderne," in Brecht, ed., *Theologen und Theologie an der Universität Tübingen* (Tübingen, 1977), 270–343.

which started a furor of linguistic, alchemical, and religious speculations across the Continent and in England. The Manifestos were allegedly published by a secretive society, the followers of the fourteenth-century German traveler and mystic Christian Rosenkreuz, who had supposedly gained insights into the divine secrets of the universe during his sojourn in the Middle East. Asserting that the society had already communicated with European heads of state and requesting that learned readers make contact with the "Fraternity," the Manifestos kicked off hysterical speculations about the identity of these "brothers" and widespread attempts to earn initiation into the society. Though Andreae eventually disclaimed the Manifestos as an elaborate hoax, they had appealed to the utopian desires of the time by claiming to have forged a "new language" that offered insights into the divine essences of nature.[12]

The title page of the first printed edition of the *Fama* foregrounds the utopian goals of the Rosicrucian Manifestos—the "Universal and General Reformation of the Whole Wide World." Although this call for a global transformation seems to contradict the secrecy of the Fraternity, the strategy was to communicate the Fraternity's wisdom and mystical insights to "all the scholars and heads of state in Europe" and consecutively educate future rulers in everything that "God allowed human beings to know." These rulers would, in turn, implement this wisdom throughout the world. At the end of the *Fama*, the writer claims to have sent out the manuscript "in five languages"—which are not named—along with the Latin text of the *Confessio* to all learned people of Europe, asking them to examine them diligently and to communicate their response either in a closed correspondence or to publish their opinions in print (the latter resulting in a veritable flood of publications by individuals trying to contact the Fraternity).[13]

Although the presumably multilingual dissemination of the Manifestos

12. Frances A. Yates, *The Rosicrucian Enlightenment* (London, 1972), 92; Richard von Dülmen, "Einleitung," in Johann Valentin Andreae, *Fama Fraternitatis (1614), Confessio Fraternitatis (1615), Chymische Hochzeit: Christiani Rosencreutz, Anno 1459 (1616),* ed. Dülmen, Quellen und Forschungen zur Württembergischen Kirchengeschichte, eds. Martin Brecht und Gerhard Schäfer, VI (Stuttgart, 1973), 7–14; John Matthews et al., *The Rosicrucian Enlightenment Revisited* (Hudson, N.Y., 1999); Christoper McIntosh, *The Rose Cross and the Age of Reason: Eighteenth-Century Rosicrucianism in Central Europe and Its Relationship to the Enlightenment* (Leiden, 1992); McIntosh, *The Rosicrucians: The History, Mythology, and Rituals of an Occult Order* (Wellingborough, U.K., 1987); Benedict J. Williamson, ed., *The Rosicrucian Manuscripts* (Arlington, Va., 2002).

13. Andreae, *Fama,* ed. Dülmen, 16, 20, 29. In a later publication, Andreae himself likened the response to the Manifestos to the confusion at Babel. See Andreae, *Turris Babel sive Judiciorum de Fraternitate Rosaceae Crucis Chaos* (Strassburg, 1619).

already signals the goal of overcoming linguistic divisions, the primary tool for reaching this end was the construction of a new language. Beginning with the account of Christian Rosenkreuz's travels, the *Fama* takes him on a journey of language acquisition; in learning Greek, Latin, and eventually Arabic (although Hebrew was surprisingly absent), Rosenkreuz epitomizes the Renaissance retrieval of ancient knowledge. Upon his return to Germany, he gathers three confidants (forming the original "Fraternity R.C.") to whom he dictates the entire account of his learning and insights. At this crucial juncture, Rosenkreuz makes the transition from learning from others in known, human languages to revealing his knowledge in a system of magical or divine signification. The *Fama* reports: "Thus began the Fraternity R.C. first and exclusively among these four persons and was constituted through these words, a magical language and system of writing with an extensive vocabulary, which we still use today to the honor and glory of God, and we find great wisdom in it." The subject of Rosenkreuz's revelations in this "magical language" was the "Book M.," a little-veiled allusion to the "liber mundi," that is, the entirety of the known world or creation.[14]

Not surprisingly, the three original members of the Fraternity were soon overwhelmed by the scope of this work and "decided to draw others into their society and fraternity," emphasizing the dialectical relationship between secrecy and communalism in the Rosicrucian ideology. Rosenkreuz's teachings are distilled into a mystical language that—like Adam's language in paradise—is expressive of the creation, thus enabling the members of the Fraternity to "translate" the actual "Book of Nature" (which was, of course, only metaphorically a "book," as its "letters" or "characters" were all parts of creation) into an actual, written text. Fixed into a written system by a small group of initiates, Rosenkreuz's knowledge is to be shared with "posterity" through a "special revelation." The writings also serve to protect his wisdom against any falsification, which could happen simply by changing "a single syllable or letter." Of course, the implication is that anyone changing a text of the "Book of Nature" was meddling with God's work. The Rosicrucian *Fama,* therefore, claimed nothing less than restoring the original isomorphism between creation and language and thus doing

---

14. Andreae, *Fama,* ed. Dülmen, 17–18, 21: "Also fieng an die Brüderschafft des R. C. . . . . erstlich allein unter 4 Personen und durch diese Worte zugericht, die Magische Spraache und Schrifft mit einem weitleufftigen Vocabulario, weil wir uns deren noch heutiges Tages zu Gottes Ehr und Ruhms gebrauchen und grosse Weißheit darinnen finden." For an elaboration on the history of the idea of the "liber mundi" or "Book of Nature," see Peter Harrison, *The Bible, Protestantism, and the Rise of Natural Science* (Cambridge, 1998).

away with the fallibility of human language, which was believed to obstruct human progress.[15]

Finally, the *Fama* relates the mystical transmission of Rosenkreuz's revelations to the seventeenth century. The elaborate trope of the discovery and unlocking of Rosenkreuz's grave "typifies the opening of a door in Europe which is greatly desired by many." The Rosicrucian brothers claimed to have discovered a door to a crypt, where they found an "altar" under which rested the body of Christian Rosenkreuz, holding in his hand a "little book written in parchment with gold, entitled T. [Testament or Thesaurus], which is now, after the Bible, our most precious treasure, and it shall not easily be submitted to the censure of the world." The comparison of Rosenkreuz's "little book" to the Bible is instructive; the *Fama* here claims for Rosenkreuz's writings the same status of divine revelation as was presumed for the scriptures. The reference to his corpse as "the beautiful and admirable body, unblemished and without any decay," links, as a double entendre, the body *and* word of Christian Rosenkreuz to the paradigmatic account of the incarnation in John 1:1, in which Jesus Christ is seen as the "word made flesh."[16]

The Fraternity also published the *Confessio Fraternitatis*, which promises initiates universal knowledge: "Wouldn't it be a precious thing if you could find, read, understand, and remember in one book everything contained in all the books that have ever been or will be written and published?" The *Confessio* surmised that God had placed secret characters and letters in the scriptures and in creation. Fulfilling the dream of rediscovering the full signification of the Adamic tongue, the Fraternity claimed to have taken their

magical writing from these letters and invented for ourselves a *new language,* in which simultaneously the nature of all things is being expressed and explained, which makes it less surprising that we are not so interested in other languages, because we know that they cannot be compared to our first father's, Adam, or Enoch's language, but are obscured through the confusion at Babel.

---

15. Andreae, *Fama,* ed. Dülmen, 21: "Sie machten auch den ersten Theil des Buchs M. weil ihnen aber die Arbeit zu groß worden und der Krancken unglaublichen zulauff sie sehr hinderten, auch allbereit sein newes Gebäw Sancti Spiritus genennet, vollendet war, beschlossen sie noch andere mehr in ihr Gesell: und Brüderschafft zu ziehen . . . damit die posteritet, so durch besondere Offenbarung künfftig sollen zugelassen warden, nicht mit einer Silben oder Buchstaben betrogen würde."

16. Yates, *Rosicrucian Enlightenment,* 44; Andreae, *Fama,* ed. Dülmen, 26.

The "new language" of the Rosicrucians expresses all things in nature; thus, it restores the original isomorphism between language and creation. It enables perfect communication among all initiates and makes the knowledge of other languages obsolete.[17]

The third of the Rosicrucian Manifestos, the *Chymische Hochzeit (Chymical Wedding)*, begins with a vision (apparently the first-hand account of Christian Rosenkreuz) that could easily serve as a metaphor for the multilingual promotion of early Pennsylvania. The purported author describes a vision of a beautiful woman dressed in blue, with golden stars all over, appearing to him in his study or hermit's cell on "an evening before the Easter day." The woman carried in one hand a golden trumpet with a name engraved that the author was not allowed to reveal and in the other "a large bundle of letters in *all kinds of languages,* which (as I found out later), she had to carry into all countries." He received a small letter that contained an invitation to a wedding—a trope for the Second Coming of Christ or the final reunion of the Church (the bride) with Christ (the heavenly bridegroom). Radical immigrant groups in early Pennsylvania felt they had received a similar vision that commanded them to aggregate for such a "wedding" in the wilderness of Pennsylvania, and promotional tracts were sent across Europe in *"all kinds of languages."* On an eschatological level, the *Chymische Hochzeit* represents the hope that Christ's coming would not only reunite all believers in a single faith but, significantly, unite the speakers of all languages, in "all countries," thus overcoming the heritage of Babel.[18]

Jan Amos Comenius (1592–1670)—the last bishop of the "Old" Unitas Fratrum and reformer of pedagogy and linguistics—probably shared more than any other seventeenth-century individual the Rosicrucians' utopian hope for a universal restoration of divine knowledge and an end to religious

17. Andreae, *Fama,* ed. Dülmen, 35 ("Wehre es nicht ein köstlich Ding, daß du also lesen kündtest in einem Buch, daß du zugleich alles, was in allen Büchern, die jemals gewesen, noch seyn oder kommen und außgehen werden, zu finden gewesen, noch gefunden wird und jemals mag gefunden werden, lesen, verstehen und behalten möchtest?"), 39 (emphasis added) (". . . von welchen Buchstaben wir denn unsere Magische Schrifften entlehnet und uns ein newe Sprache erfunden und zuwege gebracht haben, in welcher zugleich die Natur aller dinge außgedrucket und erkläret wird, daß es daher kein Wunder, daß wir in andern Sprachen nicht so zierlich seyen, welche wir wissen, daß sie keines weges mit unsers ersten Vatters Adams oder Enochs Sprache sich vergleichen, sondern durch die Baby- . . . Ionische Verwirrung gantz verdecket worden").

18. Andreae, *Fama,* ed. Dülmen, 45–46 (emphasis added): "In der lincken Hand hatte sie ein grosses büschel Brieff von allerley sprachen, die sie (wie ich hernach erfahren) in alle Land tragen muste." "Chymical" is an obsolete form of "chemical." The *Oxford English Dictionary* lists "alchemical" as the corresponding meaning from the sixteenth to the eighteenth century.

strife. Yet Comenius turned away from Rosicrucianism after the responses to the Manifestos reenacted the religious and linguistic confusion of the time. In his early work *The Labyrinth of the World,* Comenius allegorically described how the Rosicrucian phenomenon abused people's longings and led them ever deeper into spiritual darkness.[19]

Unlike the Rosicrucians, Comenius promoted the construction of an actual universal language *(panglottia)* and the acquisition of multiple human languages. Specifically, Comenius deployed language learning to facilitate universal education *(pampaedia)* and universal knowledge *(pansophia).* He understood his panglottia as a "way to end the confusion of languages." Like Boehme, the Rosicrucians, and other mystical language reformers, Comenius subscribed to the Neoplatonist notion that human language had lost its original connection to the divine signified. Broken ties between man, language, and God resulted in a virtual contamination of the whole "body" of human society and human affairs. Since Babel, human languages had been affected by "worms . . . [that] may be religious, political, economic or philosophical. . . . If they could only be eliminated (so that there would be one common spirit for the whole body), there would be real hope of a return to healthy living." Comenius targeted not so much the multiplicity of languages but the separation of human language from divine or spiritual truth. That Comenius regarded his universal language as a global missionary tool is revealed in the preface to *Panglottia,* written as a "Letter from the Continent of Europe to Peoples and Nations of Every Tongue Dispersed All over the World!" He describes his addressees as "Honoured Friends, Fellow-Dwellers on Earth, Beloved Kinsmen" and wishes "Peace and Salvation to You All." The eschatological motivation of his linguistic endeavors stands out even more clearly in the dating of the "Letter": "We are presenting our proposals six thousand years after the Creation in the Garden of Eden, 4344 years after the world was destroyed in the Flood, 4220 years after the Tower of Babel and the dispersal of the nations, and 1666 years after the advent of our Redeemer." The *Panglottia* thus distills Comenius's ideas about the nature and specific purpose of his universal language, which he requires to be "pleasing to the ear like harmony in music, associating things with ideas

19. Howard Louthan and Andrea Sterk, "Introduction," in John [Jan Amos] Comenius, *The Labyrinth of the World and the Paradise of the Heart,* trans. Louthan and Sterk (New York, 1998), 7–54; also "Comenius, Johann Amos," in Herbert Jaumann, *Handbuch Gelehrtenkultur der frühen Neuzeit,* I, *Bio-bibliograpisches Repertorium* (Berlin, 2004), 191–192; Yates, *Rosicrucian Enlightenment,* 167–168.

and ideas with words so closely that things are obviously conceived as they really are and are expressed in conversation exactly as they are conceived, without fault or omission or discord or error." He thus retained the mystical idea that human language—in conjunction with music—could recapture its original harmony with the divine essence of the universe.[20]

Throughout his life, Comenius conceived a number of innovative pedagogical projects and tools designed to simplify and generalize language learning. He tried to accomplish this goal by illustrating the common grammatical principles of different European languages and by linking linguistic study to concrete images. One of Comenius's most widely known publications was *Janua Linguarum Reserata* (also issued as a trilingual edition titled *Porta Linguarum Trilinguis Reserata*), published in England in 1631 as *The Gate of Tongues Unlocked and Opened, or Else a Seminarie or Seed-Plot of All Tongues and Sciences*. The *Janua Linguarum Reserata* was originally published in Czech and Latin and was designed to facilitate the learning of Latin as a European lingua franca. *Janua Linguarum Reserata* hoped to harness Latin for facilitating universal knowledge and to promote peaceful understanding among contending religious and political forces. Thus, it needs to be primarily understood in the context of the turmoil of the Thirty Years' War and in Comenius's forced exile from his native Bohemia after the Habsburg proclamation declaring Catholicism the state religion in 1627. The appeal of Comenius's textbook in a Europe shaken by warfare is attested by the eighty editions—in various European languages—published during Comenius's lifetime. In its various translations, the *Janua* became so widely used in many European schools that its dialogic arrangement of languages influenced foreign-language instruction for centuries.[21]

Comenius's *Janua Linguarum Reserata* and *Porta Linguarum Trilinguis Reserata* are practical linguistic handbooks built upon Neopla-

20. Jan Amos Comenius, *Panglottia; or, Universal Language: Being Part Five of His Universal Deliberation on the Reform of Human Affairs* . . . , trans. A. M. O. Dobbie (Shipston-on-Stour, U.K., 1989), 2–3, 12–13; John Edward Sadler, *J. A. Comenius and the Concept of Universal Education* (New York, 1966), 154–155; Sarah Rivett, "Empirical Desire: Conversion, Ethnography, and the New Science of the Praying Indian," *Early American Studies*, IV (2006), 24.

21. Sadler, *J. A. Comenius*, 267–268. Sadler quotes a survey conducted for the duke of Württemberg, which found the *Janua* in use "in more than 250 German grammar schools" (268). See Jan Amos Comenius, *Porta Linguarum Trilinguis Reserata et Aperta* . . . / *The Gate of Tongues Unlocked and Opened* . . . (London, 1631); *Janua Linguarum Reserata; or, A Seed-Plot of All Languages and Sciences: I.E.A Compendious Method of Learning Latine (as Also Any Other) Tongue, Together with the Foundations of Sciences and Arts: Comprehended in an Hundred Titles, and a Thousand Periods* (London, 1636). In Czech, the book was published as *Brána jazyků otevřená* (Leszno, Poland, 1631).

tonic principles. Two or three languages—in this case Latin, English, and French—are usually presented in parallel columns (Figure 1). This design was supposed to accelerate the learning of several languages; one English edition hyperbolically advertised the organization and method as "a short way of teaching and thorowly learning within a yeare and a halfe at the farthest, The Latin, English, French, (and any other) tongue, together with the ground and foundation of Arts and Sciences." Comenius's main structural innovation was the conversational presentation of words and concepts within a material, social, or religious context. Thus, the presentation of vocabulary was not alphabetical but followed the *nomenclator* principle, that is, the ordering of words according to thematic areas. The progression of topics or categories reveals that the *Porta Linguarum* was guided by metaphysical as much as pedagogical principles. Following a belief in a "separate creation of all the species" and Adam's subsequent naming of all animals and plants in paradise, Comenius chose subject areas and section titles following the account of the creation in Genesis: "Of the beginning of the World," "Of the Elements," "Of the Firmament," and so forth. In explaining this structure, Comenius writes: "I planned a book in which all things, the properties of things, and the actions and passions of things should be represented, and to each should be assigned its proper work, believing that in one and the same book the whole connected series of things might be surveyed historically, and the whole fabric of things and words reduced to one continuous context."[22]

Like Boehme, Comenius maintained that the power of naming presupposed the knowledge of the essential or divine meanings of the universe. In the first unit of the *Porta Linguarum,* the teacher tells the student or "Reader": "Hee hath laid the grounds and foundation of all learning, that hath throughly [sic] learned the nomenclature or surname of things." The parallel arrangement of three different languages signaled that a hidden concordance between words and the objects they designate existed equally in these three tongues. Following the mystical notion of "openings," the *Porta Linguarum* served as the key that would unlock the gates barring humankind from true knowledge. Comenius's method of spiritual and linguistic integration was twofold: horizontally, words, phrases, sentences, and ideas were integrated among the three languages on the page; vertically, the languages and their parts agreed with the divine meanings that Babel had ob-

22. Comenius, *Gate of Tongues,* 3, 4, 5, 7; Sadler, *J. A. Comenius,* 65; Will S. Monroe, *Comenius and the Beginnings of Educational Reform* (New York, 1971), 125.

PORTA
LINGVARVM
referata.

THE GATE
OF TONGVES
opened.

LA PORTE
DES LANGVES
ouuerte.

I. *Introitus.*

I. *The Entrie, or Entrance.*

I. L'Entree.

1. SAlue Lector a. mice.

1. GOD faue thee louing Reader.

1. DIEV te gard amy Lecteur.

2. Si rogas quid fit eruditum effe ? Refponfum habe , *Noffe rerum differentias , & poffe vnum quodque fuo infignire nomine.*

2. If thou askeft, whats to bee learned? haue for anfwer, *To know the differences of things, and to bee able to giue its name vnto euery thing.*

2 *Si tu demandes que c'eft, que d'eftre docte, m'a refponce, eft ou aye pour refponce, que c'eft,* Scauoir la difference des chofes, et de pouuoir attribuer a chacune fon propre nom.

3 Nihil ne præterea? nil certè quicquam.

3. Is there nothing more? Truly nothing at all.

3. *N'y a il rien d'auantage? Certes rien du tout.*

4. Totius erudirionis pofuit fundamenta, qui Nomenclaturam rerum perdidicit.

4. Hee hath laid the grounds and foundation of all learning, that hath throughly learned the nomenclature or furname of things.

4. *Celuy a pofé ou mis les fondemens de toute loctrine, qui a appris parfaictement la Nomenclature des chofes.*

5. Sed id difficile forfan?

5. But it may be, its a hard thing?

5. *Maic c'eft peut eftre vne chofe difficile?*

B

Figure 1. Trilingual Page from Jan Amos Comenius, The Gate of Tongues
Unlocked and Opened . . . *(London, 1631). This item is reproduced by permission of
The Huntington Library, San Marino, California*

scured but that might be reilluminated with Comenius's pansophist approach to language learning.[23]

Comenius's other popular linguistic textbook was the *Orbis Sensualium Pictus*. The book was designed to teach children Latin by coupling it with a vernacular language as well as iconographic illustrations (Figure 2). The images expanded the idea of contextual learning begun in the *Porta Linguarum* by appealing to sensory perception. In keeping with Comenius's Neoplatonist ideas, this textbook recalls Adam's original act of naming in Eden. The epigraph to *Orbis Sensualium Pictus*—taken directly from Genesis—makes the spiritual or metaphysical significance of the material images explicit: "The Lord God brought unto *Adam* every Beast of the Field, and every Fowl of the air, to see what he would call them. And *Adam* gave names to all Cattell, and to the Fowl of the air, and to every beast of the Field." Children beholding the images and pronouncing their names in English and Latin restaged the original moment of naming and concomitantly erased the disjunction between language and divine essences caused by Babel. The onomatopoeic transcriptions of the sound of the respective animals or actions, moreover, boiled language down to the basic emulation of natural sounds by the human voice. Structurally, images and their respective names are *not* organized alphabetically following their first letter; rather, they are illustrated by an animal whose voice or sound resembles the phonetic quality of the letter *A* ("The Crow cryeth"), *B* ("The Lamb blaiteth"), *C* ("The grashopper chirpeth"), and so forth. In resembling the sounds of nature, the phonetic qualities of the alphabet are—putatively—universal. Language is once more redeemed through its direct association with creation and the recovery of the Adamic tongue.[24]

While inserting words and their pictoral representation into the religious scheme of biblical creation, Comenius evokes grammar as the metaphysical and universal element governing language. Material images teaching nouns

23. Comenius, *Gate of Tongues*, 1. On Comenius's possible influence on Roger Williams's *Key into the Language of America* (1643), see J. Patrick Cesarini, "The Ambivalent Uses of Roger Williams's *A Key into the Language of America*," *Early American Literature*, XXXVIII (2003), 469–494; Anne G. Myles, "Dissent and the Frontier of Translation: Roger Williams's *A Key into the Language of America*," in Robert Blair St. George, ed., *Possible Pasts: Becoming Colonial in Early America* (Ithaca, N.Y., 2000), 88–108.

24. Joh. Amos Comenii, *Orbis Sensualium Pictus* . . . (London, 1659), 4. According to Patricia Crain, the *Orbis Pictus Sensualium* went through 244 editions between 1658 and 1964. See Crain, *The Story of A: The Alphabetization of America from "The New England Primer" to "The Scarlet Letter"* (Stanford, Calif., 2000), 27–37.

Cornix cornicatur.   á á | A a
𝕿𝖍𝖊 𝕮𝖗𝖔𝖜 𝖈𝖗𝖞𝖊𝖙𝖍.

Agnus balat.   bé é é | B b
𝕿𝖍𝖊 𝕷𝖆𝖒𝖇 𝖇𝖑𝖆𝖎𝖙𝖊𝖙𝖍.

Cicáda ſtridet.   cí ci | C c
𝕿𝖍𝖊 𝖌𝖗𝖆ſ𝖍𝖔𝖕𝖕𝖊𝖗 𝖈𝖍𝖎𝖗𝖕𝖊𝖙𝖍.

Upupa dicit.   du du | D d
𝕿𝖍𝖊 𝖂𝖍𝖔𝖔𝖕𝖕𝖔𝖔 ſ𝖆𝖎𝖙𝖍.

Infans éjulat.   é é é | E e
𝕿𝖍𝖊 𝕴𝖓𝖋𝖆𝖓𝖙 𝖈𝖗𝖞𝖊𝖙𝖍.

Ventus flat.   fi fi | F f
𝕿𝖍𝖊 𝖜𝖎𝖓𝖉 𝖇𝖑𝖔𝖜𝖊𝖙𝖍.

Anſer gingrit   ga ga | G g
𝕿𝖍𝖊 𝕲𝖔𝖔ſ𝖊 𝖌𝖆𝖌𝖌𝖑𝖊𝖙𝖍,

Os halat.   háh háh | H h
𝕿𝖍𝖊 𝖒𝖔𝖚𝖙𝖍 𝖇𝖗𝖊𝖆𝖐𝖊𝖙𝖍
    𝖔𝖚𝖙.

Mus mintrit.   íi íi | I i
𝕾𝖍𝖊 𝕸𝖔𝖚ſ𝖊 𝖈𝖍𝖎𝖗𝖕𝖊𝖙𝖍.

Anas tetrinnit.   khá khá | K k
𝕿𝖍𝖊 𝕯𝖚𝖈𝖐 𝖖𝖚𝖆𝖈𝖐𝖊𝖙𝖍.

Lupus úlulat.   lu ulu | L l
𝕿𝖍𝖊 𝖂𝖔𝖑𝖋 𝖍𝖔𝖜𝖑𝖊𝖙𝖍.

Urſus múrmurat.   mum mum | M m
𝕿𝖍𝖊 𝕭𝖊𝖆𝖗 𝖌𝖗𝖚𝖒𝖇𝖑𝖊𝖙𝖍.

Figure 2. Page from Joh. Amos Comenii, Orbis Sensualium Pictus . . .
(London, 1659). © *The British Library Board*

appear within short phrases coupled with a verb. Students would presumably process not only a static connection between word and thing but a dynamic relationship between representation and object, between thought and action. By joining the material images of the animals, their presumably universal sounds, their names, and grammatically simple phrases expressing the animals' verbalization, Comenius hopes to recapture Augustine's association of the voice (human and nonhuman) and the material images that accompany our inner language or silent speech. The simplest grammatical construction—a noun / subject coupled with a verb / predicate—is linked directly to nature and thus to the divine order of the universe. If grammar expresses the structures of the universe, then speech once more reflects the Word of God that called creation into being.

Comenius's Neoplatonist linguistics put a concrete foundation under the utopian visions proposed by Rosicrucians, Christian alchemists, and Behmenists. His proposals "envisioned the creation of a publicly acknowledged, collaborative network of Christian natural philosophers who would take on the mission of improving the world for the coming of Christ." Samuel Hartlib, a German educational reformer living in England, corresponded with Comenius and eventually invited him to England to create a universal college. Comenius arrived in England in September 1641, where he wrote his *Via Lucis*, a "detailed account of the overall pansophic program." Although Comenius's plans and visit to England were interrupted by the beginning of the English Revolution in 1642 (and he accepted an invitation to reform the Swedish school system), his impact on English thought on education, language reform, and an overall restructuring of human affairs was immense. His pansophist plans met with great enthusiasm among philosophers, theologians, and reformers ranging from John Gauden, future bishop of Worcester, to the mathematician John Pell. Comenius's influence was also reflected in the English book market, with a total of sixty-one separate titles and editions appearing under his name until 1700 and forty-four titles during and after his stay in England. His works for practical language instruction— such as the *Janua Linguarum Reserata, The Gate of Tongues Unlocked and Opened,* and the *Orbis Sensualium Pictus*—enjoyed the greatest popularity, with forty-six titles and editions published between 1631 and 1700. Comenius's linguistic works and theories, in other words, found acceptance far beyond a small circle of esoteric reformers and Christian alchemists.[25]

25. Walt W. Woodward, *Prospero's America: John Winthrop, Jr., Alchemy, and the Creation of New England Culture, 1606–1676* (Chapel Hill, N.C., 2010), 43–74 (esp. 57, 63, 72); Louthan and

Continental mysticism had influenced English speculations about language and religious reform even before the widespread reception of Comenius, Boehme, and the Rosicrucian Manifestos in the mid-seventeenth century. The medieval German tradition of the *Theologia Germanica*, often attributed to Johannes Tauler (circa 1300–1361), received renewed interest in Civil War and Interregnum England owing to its emphasis on an interior experience of faith. Puritan theologian John Everard (1575–1650), for instance, distinguished between letters made by human beings and a spiritual language that expresses the mind of God. In creating theories of divine signification, English radical Protestants absorbed German ideas and translated German writers proliferously. Translation became the primary means by which English religious radicals imbibed German mystical notions about language. Eventually, the interpenetration of linguistic and spiritual reform efforts advanced by Boehme, Comenius, and the Rosicrucians impacted the mutual vocabulary of those German and English radical Protestants who conceived Pennsylvania as a holy experiment.[26]

In the radical religious environment of the English Civil War and Interregnum, the works of Jacob Boehme—along with the Rosicrucian Manifestos—became some of the most frequently translated texts of German spiritualism, and they exerted a definitive impact on English radical Protestantism. Translated in 1652 by the alchemist Thomas Vaughan, the *English* version of the Rosicrucian Manifestos continued the pretense of a hidden society that had reached mystical insights into the divine secrets of the universe. The fictive publisher of the translation, Eugenius Philalethes, positioned the tracts in the widespread speculations over the nature of the Adamic language and its supposed isomorphism with divine creation: "After God had brought before him [Adam] all the Creatures of the Field, and the Fowls under Heaven, he gave to every one of them their proper names, according to their nature." The preface then followed Kab-

Sterk, "Introduction," in Comenius, *Labyrinth of the World,* trans. Louthan and Sterk, 14; Rivett, "Empirical Desire," *Early American Studies,* IV (2006), 24–25. For a collection of source documents on Comenius's visit to England, see Robert Fitzgibbon Young, *Comenius in England* (Oxford, 1932). Numbers are based on an author search for "Comenius" in Early English Books Online, Chadwyck-Healey, Feb. 20, 2009.

26. Nigel Smith, *Perfection Proclaimed: Language and Literature in English Radical Religion, 1640–1660* (Oxford, 1989), 115–143, 265; Ormsby-Lennon, "Rosicrucian Linguistics," in Merkel and Debus, eds., *Hermeticism and the Renaissance,* 318; Reiner Smolinski and Kathleen B. Freels, "'Chymical Wedding': Rosicrucian Alchemy and Eucharistic Conversion Process in Edward Taylor's Preparatory Meditations and in Seventeenth-century German Tracts," in Udo J. Hebel and Karl Ortseifen, eds., *Transatlantic Encounters: Studies in European-American Relations* (Trier, 1995), 40–61.

balistic and esoteric language philosophy, especially in its reference to hidden divine meanings underlying "words," "dark sentences," and "Signs and Wonders"—all of which the "Wisdom" presumably offered by the Rosicrucian society would penetrate.[27]

The first Behmenist tract to appear in English translation was Abraham von Franckenberg's *Life of One Jacob Boehmen*, published in 1644. Between 1644 and 1662, thirty-two separate translations of certain portions of Boehme's overall work appeared in England, but manuscript extracts circulated as early as the 1630s. Accounts of Boehme's reception and dissemination nevertheless vary. According to literary scholar Nigel Smith, "Boehme had a significant influence upon a handful of important sectarians who each gave their own forms of expression and shapes to Boehme's ideas, making Boehme's unique statements part of a wider knowledge." Many influential religious reformers and radicals—such as George Fox, founder of the Society of Friends—might have sounded like Boehme without having read Boehme directly.[28]

Theories of language, scriptural interpretation, and spiritual communication among the Society of Friends mirrored German mystical hopes for a reuniting of human language with its divine referents. The Quaker insistence that the spirit or Inward Light was the wellspring of all religious testimony recognized as truth closely resembled the Behmenist and Rosicrucian claims for a Natursprache or new language. The transformation of Quaker speechways in the mid-seventeenth century was driven by the desire to strip away the dead letters of orthodox Christianity and speak with the knowledge of the divine essences of the world. Most important for the transmission of such ideas to Pennsylvania, Quaker theories of language reform always had profoundly communal dimensions. Indeed, Quakers attempted to build a community, a Society of Friends, in which Augustine's inner and outer speech—the silent language of the soul and outward language of human speech—would be virtually the same. Friends would be filled with mutual love, because they were united by such a language of the spirit.

27. "To the Wise and Understanding Reader," in Eugenius Philalethes [Thomas Vaughan], ed., *The Fame and Confession of the Fraternity of R: C: Commonly, of the Rosie Cross; with a Praeface Annexed Thereto, and a Short Declaration of Their Physicall Work* (London, 1652), n.p.

28. Smith, *Perfection Proclaimed*, 185–186. Also see Jones, *Spiritual Reformers*, 190–234; Margaret Lewis Bailey, *Milton and Jakob Boehme: A Study of German Mysticism in Seventeenth-Century England* (New York, 1914); Wilhelm Struck, *Der Einfluss Jakob Boehmes auf die englische Literatur des 17. Jahrhunderts* (Berlin, 1936); Nils Thune, *The Behmenists and the Philadelphians: A Contribution to the Study of English Mysticism in the Seventeenth and Eighteenth Centuries* (Uppsala, 1948).

Language that was not filled with the spirit destroyed mutual cohesion and should thus be supplanted with silence.[29]

Fox and the Quakers rehearsed German language mysticism by believing in the fallenness of all human languages resulting from the moral and spiritual confusion of Babel. Friends conflated the Old Testament Babel and the New Testament Babylon to emphasize that the corruption of language and faith went hand in hand. Babel prefigured Babylon in the Quaker imagination, because the spirit had become divorced from the divine Word, necessitating the creation of human languages through convention. Human tongues, in turn, had been corrupted by pagan influences and the power structures of church and state. The Quakers' plain language was not only an attempt to expurgate signifiers of church and state authority and the effusions of human pride; it was also the construction of a new language filled with the knowledge of the divine. Thus, Fox's accounts of his divine openings and his vituperative attacks on the languages of Babel go together; immediate revelations provided access to a spiritual language that could replace the language of Babylon and undo the confusion of Babel.

Fox's most direct invective against the language of Babel / Babylon appears in his brief pamphlet *A Battle-Door for Teachers and Professors to Learn Singular and Plural,* which he authored in collaboration with Quaker leaders John Stubs and Benjamin Furly. On one level, the *Battle-Door* propounds the Quakers' idiosyncratic pronoun usage, designating *"You* to *Many,* and *Thou* to *One:* Singular *One, Thou;* Plural *Many, You."* By replacing the "you" used in early modern English society as a show of subservience toward power and status, the Quaker "thee" and "thou" represented an attack on "vain customs and fashions" in language. Beyond an attack on secular and sacred institutions of power, language was to be a re-

---

29. Richard Bauman, *For the Reputation of Truth: Politics, Religion, and Conflict among the Pennsylvania Quakers, 1750–1800* (Baltimore, 1971); Bauman, *Let Your Words Be Few: Symbolism of Speaking and Silence among Seventeenth-Century Quakers* (Cambridge, 1983); Rosemary Moore, *The Light in Their Consciences: Early Quakers in Britain, 1646–1666* (University Park, Pa., 2000); Hugh Ormsby-Lennon, " 'The Dialect of Those Fanatick Times': Language Communities and English Poetry from 1580–1660" (Ph.D. diss., University of Pennsylvania, 1977), chap. 2; Ormsby-Lennon, "From Shibboleth to Apocalypse: Quaker Speechways during the Puritan Revolution," in Peter Burke and Roy Porter, eds., *Language, Self, and Society: A Social History of Language* (Cambridge, 1991); Kate Peters, *Print Culture and the Early Quakers* (Cambridge, 2005); Nancy E. Rosenberg, "The Sub-Textual Religion: Quakers, the Book, and Public Education in Philadelphia, 1682–1800" (Ph.D. diss., University of Michigan, 1991); Hermann Wellenreuther, "The Quest for Harmony in a Turbulent World: The Principle of 'Love and Unity' in Colonial Pennsylvania Politics," *Pennsylvania Magazine of History and Biography,* CVII (1983), 537–576.

flection of an inner state; along with dress codes and simplicity, language reform contributed to the eschatological fulfillment of millenarian hopes here and now.[30]

But Fox also responded tersely to the linguistic theories and speculations of the age. Ultimately, humans should not quarrel at all about languages but aspire exclusively to a life of the spirit. Fox associated language with the mortal state of the human flesh; almost Christlike, human beings come into human form—and *into* human languages—only temporarily, to be redeemed by the ultimate "word made flesh," Jesus Christ: "All Languages are to me no more than dust, who was before Languages were, and am come'd before Languages were, and am redeemed out of Languages into the power where men shall agree." Yet Fox switched from the undifferentiated dismissal of "languages" to a distinction between "word" and "Word" reminiscent of standard Neoplatonist theory:

> But this is a whip, and a rod to all such who have degenerated through the pride, and ambition, from their natural tongue, and Languages, and all Languages upon the earth is but Naturall, and makes none divine, but that which makes divine is the Word, which was before Languages, and Tongues were.
>
> Men, crying up Tongues to be the Original, and they have degenerated from the Tongues which they call the Originall, which is not the Originall, which be the Naturals, I look upon the natural Languages no more than men to learn to dress a horse, or women to sweep a house, as to divine things; For in the beginning was the word, which was before Natural Languages were.

Admittedly, Fox struggles with the arcane definitions and terms tossed about in the confusion of language theories at the time, thus creating a syntactically and semantically confusing passage. Yet he tries to drive home his point about the difference between fallen, human languages and an ultimate, spiritual "Word." Somewhere, he says, they are connected. Although human language is fallen, it nevertheless *does* matter. His tract is a "whip" or "rod" insofar as it tries to purge the English language of its degenerate ele-

---

30. George Fox, John Stubs, and Benjamin Furley, *A Battle-Door for Teachers and Professors to Learn Singular and Plural . . .* (London, 1660), [i]. This publication uses the spelling "Furley," but the most common spelling of the name, especially in his later translations of Penn's promotional tracts, is "Furly." See also Ormsby-Lennon, "From Shibboleth to Apocalypse," in Burke and Porter, eds., *Language, Self, and Society,* 91.

ments caused by "pride" and "ambition"—the key elements of the Tower of Babel. If the currently spoken language is degenerate, there has to be a more ideal state that has been left behind.[31]

Fox here comes close to asserting that human beings once spoke a perfect language, which he calls the "natural tongue." But Fox does not mean Boehme's Natursprache, and much less an "Originall" tongue supposedly spoken in Eden. Instead, Fox finds that normal folk speak a language— a *plain* English—that is then marred by "the Teachers of the world, and Schollars" who "are them which corrupts the Languages, and are exalted, taking glory to themselves, and have the Plural put upon them, for the singular, which is vulgar." Still, Fox insists that no human language—not even a pure Quaker speech free of pride and pagan influences—can help bring about salvation, for "all Languages upon the earth is but Naturall, and makes none divine." Salvation, Fox asserts (and here he finally meets the theolinguistic hopes of contemporary mystics in England and the Continent), will finally be achieved when the words of human language collapse into the ultimate signifier, "the Word," "that which makes divine" and "was before Natural Languages were." In spite of his folksy pragmatism and anti-intellectualism, Fox was also gripped by the recurring question whether human language could ever approximate the divine Word glimpsed through immediate revelation.[32]

Indeed, Fox's journal described divine openings that allowed him to tap into the script in which the universe was written and thus bridge the gap between human language and the divine Word. In the most paradigmatic passage, Fox wrote:

Now was I come up in spirit through the flaming sword into the paradise of God. All things were new, and all the creation gave another smell unto me than before, beyond what words can utter. I knew nothing but pureness, and innocency, and righteousness, being renewed up into the image of God by Christ Jesus, so that I say I was come up to the state of *Adam which he was in before he fell.* . . . Great things did the Lord lead me into, and wonderful depths were opened unto me, beyond what can by words be declared; but as people come into subjection to the spirit of God, and grow up in the image and power of the Almighty, they may *receive the Word of wisdom, that opens all things,*

31. Fox, Stubs, and Furley, *Battle-Door,* [iii].
32. Ibid.

and come to know the hidden unity in the Eternal Being. . . . These things I did not see by the help of man, nor by the letter, though they are written in the letter, but I saw them in the light of the Lord Jesus Christ, and by his immediate Spirit and power, as did the holy men of God, by whom the Holy Scriptures were written. Yet I had no slight esteem of the Holy Scriptures, but they were very precious to me, for I was in that spirit by which they were given forth, and what the Lord opened in me I afterwards found was agreeable to them.

Fox's belief in openings into the divine script in which the universe was written provided intriguing possibilities for building the foundation of a radical Protestant theory of translation and a common spiritual language. Translation is always concerned with the loss of meaning (in other words, the *spirit* of the text) from one language into the other. Depending on the nature of the material to be translated, such a loss of meaning could be spiritual, cultural, philosophical, or intellectual. The task of the translator, therefore, is the carrying over of this spiritual or cultural content from one system of linguistic signification to the next. Even if the translator was able to partake in the cultural contexts and spiritual states in which the original text was written, the readers of the translation presumably would *not*. To put it in clerical terms, the translator of religious or spiritual texts functions as a minister who attempts to interpret and *translate* the spirit in which the scriptures were written into a language that is ultimately incapable of containing the same spiritual meaning. Some Protestant denominations—such as the New England Puritans—attempted to solve the problem of the incumbent loss of meaning (or spirit) by increasing the spiritual and scholarly competency of the clergy; ministers had to be both regenerate (that is, converted, and thus filled with the assurance of salvation) and university trained. Radical Protestant groups such as German radical Pietists and Quakers, however, believed not just in the regeneration of the translator (the person interpreting the divine text or will) but also in the prerequisite transformation of the *readers* receiving the translated version. Much more, all the faithful had to be translators themselves, that is, they had to be equally capable of partaking in the spirit of the original.[33]

Fox claimed this status of being an ideal translator of the divine when

33. "The Journal of George Fox," in Douglas V. Steere, ed., *Quaker Spirituality: Selected Writings* (New York, 1984), 68–69 (emphasis added). On Fox's "openings," also see William C. Braithwaite, *The Beginnings of Quakerism*, 2d ed., rev. Henry J. Cadbury (Cambridge, 1961), 33–39.

he says that he viewed all mysteries of the universe "as did the holy men of God, by whom the Holy Scriptures were written." Fox did not have to rely on a secondhand or thirdhand interpretation of the scriptures because he could read them with the same degree of divine inspiration as the original writers. And, if the writers of the Gospels were still alive, Fox could presumably converse with them about the divine meaning of the universe and the scriptures without a loss of meaning, for they would all partake equally in this spirit. As a Quaker, Fox does not claim such a status for himself alone; his *Journal* (and other writings and preaching) invites others to ascend to the same position. In the ideal case, all those individuals sharing with Fox a state of opening to the divine mysteries would no longer need a translation, for they would all partake in a spiritual language that precedes or supersedes any human utterance. If such a community were gathered, its language would in fact be identical with the spiritual language, for all would have access to the ultimate divine referents.

The repercussions of such a religious or spiritual theory of linguistic translation are immense. The text of the translated and the translating version would no longer be tied together merely through the tenuous and fallen bonds of human signifiers. Instead, the link between both textual versions would lie entirely outside the realm of language. These ties, therefore, would not be ensured through the linguistic accuracy of the translation but rather in the spiritual ties to the divine referent or opening to the Holy Spirit presumably shared by members of both linguistic groups. To put it differently, because the writers and readers of the original text had access to the same spiritual plane as the writers and readers of the translated text, the loss of spiritual meaning would be negligible. For Fox and other radicals, the language of a true church had to partake fully of the divine spirit and, thus, resemble the language of the scriptures.

Yet there was a flipside to such claims: what counted as spiritual language for those claiming continued access to the divine was incomprehensible gibberish for outsiders. In trying to achieve this ideal state of language and community, one opened the doors to a perfect confusion. Many of those individuals and groups in early Pennsylvania who deployed translation and multilingualism as the means for achieving a spiritual language reflected on this central dilemma. Discussions about linguistic and spiritual compatibility tempered a pure theory of spiritual language with two caveats: human language was still fallible, even if it reverberated with the spirit, and individuals may be deceived in their claims of having access to the spirit. To confront these conditions, translators and authors asked readers to disregard linguistic incongruities and focus only on the spiritual foundation in which the original text was conceived. Nothing guaranteed the proper reception of the translation as much as ensuring that the translator and the readers partook in the same spirit as the writers and readers of the original. In turn, the frequent production and use of translations helped writers and readers on both sides (the original side and the translation side) to train one another in recognizing spiritual similarities in spite of linguistic dissimilarities. The relationship was, again, dialectical: spiritual community could be harnessed to ensure the proper reception of translations; translations could be deployed to create or bolster religious community.

Beside Fox, one of the most influential Quaker writers was Robert Barclay (1648–1690), the so-called Quaker apologist. Barclay's *Apology for the True Christian Divinity* shaped the reception of Quakerism inside and outside the community throughout the late seventeenth and eighteenth centuries. Even more clearly than Fox, Barclay developed a theory of spiritual language that would be rehearsed by Quakers and other religious radicals in Pennsylvania and throughout the Atlantic world. Barclay's attempt to shift attention from outward rhetorical expressions — in spite of his own eloquence — to inward spiritual content (or truth) was echoed in most translations discussed in this book. In his preface to the *Apology*, Barclay wrote:

For what I have written comes more from my heart than from my head; what I have heard with the Ears of my Soul and seen with my inward Eyes and my hands have handled of the Word of Life. And what hath been inwardly manifested to me of the things of God, that do I declare, not so much minding the Eloquence and Excellency of Speech as desiring to demonstrate the efficacy and operation of Truth, and if I err sometime in the former it is no great matter; for I act not here the Grammarian or the Orator, but the Christian; and therefore in this have followed the certain Rule of the Divine Light, and of the Holy Scriptures.

Barclay's juxtaposition of "the Grammarian or the Orator" with "the Christian" reflects two types of translation evoked in the spiritual writings of European and American radical Protestantism. The first translation occurred when writers transferred "what hath been inwardly manifested" into spoken or written language. In fact, Quakers carefully mediated and oftentimes restricted the type or amount of testimony written or printed, trying to limit the attention to the human word instead of the truth or divine Word. Secondly, Barclay's concept held crucial implications for the actual translation of spiritual content from one human language into another. Translators and readers had the obligation to search for the spirit in which the original was conceived rather than splitting hairs over specific rhetorical expressions. Of course, the fear was that a change in wording could destroy or distort the very spiritual content to be transmitted. According to Barclay, both the translator and the readers of the translation had the responsibility of recapturing the spirit of the original, just as the church tried to reconstitute the spirit in which the Bible was conceived. Unlike orthodox churches, Quakers and other radical Protestants claimed that the process of creating community through spiritually endowed language was still continuing.[34]

In building on Fox, Barclay declared the authority of the Bible as coeval with the operations of the spirit within. Accused by many critics of devaluing the scriptures, Barclay responded with an explanation that places the Holy Spirit in the position of ultimate authority, while conceiving any human, linguistic expressions, including the words of the Bible, as equally flawed. Like Neoplatonist and radical Protestant reformers before him, Barclay held Augustine's distinction between inner and outer speech as fundamental to the development of a spiritual language: " 'It is the inward master (saith Augustin) that teacheth, it is Christ that teacheth, it is inspiration that teacheth: where this inspiration and unction is wanting, it is in vain that words from without are beaten in.' And therefore: 'for he that created us, and redeemed us, and called us by faith, and dwelleth in us by his Spirit, unless he speaketh unto us inwardly, it is needless for us to cry out.' " All language—whether in translation or original—needed to stand the test of divine inspiration. If it was not filled by the Holy Spirit, it was to cease and be replaced by the characteristic silence of Quaker worship.[35]

For translators and translations of writings considered to contain a divine authority, the same test had to be applied; rather than a simple carrying over of spiritual content from one version into another, translations had to become renewed outpourings of the spirit that "speaketh unto us inwardly." By the same token, they could then become equal purveyors of spiritual truth with the presumed originals. In fact, Barclay asserted, the spirit allowed any individuals—even the untutored or illiterate—the same authority in interpreting the scriptures. In his "Third Proposition; Con-

34. Robert Barclay, *An Apology for the True Christian Divinity, as the Same Is Held Forth, and Preached by the People, Called, in Scorn, Quakers* . . . ([London?], 1678), "R.B. unto the Friendly Reader Wisheth Salvation," B2.
35. Ibid., 5, 38.

cerning the Scriptures," Barclay argued at length that all translations of the Bible thus needed to be subjected to the guidance and correction of the spirit; knowledge of the "original languages" did not guarantee a knowledge of the spirit in which the scriptures were written.[36]

German and English radical Protestants usually condemned the supposed vanity of learning classical and even scriptural languages. In his *Journal,* Fox recounted meeting a government representative, who was on his way to "to set up a college [in Durham] to make ministers of Christ." Fox tried to make this official understand his folly and

> let him see that this was not the way to make them Christ's ministers by Hebrew, Greek, Latin and the Seven Arts, which all were but teachings of the natural man. For the many languages began at Babel . . . and they set them atop Christ the Word when they crucified him. And John the Divine, who preached the Word that was in the beginning, said that the beast and the whore have power over tongues and languages . . . *which are in mystery Babylon, for they began at Babel.* . . . But [Christ] is risen over them all, who was before Babel was. And did he think to make ministers of Christ by these natural, confused languages, at Babel and in Babylon, set a-top Christ the Life by a persecutor? Oh no!

Fox conflated the linguistic corruption of Babel with the moral or spiritual corruption of Babylon, thus creating an eschatological arch from the beginning of human pride at the Tower to its apocalyptic end. Fox turned the languages purportedly placed above Christ on the cross as emblems for all human languages into the antithesis of the divinely inspired and creative Word. In the resurrection, "Christ the Word" reversed this relationship and, according to the Book of Revelation, would return to rule earth for a thousand years before the final judgment. Christ's atonement thus undid man's fall into sin *and* into linguistic confusion.[37]

Providing a somewhat more nuanced position on language learning, Barclay joined Augustine's pragmatic quest for a unification of human languages and his differentiation between spiritually dead human language and inspired divine language. Barclay praised the efforts of Reformation linguists and translators for fostering the study of Hebrew and Greek, and thus

---

36. Ibid., 38–57.

37. Fox quoted in Ormsby-Lennon, "From Shibboleth to Apocalypse," in Burke and Porter, eds., *Language, Self, and Society,* 89.

for correcting the Catholic error of treating the Bible like a "sealed book" in order to keep the people in a "Babylonish darkness." Similar to Comenius, Barclay advocated the use of a "common language"—such as Latin—in order to improve communication among different nations. He even judged "it necessary and commendable, there be publick Schools, for the teaching and instructing youth, as are inclinable thereunto, in the languages." Nevertheless, Barclay rejoined that such a "knowledge can no ways make up the want of the Spirit in the most learned and eloquent. For all that, which man by his own industry, learning, and knowledge in the languages, can interpret of the Scriptures, or find out, is nothing without the Spirit."[38]

August Hermann Francke (1663–1727), German Pietist pastor and founder of the orphanages and schools in Halle-Glaucha, developed a similar system of biblical hermeneutics that differentiated between the promotion of language study to produce more accurate interpretations and the experience of the inner, spiritual meanings of the Bible. Using the metaphor of shell and core, Francke defined the shell as the "historical, grammatical, and analytical study of the Scriptures"; the core, however, is the "deeper, spiritual insight" one reaches by penetrating through linguistic, historical, and exegetic levels of reading. Francke stated his preference for inner, spiritual insights over the outward understanding of its content. As the "core" satisfies the needs of the heart, the deeper understanding of the scriptures proceeds on a sublinguistic level. Like Fox, Francke also differentiated between the "fallen and human word" and the divine Word that *is* God. Francke's argument is ontological: the divine Word is coeval with the creative power that is God; thus, it is both eternal and immune to the errors of human language. As the "word made flesh" of the Gospel, Christ is the "core of the Holy Scriptures." Francke listed a total of seventy-five names or titles the Bible gives Christ, illustrating the relationship between language and the divine: the multiplicity of human signifiers is subsumed in Christ, the divine signified. The eschatological significance of the diversity of human language is its collapsing into the unity of the Word.[39]

Similar to Fox and Barclay, Francke also targeted the role of language learning in the preparation for the ministry. At "schools and universities," he wrote in "Observationes Biblicae," he wished for a "consequential continuation of

38. Barclay, *Apology,* 207. Also see William Braithwaite, *The Second Period of Quakerism,* 2d ed., prepared by Henry J. Cadbury (Cambridge, 1961), 533.

39. Erhard Peschke, "Introduction," in August Hermann Francke, *Schriften zur biblischen Hermeneutik I,* ed. Erhard Peschke (Berlin, 2003), xv; see also 229, 313–322.

the Reformation" by "making God's Word again the primary and not the sec- ondary focus." Although praising the study of the biblical languages, which he calls "foundational languages," Francke warns against making philological work the primary focus of religious training instead of the "substance itself, which is being presented to us in God's Word." For this purpose, Bible schol- ars as well as readers of the Bible in general must ask for the "illumination of his Holy Spirit." As in translation, understanding scriptural language was to penetrate beneath the level of linguistic and philological comprehension to gain a physical ("sweet") and spiritual sense of its meaning.[40]

Barclay and Francke thus differentiated between a use of languages for practical human communication as well as biblical scholarship on the one hand and the supreme language of the spirit on the other hand. What united Barclay and Francke, as well as the Quaker and Pietist movements in early modern Europe, was the effort to escape Babel / Babylon and create a more perfect society through linguistic and spiritual reform. Their common logo- mystical beliefs were also at the center of the utopianism that created the idea of Pennsylvania as an antitype to the linguistic and spiritual separa- tion from the divine signified or Word. Unfortunately, the utopianism of Pennsylvania's founding has become such a cliché that its explanatory value has waned. One of the reasons is that few accounts search deeper into the causes and meanings of this utopianism. Indeed, during the decades pre- ceding the founding and settlement of Pennsylvania, the religious and lin- guistic undoing of the heritage of Babel and Babylon—along with the prin- ciple of Philadelphia—was one of the most widely exchanged ideals among English and German radical reformers, turning it into a transnationally and translingually recognized concept. The concept of Philadelphianism at the core of this experiment did not merely espouse vague notions of universal brotherhood but constructed Pennsylvania as the embodiment of theologi- cal and linguistic reform movements.[41]

Translating the Philadelphian Ideal

Although the Philadelphian ideal was most openly espoused by the Phila- delphian Society, it found broad acceptance in radical Protestant commu-

---

40. Francke, *Schriften*, ed. Peschke, 484.

41. Melvin B. Endy, Jr., *William Penn and Early Quakerism* (Princeton, N.J., 1973), 349; Edwin B. Bronner, *William Penn's "Holy Experiment": The Founding of Pennsylvania, 1681–1701* (New York, 1962), 14.

nities of late-seventeenth-century England and Germany. The key word "Philadelphia" thus evoked a host of eschatological and apocalyptical speculations. Philadelphians specifically interpreted and looked to the Book of Revelation (chapter 3), in which seven letters sent to seven churches presumably evoked periods in the history of the Christian church. During the time of Philadelphia (Rev. 3:7–13), the true children of God would be gathered and become the betrothed to the lamb or Christ. Eventually, the orthodox churches or "sects" would be eliminated as part of "Babel." The end of human history would be followed by the restoration of all things *(Apokatastasis panton)*. In the meantime, "Philadelphia" was to be understood and lived as the unpartisan, brotherly love that countermands doctrinal wrangling and distinguishes true Christianity. Pennsylvania would be founded on this notion of "Philadelphia," which was not merely the general espousal of brotherly love and religious tolerance but also a set of eschatological, radical Protestant ideals, most prominently the exit from and undoing of Babel and Babylon.[42]

The activities of "Philadelphians" in late-seventeenth-century England and Germany demonstrate that a common interest in the "restoration of all things" as well as a concrete cooperation through translation did not for the first time develop in Pennsylvania. It was rather a continuation of practices based on linguistic and spiritual reform and, more specifically, the ideal of "Philadelphia." Members of the English and German Philadelphian movements connected through an active correspondence and frequent, reciprocal translation of theological and mystical writings, leading to "a certain unification of radical Pietist thought." Indeed, translation and correspondence brought English and German radical Protestants so close together that they regarded themselves as "branches of the same tree." Based on the practice first introduced by Philipp Jakob Spener, the "father" of German Pietism, Philadelphians and radical Pietists in England and Germany met in small groups called "conventicles," which discussed a variety of religious ideas, introduced writings in translation, and corresponded with likeminded meetings at home and abroad. In the 1680s and 1690s, such groups also became hubs for the dissemination of concrete news as well as more

---

42. Schneider, "Der radikale Pietismus," in Brecht, ed., *Der Pietismus*, 405. Mary K. Geiter cites three reasons William Penn chose to name the city "Philadelphia": the word's Greek meaning, "City of Brotherly Love," that the ancient city of Philadelphia was "the site of one of the seven churches in Asia Minor to which the Book of Revelation was dedicated by St. John," and it was a "modern city with which merchants in the Levant Company, many of whom invested in Pennsylvania, currently traded" (*William Penn* [New York, 2000], 115).

esoteric speculations about emigration to Pennsylvania. For instance, the German immigrant leader and eventual founder of Germantown Francis Daniel Pastorius received his motivation for immigrating to Pennsylvania from the Frankfurt Pietists, the first of these radical Pietist and Philadelphian groups to consider "emigration as an attractive possibility for a consequential exit from 'Babel.'" Although the actual founding of Pennsylvania also emerged from a variety of complex political, imperial, and economical considerations, the spread of Philadelphian and radical Pietist hopes for leaving behind the linguistic and moral Babel / Babylon provided some of the most important theological and intellectual underpinnings. Religious radicals immigrating to Pennsylvania in the late seventeenth and early eighteenth centuries carried with them mystical ideals about the spiritual and communal significance of this experiment. Most certainly, they believed that their common search for a spiritual language was a direct means to counter the heritage of Babel.[43]

Translation was the driving force of the spread of Philadelphian ideals in England and Germany. Initially, the most prominent leaders of the Philadelphian Society in England — Jane Leade, John Pordage, and Thomas Bromley — received their mystical stimulus from translations of Boehme's work. John Pordage was already known as one of the most prominent "Behmenists" in England when he first met Jane Leade in the 1670s. Under the influence of Boehme's experiences, Leade recorded many "prophetic visions" in her spiritual diary, *A Fountain of Gardens* (published 1696–1701). Her visions of "God's Eternal Virgin, Wisdom" recalled Boehme's notion of the "Virgin Sophia." Both presumed that the Holy Spirit was a female quality of God that inhabited the first humans but fled as a result of the fall. Although Quaker beliefs in the indwelling spirit or Inward Light differed considerably from the radical Pietist idea of an aloof "Virgin Sophia," both groups agreed in their assumption that the connection to this spirit or divine wisdom resulted in fundamental changes in the behavior and speech of individuals and entire communities.[44]

43. Schneider, "Der radikale Pietismus," in Brecht, ed., *Der Pietismus,* 400, 405, 418–421.

44. Jones, *Spiritual Reformers,* 227–228; Thune, *The Behmenists,* 49, 64–65. Pordage's *Theologia Mystica; or, The Mystic Divinitie of the Eternal Invisibles* (1683) is considered one of the constituting texts of the movement. For differences between Quakers and Pietists, see Klaus Deppermann, "Pennsylvanien als Asyl des frühen deutschen Pietismus," *Pietismus und Neuzeit: Ein Jahrbuch zur Geschichte des neueren Protestantismus,* X (Göttingen, 1984), 190–226; Rüdiger Mack, "Franz Daniel Pastorius, sein Einsatz für die Quäker," *Pietismus und Neuzeit,* XV (1989), 132–171.

In turn, Philadelphian writings found an enthusiastic audience in Germany, where the first complete publication of Boehme's writings by Gichtel was reenergizing the radical Pietist movement, such as the Pietist conventicle founded by Spener at the so-called Saalhof in Frankfurt. Particularly fruitful was Leade's exchange with two chiliastically inclined members of this group, Johann Wilhelm Petersen and his wife Johanna Eleonora Petersen (née Merlau). Leade and other members of the Philadelphian Society sent their manuscripts for commentary and translation to the Petersens; in turn, writings by the Frankfurt Pietists were translated and published by the Philadelphians in England. Besides outlining the mystical beliefs of the society, these publications promoted a communitarian and interdenominational program, including the mandate to "prepare for that great and solemn Time [the Coming of Christ] by a good Life, universal Charity, and Union amongst the Protestant Churches."[45]

Similar to Boehme, the Philadelphians also likened the spiritual illumination received through unification with the "heavenly Sophia" to the divine music of the spheres. Published in the *Theosophical Transactions,* the short-lived journal of the Philadelphian Society, Francis Lee's tract "A New Theory of Music" (1697) explained the Philadelphians' mystical theory of music, which they regarded as a conduit to the hidden, divine mysteries of the universe. Accordingly, the relation of musical notes to each other was a reflection of the "Harmony of the Divine Powers and Properties in the Nature of God: who exists and manifest *[sic]* himself in infinite variety and multiplicity, all in perfect Concord and Unity." Most important, Lee located this divine harmony not only in music but also in the sounds of spoken language:

The Ground on which we proceed, is a New Discovery arising from this Theory; Which is This: That the Natural Pronunciation, or the Tone, Accent, and Emphasis, which we use in speaking our Words; and that variety of it that appears in the Expression of our Passions; is nothing else but Musick; it is True and natural Harmony.

Lee's theories promised a soteriological effect of language *perceived* as music, but especially of language *performed* as music. In essence, Lee suggested an elevation of human expression through music to the level of angelic singing, which must have created nothing short of euphoria among

---

45. Thune, *The Behmenists,* 81, 93–94, 100; Schneider, "Der radikale Pietismus," in Brecht, ed., *Der Pietismus,* 394, 405.

mystical Pietists trying to perfect their earthly existence in anticipation of Christ's Second Coming.[46]

The culmination of the Philadelphian and Neoplatonist visions of the seventeenth and early eighteenth centuries can be found in the thought and work of Count Nikolaus Ludwig von Zinzendorf. In founding the Renewed Unitas Fratrum or Moravian Church in 1727, Zinzendorf joined the mystical currents of radical Pietism with the heritage of the Bohemian Brethren, a pre-Lutheran Reformation church that originated in the teachings of Jan Hus (circa 1372–1415) and was carried on by a small group of Moravian refugees who settled on Zinzendorf's estate. Although the Moravians under Zinzendorf practiced a "heart religion" that placed the individual believer in an intensely personal and emotional relationship with Christ, especially through the complete immersion in the cult of Jesus's blood and wounds, it was within the communal expression and celebration of this individualistic faith that the full power of Moravian spirituality took shape. Concretely, love feasts and hymn singing galvanized a "community of the cross" through the joint experience and expression of Christ's love. Although recent scholarship has teased out the theological and communal underpinnings of Moravian beliefs and practices, it has neglected the impact of Zinzendorf's ideas concerning the linguistic multiplicity of the Moravian Church. Zinzendorf championed the earlier, seventeenth-century fervor about the reformation of human language, society, and religion represented by Jacob Boehme, Jan Amos Comenius, and the Philadelphians, and he applied their thought to the expansion of the Moravian Church—fostered through a dynamic missions program—into a global, transnational, and translingual community.[47]

---

46. Francis Lee, "A New Theory of Musick," *Theosophical Transactions: Consisting of Memoirs, Conferences, Letters, Dissertations, Inquiries, etc. for the Advancement of Piety, and Divine Philosophy,* I, no. 1 (March 1697), 65. For further background on Lee, see Jones, *Spiritual Reformers,* 231; Thune, *The Behmenists,* 82. Also see Arthur Versluis, "Mysticism and Spiritual Harmonics in Eighteenth-Century England," *Esoterica,* IV (2002), 2, 6, 102, 103, www.esoteric.msu.edu/VolumeIV/Harmonic .htm.

47. Craig D. Atwood, *Community of the Cross: Moravian Piety in Colonial Bethlehem* (University Park, Pa., 2004). For other works on Moravian spirituality and communal formation, see Aaron Spencer Fogleman, *Jesus Is Female: Moravians and the Challenge of Radical Religion in Early America* (Philadelphia, 2007); Paul Peucker, "Inspired by Flames of Love": Homosexuality, Mysticism, and Moravian Brothers around 1750," *Journal of the History of Sexuality,* XV (2006), 30–64; Peucker, "The Songs of the Sifting: Understanding the Role of Bridal Mysticism in Moravian Piety during the Late 1740s," *Journal of Moravian History,* III (2007), 51–87. For biographical scholarship on Zinzendorf, see Erich Beyreuther, *Der junge Zinzendorf* (Marburg, 1957); Beyreuther, *Zinzendorf und die sich allhier beisammen finden* (Marburg, 1959); Beyreuther, *Zinzendorf und die Christenheit, 1732–1760* (Marburg, 1961); Martin Brecht and Paul Peucker, eds., *Neue Aspekte der Zinzendorf-*

Zinzendorf had grown up at a crossroads of Pietist and radical Protestant thought. He was raised by his grandmother Henriette Katharina von Gersdorf (1648–1726), who was known for her language learning and independent thought on religious matters. She participated in a vigorous communication with the most well-known figures in Lutheran Pietism, including Phillip Jacob Spener and August Hermann Francke, who visited her residence when Zinzendorf was still a child. Henriette was also well read in the writings of radical Pietism and Philadelphianism, including Jacob Boehme, Jane Leade, and Johann Wilhelm Petersen. These Pietist and mystical influences as well his experiences during his "Grand Tour" led the young Zinzendorf to embrace the idea of a "trans-denominational heart religion and a universal church, that is tied to the heart and suffering of Jesus." His early travels apparently helped inspire the strongly ecumenical idealism that would drive Zinzendorf for the rest of his life; he claimed that "from this time on, I tried to discover the best in all religions . . . for I knew that the Lord wanted to have his own among all different peoples." Motivated by a mystically oriented love of Christ, Zinzendorf increasingly developed the desire to join or form a community built according to Philadelphian principles.[48]

Beyond the influence of Behmenist mysticism and Philadelphianism, Zinzendorf soon encountered another radical Protestant tradition through his meeting with the descendents of the Bohemian Brethren and their joint founding of the new Unitas Fratrum in 1727. As the last "bishop" of this pre-Lutheran reformation church, Jan Amos Comenius had written the history of the Bohemian Brethren, which Zinzendorf read in July 1727 on a journey to Silesia and, in part, translated from Latin to German. Zinzendorf also modeled some of the rules of the Renewed Unitas Fratrum on Comenius's *Historia Fratrum Bohemorum* and was thus able to give

---

Forschung (Göttingen, 2006); Mari P. van Buijtenen, Cornelis Dekker, and Huib Leeuwenberg, eds., *Unitas Fratrum: Herrnhuter Studien/Moravian Studies* (Utrecht, 1975); Dietrich Meyer, "Zinzendorf und Herrnhut," in Martin Brecht and Klaus Deppermann, eds., *Der Pietismus im achtzehnten Jahrhundert*, vol. II of *Geschichte des Pietismus* (Göttingen, 1995), 3–106; Peter Vogt, "Nicholas Ludwig von Zinzendorf (1700–1760)," in Carter Lindberg, ed., *The Pietist Theologians: An Introduction to Theology in the Seventeenth and Eighteenth Centuries* (Malden, Mass., 2005), 207–223. Even in the most recent scholarship on the Moravian expansion across the Atlantic world, language contact and language difference has played virtually no role. See, for example, Michele Gillespie and Robert Beachy, *Pious Pursuits: German Moravians in the Atlantic World* (New York, 2007).

48. Meyer, "Zinzendorf und Herrnhut," in Brecht and Deppermann, eds., *Der Pietismus*, 6–7, 16, 18; Zinzendorf, quoted ibid., 17: "Von der Zeit an bemühte ich mich, daß beßte in allen Religionen zu entdecken . . . dann ich wußte, daß in allerley Volck der Herr die seinigen haben wolle."

the new church a sense of continuity and respectability. Zinzendorf became Comenius's heir when Friedrich Wilhelm I recognized the Moravian Church and Bishop Daniel Ernst Jablonski (1660–1741) ordained Zinzendorf as bishop on May 20, 1737. Jablonski was not only a court preacher in Berlin and bishop of the Polish portion of the Unitas Fratrum but also the grandson of Jan Amos Comenius. Although no direct evidence exists for Zinzendorf's study and embrace of Comenius's linguistic thought and writings, he certainly embraced the principles of pacifism and a universal reform of faith and language that Comenius had espoused. Comenius's writings on pansophism and his practical linguistic works were so widely received throughout the late seventeenth and eighteenth centuries that Zinzendorf must have come into contact with the foundations of Comenius's projects. Zinzendorf's thought about the spiritual and linguistic renewal and unity driving the worldwide Moravian Church certainly reverberated with the spirit of Comenius's pansophism.[49]

During the 1730s and 1740s, Zinzendorf began to adapt Boehme's Neoplatonist language mysticism and Comenius's pansophism to the concrete, communal developments within a Moravian Church expanding across Europe and into the worldwide mission field. Zinzendorf built on Boehme's distinction between actual, spoken languages and a spiritual language contiguous to or inspired by the Holy Ghost, even adopting the concept of Natursprache. During a Moravian synod at Zeist, Holland, in May-June 1746, Zinzendorf delivered a sermon on language difference and unity within the Moravian Church. Reverberating with Boehme's Natursprache, Zinzendorf's speech evoked Augustine's Pentecostal global church as well as Comenius's linguistic universalism:

It has been said: unite all languages, etc. This is such a reality that, I believe, speaking in tongues does not mean one should babble some-

---

49. Beyreuther, *Zinzendorf und die sich allhier besammen finden*, 188; Meyer, "Zinzendorf und Herrnhut," in Brecht and Deppermann, eds., *Der Pietismus*, 18, 21. For Comenius's church history, see *Kurz-gefaßte Kirchen-Historie der böhmischen Brüder, wie solche Johann Amos Comenius, Weyland letzter Bischoff der vereinigten Brüder-Gemeine in Böhmen, lateinisch beschrieben, dernach aber, um des erbaulichen Innhalts willen, Nebst einem Glaubens-Bekänntniß, Etlichen zur Erläuterung dienlichen Briefen, und der fürtrefflichen Kirchen-Ordnung derselben* (1739), in Alfred Eckert and Werner-Friedrich-Aloys Jakobsmeier, eds., *Quellen zur Geschichtsschreibung der Böhmischen Brüder . . .* (Hildesheim, 1980). On Jablonski, see Joachim Heubach, "Jablonski, Daniel Ernst," *Biographische-Bibliographisches Kirchenlexikon*, II (1990), columns 1395–1396. Along with G. W. Leibniz, Jablonski founded the Berliner Akademie der Wissenschaften (Berlin Academy of Sciences) in 1700. The name is also sometimes spelled "Jablonsky."

thing in a language that no one understands; but, first, that one unites the languages as we do in "Lamb, Lamb, oh Lamb etc." [that is,] that everyone praises the lamb in his or her own language; secondly, that one brings to bear the force of a language onto the *spiritual language.* If in our language a word is clearer, it is used in German in another country; but if it is clearer in Dutch, one uses — in the middle of the German — the Dutch, or the Latin or the French or the Greek language. And to understand this, one does not have to do anything but ask "what does this part of a line mean?" There are at least one hundred brothers and sisters present who understand it just like that and for whom it is even clearer and more evocative; and, 20 years later no one will understand us, which will be right, for we won't speak unclearly or absurdly, but instead we will speak a *natural Language, a central language.*

Following the dictum of linguistic unity given by a variety of Neoplatonist philosophers and theologians before him, Zinzendorf defined how the Moravian Church addressed the dilemma of Babel. He distinguished his ideas of divinely inspired language from ultramystical forms of "speaking in tongues" and described a gradual approximation of the language spoken by the community to the ideal or spiritual language pervading all church members.[50]

Zinzendorf understood the development of linguistic unity among the Moravians as twofold. First was a parallel multilingualism anchored in the joined exultation of Christ. Zinzendorf mentioned the widespread practice of selecting a specific hymn that would be sung in all the vernaculars of the

---

50. "Protokoll der Synode in Zeist, Mai–Juni 1746," Moravian Archives, Bethlehem, Pa., 90, copy of the original at the Moravian Archives, Herrnhut (underline in the original, italics added): "Daher heißts: bringt alle Sprachen zusammen etc. das ist eine solche realitaet, daß ich glaube, das mit Zungen redden heißt nicht daß man soll was hinplappern in einer Sprache, die niemand versteht, sondern erstens, daß man die Sprachen zusammen bringt wie wir in Lamm, Lamm, o Lamm etc. daß ein jeder in seiner Sprache das Lamm lobet; zweitens, daß man der Sprache ihre Force auch mit in die Geistes Sprache hin einbringe. Ist in unserer Sprache ein Wort deutlicher, so sagt mans in einem andern Lande teutsch ists aber im Holländischen deutlicher so sagt mans mitten im teutschen Holländisch oder lateinisch oder Französisch oder griechisch, und das zu verstehen, braucht nichts mehr als daß man einmal frage, was heißt die halbe Zeile? Es sind ohne dem hundert Geschwister da, die es so verstehen und denen ists gleich noch einmal so deutlich und eindrücklich und in 20 Jahren hernach versteht uns gar kein Mensch, und das ist recht, nicht als ob wir undeutlich oder absurd redten, sondern wir reden eine *naturSprache, eine central-sprache.*" I am indebted to Paul Peucker, archivist of the Moravian Archives in Bethlehem, for pointing out this passage to me and providing several other references on Zinzendorf's thought on language.

members of the global Moravian Church present at a given time and place. The parallels to the scriptural Pentecost were obvious: speakers from different nations did not lose their respective language; they "unite[d] all languages." Within a multilingual, global church community, Christ spawned a multiplicity of linguistic expressions; he was both signifier and signified in *any* national or ethnic community. In a speech given before his departure to America in 1741, Zinzendorf said: "Everything is created by him and through him and toward him: from the smallest worm to the highest archangel, everything exists for his sake. Thus, the poor man Jesus has such superlative and infinitely excessive by-names, for he is the creator of all times and all beings." The linguistic multiplication of representations of Christ's suffering and death confirmed the status of Christ as logos and thus the linguistic and spiritual unity of the Moravian Church.[51]

Secondly, Zinzendorf's speech to the synod at Zeist illustrated his expectation that the Moravian Church would ultimately build a language that combined the spiritual elements of all languages represented in the community—such as German, Dutch, Latin, French, or Greek—in a single tongue spoken and understood by everyone within, but by nobody without, the *Gemeine* (the term German Moravians used for spiritual or religious community). Zinzendorf followed to a certain degree the conventionalist approach to language formation: a prolonged exchange of words and meanings within a multilingual and multicultural community resulting in a language mosaic (which reverses Babel by validating language difference). On a more mystical level, Zinzendorf relied on Boehme's Neoplatonist theory that existing languages retain traces of the spiritual language spoken by Adam in paradise. After all, the measure for determining which linguistic expression is "clearer" in communicating a given thought or idea could only be found in the "spiritual language" presumably spoken or understood by those united in faith. Therefore, the Moravian language formation Zinzendorf described continued the search for insights into the divine "text" underlying language and being. Unlike seventeenth-century Neoplatonists, the Moravian community did not seek to recover an "original" language lost at Babel but rather hoped to create a new language; this language was "natural," not primarily because it returned to childlike diminutives, but rather because it captured a spiritual connection between human language and the divine. It

---

51. Zinzendorf quoted in Helmut Bintz, *Nikolaus Ludwig von Zinzendorf: Texte zur Mission* (Hamburg, 1979), 22.

was "central" because it expressed the spiritual and linguistic unity of the Moravian Church within its national or cultural diversity.[52]

Zinzendorf thus articulated a solution to the crucial paradox between spiritual unity and linguistic multiplicity that not only took stock of concrete experiences with diversity but also predicated any future cohesion of the Gemeine on the embrace of its many parts. Although Zinzendorf's idea of a Natursprache emerging from or through the diversity of the Moravian Church retained the earlier, Neoplatonist notion of a common spiritual language, it no longer followed the mystical hopes of either rediscovering an original *lingua adamica* or constructing a universal or perfect language. By inserting visions for linguistic and spiritual renewal into the communal context of the church, Zinzendorf and the Moravians developed a mature model of earlier language mysticism that allowed a universalist expansion of the church among the many peoples and languages of the world to be interpreted as a direct undoing of the spiritual and linguistic heritage of Babel. By experiencing spiritual cohesion in the community, Moravians could build a "spiritual language" that is *natural* because it expressed, not the essence of creation, but rather the essence of the Moravians' joint experience of faith. The "key" to the undoing of the heritage of Babel, in other words, did not lie in confronting linguistic multiplicity but in embracing it. On a communal level, the intense focus on Christ, "the Word made flesh," made actual linguistic differences insignificant.

Linguistic Utopianism and the Founding of Pennsylvania

The interpenetration of religious and linguistic reform movements in Europe affected early Pennsylvanian attitudes toward the spiritual and communal life of the province indirectly and directly: the English Quakers, radical German Pietists, and German and Dutch Anabaptists who dominated the earlier waves of immigration to Pennsylvania—and thus determined its spiritual and cultural makeup—condemned European society in general and the orthodox Protestant churches in particular as an outgrowth

---

52. On Zinzendorf's concepts of language, see Wilhelm Bettermann, *Theologie und Sprache bei Zinzendorf* (Gotha, 1935); Meyer, "Zinzendorf und Herrnhut," in Brecht and Deppermann, eds., *Der Pietismus*, 49; Jörn Reichel, *Dichtungstheorie und Sprache bei Zinzendorf: Der 12. Anhang zum herrnhuter Gesangbuch* (Bad Homburg v.d.H., 1969); Carola Wessel, "'Es ist also des Heilands sein Predigtstuhl so weit und groß als die ganze Welt': Zinzendorfs Überlegungen zur Mission," in Martin Brecht and Paul Peucker, eds., *Neue Aspekte der Zinzendorf-Forschung* (Göttingen, 2006), 172.

of Babel and Babylon, two biblical types they conflated in their rhetoric. Although the members and the later descendants of this wave of religious immigration might not have directly studied and understood Philadelphian, mystical, esoteric, and chiliastic theologies and linguistic theories, they nevertheless continued a spiritual and linguistic sensibility steeped in an earlier enthusiasm for religious and linguistic renewal. Moreover, many educated representatives of radical Pietist and sectarian groups — such as Francis Daniel Pastorius, Johannes Kelpius, Christopher Witt, Peter Miller, Anthony Benezet, David Zeisberger, and John Heckewelder — studied and disseminated seventeenth-century mystical, utopian, and esoteric ideas about religion and language. They tried to reconcile these traditions with the diverse ethnic, linguistic, and religious composition of early Pennsylvania.[53]

On the surface, linguistic and religious diversity in Pennsylvania resembled the confusion of languages and scattering of peoples at Babel. On a deeper, mystical level, Pennsylvania was regarded by many as a communal experiment where outward, spoken languages and the inward, spiritual languages could be reunited. Most of the radical Protestant immigrants who shaped the early spiritual and cultural composition of the province considered Pennsylvania a testing ground for the theories developed by reformers, mystics, linguists, and theologians in the seventeenth century. The "holy experiment" could only become a reality — and its members could only be united in "brotherly love" — if the different components of society could be joined in a common language of the spirit. Spiritual language was that which remained after linguistically or denominationally specific expressions of faith had been made interchangeable through translation. To translate was to find the language of the spirit.

In Pennsylvania, the texts, writers, and translators most concerned with the emergence of this spiritual language through translation frequently cited the scriptural tenet from Paul's first letter to the Thessalonians that had been the motto of Johann Arndt and of radical Pietism: "Prove all things; hold fast that which is good" (1 Thess. 5:21). From Francis Daniel Pastorius's multilingual "Bee-Hive" manuscript, to the first Mennonite translation of the Dordrecht Confession of Faith published in America, to

---

53. For the successive waves of German immigration, see Aaron Spencer Fogleman, *Hopeful Journeys: German Immigration, Settlement, and Political Culture in Colonial America, 1717–1775* (Philadelphia, 1996), 4–6.

Anthony Benezet's translation of Johannes Tauler's works, translations and translators directly evoked Paul's letter and Arndt's motto to emphasize the spiritual and communal significance of writing and reading in translation: translators and the readers of translations inherently tested the spiritual veracity of everything carried from one language to another, trying to establish linguistic and spiritual correspondences.[54]

Arriving in Pennsylvania as the vanguard of German immigration, the polymath, lawyer, and Lutheran Pietist Francis Daniel Pastorius (1651–1719) exemplified the continued study of the philosophical and theological questions on language characteristic of seventeenth-century Europe; in his extensive work in translation and multilingual composition, he also revealed the application of this thought to the linguistic and religious diversity of early Pennsylvania. Pastorius generally perceived his multilingual manuscript writings—especially the commonplace book and encyclopedia known as the "Bee-Hive"—as an effort to collect European knowledge and grapple with its relevance in a New World society. In the encyclopedic section of the "Bee-Hive," Pastorius assembled religious and secular ideas from a wide spectrum of authors. Several entries concerning language demonstrate his continued interest in seventeenth-century notions of religious and linguistic reformation, specifically the desire to overcome linguistic divisions as both symptoms of and impediments to spiritual unity.[55]

54. Schneider, "Der radikale Pietismus," in Brecht, ed., *Der Pietismus*, 394.

55. Francis Daniel Pastorius was born on September 26, 1751, in Sommerhausen, Germany, and he spent most of his youth in the imperial city of Windsheim (Franconia), where his father, Melchior Adam Pastorius, held prominent public offices. After several years in the Latin school in Windsheim, Pastorius studied at various European universities, including Altdorf, Strassburg, Basel, Jena, and Regensburg. He graduated with a doctorate in law from Altdorf in 1676. Pastorius briefly practiced law in his hometown before moving to Frankfurt am Main and becoming closely associated with Pietist circles. From 1680 to 1682, Pastorius accompanied a German nobleman on a grand tour and visited various European countries. Returning to Frankfurt, Pastorius learned about the Pietists' plans to purchase land in Pennsylvania, and he enthusiastically agreed to function as their agent. He left Frankfurt in April 1683, and, on his way to Rotterdam, he visited the group of Krefeld Quakers who later that year joined him in Pennsylvania. Pastorius arrived in Philadelphia in August 1683, and he immediately negotiated the location and size of the German settlement with William Penn. While he became increasingly alienated from the Frankfurt Pietists (who failed to join him in Pennsylvania), Pastorius assumed a central position in the life of the Germantown community, and he forged a number of friendships with English Quakers. He married Anna Klostermann in 1688, and the couple had two sons, Johann Samuel and Heinrich. Pastorius died in Germantown sometime between December 26, 1719, and January 13, 1720.

For biographical details in Pastorius's own work, see *Circumstantial Geographical Description of Pennsylvania*, trans. Gertrude Selwyn Kimball, in Albert Cook Myers, *Narratives of Early Penn-*

Pastorius continued to invest in approximating human communication and the language of the spirit, which, he hoped, would result in greater harmony in all human affairs. In the following encyclopedia entry, he touched upon the hallmarks of the seventeenth-century religious occupation with language:

456. *Language, add Speech, Tongue, Original Tongue, English Tongue:* linguae differentes (:expressa Babylonis vestigial:) numerantur ab audoribus septuaginta due, non connumerando diveras adjustu jury dialectos, true Canting. A linguist rather than a realist. Strange gibberish. State English, Court English, Secretary English, Plain English; the last the best. Whatsoever tongue will gain the race of perfection must run on these four wheels, Significancy, Easiness, Copiousness and Sweetness, so that we may express the meaning of our minds aptly, readily, fully and handsomly *[sic].* . . . The language of Canaan for purity and verity. . . . Hebrew—Greek and Latin makes no minis-

sylvania, West New Jersey, and Delaware (New York, 1912) (translation of *Umständige geographische Beschreibung der zu allerletzt erfundenen Provintz Pensylvaniae, in denen End-Gräntzen Americae in der West-Welt gelegen* . . . [Frankfurt and Leipzig, 1700]); and two sketches in manuscript, "Kurtzer Lebens Lauff" in his inventory "Res Propriae," 5-12, Pastorius Papers, Historical Society of Pennsylvania, Philadelphia, and "Genealogia Pastoriana," in "Bee-Hive," MS Codex 726, 221-226, Rare Book and Manuscript Library, University of Pennsylvania. The most comprehensive biographical works on Pastorius are Margo M. Lambert, "Francis Daniel Pastorius: An American in Early Pennsylvania, 1683-1719/20" (Ph.D. diss., Georgetown University, 2007); Marion Dexter Learned, *The Life of Francis Daniel Pastorius, the Founder of Germantown* (Philadelphia, 1908); John David Weaver, "Franz Daniel Pastorius (1651-c. 1720): Early Life in Germany with Glimpses of His Removal to Pennsylvania" (Ph.D. diss., University of California, Davis, 1985); DeElla Victoria Toms, "The Intellectual and Literary Background of Francis Daniel Pastorius" (Ph.D. diss., Northwestern University, 1953). For brief biographical sketches, see Alfred L. Brophy, "Bee-Hive, 1696, Francis Daniel Pastorius," in Marc Shell and Werner Sollors, eds., *The Multilingual Anthology of American Literature: A Reader of Original Texts with English Translations* (New York, 2000), 12-15; Rosamund Rosenmeier, "Francis Daniel Pastorius," in Emory Elliott, ed., *American Colonial Writers, 1606-1709, Dictionary of Literary Biography*, XXIV (Detroit, 1984), 245-247; Marianne S. Wokeck, "Francis Daniel Pastorius," Craig Horle et al., eds., *Lawmaking and Legislators in Pennsylvania: A Biographical Dictionary*, I, *1682-1709* (Philadelphia, 1991), 586-590.

On the "Bee-Hive," see Alfred Brophy, "'The Quaker Bibliographic World of Francis Daniel Pastorius's Bee-Hive," *PMHB*, CXXII (1998), 241-291; Patrick M. Erben, "'Honey-Combs' and 'Paper-Hives': Positioning Francis Daniel Pastorius's Manuscript Writings in Early Pennsylvania," *EAL*, XXXVII (2002), 157-194; Brooke Palmieri, "'What the Bees Have Taken Pains For': Francis Daniel Pastorius, The Beehive, and Commonplacing in Colonial Pennsylvania," 2008-2009 Penn Humanities Forum on Change, University of Pennsylvania, April 2009, http://repository.upenn.edu/uhf_2009/7/; Lyman W. Riley, "Books from the 'Beehive' Manuscript of Francis Daniel Pastorius," *Quaker History*, LXXXIII (1994), 116-129.

ter of God. *G.F. Journal.* The languages began at Babel; and the beast and whore have power over them. etc. Ad. P. 281, a linguist: In heaven all speak the L: of Canaan (: which some think is the Hebrew tongue:) if indeed they make any articulate sound. . . . We first learn to read our Native tongues, which [we] speak without teaching. . . .

The dead and living *Languages.* Hebrew the ancientest, Greek the most Copious, and Latin the finest. Hebrew and Greek S. Augustine calls the precedent or Original Tongues. . . . L: by attention and use may be learned, all the L: of the world signify nothing to us, unless we learn also, God's language, thereby to converse with him, Ludolf, p. 51. 'tis the Speech of the heart only, which is acceptable to God, bare words are too outward, and the strength of the Spirit often loses by the great Care of fine language.

As an encyclopedist, Pastorius did not write an argument for or against a particular position toward language, but he surveyed various religious, linguistic, and popular notions. His entry demonstrates his fascination and identification with linguists, especially polyglot individuals like himself. Pastorius wrote predominantly in German, English, Latin, and Dutch, but he also knew French, Italian, and Greek. His "Bee-Hive" manuscript included a title page in seven languages and is interspersed with multilingual poetry.[56]

At the same time, Pastorius echoed the widespread notion that the multiplicity of human languages originated at Babel and the spiritual fall associated with this scriptural event tainted linguistic diversity; the acquisition of classical languages was considered a particular symptom of spiritual corruption. Paraphrasing the Quaker founder George Fox, "The languages began at Babel; and the beast and whore have power over them," Pastorius highlighted the conflation of linguistic and religious degradation explicit in the Babel / Babylon complex that dominated seventeenth-century thought on both topics. He also revealed his own ambivalence about the intellectual

---

56. Translation of the Latin: "The different languages (expressions of the remainders [vestiges] of Babel) are numbered by the authors as seventy-two, not counting any adjustments for many others judged to be dialects." "Ludolf" probably refers to Hiob Ludolf, a German jurist and linguist, who dedicated the latter part of his life to the study of African languages. He moved to Frankfurt am Main in 1678, where Pastorius could have met him or at least heard of his work. See Jürgen Tubach, "Hiob Ludolf," *Biographisch-bibliographisches Kirchenlexikon,* V (1993), columns 317-325, http://www.bautz.de/bbkl/l/ludolf_h.shtml.

culture of elite European society and his complex allegiances to German Pietist and English Quaker sensibilities.

Pastorius's encyclopedia entry further traced the fascination with and speculation over two concomitant linguistic ideals—the identification of Hebrew as the original language purportedly spoken in Eden (and possibly in heaven) and the development of an ideal or artificial language possessing specific qualities such as "Significancy, Easiness, Copiousness and Sweetness." That Pastorius and other seventeenth-century Protestants were not satisfied with finding a language that would merely present the best possible way of communicating among *humans* becomes obvious in his assertion that one must "learn also, God's language, thereby to converse with him." Pastorius's maxim thus provides the linchpin for applying the European linguistic theories to the discourses on language and community in Pennsylvania: language reform, for Pastorius and many others before and after him, was in vain if it did not bring human expression closer to the divine meaning or truth. Theologians, philosophers, and religious reformers evoked the ideal of a spiritual language in which human beings could, once more, communicate with God. Pastorius's statement that "'tis the Speech of the heart only, which is acceptable to God" epitomizes the focus of virtually all seventeenth-century Christian reform movements—from Pietism in Germany to Quakerism and later Methodism in England to Quietism in the Catholic countries. Almost uniformly, they emphasized that true faith could not come from the acceptance of religious doctrine—even the literal acceptance of the Bible—but had to spring from a deep, emotional conviction. The projects of linguistic and spiritual reformation were so closely intertwined because they were believed to originate in a common locus. True faith spoke the language of the heart and soul. Colonial Pennsylvanians knew that the work of building an exemplary community distinguished by brotherly love and religious liberty required a constant attention to and negotiation of the language they used. Building community in early Pennsylvania was always a religious and a linguistic enterprise.

The story of the influence of seventeenth- and early-eighteenth-century theories of the confusio linguarum on the development of literature, culture, religion, and especially the formation of communities in Pennsylvania has never been told. Scholarship has never analyzed how individuals and groups in Pennsylvania (or other British colonies in North America) adapted traditional and recent interpretations of Babel to the concrete problems of spiritual and linguistic difference in the New World. An examination of discourses of community in the province, therefore, reveals the story of the ultimate intertwining of the theory and reality of linguistic and spiritual confusion. Pennsylvanians sought to overcome the effects of Babel by communicating across linguistic divisions, while simultaneously developing or searching for a common spiritual language that could operate and build community regardless of linguistic diversification and religious denomination.

Translating Pennsylvania

VISIONS OF SPIRITUAL COMMUNITY IN
PROMOTIONAL LITERATURE

fter William Penn had received the charter to a huge tract of land in the spring of 1681, he and other English Quakers embarked on an unprecedented project of promoting and building a new settlement. For the first time in the history of British coloniza- tion in America, Pennsylvania was envisioned as a refuge for linguistically, culturally, and religiously diverse immigrants. Penn's colony attracted a "mix'd multitude," resulting in a remarkably pluralistic society. Yet scholars know little about promotional literature on Pennsylvania itself, especially how it anticipated, theorized, and prepared structures of translin- gual and intercultural communication and communal construction. Penn, his promoters in England and on the Continent, and a network of radical Protestant—especially Pietist—sympathizers developed the first translin- gual project of advertising and settling a New World colony. Translation and multilingual dissemination became the central tools and tropes for con- structing and representing such a project.[1]

1. On Penn's activism for religious toleration and freedom of conscience, see Hugh S. Barbour, "Penn's Arguments for Toleration," in Barbour, ed., *William Penn on Religion and Ethics: The Emer- gence of Liberal Quakerism* (Lewiston, N.Y., 1991), 393–399; Edwin B. Bronner, "'Truth Exalted' through the Printed Word," in Bronner and David Fraser, eds., *William Penn's Published Writings, 1660–1726: An Interpretive Bibliography*, vol. V of Mary Maples Dunn and Richard S. Dunn et al., eds., *The Papers of William Penn* (Philadelphia, 1981–1986), 24–45 (hereafter cited as *Penn Papers*); Bronner, *William Penn's "Holy Experiment": The Founding of Pennsylvania, 1681–1701* (New York, 1962); William J. Buck, *William Penn in America; or, An Account of His Life* (Philadelphia, 1888); Mary Maples Dunn, *William Penn: Politics and Conscience* (Princeton, N.J., 1967); Richard S. Dunn and Mary Maples Dunn, eds., *The World of William Penn* (Philadelphia, 1986); Melvin B. Endy, Jr., *William Penn and Early Quakerism* (Princeton, N.J., 1973); Jean R. Soderlund et al., eds., *William Penn and the Founding of Pennsylvania, 1680–1684: A Documentary History* (Philadelphia, 1983), 48–86; Mary K. Geiter, *William Penn* (New York, 2000); Harry Emerson Wildes, *William Penn* (New York, 1974). Regarding religious liberty and toleration in Pennsylvania, see J. William Frost, "Reli- gious Liberty in Early Pennsylvania," *Pennsylvania Magazine of History and Biography*, CV (1981), 419–451; Sally Schwartz, *"A Mixed Multitude": The Struggle for Toleration in Colonial Pennsylvania*

Translation had spread reports of the New World throughout earlier phases of Spanish, Portuguese, French, Dutch, Swedish, and English exploration and discovery and thus made the European imagination of America an integral part of the intellectual, political, and social development of early modern Europe. Like the land itself, no accounts of the New World remained the sole property of one nation or people. Yet most European powers were as opposed to sharing the textual representation of the New World as they were unwilling to share the land they claimed. Texts reporting on the discovery, exploration, and settlement of America became "captives" to imperial contenders just like the people involved. The promotion of early Pennsylvania was remarkably different. Although Penn certainly styled himself a governor and proprietor who would rule over and also profit from the colony similar to an aristocratic landholder, he and other Quaker promoters and land agents specifically asked members of various Christian denominations (excluding Catholics) and other nations to join the settlement and communal development of the nascent society.[2]

(New York, 1987); Frederick B. Tolles, "The Culture of Early Pennsylvania," *PMHB*, LXXXI (1957), 119–137; Michael Zuckerman, "Introduction: Puritans, Cavaliers, and the Motley Middle," in Zuckerman, ed., *Friends and Neighbors: Group Life in America's First Plural Society* (Philadelphia, 1982), 3–25.

2. On the translingual circulation of exploration narratives and promotional accounts, see Ralph Bauer, *The Cultural Geography of Colonial American Literatures: Empire, Travel, Modernity* (Cambridge, 2003); Lisa Voigt, *Writing Captivity in the Early Modern Atlantic: Circulations of Knowledge and Authority in the Iberian and English Imperial Worlds* (Chapel Hill, N.C., 2009).

In comparing English and German immigrant writings, I frequently refer to "national" differences and use the term "transnational" to describe a crossing or bridging of divisions between both groups. I consciously apply this vocabulary to describe communal positions and group relationships in a period before the emergence of "nationalism" and the modern nation-state. Essentially, I follow contemporary (that is, late-seventeenth- and early-eighteenth-century) uses of the terms "nation." Writers and immigrants recognized "national" difference in the "ethno-symbolic" sense described by Anthony D. Smith. Accordingly, the term "nation" before the emergence of nationalism evoked a host of cultural, mythographic, and ethnic signifiers—including language, geography, and consanguinity—that helped members of a specific group to identify themselves and others. Even though this definition of "nation" or "nationality" embraces our present use of "ethnicity," I prefer to use the term "nation" because it was meaningful and widely used in the period I investigate. For example, the Lutheran pastor Justus Falckner wrote in 1701 in a report to church authorities in Germany about the different "nations" present in early Pennsylvania and their respective religious allegiances: "Und so ist die Protestantische Kirche auch hier in drey Nationen getheilet, denn es ist hier eine Englische protestantische Kirche, es ist eine Schwedische protestantische Lutherische Kirche, und sind hier Leute Teutscher Nation von der Evangelischen Lutherischen auch reformirten Kirchen" ["And thus the Protestant church here is also divided into three nations, for there is here an English Protestant church, there is a Swedish Protestant Lutheran church, and here are also people of the German nation of the evangelical Lutheran church and also the reformed church."] See *Abdruck eines*

The promotional literature on Pennsylvania appealed to the existing search for a Philadelphian society among religious radicals in Europe. Rather than clothing the new colony in fantastic descriptions of wealth and abundance, the promotional literature on early Pennsylvania gave voice to contemporary hopes for a Philadelphian, anti-Babylonian community, which it mapped onto a nondescript colonial space. Just as with the development of Behmenism or Philadelphianism in England and Germany a few years before, the promotion of Pennsylvania became a complex intellectual and textual construction in which linguistic and denominational differences were blurred through a broadscale longing for religious and linguistic universalism. This language of spiritual community became most visible in moments of linguistic and cultural translation. In promoting the colony to religious radicals in Germany and Holland, Penn and his representatives on the Continent—especially Benjamin Furly, a polyglot English Quaker and merchant living in Rotterdam—had to emphasize a common purpose, which, at least in the beginning of the experiment, was almost always utopian.

The prevalence of the discourse of spiritual and linguistic utopianism can easily be missed by readers who solely rely on the *English*-language materials, thus failing to account for the prolific and influential production, dissemination, and discursive construction of Pennsylvania in Germany. A comparative reading of English and German promotional tracts

---

Schreibens an Tit. Herrn D. Henr. Muhlen, aus Germanton, in der americanischen Province Pensylvania, sonst Nova Suecia, den ersten Augusti, im Jahr unsers Heyls eintausend siebenhundert und eins; Den Zustand der Kirchen in America betreffend (n.p., 1702), 5.

Ultimately, shared linguistic systems allowed Pennsylvanians to categorize and comprehend difference. Although the regional heritage of German immigrants meant little to English settlers in Pennsylvania, linguistic difference structured their everyday interaction. Moreover, the promotional tracts transmitted to Germany by individuals such as Pastorius, Daniel Falckner, and Justus Falckner made very little reference to regional differences among German immigrants. Instead, they focused on the national, linguistic, and especially denominational differences that reverberated in the context of early Pennsylvania. Justus Falckner wrote in his report: "There are a great number of *Germans* here, who, however, have crept in with other sects which have the English language, which is being learned immediately by all who come here. Many of them are Quakers, Anabaptists, and some of them Free Thinkers, who are not aligned with anybody and let their children grow up in the same spirit" (6, emphasis added). Here, Falckner can speak summarily of "Germans" because what matters most to him is that they learned English and joined the Quakers. Thus, the linguistic contact and religious diversity of colonial Pennsylvania blurred or concealed regional differences that might have been significant in the home country. See Martin Krieger, " 'Transnationalität' in vornationaler Zeit? Ein Plädoyer für eine erweiterte Gesellschaftsgeschichte der Frühen Neuzeit," *Geschichte und Gesellschaft*, XXX (2004), 125–136; Anthony D. Smith, *Myths and Memories of the Nation* (New York, 1999).

reveals a preoccupation with questions of linguistic, cultural, and national difference as well as the hope for a widely accepted communal ethics to make life more harmonious and ordered. Before settlers began to interact with one another, the writers, editors, translators, and booksellers involved in the promotion of the province paved a textual path of exchange that allowed immigrants to imagine not only their encounter with strange cultures, languages, and political systems but also the possibility for their own transcultural or translingual mobility. Accounts of early Pennsylvania written by William Penn, Francis Daniel Pastorius, and other authors passed through a process of translation, editorial amendment, and dissemination that adjusted the promotional discourse to culturally and linguistically specific sensibilities. In reading these tracts, prospective German and English immigrants encountered textual examples of cultural flexibility while coming to expect a degree of partisan confrontation. Since the new province was textually represented to various constituencies as a malleable space adapted to their interests, immigrants could feasibly hope to become involved in the future construction of the new community as well. A colonial and promotional project that could have been purely geared toward English imperial expansion devolved power and textual authority to non-English promoters and writers who appealed to diverse audiences.[3]

Specifically, the production and dissemination of German tracts relied on the intercession of local agents and interest groups who were themselves considering settlement in Pennsylvania and distributed Penn's writings among other prospective immigrants. Along with the translation and editorial amendment of the original English accounts, manuscript circulation further decentralized the power structure of English colonization. Personal

3. While assuming that "promotional literature acquainted large numbers of people with settlement opportunities," historian Marianne S. Wokeck admits in her study of German immigration to colonial America that "no systematic survey and analysis of the promotional literature in the Rhine lands in the eighteenth century exists." See Wokeck, *Trade in Strangers: The Beginnings of Mass Migration to North America* (University Park, Pa., 1999), 26. John Smolenski includes some of the German promotional accounts on early Pennsylvania in *Friends and Strangers: The Making of a Creole Culture in Colonial Pennsylvania* (Philadelphia, 2010), esp. "Narratives of Early Pennsylvania, I: Life on the Colonial Borderlands," 178–212, and "Narratives of Colonial Pennsylvania, II: The Founding of Pennsylvania," 215–248. I use the terms "translingual" and "transcultural" to describe the quality or subjectivity of individuals, groups, communal activities, and texts that results from the practice of translation, both in a linguistic and cultural sense. I prefer the prefix "trans" to "inter" in terms such as "transcultural" because it denotes a bridging of differences resulting to a certain degree in the *trans*formation of the individuals.

letters from immigrants or colonial agents as well as handwritten copies of printed tracts evoked feelings of communal affect. In turn, promotional literature highlighted personal relationships among prominent German and English individuals involved in the settlement of Pennsylvania as the embodiment of community. For German readers, in particular, the friendship between William Penn and Francis Daniel Pastorius metaphorically linked both segments of the population. The representation of their relationship emphasized the key role of personal and spiritual congeniality in generating communal cohesion. The promotional writings by Penn and Pastorius were eventually combined in multiauthor publications and left a lasting impression of transnational cooperation among subsequent waves of immigrants.[4]

The Founder

During the 1670s, English Quakers sought to intensify ties to like-minded groups on the Continent by conducting missionary journeys to Holland and Germany in 1671 and 1677. How important these visits were is proven by the illustrious cast of Friends participating in the trips: William Penn, George Fox, Robert Barclay, George Keith, and Benjamin Furly. These journeys created international and interdenominational communication networks among dissenters in England and Europe while establishing the structures that Penn and his agents could harness to promote the settlement of Pennsylvania a few years later. Similar to the spiritual and intellectual exchanges characterizing the contacts between England and Germany throughout the seventeenth century, the Quaker visits explored, renewed, cemented, or established compatibilities among related religious groups, including Dutch Quakers, Mennonites, Pietists, and Labadists. Unlike missionaries attempting to convert followers of different faiths, Penn and his fellow travelers acted more like ministers tending to their flock. In keeping with the fundamental Quaker doctrine of the Inward Light working in all human beings, the missionaries were on a quest to find spiritual community among like-minded individuals. Thus, the particular meetings and exchanges Penn recorded in his journal describe a process of mutual opening. Although translation served as a practical, linguistic tool during the entire journey, spiritual community always appeared in the form of, or was facilitated by, supralinguistic bonds established during the meetings and culti-

4. Beatrice Pastorius Turner, "William Penn and Pastorius," *PMHB*, LVII (1933), 66–90.

vated later through correspondence and the exchange of religious writings. Hardly knowing that the word would become flesh in the form of Pennsylvania only five years later, Penn and his associates searched for a Philadelphian community among congenial Protestant groups and a common language of the spirit that would make such a fellowship possible. The literature of promotion eventually attempted to recapture this language and translate it to the discourse of colonial settlement.[5]

Surprisingly, Penn's journal largely eclipsed the role translators played during the journeys through Holland and Germany. Although he regularly mentioned the "Friends" who interpreted for him — Benjamin Furly and Jan Claus — Penn never described directly how communication with Dutch Quakers or German Pietists worked on a concrete level. Did Furly and Claus translate simultaneously while Penn or Keith preached? In a faith emphasizing the direct workings of the spirit within and its outpouring into spoken language, this practice could potentially have been disruptive to the spiritual goals of the journey. Or did Penn's translators wait until he was finished speaking and then repeat, paraphrase, or merely summarize his efforts? In any case, spiritual content might have gotten lost in translation, which potentially explains Penn's unwillingness to mention the interpreters' work. Primarily, Penn's journal eclipsed translation because he tried to recreate linguistic and spiritual universalism. Speech, in the most paradigmatic moments of his journal, appears as a mutual outpouring of spiritual language. The most frequent word Penn employs in describing such moments is the word "opening," which, in going beyond Jacob Boehme and George Fox's *individual* insights into the divine language of the universe, evoked a *communal* access to a divine language or idiom.

Concretely, of course, evocations of such linguistic and spiritual unanimity simply served to heal divisions or even squelch disagreements regarding religious discipline and doctrine. At the start of Penn's longer journey in 1677, the Dutch Friends at Amsterdam formulated a resolution designed to pursue a unified language of the spirit and thus prevent disputes:

5. [William Penn], *An Account of William Penn's Travels in Holland and Germany* . . . (London, 1714); *Penn Papers,* I, 425–508; Rosalind J. Beiler, "Bridging the Gap: Cultural Mediators and the Structure of Transatlantic Communication," in Norbert Finzsch and Ursula Lehmkuhl, eds., *Atlantic Communications: The Media in American and German History from the Seventeenth to the Twentieth Century* (Oxford, 2004), 45–64; Beiler, "Distributing Aid to Believers in Need: The Religious Foundations of Transatlantic Migration," *Pennsylvania History,* LXIV (1997), 73–87; William I. Hull, *William Penn and the Dutch Quaker Migration to Pennsylvania* (Baltimore, 1970), 1–177.

It is also agreed, that the care of reading and approving books be layd upon some of every meeting, to the end, no book may be publisht; but in the unity: Yet any other faithful Friends not so nominated are not thereby excluded. Though in all those cases it is desired, that all would avoyd *unnecessary disputes about words,* which profitt not; but keep in the love, that edifyeth.

The dialectics (or, potentially, contradictions) between difference and unity encapsulated in this passage hint at the conflicted Quaker attitudes toward language. Words, individually spoken or published in books, are to create rather than divide the community of love. Yet such testimonials of unity also display the awareness of the possible suppression of the individual by the community. Although reading and approving future publications seems like communal censorship, the group monitoring this process may virtually include anyone, since "other faithful Friends not so nominated are not thereby excluded." On one level, this is circular reasoning that exposes the potential futility of such efforts: the committee in charge of assuring communal love through unity is itself opened up to dissolution. This particular meeting—consisting of a heterogeneous membership—thus debated a paradigmatic question for the later struggles among Quakers and related groups in Pennsylvania: How can a faith built on the primacy of individual conscience and a personal relationship to God ensure the unity of love within the community? In moments of conflict or disagreement, can unity be created without suppressing the Inward Light? Is love always an outpouring of the spirit, or is it a function of the community? Ultimately, the answer could be found only in continuous evocations of a unified language of the spirit. If the spirit dwelling within each individual could be expressed in a common language, unity and love would follow. Communal success, in other words, would depend on the degree in which individual members were equipped to distinguish spiritual communication from mere "disputes about words."[6]

Notwithstanding such fundamental contradictions, Penn attempted to cultivate a language that harnessed an immediate connection with the divine as a medium for creating spiritual community. Coming into contact with different denominations and languages highlighted for Penn the necessity to reach deeper into a common storehouse of spiritual signifiers. In particular, Penn was interested in outward evidence of the inward breaking down

6. *Penn Papers,* I, 425 (emphasis added), 435.

of a fallen, human self-will or self-determination and thus an "opening" to the workings of the spirit. A follower of the spiritualist ideas of Jean de Labadie (1610–1674), the Princess Elizabeth of the Palatinate (1618–1680) became Penn's poster child for the power of the spirit upon the individual. The princess might first have come in contact with Quaker principles during a visit from William Ames to her brother's court in Heidelberg in 1659. In 1676, Robert Barclay and Benjamin Furly had visited her in Herford and begun an extensive communication and exchange of religious materials with her as well as Elizabeth's close friends, the Labadist leader Anna Maria van Schurman and the Dutch countess Anna Maria van Hoorn. These exchanges and correspondences prepared structures of linguistic and spiritual transfer later repeated and expanded in spreading promotional literature on Pennsylvania in Germany and Holland: Benjamin Furly translated Barclay's and other Quaker writings into Dutch and German for the Princess Elizabeth and the Countess van Hoorn. Eager to spread Quaker writings, van Hoorn—who was becoming increasingly proficient in English— "translated out of English into Dutch a book of Isaac Pennington's"; in turn, Barclay had Furly translate van Hoorn's Dutch-language letters into English and forwarded them to the daughters of English Quaker leader Margaret Fell. Even before Penn's own visit to the Princess Elizabeth, therefore, Quakers had set up a translingual network of spiritual correspondence, establishing a spiritual community among Quakers in England and Holland and their sympathizers among Labadists, Pietists, and other radical Protestants.[7]

Penn's journal of his personal visit to the princess reverberates with the attempt to strive for an even higher, mystical level of spiritual communication that would—at least for a moment—do away with linguistic signification altogether. Upon concluding the first meeting at the princess's residence in Herford, Penn described the effect of this supralinguistic communion by evoking the Johannine equation of Christ with the "living word," which restores humankind's direct relationship to God. Penn elaborated on the qualities of the revelation of divine meaning in olfactory language appealing to the senses rather than the intellect:

7. Hull, *William Penn*, 2–19. On Labadie and his followers, see T. J. Saxby, *The Quest for the New Jerusalem: Jean de Labadie and the Labadists, 1610–1744* (Dordrecht, 1987). On Elizabeth of the Palatinate, see *Penn Papers*, I, 503 n. 62; Hull, *William Penn*, 21–22. On Schurman and van Hoorn, see ibid., 22–35. Van Hoorn was able to translate from English into Dutch, but not vice versa. Elisabeth was apparently proficient in English, German, and Dutch (26).

O the word that never faileth them, that wait for it, and abide in it, opened the way, and insealed the book of life. Yea, the quickening power and life of Jesus wrought and reach'd to them; and Virtue from him, in whom dwelleth the Godhead bodily, went forth, and blessedly destilled upon us his own heavenly {life} [illegible deletion] sweeter then the spices with pure Franckincense; yea then the sweet smelling myrrh, that cometh from a far Country.

The language of God manifested itself by appealing to the nonlinguistic sensory functions of all those present, thus transcending any linguistic or denominational differences. The communion Penn and Elizabeth experienced apparently went beyond linguistic mediation.[8]

In radical Protestant thought, the ultimate failure of human language was interpreted as a sign of mystical fullness. As the ineffable qualities of the divine confounded speech, loss of language was evidence of direct contact with the divine. After the meeting, Penn suddenly found himself in a more intimate spiritual moment with the princess. The journal poignantly linked the princess's failure to express herself to her physical, outward manifestation of deep inner turmoil and, finally, to Penn's own spiritual transformation:

The Princesse came to me, and took me by the hand . . . and went to speak to me of the sense she had of that power and presence of god, that was amongst us; but was stopd: and turning herself to the window broke forth in an extraordinary {passion}, [illegible deletion] crying out, *I can not speak to you, my heart is full; clapping her hand upon her breast.* It melted me into a deep and calm tenderness, in wch I was moved to minister a few words softly to her.

According to the apophatic tradition in mysticism, in approaching an ultimately unknowable and transcendent God human beings would find themselves speechless; the experiences of the divine, in other words, were ineffable. Penn's narrative interprets the princess's speechlessness, not as a sign of her failure to comprehend the Holy Spirit's working upon her, but rather as testimony of the intensity of her mystical experience.[9]

8. *Penn Papers,* I, 445.

9. Ibid., I, 445; Steven Fanning, *Mystics of the Christian Tradition* (London, 2001). According to Fanning, Christian mysticism distinguised between apophatic (also know as *via negativa*) and cataphatic *(via positiva)* theology, with the former stating what God is by way of negation and the latter by way of affirmation (36–38). Fanning cited a passage from the work of an early follower of the

The passage masterfully constructed a spiritual reciprocity between the princess and Penn, mediated by a set of physical and emotional gestures that ultimately dissolve the borders between self and other. Though language failed here, communication succeeded on a spiritual level. That the princess indeed felt the "power and presence of god" is proven by her inability to describe it. Tears and other physical manifestations of deep spiritual and emotional turmoil were among the stock features of radical Protestant religious literature, especially poetry and hymnody. The divine fullness that affected the princess's heart and transported her into an "extraordinary {passion}" corresponded to physical passions regularly harnessed by Baroque poets to heighten the transforming power of divine love. That this passage spoke with a strongly erotic undertone is therefore no accident. The princess's divinely inspired passion had a commensurate effect on Penn, who described his response in terms that show him as particularly open to the spirit. Although the passage is ripe for satirizing, Penn's description has nothing to do with romantic love. Rather, if both seemed transported into passionate and tender states of body and mind, it was because they were absorbed into a spiritual union with God that erased all barriers between human beings. Penn and the princess become one with each other because they have become one with God.

Throughout his travels in Germany, Penn attempted to create and describe such moments of spiritual union with God—manifested, not in language, but in outward, physical signs and expressions—that would simultaneously induce the perfect condition of spiritual communion with others. After Herford, Penn sought out members of the most active and well-known radical Protestant or Philadelphian circles in Germany, the "Saalhof Pi-

---

apophatic method, the Pseudo-Dionysian Maximus the Confessor (580–662), that defines an apophatic experience of the divine that closely resembles Penn's description of the princess's experience: "When in the full ardor of its love for God the mind goes out of itself, then it has no perception at all either of itself or of any creatures. For once illumined by the divine and infinite light, it remains insensible to anything that is made by him, just as the physical eye has no sensation of the stars when the sun has risen" (37). Apophatic notions of mysticism, in other words, stress the unknowability of God and demand self-denial to remove physical or fleshly obstructions against a union with the divine. In describing the application of apophatic language by the German mystic and founder of Ephrata, Jeff Bach wrote: "A seeker prepares for the immediate presence of God through the denial and loss of self" (*Voices of the Turtledoves: The Sacred World of Ephrata* [University Park, Pa., 2003], 36–37). Moravian and other Christo-centric mystical groups in this period, however, stressed the cataphatic approach in their adoration for the physical sacrifice of Christ and his physical attributes, resulting in the *outpouring* of language describing mystical longing and union with the divine (for instance, in blood and wounds litanies and hymnody).

etists." Originally created as one of Philipp Jakob Spener's Pietist conventicles during the late 1670s, the Frankfurt Pietists moved toward a more radical chiliastic and mystical orientation under the leadership of Johann Jakob Schütz, Johann Wilhelm Petersen, and his (later) wife Johanna Eleonora von Merlau. Again trying to bridge linguistic differences by transcending language altogether, Penn instructed the Pietists in the methods of a "silent meeting," which entailed the suspension of all human-image making and thus a listening to the language of the soul:

> We recommended a silent meeting unto them that they might grow into an holy Silence into themselves; that the mouth, that calleth god Father, that is not of his own birth, may be stopped, and all Images confounded. That they might hear the soft voice of Jesus to instruct them, and receive his sweet life to feed them, and to build them up.

Penn here espoused a radically Neoplatonist division between inner and outer language. He asked the Frankfurt Pietists to suspend all human language so that the inner language, or "soft voice of Jesus," could be heard. Eventually, Penn and his associates felt they had accomplished their "mission" among the Frankfurt Pietists when the breaking of the human self-will resulted in a particular perceptiveness to the language of the divine: "The Lord did so abundently *[sic]* appear amongst us, that they were more broken, then we had seen them at any time. Yea, they were exceeding tender and low; and the Love of god was much raised in their hearts to the Testimony. In this *sensible Frame* we left them; and the blessings and peace of our Lord Jesus Christ with {and among} them." Penn created, in his estimation, the perfect spiritual communion; through his facilitation, both sides reached a state in which they could freely partake in spiritual openings. Rather than tying the Pietists to the Quakers by outlining common articles of faith, the missionaries induced a state of mystical lowliness where spiritual reception was freed from the human will and human language was confounded.[10]

Among the Pietists, Penn apparently felt most connected to Merlau, with whom he initiated a lively correspondence after the visit to Frankfurt. In a

10. *Penn Papers*, I, 455 (emphasis added). On Spener and his work in Frankfurt, see Martin Brecht, "Philipp Jakob Spener, sein Programm und dessen Auswirkungen," in Brecht, ed., *Der Pietismus vom siebzehnten bis zum frühen achtzehnten Jahrhundert*, vol. I of *Geschichte des Pietismus* (Göttingen, 1993), 281–328; Andreas Deppermann, *Johann Jakob Schütz und die Anfänge des Pietismus* (Tübingen, 2002).

letter written from Düsburg on September 11, 1677, Penn defined Merlau and the rest of her community as a mystical society receiving divine communications binding them to God and to each other: "For this know, it was the life in your selves, that so sweetly visited you by the ministry of life through us." Rather than Penn and the other "missionaries" teaching or instilling in the Pietists a Christian faith, they opened an awareness of the spirit within themselves. Spiritual community, for Penn, was thus the mutual discovery of the residence of the spirit within individuals. It could be facilitated through various kinds of ministry, but, most important, it consisted of the mutual ability to listen to the language of the soul. Although the Quaker and radical Pietist quest for spiritual community sought divine openings through a suspension of language, personal correspondence clearly harnessed textuality as a stand-in for relationships operating outside language. Yet the epistolary genre itself was for Quakers and other radical Protestants no more than the dead "letter" of human language if it was not filled with the spirit. Letters could reverberate with the spiritual community established earlier in their personal interaction. In addition, letters could be deployed to evoke common religious experiences and thus project a degree of spiritual compatibility well in excess of the letter and its message.[11]

Letter writing thus served to cement spiritual bonds already established through physical acquaintance and fellowship but also to prepare new ties. Certain letters Penn wrote to individuals and groups, such as the Frankfurt Pietists, would eventually be printed or distributed in manuscript form, thus infusing wider communication with an impression of the spiritual bonds established in person or through correspondence. In turn, texts published by Penn as promotional tracts, for instance, would eventually be circulated in manuscript or even letter form among the networks established during these journeys, thus harnessing the seemingly impersonal medium of print to facilitate personal, spiritual relationships. During the actual missionary journey, the exchange of printed books served to expand and deepen nonlinguistic, spiritual bonds already established in person. Unlike traditional missionaries exclusively providing their prospective converts with appropriate reading materials, Penn and his associates both provided and received books. After leaving a group in Worms, Penn immediately sent them books in order to continue and deepen the impact of personal spiritual fellowship: "After we had discourst about an hour with him of the true and heavenly ministry, and worship, and in what they stood; and wt all

11. *Penn Papers,* I, 470–471.

people must come unto, if ever they will know {how} to worship god aright, we departed: and immediately sent them several good books of Friends in high dutch." Importantly, this statement stressed the significance of translation in facilitating textual exchanges between Quakers and non-Quakers, English and German Christians. Penn and the other missionaries apparently tapped into an existing market or trade in Quaker books for individuals and groups on the Continent. The production of translated books and edited compilations of promotional materials on Pennsylvania a few years later continued existing practices of Quaker books circulated — *in translation* — across Germany, Holland, and other countries on the Continent.[12]

During their travels, Penn and other prominent Quakers thus not only established the specific communication networks that would a few years later allow them to promote the founding and settlement of Pennsylvania among radical Protestant groups across Holland and Germany. More important, their visits, meetings, correspondence, and exchange of devotional books promoted the ideal of spiritual communication and spiritual community, which would soon become the foundation of the literature promoting settlement in Pennsylvania. The central activities of the missionaries always focused on the deployment of human language and human communication for the sake of facilitating nonverbal or nonlinguistic connections. Whether preaching, making contact through letters, ministering a few soft words to souls in turmoil, or instructing congregations in the art of holding silent meetings, the function of language was always to point beyond itself, toward a spiritual communion beyond the realm of speaking, reading, and writing. Here, spiritual community was accomplished precisely at the moments when human language had failed or was meant to fail.

Ostensibly, the literature promoting settlement in Pennsylvania would perform the opposite function: deploying language to represent the real — that is, the geography, vegetation, climate, native and European inhabitants, economy, civic institutions, and laws of the new province. With claims to authenticity made by supposed eyewitnesses, promotional literature pretended to create a stable relationship between word and thing, between signifier and signified. The promotional literature on Pennsylvania, however, frequently shifted the focus from this mimetic function of language to the nonlinguistic, spiritual, and visionary goals of settlement and communal formation. Translation and translingual dissemination pointed away from representational authenticity and toward preexisting, spiritual ideals to be

12. Ibid., I, 454.

created in Pennsylvania. It stressed the difficulties in carrying over concepts or ideas from one language and culture to another or in conveying the full spiritual and emotional weight of the bonds of Christian community projected onto Pennsylvania. While proposing civic institutions and describing economic opportunities, promotional literature reiterated the intangible and often indescribable nature of spiritual community.

The circulation and reception of these materials not only followed the networks Penn and his fellow missionaries had established but tried to recapture the supralinguistic ideals the Quaker travelers had promoted. The promotional writings that eventually triggered the Frankfurt Pietists to purchase land from Penn and send Pastorius to establish a settlement appealed to their readers because of the promise of spiritual fellowship. Even among groups and individuals whom Penn had not met in person during his travels, promotional writings on Pennsylvania would have a similar effect. When promotional literature slipped into a more conventional discourse of colonization and civic engineering, individuals like Benjamin Furly ensured its appeal to radical Protestant groups on the Continent by reintroducing, strengthening, or adding in translation the language of radical reform and spiritual community.

The Translators

In one of his first promotional tracts, entitled *Some Account of the Province of Pennsilvania* (1681), Penn specified as his audience "those of our own, or other Nations, that are inclin'd to Transport themselves or Families beyond the Seas." The targeting of those "other Nations" relied on the adaptation and translation of the English Quaker promotional discourse to the sensibilities of radical Protestants on the Continent, especially the Dutch and German groups Penn had visited a few years prior. Entitled *Eine Nachricht wegen der Landschaft Pennsilvania,* the German edition followed the general structure of Penn's *Some Account;* its departures and additions, however, addressed the shortcomings of the English original as a promotional tool for a German Protestant audience while highlighting the importance of the translation process in negotiating differences and distilling a common understanding. Whereas Penn's journal of his travels through Germany had eclipsed his translators' role in order to emphasize the transcendent quality of spiritual community, his promotional materials granted more influence to linguistic and cultural mediators. In distilling what mattered most to both English Quaker and German radical Protestant immigrants, translations and translators emphasized common spiritual denominators, particularly the desire for toleration and interdenominational harmony. As translator, editor, and distributor of Penn's promotional materials on the Continent, Benjamin Furly, in particular, wielded his influence in heightening reformist elements; he used prefaces and other metatextual devices to prepare non-English readers for the encounter with difference and to appeal to their desire for spiritual community.[13]

In adopting the English promotional discourse to a transnational and translingual audience, *Eine Nachricht* inserted English words and phrases — especially legal and historical terms — parenthetically in the German text and provided a glossary of the most difficult concepts (Figures 3 and 4). The anonymous translator (probably Furly or Clauss) introduced this bilingual feature in a preface that foreshadowed the linguistic and cultural incongruities German immigrants would encounter in America:

> How difficult, I dare not say impossible, it is to translate adequately and clearly the meanings of many expressions, particularly in the ancient laws and customs of a foreign country and its language, into the High-German, is sufficiently known to those who have dealt with this problem themselves. Therefore, I did not deem it inconvenient here to add both the English words in several instances as well as a short glossary of some of them in the end, hoping that the well-inclined reader will not be offended, but rather to receive it, as it is intended, favorably.

The preface justified the parenthetical insertions of English terms and the glossary as a crutch for overcoming the translator's self-avowed difficulties in transferring specific historical and legal terms from English to German. While asking the readers for their forbearance, the translator obliquely yet cleverly instructed prospective immigrants that it would be in their own interest not to rely on seemingly straightforward translations but to learn the English terms and their various connotations. The preface addressed the

---

13. William Penn, *Some Account of the Province of Pennsilvania in America* . . . (London, 1681), 1. For an overview of Penn's accounts of Pennsylvania and their spread on the Continent, see Hull, *William Penn,* 311–316. See also Penn, *Eine Nachricht wegen der Landschaft Pennsilvania in America* . . . (Amsterdam, 1681). The Dutch translation of this tract was made by Furly, but no translator of the German is listed. Hull speculates that it was Jan Claus (*William Penn,* 312). The preface cited below is simply signed "The translator." For a brief biographical note on Furly, see Albert Cook Myers, ed., *Narratives of Early Pennsylvania, West New Jersey, and Delaware, 1630–1707* (New York, 1912), 405n.

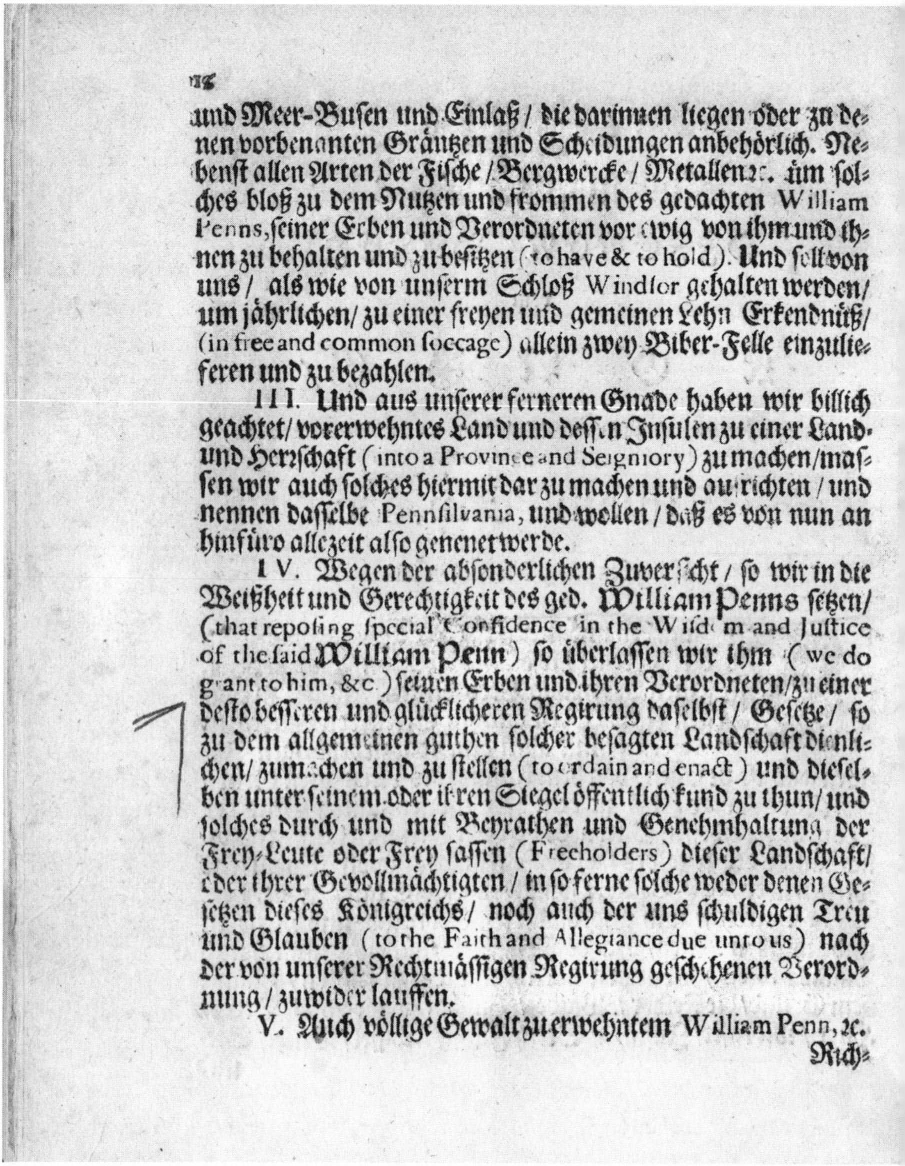

und Meer-Busen und Einlaß/ die darinnen liegen oder zu denen vorbenanten Gräntzen und Scheidungen anbehörlich. Nebenst allen Arten der Fische/ Bergwercke/ Metallen ꝛc. üm solches bloß zu dem Nutzen und frommen des gedachten William Penns, seiner Erben und Verordneten vor ewig von ihm und ihnen zu behalten und zu besitzen (to have & to hold). Und soll von uns/ als wie von unserm Schloß Windsor gehalten werden/ um jährlichen/ zu einer freyen und gemeinen Lehn Erkendnüß/ (in free and common soccage) allein zwey Biber-Felle einzuliefern und zu bezahlen.

III. Und aus unserer ferneren Gnade haben wir billich geachtet/ vorerwehntes Land und dessen Insulen zu einer Land- und Herrschaft (into a Province and Seigniory) zu machen/ massen wir auch solches hiermit dar zu machen und aurichten / und nennen dasselbe Pennsilvania, und wollen / daß es von nun an hinfüro allezeit also genenet werde.

IV. Wegen der absonderlichen Zuversicht / so wir in die Weißheit und Gerechtigkeit des ged. William Penns setzen/ (that reposing special Confidence in the Wisdom and Justice of the said William Penn) so überlassen wir ihm (we do grant to him, &c.) seinen Erben und ihren Verordneten/ zu einer desto besseren und glücklicheren Regirung daselbst / Gesetze/ so zu dem allgemeinen guthen solcher besagten Landschaft dienlichen/ zu machen und zu stellen (to ordain and enact) und dieselben unter seinem oder ihren Siegel öffentlich kund zu thun/ und solches durch und mit Beyrathen und Genehmhaltung der Frey-Leute oder Frey sassen (Freeholders) dieser Landschaft/ oder ihrer Gevollmächtigten / in so ferne solche weder denen Gesetzen dieses Königreichs/ noch auch der uns schuldigen Treu und Glauben (to the Faith and Allegiance due unto us) nach der von unserer Rechtmässigen Regirung geschehenen Verordnung/ zuwider lauffen.

V. Auch völlige Gewalt zu erwehntem William Penn, ꝛc.

Rich-

Figure 3. Page from William Penn, Eine Nachricht wegen der Landschaft Pennsilvania in America . . . *(Amsterdam, 1681), including parenthetical English insertions in German translation. By permission of The Historical Society of Pennsylvania (HSP)*

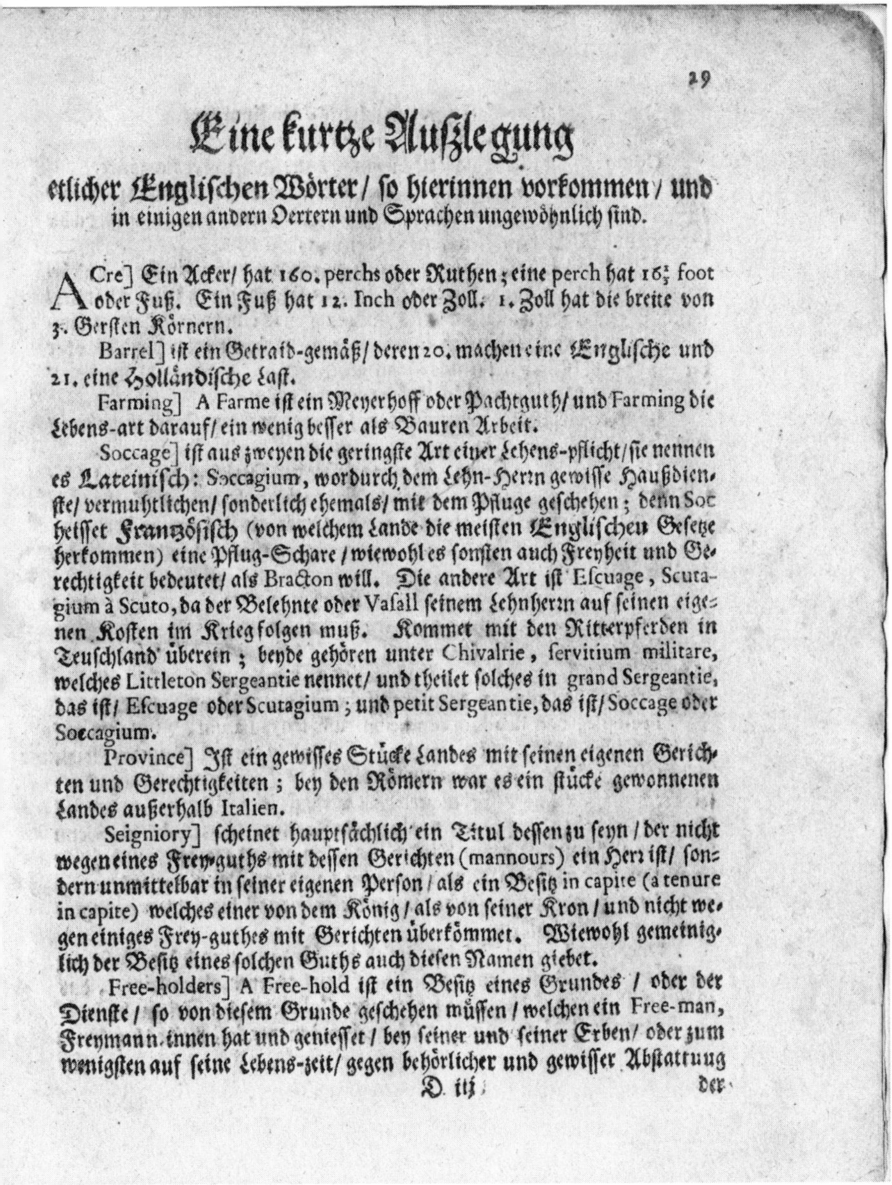

Eine kurtze Außlegung

etlicher Englischen Wörter/ so hierinnen vorkommen/ und in einigen andern Oertern und Sprachen ungewöhnlich sind.

Acre] Ein Acker/ hat 160. perchs oder Ruthen; eine perch hat 16½ foot oder Fuß. Ein Fuß hat 12. Inch oder Zoll. 1. Zoll hat die breite von 3. Gersten Körnern.

Barrel] ist ein Getraid-gemäß/ deren 20. machen eine Englische und 21. eine Holländische Last.

Farming] A Farme ist ein Meyerhoff oder Pachtguth/ und Farming die Lebens-art darauf/ ein wenig besser als Bauren Arbeit.

Soccage] ist aus zweyen die geringste Art einer Lehens-pflicht/ sie nennen es Lateinisch: Soccagium, wordurch dem Lehn-Herrn gewisse Haußdienste/ vermuhtlichen/ sonderlich ehemals/ mit dem Pfluge geschehen; denn Soc heisset Frantzösisch (von welchem Lande die meisten Englischen Gesetze herkommen) eine Pflug-Schare/ wiewohl es sonsten auch Freyheit und Gerechtigkeit bedeutet/ als Bracton will. Die andere Art ist Escuage, Scutagium à Scuto, da der Belehnte oder Vasall seinem Lehnherrn auf seinen eigenen Kosten im Krieg folgen muß. Kommet mit den Ritterpferden in Teuschland überein; beyde gehören unter Chivalrie, servitium militare, welches Littleton Sergeantie nennet/ und theilet solches in grand Sergeantie, das ist/ Escuage oder Scutagium; und petit Sergeantie, das ist/ Soccage oder Soecagium.

Province] Ist ein gewisses Stücke Landes mit seinen eigenen Gerichten und Gerechtigkeiten; bey den Römern war es ein stücke gewonnenen Landes außerhalb Italien.

Seigniory] scheinet hauptsächlich ein Titul dessen zu seyn/ der nicht wegen eines Frey-guths mit dessen Gerichten (mannours) ein Herr ist/ sondern unmittelbar in seiner eigenen Person/ als ein Besitz in capite (a tenure in capite) welches einer von dem König/ als von seiner Kron/ und nicht wegen einiges Frey-guthes mit Gerichten überkömmet. Wiewohl gemeiniglich der Besitz eines solchen Guths auch diesen Namen giebet.

Free-holders] A Free-hold ist ein Besitz eines Grundes/ oder der Dienste/ so von diesem Grunde geschehen müssen/ welchen ein Free-man, Freymann innen hat und geniesset/ bey seiner und seiner Erben/ oder zum wenigsten auf seine Lebens-zeit/ gegen behörlicher und gewisser Abstattung

D. iij   der

Figure 4. Glossary of English Terms with German Definitions in William Penn,
Eine Nachricht wegen der Landschaft Pennsilvania in America . . . *(Amsterdam, 1681).*
By permission of The Historical Society of Pennsylvania (HSP)

awareness of the cultural complexity of language that translators or bilingual individuals may possess but that he or she can hardly reflect in a direct translation from one word to another.[14]

Faced with this problem, the translator chose not to cover up the remoteness between signifier and signified but to reproduce among his readers his own awareness for the tenuous and vague correspondences between the English and German languages and their respective systems of cultural and historical meanings. Thus, the German edition of Penn's *Some Account* apprised German readers that immigration to Pennsylvania would entail the confrontation with an unknown country and sets of foreign linguistic, legal, and social systems. The translator's preface hinted at the limitations of any promotional treatment—particularly in translation—in anticipating the immigrant experience. At the same time, the partially bilingual structure also fulfilled the seemingly opposite didactic purpose of preparing these immigrants for their experience by anticipating words and expressions they would need. The translator thus rendered difference comprehensible and transparent. The translator's glossary—entitled "A Short Explanation of a Number of English Words Which Appear Herein and Are Uncommon in Several Other Languages and Countries"—continued the task of adopting the linguistic representation of Penn's account to the needs of prospective immigrants in German. Referring exclusively to words in the "Patent," the glossary explains in detail specific legal or social terms that are particularly difficult to translate because there may not be a German analogue or the implied concept and historical background do not exist in German culture. In the example of the term "View of Franke-pledge," the glossary provided a lengthy entry describing not only the current meaning but also its former usage. The cumbersome definition illuminated the interplay between familiarization and estrangement inherent in the project of translating promotional texts. An exclusively monolingual translation would obscure incongruities between English and German terms and thus erase the differences between the respective legal and cultural systems. By calling attention to

14. Penn, *Eine Nachricht*, 2: "Wie schwer, ich will nicht eben sagen, unmüglich es sey, die eigentliche Bedeutung etlicher Redens-arten, sonderlich in denen alten Gesetzen und Gebräuchen, eines frembden Landes und derselben Sprache in die Hoch-Teutsche behörlichen und deutlichen überzutragen, ist denen, so dergestalt darmit umbgangen, satsam wissend; Derohalben habe ich alhier nicht vor unbequehm zu seyn erachtet, so wohl an etlichen örtern die Englische Wörter, als auch am Ende eine kurtze Auslegung über einige wenige derselben beyzufügen, der guten Hofnung, es werde der freundlich-gewillete Leser mir solches nicht allein nicht [sic] verargen, sondern vielmehr, gleichwie es von mir gemeinet, im besten aufnehmen."

this incongruity and adding a historical apparatus, the translator attempted a more complete translation from one culture to another, thereby familiarizing the English system for German readers.[15]

Confronting the difficulty of representing the strange in familiar language, promotional treatments on Pennsylvania turned inward—toward a more spiritual plane of conceptualizing community in the new province. Faced with the kind of incongruities mentioned in the preface, the translator—as well as the entire promotional network—had to focus on elements that united the different constituencies involved in the settlement. Thus, translators and editors adapting the promotional literature for a radical Protestant readership in Germany tried to wield a common language of spiritual and moral renewal. Rather than inventing this feature for German readers, the translators and promoters on the Continent reemphasized Penn's or the Quakers' earlier activism for religious toleration throughout Europe. Translators and promoters wanted German and Dutch readers to know that fundamentally they already shared with Penn, as well as other English settlers, a common vocabulary and experience of persecution, piety, personal faith, and, especially, a quest for religious toleration.

Possibly for reasons beyond his control, however, Penn's first promotional tract nowhere mentioned religious toleration. *Some Account* promised the adoption of a constitution but did not specify that freedom of conscience would be part of it: "[As] soon as any are ingaged with me, we shall begin a Scheam or Draught together, such as shall give ample Testimony of my sincere Inclinations to encourage Planters, and settle a free, just and industrious Colony there." Adapting the tract to the sensibilities of German dissenters, the editor or translator of *Eine Nachricht* added the following clause to Penn's sentence: ". . . and also there to institute the freedom of conscience for anyone to practice their faith and to worship publicly." In grafting the clause on religious liberty onto *Some Account,* the translator or editor was drawing from the precedent Penn had set with his extensive writings on religious freedom before his acquisition of Pennsylvania. In order to bolster the emphasis on religious toleration even more, the German edition of *Some Account* included a letter arguing in favor of toleration for local Quakers that Penn had sent to the magistrates of Emden and Danzig, published in English as *Christian Liberty . . . Desired in a Letter to Certain For-*

15. Ibid., 29: "Eine kurtze Außlegung etlicher Englischen Wörter, so hierinnen vorkommen, und in einigen andern Oertern und Sprachen ungewöhnlich sind."

eign States (1674) and in German as *Send-Brieff an Die Bürgermeister und Rath der Stadt Danzig* (1675).[16]

How important a written guarantee of religious toleration in Pennsylvania was for European dissenters became evident in Benjamin Furly's critique of subsequent changes made in several drafts of the *Frame of Government*. The first *Frame of Government of the Province of Pennsilvania in America*, published in May 1682, was the result of some intense political and textual wrangling over the specific rights of the proprietor and the new settlers. The drafting process produced at least twelve preliminary documents and involved Penn's collaboration with several other interested individuals. Furly severely criticized the changes made between the initial draft, "The Fundamentall Constitutions of Pennsilvania," and the *Frame of Government* published in 1682. "Fundamentall Constitutions," the most liberal of all the drafts, opened with a proclamation of religious freedom. In the published *Frame of Government,* however, liberty of conscience was downgraded from the prominent status of a preamble to an almost insignificant position as item thirty-five. In a letter to Penn, Furly expressed his indignation over the changes: "Who has turned you aside from these good beginnings, to [establish] things unsavory and unjust; as fundamental to wch all Generations to come should be bound?" Furly objected to the less prominent position of religious toleration as well as to the absence of any regulation against excessive litigation, communicating to Penn his insight into the interpenetration of legal and religious sensibilities of German and Dutch immigrants: "Consider further that there are many Christians in holland *[sic]* and Germany that look upon it as unlawfull to sue any man at the Law, as to fight wth armes[.] These then having no other fence but their prudence in intrusting none but honst *[sic]* men." Furly also claimed that inheritance laws and a xenophobic naturalization policy disadvantaged non-English immigrants. Just as Penn's subsequent drafts of the *Frame of Government* had toned down the progressive social framework many prospective settlers had expected, the adopted version also limited its use as a spiritually unifying tool, as his earlier letters on toleration had been. As

16. Penn, *Some Account,* 5; Penn, *Eine Nachricht,* 10. The entire passage in German is (italics added for the inserted section): "So bald als sich einige mit mir eingelassen haben, so wollen wir zusammen einen Entwurff tuhn, welches ein völliges Zeugnüs meiner aufrichtigen Genegenheit geben soll, um die neu-anbauende aufzumuntern, und um eine freye, gerechte, und fleissige Erbauung (Colony) *auch die Gewissens-Freyheit eines jedwedern nach seinem Glauben und zu dessen öffentlichen übung des Gottesdienstes aldar* zu stifften." For Penn's original manuscript journal of his travels in 1677, entitled "An Account of My Journey into Holland and Germany," see *Penn Papers,* I, 425–508.

a translator and Quaker living in Rotterdam, Furly represented the middle ground or space in-between where, in translation, differences became apparent and commonalities needed to be forged.[17]

Furly's life in the cosmopolitan port city of Rotterdam, as well as his wide-ranging intellectual interests and illustrious friends—ranging from John Locke to the first earl of Shaftesbury—placed him in a unique position to become mediator of the spiritual and utopian principles underlying the founding of Pennsylvania. Even among fellow Quakers, Furly stood out through his strong anti-authoritarianism, but he also donned a broad and eclectic learning, especially in classical and foreign languages. Settling permanently in Rotterdam in 1661 to take advantage of the city's status as nexus of Atlantic and Continental trade, Furly began to amass a huge library. His collection reveals his interest in the work of German mystics, including Jacob Boehme and Francis Mercurius van Helmont, a German philosopher who reached prominence through his theories on the transmigration of souls. Through Helmont, Furly also came in contact with the mystical German theologian Christian Knorr von Rosenroth, whose publication of the Kabbalist text *Kabbala Denudata* (1677-1684) deeply impacted the development of German radical Pietism.[18]

Furly's readings in mystical theology and the Christian Kabbalah were in line with his strong interest in language, particularly questions of the deeper, divine significance of the scriptures as an inspired text. In a letter to Pierre Desmaizeaux, Furly alleged that mysteries were hidden in the text of the Bible and that there are "many such passages, wch to us seem insoluble by any knowne principles or systeme." Kabbalist modes of reading and interpreting the text of the Torah or even the Christian Bible as a code

17. *Penn Papers*, II, 140, 233, 235. The draft's commitment to religious toleration is unequivocal, granting to any person residing in Pennsylvania "the Free Possession of his or her faith and exercise of worship towards God, in such way and manner As every Person shall in Conscience believe is most acceptable to God" (143). See also Julius Friedrich Sachse, *Benjamin Furly, "an English Merchant at Rotterdam," Who Promoted the First German Emigration to America* (Philadelphia, 1895), 23-32; Luisa Simonutti, "English Guests at 'De Lantaarn': Sidney, Penn, Locke, Toland, and Shaftesbury," in Sarah Hutton, ed., *Benjamin Furly, 1646-1714: A Quaker Merchant and His Milieu* (Florence, 2007), 42-43.

18. On Furly's anti-authoritarianism, see Sarah Hutton, "Introduction," in Hutton, ed., *Benjamin Furly*, 7. For an analysis and description of Furly's library and reading practices, see Hutton, "Mercator Theologico-Philosophicus: Benjamin Furly Reading," ibid., 149-170. Hutton gives a detailed outline of Furly's "remarkable library of over 4,000 books" (Hutton, "Introduction," ibid., 2). A catalog of Furly's library was printed as *Bibliotheca Furliana; sive, Catalogus librorum honoratiss. et doctiss. viri Benjamin Furly* . . . (Rotterdam, 1714).

or divine script appealed to Furly on a spiritual and intellectual level. The mystical semiotics practiced in Kabbalist hermeneutics allowed trained or initiated readers to make sense of otherwise difficult or obscure passages; as language theory, Kabbalist reading practices accounted for the remoteness of the human signifier from the divine signified while promising a rediscovery or reuniting with divine signification. Similar to Boehme, Furly believed that spiritual meaning was still hidden beneath and accessible through human language. In a Philadelphian manner, Furly linked different languages through his translation work, but he also desired a deeper, mystical union of human language with the divine Word or "logos." His Philadelphian sentiments, moreover, were complemented by his belief in *"Universal Love,* a principle posited by God in man, 'in his heart and mouth.'" This divine principle, according to Furly, allowed the Inward Light to function as "an essential guide for following divine dictates." *Universal Love* pervaded the inner language of the soul and, if freed, would manifest itself in outward speech and actions.[19]

Even when political and economic business in the colony began to overshadow spiritual principles, Furly continued to remind Penn of the Philadelphian idealism responsible for its founding. Along with a 1684 letter to Penn, Furly sent the proprietor "3 or 4 books from V. Helmont, being 200 queries concerning the {doctrine of the} Revolutions of humane soules." In his letter, Furly first explained why he considered Helmont's theory a valuable tool for comprehending otherwise contradictory elements of the Christian faith. Helmont's theory specifically allowed him to render "compatible the justice of God with the punishment of apparently innocent souls." Furly did not say that he subscribed to Helmont's theory; rather, he emphasized its merit as a universalist interpretive tool for a central Christian mystery. Furly was appalled that Helmont was being maligned and ostracized in England. Much of Furly's letter, therefore, indicted the un-Christian treatment of the German theologian there and made a serious appeal to Penn that Pennsylvania should defy the hate mongering of religious orthodoxy. Furly's appeal to Penn's Philadelphian spirit thus culminated in a call for ex-

19. Furly quoted in Hutton, "Mercator," 160, and Simonutti, "English Guests," 37, both in Hutton, ed., *Benjamin Furly.* Having left France with his family after the revocation of the Edict of Nantes in 1685, the philosopher, journalist, and translator Pierre Desmaizeaux (1673–1745) spent much of his life in Holland (where he met Furly) and England. Desmaizeaux became most well known for his English translation of Pierre Bayle's *Dictionaire historique et critique* (1734–1738). See Herbert Jaumann, *Handbuch Gelehrtenkultur der frühen Neuzeit,* I, *Bio-bibliographisches Repertorium* (Berlin, 2004), 224; Benjamin Furly, *The Worlds Honour Detected . . .* (London, 1663).

tending Christian love across national boundaries. Mistreating a foreigner would reflect poorly on English hospitality and manners while betraying any aspirations of brotherly love professed by many religious dissenters, particularly Furly's fellow "Friends."[20]

To make explicit his vision for Pennsylvania as an antidote to European wickedness, Furly constructed a powerful rhetorical antithesis between both:

> I hop[e] if he [Helmont], or any of his perswasion in some of those things should come thither they shall not be so hunted as Foxes, but received as Christians, and not be unchristian for an opinion wch if christ did not [teach?] his disciples he at lest did bear[est?] with in them, and therefore must neither be in it self destructive of faith in [god?] nor of a holy conversation.

Literally speaking, Quakers had condemned foxhunting as a vain and cruel form of pleasure unbecoming a Christian people, but foxhunting is also a pun on the persecution of the Quaker founder, George Fox. Metaphorically, the foxhunt represented the false maligning of someone innocent of supposed deceptiveness or falseness. Fundamentally, Furly advanced a vision of Christian society as an antitype to a society that victimizes or ostracizes religious or national difference. As such a community, Pennsylvania was supposed to mend the anti-Christian behavior of England and forge a community characterized by universal love, charity, and a transdenominational harmony.[21]

It is difficult to measure Furly's success in advising Penn and trying to emphasize the reformist and exemplary characteristics of the new colony. His success in molding the laws of Pennsylvania to the advantage of German and Dutch immigrants, for instance, was limited. The second *Frame*

20. Benjamin Furly to William Penn, July 23, 1684, *Penn Papers,* II, 566; Hutton, "Mercator," in Hutton, ed., *Benjamin Furly,* 161.

21. Furly to Penn, July 23, 1684, *Penn Papers,* II, 567. Quakers were generally opposed to shooting and hunting for recreation but were especially against the pursuit of one creature by another, such as hunting with dogs. Quakers believed this practice debased the Christian sensibility of human beings and unnecessarily tormented fellow creatures. English Quaker Thomas Taylor protested against all those who pleased themselves "with beholding one creature hurt and torment another, yea, sometimes even to death, as at bull-baitings, bear-baitings, cock-fightings and the like. Oh, what minds have ye; and how contrary are ye herein to the tender nature of Christ and all Christians, truly so-called, who could never rejoice in any such things, by reason of their tender, pitiful and merciful nature" (quoted in William C. Braithwaite, *The Second Period of Quakerism,* 2d ed., prepared by Henry J. Cadbury [Cambridge, 1961], 565).

of Government adopted in Pennsylvania in 1683 did not grant Furly's open naturalization policy, yet it conferred the "property and inheritance rights of citizens" to all foreigners who had purchased land in Pennsylvania. Rather than making a direct impact on Penn's policies, Furly more likely determined the future spiritual and cultural landscape of Pennsylvania by promoting his vision among religious dissenters on the Continent, especially by confirming that their quest for religious toleration and a pious lifestyle would be met. For Furly, the promotional literature on early Pennsylvania could not just be *descriptive;* it had to become a *prescriptive* device for constructing the colony as an antidote to the ills of European society and religion.[22]

Concretely, Furly used his role as editor, translator, and distributor of subsequent promotional pamphlets to highlight existing provisions that were attractive for his constituents in Germany and Holland but had been demoted in English laws and promotional tracts. After his arrival in Pennsylvania in 1682, Penn published his *Letter to the Free Society of Traders* (1683), which became a textual focal point for promoters in England, Holland, and Germany. In his preface to the translations into Dutch and German (*Beschreibung der in America neu-erfundenen Provinz Pensylvanien,* 1684), Furly highlighted, somewhat self-servingly, his disputes with Penn; more important, he also elevated the qualities of the new province he deemed most attractive to potential Dutch and German immigrants and assured them that their sensibilities influenced the construction of community. Furly's extensive preface added much practical information regarding the purchase of land and the laws of the province—particularly religious toleration, which had been stipulated in the *Frame of Government* but was again missing from Penn's latest promotional tract. For instance, the preface specified at length what immigrants from different social positions—landowners, tenants, servants, and children—would have to expect in the province. Tenants and servants, for example, would become freeholders with extensive political rights, including the right to vote and hold offices, "all without discrimination with regard to the nation or religion to which they belong." Familiar with the lack of political rights among the peasantry in German principalities, Furly highlighted the laws of the new province that would elevate these disenfranchised groups to the status of citizens with a political voice. He also underscored the crucial link between political and religious freedom by explicitly mentioning that discrimination

22. Soderlund et al., eds., *William Penn,* 266.

against individuals based on religious affiliation would be eliminated in Pennsylvania.[23]

Finally, Furly summarized or paraphrased the laws that most concerned prospective German immigrants. This section included the provisions stipulating freedom of conscience and ordinances for public morality. In order to separate the affairs of church and state, Furly explained, the laws of Pennsylvania specified that "no official church shall be introduced, and no one shall be threatened or forced to pay any contribution for any religious gathering or any preacher." The laws of Pennsylvania, in other words, eliminated the tithes German citizens were forced to pay in support of a state-sponsored church. The separation of church and state was also to prevent the domination of certain government offices by members of specific denominations. Freedom of conscience not only granted individual liberty in matters of faith but also freed political culture from religious sectionalism.[24]

While the axiom of religious freedom determined political culture, it also influenced the life and manners of the community in a more general sense. Furly knew that religious dissidents from Germany particularly welcomed freedom from religious oppression but—like English Quakers—hoped to build a society that checked public indecency, crime, or any antisocial and amoral behavior. Although English Quakers shared similar expectations and anxieties about the new province, the original English text of Penn's *Frame of Government* obscured or relegated to less prevalent places the passages that addressed the balance between liberty and social restraint. In his preface, Furly highlighted that the proper balance between freedoms and social controls would be instituted in the new province. On the one hand, the laws of Pennsylvania promised that "everyone may enjoy liberty of conscience, which all meek and peaceful people should have and are entitled

23. William Penn, *A Letter from William Penn Proprietary and Governour of Pennsylvania in America, to the Committee of the Free Society of Traders of That Province, Residing in London . . . as Also an Account of the City of Philadelphia . . .* ([London], 1683). Furly translated Penn's *Letter* from English to Dutch and wrote the preface. The translator of the German version is merely identified as "J. W." See William Penn, *Beschreibung der in America neu-erfundenen Provinz Pensylvanien . . .* ([Hamburg], 1684), 4: ". . . und solches ohne einiges Absehen zunehmen, von was Nation und Religion die selbige auch sein mögen."

24. Penn, *Beschreibung*, 5. The entire section in German reads: "Umb zu hindern das keine Secte, ihr Haubt über die andere erhebe, ümb einige öffentliche Plätze und Besoldung, welches die eine über die andere möchte heben, auß dem Gelde der Gemeinen Einkünfften der Kammer, welches von allen Einwohnern, ohne Unterschiede einkompt. So soll da keine Haubt-Kirche eingeführet werden, und wessen Versamblung oder Prediger, Niemand soll angestrenget oder gezwungen sein etwas zu geben."

to by nature, it has been determined that not only should nobody be forced to attend a certain public performance of worship, but further everyone should possess the full liberty to conduct their own public worship." On the other hand, rules were established to "prevent everything that could cause and provide occasion to bring people to vanity, frivolity, impudence and audacity, godlessness, and a dissolute life and tempt them to desecrate the name of the Lord." Furly thus inscribed the English laws of the province with German radical Protestant interests and transformed Penn's *Letter to the Free Society of Traders* into a tool for promoting immigration and creating a vision of civic and spiritual community in Pennsylvania among his German and Dutch constituents. The emphasis on establishing a moral society free of religious coercion directly answered the hope of Continental and English radical Protestants to find an exit from Babylon. Furly helped to make sure that promotional literature on Pennsylvania spoke the language of religious and linguistic utopianism.[25]

The German Founders

With the textual changes made by Furly and other translators or editors, the German versions of English promotional accounts of Pennsylvania specifically catered to the expectations of those German religious dissenters whom Penn had visited during his mission trip down the Rhine in 1677.

---

25. Penn, *Beschreibung*, 6: "Zum abwenden und verhüten, alles dessen, welches verursachen und anlaß geben möchte, ümb das Volck zur Eitelkeit, Leichtfertigkeit, Frech- und Kühnheit, Gottlosigkeit, und zu einem lästerlichen Leben zu bringen, und verleiten, zu entheiligung des Nahmens Gottes. . . ." English Quakers and German Pietists shared resentments against civic immorality and fears of lacking social controls in America. As Hermann Wellenreuther has shown, however, frictions between German and English immigrants in colonial Pennsylvania often resulted from different expectations of social hierarchy and control: "Germans were used to living in a society structured by hierarchy, in which large but not all areas of public life were ordered by decrees, ordinances, and laws. Yet governments in Germany did not . . . restrict their activities to worldly affairs; since the sixteenth century, they had invaded the religious life, too. Order, submission, cooperation, and stability were by and large values structuring German lives in secular as well as religious affairs." See "Contexts for Migration in the Early Modern World: Public Policy, European Migration Experiences, Transatlantic Migration, and the Genesis of American Culture," in Hartmut Lehman, Wellenreuther, and Renate Wilson, eds., *In Search of Peace and Prosperity: New German Settlements in Eighteenth-Century Europe and America* (University Park, Pa., 2000), 31. For a more extended comparison between the German and English settlers in Pennsylvania and their different social and moral codes, see Wellenreuther, "Image and Counterimage, Tradition and Expectation: The German Immigrants in English Colonial Society in Pennsylvania, 1700–1765," in Frank Trommler and Joseph McVeigh, eds., *America and the Germans: An Assessment of a Three-Hundred-Year History*, 2 vols. (Philadelphia, 1985), I, 85–105.

A few years later, Penn's agents relied on these personal contacts and networks in disseminating his promotional tracts in Germany and Holland. When a strong demand made printed volumes scarce, German promoters circulated handwritten transcriptions among their friends. For instance, Furly sent both personal letters and printed accounts to the Frankfurt Pietists whom Penn had visited in 1677 or to interested individuals such as the Lübeck pastor Jaspar Könneken. In turn, these groups or individuals produced manuscript transcriptions of printed texts or personal letters. Könneken assembled a collection of primary accounts in transcription, including letters or tracts by Penn, Pastorius, and other English, German, and Dutch writers. Passing through this network, the promotional discourse was not only adapted to the social and political situations of local audiences; it also gained a personal dimension. Penn's presence in these accounts was paired with the social and spiritual bonds among local communities. The forging of spiritual community in Pennsylvania, in other words, would harness similar communal connections in Germany or England and expand them to a multilingual, multiethnic, and multidenominational arena in the new province.[26]

Francis Daniel Pastorius's retrospective account of his decision to immigrate to Pennsylvania contains the projection of community in the new province as a transplantation and expansion of existing spiritual bonds mediated by the translation and circulation of promotional texts. Pastorius's experience of first learning about Penn's province from his Pietist friends in Frankfurt was modulated by different types of transmission—oral, manuscript, and print—as well as a local community of affect that triggered his desire to emigrate. Having just returned from a two-year "Grand Tour" with a German nobleman, Pastorius described the community of Pietists at

26. Rosalind J. Beiler, "German-Speaking Immigrants in the British Atlantic World, 1680–1730," *OAH Magazine of History,* XVIII, no. 3 (April 2004), 19–22; Hull, *William Penn,* esp. 311–335. For a specific elaboration of transatlantic migration and communication networks, see Beiler, *Immigrant and Entrepreneur: The Atlantic World of Caspar Wistar, 1650–1750* (University Park, Pa., 2008). Jaspar Balthasar Könneken (or Casper Balthasar Köhn), bookseller in the northern German city of Lübeck and later pastor in the town of Behlendorf, was one of the individuals who received the most recent reports from Pennsylvania through Furly, copied the tracts or letters, and passed them on to interested individuals throughout Germany. Könneken's manuscript collection concerning Pennsylvania comprises thirteen different texts and is today located in the collection Geistliches Ministerium in the Archiv der Hansestadt Lübeck (Archive of the Hanseatic City of Lubeck), fols. 356–372. Also see Julius Friedrich Sachse, *Letters Relating to the Settlement of Germantown in Pennsylvania, 1683–4; from the Könneken Manuscript in the Ministerial-Archive of Lübeck* (Lübeck and Philadelphia, 1903).

the "Saalhof" in Frankfurt (whom he had joined after Penn's visit in 1677) as a great respite from or even an antidote to the moral degeneration he had experienced on his travels. Notably, he eventually transferred the locus of this community from Germany to Pennsylvania:

> And forasmuch as I after this my Return was glad to enjoy the ancient familiarity of my former Acquaintances (rather than to be with the aforesd. von Bodeck feasting, dancing, etc.) especially of those Christian Friends who frequently assembled together in a house, called the Saalhof, viz. Dr. Spenner [sic], Dr. Schutz, Notarius Fenda, Jacobus van de Walle, Maximilian (bynamed the pious) Lersner, Eleonora von Merlau, Maria Juliana Baurin, etc. who sometimes made mention of William Penn and of Pennsylvania, and moreover communicated unto me as well some private letters from Benjamin Furly, as also a printed Relation concerning the sd. province, and finally the whole Secret could not be withholden from me, viz. that they purchased 15000. Acres of land in this remote part of the world, some of 'em entirely resolv'd, to transport themselves, families and all; this begat such a desire in my Soul to continue in their Society, and with them to lead a quiet, godly and honest life in a howling wilderness, (which I observed to be a heavy Task for any to perform among the bad examples and numberless Vanitates Vanitatum in Europe).

According to the account of his immigration and letters to his family published later, Pastorius had for years been unsatisfied with the orthodox religion practiced among German Lutherans. During his studies at various European universities and his travels, Pastorius had developed a deeply negative view of academic and upper-class culture in Europe. While practicing law in Frankfurt, Pastorius came into contact with increasingly more radical and chiliastic Pietists around Schütz, Merlau, and Petersen. In becoming friends with the Saalhof Pietists, Pastorius entered a larger spiritual network that already comprised Penn, Furly, and other English Quakers as well as other Lutheran Pietists across Germany.[27]

Most striking about Pastorius's account is the prominence he alloted to the local community of the Pietists and the lure of continuing in its company. At the same time, Penn's textual communication—in letters and his printed accounts—played a central role in creating a coherence and specific

27. Francis Daniel Pastorius, "Bee-Hive," MS Codex 726, 221, Rare Book and Manuscript Library, University of Pennsylvania.

spiritual purpose among the Pietists: immigration to Pennsylvania. Notably, Pastorius's excitement increased after he found out about the purpose of the Pietists' communication with Penn. The plan for leaving Europe apparently spoke to a deeply spiritual need, creating a "desire in [his] soul" to pursue a life in America cast as the antithesis of life in Europe. This passage reveals the interpenetration of the linguistic, especially the textual, mediation of spiritual community and the supralinguistic affinities created by common religious beliefs, experiences, and intimate fellowship. Pastorius's description is paradigmatic for the relationship between textuality and spiritual community in early Pennsylvania: various groups depended on textual exchange to increase coherence and establish new connections; in turn, various modes of writing and reading engendered spiritual community. Translation and manuscript dissemination were the textual means most aptly establishing translingual and interdenominational links.

Promotional tracts thus harnessed existing spiritual affinities while projecting supralinguistic connections into the future. In his most widely disseminated tract, *Letter to the Free Society of Traders,* Penn defined Pennsylvania as such a community of affect between himself and members of different ethnicities and nations. His preface juxtaposed the disparagement he received in his own country with an image of transnational unity:

> But if I have been *Unkindly* used by some I left behind me, I found *Love* and *Respect* enough where I came; a universal kind *Welcome,* every sort in their way. For here are some of several *Nations,* as well as divers *Judgments:* Nor were the *Natives* wanting in this, for their *Kings, Queens* and *Great Men* both visited and presented me; to whom I made suitable Returns, etc.

Whereas Penn had invited people from "other Nations" to immigrate to Pennsylvania in *Some Account,* now immigrants "of several Nations" awaited the governor upon his arrival. His detractors in England had to learn a lesson in tolerance and forbearance from foreigners and Indians. Penn's gesture in turning from domestic squabbles to a "universal kind Welcome" in Pennsylvania synecdochically linked the figure of the governor as a universally welcome person to the province as a universally welcoming community. Through this rhetorical maneuver, Penn promoted his province as a transnational community of mutual affection and spiritual affinity. Penn's emphasis on his fair dealing with the native Americans living in Pennsylvania (predominantly Lenni Lenape or Delaware) furthermore established the mythology of the proprietor—and, by extension, the colonial government—as a friend to the Indians. Discursively, this tract thus gave birth to the tradition of Pennsylvania as a peaceable kingdom, which would not be fundamentally changed until the infamous Walking Purchase shattered Delaware confidence in the benevolent intentions of the provincial government. Nevertheless, for generations of English and German immigrants the purported mutuality between European immigrants and native American residents implied in this passage symbolized the spiritual potential of Pennsylvania even when imperial warfare seemed to destroy such ideals.[28]

Pastorius's hopes to transplant to Pennsylvania the affection he had found in the Pietist community in Frankfurt were dashed by the group's failure to follow their agent into this "howling wilderness." The reasons may range from the advanced age of many members, to an attachment to physical comforts in Europe, to a shift toward their interests in Pennsylvania as an economic investment rather than spiritual refuge, to a change in their religious agenda toward reforming European society from within. By 1686, the Frankfurt Pietists had formed the Frankfurt Land Company, the primary goal of which was to administer and sell lands purchased from Penn, thus hinting at an increasingly economic motivation for their venture in Pennsylvania. Pastorius remained agent for the Frankfurt Land Company until 1700, when his disaffection from his role as business manager rather than spiritual guide led to his resignation (which he asked for but was not granted earlier) and the reassignment of his duties to the Lutheran Pietist Daniel Falckner. Pastorius's letters to friends, family, and now business associates in Germany—although reflecting a degree of disaffection and disillusionment—retooled and redeployed the language of spiritual community by projecting it onto a larger interdenominational plane. While retaining his official assignment to promote and administer a German settlement in the province, Pastorius found personal and spiritual affinity in relationships with many English immigrants.[29]

28. Penn's support for the Catholic king James II incensed English resentments against the Quaker leader and linked them to general fears of a return to Catholicism in England. See Penn, *Letter*, 1.

29. Frankfurt Land Company, "Im Nahmen und zur Ehre Gottes! . . . Welcher gegeben zu Franckfurt am Mayn, den 12, Novemb. anno 1686" (Frankfurt, 1686), Library Company of Philadelphia. Falckner became involved in a scheme of real estate fraud that resulted in the loss of the company's holdings in Pennsylvania and their eventual dissolution. All of Pastorius's manuscripts relating to the Frankfurt Land Company are located in the Pastorius Papers, Historical Society of Pennsylvania, Philadelphia. Also see Julius Friedrich Sachse, *The German Pietists of Provincial Pennsylvania, 1694–1708* (1895; rpt. New York, 1970), 299–334; Samuel Whitaker Pennypacker, *The Settlement of Germantown and the Beginning of German Emigration to North America* (1899; rpt. New York, 1970),

Pastorius's early letters—written during his journey to America and shortly upon his arrival in Pennsylvania—strongly reflect the anti-Babylonian critique of European morals and orthodox churches common among radical Protestants in England as well as Germany. The currency of this chiliastic dimension of immigration apparently remained strong among German readers and prospective immigrants even after Pastorius's estrangement from the Pietists; thus, his letters to Germany are preserved in the various *printed* editions produced by the Frankfurt Land Company and other promoters of immigration. The utopianism of Pastorius's early letters— explaining his own rationale for immigration and giving advice to future immigrants—thus sold promotional pamphlets as well as land among prospective immigrants across Germany. Even though actual events in Pennsylvania (such as the Keithian schism) and Pastorius's relationship with the Pietists no longer reflected ideals of spiritual community, promotional treatments distributed across Germany still touted immigration as the fulfillment of the spiritual and religious quest of radical Protestant groups. Pastorius's letters early on reflected disunity between himself and the Pietists while transplanting his desire for spiritual community to the Quakers, particularly William Penn. Given a considerable lag between the original composition of some of these letters and their eventual publication within compiled and edited promotional tracts, readers and prospective immigrants in Germany continued to perceive Pennsylvania as a society where spiritual affinities were crafted across linguistic and denominational divisions.

Chronologically, one of Pastorius's first letters preserved in later promotional tracts published in Germany is his letter to his father and friends, dated Deal (England), June 7, 1683. His explanations for leaving Europe and immigrating to Pennsylvania reflect the radical Protestant critique of Babel / Babylon:

After examining to my satisfaction the European provinces and countries, and the impending *motus belli,* and after taking apprehensively to heart the vicissitudes and troubles of my native country arising therefrom, I have suffered myself to be moved by the special direction of the Most High to journey over to Pennsylvania, living in the hope that this my design will work out to my own good and that of my dear

21–50; Marianne S. Wokeck, "Francis Daniel Pastorius," in Craig W. Horle et al., eds., *Lawmaking and Legislators in Pennsylvania: A Biographical Dictionary,* I, *1682–1709* (Philadelphia, 1991), 586–590.

brothers and sisters, but most of all to the advancement of the glory of God (which is my aim above all else), especially as the audacity and sin of the European world are accumulating more and more from day to day, and therefore the just judgment of God cannot be long withheld.

Besides the threat of war with France, Pastorius justified his immigration by recounting the usual charges against European immorality and vice, thus imagining the formation of a moral society in Pennsylvania as an antidote. Pastorius's chiliastic leanings at this point become apparent in his anticipation of a cataclysmic event. The original German evocation of "Straff-Gerichte Gottes" goes far beyond predicting merely a "just judgment of God"; rather, it calls to mind an apocalyptic day of judgment that condemns all those who followed the "whore of Babylon."[30]

Ironically, Pastorius very soon associated his friends at the Saalhof in Frankfurt with the European "Babylon." In his first account sent to the Pietists, Pastorius subtly shifted his definition of spiritual community to individuals and groups already in Pennsylvania — especially Penn himself — and admonished his former associates for the waning of their spiritual zeal. Pastorius's first published letter to his Frankfurt friends (written in March 1684) — later printed and distributed as a promotional tract entitled *Sichere Nachricht* (*Positive Information* or *Certain News*) — ostensibly assessed the chances of an exclusively German community, but his appraisal of Penn valued intellectual and spiritual consanguinity over national affiliation in the construction of community. According to *Sichere Nachricht,* the affection between the two men relied strongly on common visions for the spiritual and social development of the province but also on a common intellectual heritage, including the mastery of Latin and French. Penn and Pastorius apparently enjoyed each other's company in spite of protracted negotiations over the land purchased by the Frankfurt investors. Pastorius reported that Penn "often invites me to his table and has me walk and ride in his always edifying company; and when I lately was absent from here a week ... and he had not seen me for that space of time, he came himself to my

30. Francis Daniel Pastorius, *Umständige geographische Beschreibung der zu allerletzt erfundenen Provintz Pensylvaniae* ... (Frankfurt and Leipzig, 1700), 45–47. I am following the English translation in Pastorius, *Circumstantial Geographical Description of the Lately Discovered Province of Pennsylvania* . . . , trans. Gertrude Selwyn Kimball, in Myers, ed., *Narratives of Early Pennsylvania,* 411–412. Below, I analyze several key passages where the translation does not fully capture or even alter the ideas conveyed in the original.

little house and besought me that I should at least once or twice a week be his guest." Passing by the house Pastorius had built in Philadelphia, Penn read the Latin motto echoing Vergil's *Aeneid* above the door: "Parva domus sed amica bonis, procul este prophani" ("A little house, but a friend to the good; remain at a distance, ye profane"). Pastorius proudly reported that Penn was pleased by his inscription. Both having received a privileged education, Penn and Pastorius shared the cosmopolitan intellectual heritage of the late Renaissance, epitomized by their common knowledge of classical languages and literature. Elite members of the inchoate settlement were able to transfer existing bonds of European intellectualism to the new province and harness these initial ties for the construction of a transnational community in Pennsylvania.[31]

If the congeniality provided by an elite European education was beyond the reach of most immigrants, a shared vision of spiritual renewal under Pennsylvania's motto of "brotherly love" could attract religious dissenters from any class or social standing. Pastorius's praise of Penn thus moved Christian fellowship to the center of communal bonding in the province:

31. Besides Penn and other English Quakers, Pastorius also embraced the Krefeld Quakers, who were the first substantial group from German-speaking areas to arrive in Pennsylvania in October 1683 and participate in the settlement of Germantown. Although the Krefelders spoke a low-German dialect closer to modern Dutch, Pastorius apparently had no problems communicating with them. The original letter does not seem to be extant. A unique printed copy can be found in the Stadtbibliothek Zürich: Francis Daniel Pastorius, *Sichere Nachricht auß America, wegen der Landschafft Pennsylvania, von einem dorthin gereißten Teutschen, de dato Philadelphia, den 7. Martii 1684*. For a photostat reproduction of this print, see Marion Dexter Learned, *The Life of Francis Daniel Pastorius, the Founder of Germantown* (Philadelphia, 1908), 8 unnumbered pages inserted between 128 and 129. All quotations from the original German of *Sichere Nachricht* below refer to this photostat (numbered 1–8). A separate manuscript transcription not made from the printed version can be found in the Könneken MSS, fols. 356–372, Geistliches Ministerium, Archiv der Hansestadt Lübeck, Germany. In a poem written upon Penn's return to Pennsylvania in 1699, Pastorius claims that, upon his own arrival in the province in 1683, he could "talk with him [Penn] but in the Gallic Tongue" ("Bee-Hive," 177). See Francis Daniel Pastorius, *Positive Information from America, concerning the Country of Pennsylvania* . . . , in Pastorius, *Circumstantial*, trans. Kimball, in Myers, ed., *Narratives of Early Pennsylvania*, 396 ("Er lässt mich zum öfftern an seine Taffel bitten, auch in seiner jederzeit erbaulichen Gesellschafft außwandeln und reiten; und da ich letzthin 8. Tag von hier . . . aussen war, und Er mich solche Zeit über nicht gesehen, kam Er selbst in mein Häusgen, und begehrte, ich solle doch wochentlich ein paar mal bey ihme zu Gast kommen" [Pastorius, *Sichere Nachricht*, 2]), 404; Pastorius, *Sichere Nachricht*, 5. For detailed studies of Pastorius's education in Europe, see Learned, *Life of Pastorius*; Rosamund Rosenmeier, "Francis Daniel Pastorius," in Emory Elliott, ed., *American Colonial Writers, 1606–1734*, Dictionary of Literary Biography 24 (Detroit, 1984), 245–247; and John David Weaver, "Franz Daniel Pastorius (1651–c. 1720): Early Life in Germany with Glimpses of His Removal to Pennsylvania" (Ph.D. diss., University of California, Davis, 1985).

I . . . delivered to William Penn the letters that I had, and was received by him with amiable friendliness; of that very worthy man and famous ruler I might properly . . . write many things; but my pen . . . is much too weak to express the high virtues of this Christian—for such he is indeed. . . . He heartily loves the *[Germans]*, and once said openly in my presence to his councillors and those who were about him, I love the *[Germans]* and desire that you also should love them. Yet in any other matter I have never heard such a command from him. . . . I can at present say no more than that William Penn is a man who honors God and is honored by Him, who loves what is good and is rightly beloved by all good men. I doubt not that some of them will come here and by their own experience learn, that my pen has in this case not written enough.

Pastorius's elaboration of Penn's welcome corresponded to Penn's description of his own reception in the province by members of various nations. Curiously, Pastorius here espoused the notion of transnational unity crystallized in Penn as a symbolic figure while stressing the proprietor's bias in favor of the Germans in particular.[32]

Yet Pastorius's apparent joy over Penn's favoritism toward the Germans is an error of interpretation readers today would make by relying on the English translation. The early-twentieth-century translator inserted the national group marker "Germans" in the blanks left in the original printed version of Pastorius's *Sichere Nachricht,* assuming that Pastorius represented all Germans and that Penn expressed his preference for all Germans. A comparison between the printed version of *Sichere Nachricht* and a transcription of Pastorius's letter in the Könneken manuscripts yields "Ffr" or

32. Pastorius, *Positive Information,* in Pastorius, *Circumstantial,* trans. Kimball, in Myers, ed., *Narratives of Early Pennsylvania,* 396–397 (emphasis added): ". . . da ich deß folgenden Tags die mithabende Schreiben an W. Penn überliefferte, und von ihme mit Liebvoller Freundlichkeit empfangen wurde; von diesem sehr werthen Mann, und rumwürdigen Regenten, solte ich billich II. Ein und anders überschreiben; allein, meine Feder . . . ist viel zu schwach, die hohe Tugenden dieses Christen, dann solches ist Er in der That, zu exprimiren. . . . Er hat die [blank] hertzlich lieb, und sagte einst offentlich in meiner Gegenwart zu seinen Räthen und Umbstehenden: Die [blank] hab ich lieb, und wil, daß ihr sie auch lieben sollet; Wiewol ich übrigens niemalen dergleichen Befehlchswort von ihm gehöret habe; . . . Ich kan anjetzo mehr nicht sagen, als daß Will. Penn, ein Mann sey, welcher Gott ehret, und von Ihme wieder geehret wird: welcher das gute liebet, und von allen guten mit recht geliebet wird, etc. Ich zweiffle nicht, es werden noch einige selbsten anhero kommen, und im Werck erfahren, daß meine Feder hierinnfalls noch nicht genug geschrieben" (Pastorius, *Sichere Nachricht,* 2).

"Frankfurter" as the text that was erased in the printed version. Penn, in other words, praised the Frankfurt Pietists whom he had visited on his missionary trip in 1677 and who had subsequently purchased a tract of land in Pennsylvania. The Pietist sponsors who formed the Frankfurt Land Company to manage their estate in Pennsylvania might have omitted this reference in printing the letter as a promotional text because it was too specific for a tract disseminated throughout Germany. Or, the Frankfurt Pietists noticed the rhetorical goal Pastorius pursued in emphasizing Penn's preference for them.[33]

In fact, Pastorius rebuked his Frankfurt sponsors because he already sensed that they hesitated—and would ultimately fail—to live up to their promise of transplanting their Christian community to America. Recognizing the increasingly economic foundation of their relationship, Pastorius refused to turn his account into a standard promotional tract that exaggerated the features of the land. From Columbus onward, explorers and settlers in the New World deployed their own inability to do justice to the marvels of their discoveries—such as monstrous animals or luscious landscapes—as a trope to increase their readers' sense of wonder and expectation of financial exploits. Pastorius, in contrast, described the character of a seemingly familiar person—Penn—in terms of discovery and wonder, ultimately resulting in the failure of representation itself. Only personal experience, according to Pastorius, could do justice to Penn's character. Yet, unlike the dangerous encounters with the unknown that had been presaged by other promotional accounts, a meeting with Penn would not only be completely benign but also promise great spiritual advancement. In highlighting the ineffability of his admiration for Penn and of the proprietor's qualities, Pastorius emphasized the mystical union established between truly kindred spirits. Thus, Pastorius subtly faulted the Pietists' reluctance to join him, for, assuming they counted themselves among "all good men," they would find only love and affection in coming to Pennsylvania, whereas their failure to immigrate would taint their integrity and sincerity.[34]

33. Könneken MSS, fol. 358.
34. See Stephen Greenblatt, *Marvelous Possessions: The Wonder of the New World* (Chicago, 1991); Myra Jehlen, *American Incarnation: The Individual, the Nation, and the Continent* (Cambridge, Mass., 1986). For further analysis of the genre of promotional literature, see Howard Mumford Jones, "The Colonial Impulse: An Analysis of the 'Promotion' Literature of Colonization," American Philosophical Society, *Proceedings*, XC (1946), 131–161; Paul J. Lindholdt, "The Significance of the Colonial Promotion Tract," in Kathryn Zabelle Derounian-Stodola, ed., *Early American Literature and Culture: Essays Honoring Harrison T. Meserole* (Newark, Del., 1992), 57–72; Karen Schramm,

Moreover, Pastorius toyed with the stock ingredients of the promotional genre while transferring its tropes to a spiritual plane. His entire description of the material productions of the land was an extended scriptural allusion: each natural production reminded readers of a parable or emblem in the New Testament. The "apples" growing in the "wild orchard" hinted at paradise, and the frequently found snakes recalled the fall of Adam and Eve in the Old Testament, and other images typologically referred to Christ, the new Adam. Pastorius thus made two statements concerning the spiritual state of America: this part of the world was also fallen, and all hope must rest in Christ, evoked in the recurring images of the "grain" and the "vine." For instance, Pastorius described finding a "wild grape-vine, running over a tree, on which were some four hundred clusters of grapes; wherefore we then hewed down the tree and satisfied all eight of us, and took home with us a hatfull apiece besides." Used to radical Pietist imagery of the individual believer's unity with Christ through his physical sacrifice, this passage featured Pastorius and his associates cutting down the "tree" of the cross, which allowed them to satisfy their spiritual hunger and thirst by virtually celebrating Communion in consuming the metaphorical blood of Christ. Pastorius finally made the connection explicit by linking his visit to Penn's vineyard to a reflection on John 15: "I am the vine; you are the branches." Pastorius's point would have been more than clear to his pious readers: the spiritual fruitfulness of the new land entirely depended on the conduct and faithfulness of the "branches" belonging to the "vine."[35]

Given Pastorius's criticism of his "friends," one might expect that his Frankfurt sponsors would have suppressed his letter instead of publishing and distributing it as a promotional account. Yet they recognized that Pastorius's language of spiritual community in Pennsylvania and, particularly, his congeniality with Penn appealed to other potential immigrants who valued religious renewal above economic improvement. In fact, the Frankfurt Pietists deployed the friendship between Penn and Pastorius as a promotional device in later publications. In the 1700 pamphlet *Umständige geographische Beschreibung (Circumstantial Geographical Description)*, the Frankfurt sponsors attached a letter from Penn to Pastorius's father. Penn's appraisal of Pastorius mirrored Pastorius's own paean to the proprietor:

"Promotion Literature," in Kevin J. Hayes, ed., *The Oxford Handbook of Early American Literature* (Oxford, 2008), 69–91.

35. Pastorius, *Positive Information*, in Pastorius, *Circumstantial*, trans. Kimball, in Myers, ed., *Narratives of Early Pennsylvania*, 398.

"Your son was recently among the living and is even now in Philadelphia. This year he is justice of the peace, or was so very lately. Furthermore, he is called a man sober, upright, wise, and pious, of a reputation approved on all hands and unimpeached." Of course, this letter served as an authenticating device to support the truthfulness of the foregoing account by Pastorius. On another level, Penn's appraisal of Pastorius allowed prospective immigrants to picture themselves vicariously in a similar position. Since the integrity of Pastorius's character mattered most to the proprietor, their own virtue—rather than their national affiliation or prosperity—would allow them to gain access to a similar community.[36]

The rising demand for descriptions of Penn's new province led publishers and booksellers to issue compilations of various accounts. These composite texts frequently included accounts by English and German writers such as Penn, Pastorius, and Gabriel Thomas and enhanced the transnational character of the promotional discourse. For instance, Pastorius's *Umständige geographische Beschreibung*, published in 1700, was a compilation of various reports and letters he had written over fifteen years printed alongside translations of an excerpt of Penn's *Letter to the Free Society of Traders* and Thomas Paskell's *Abstract of a Letter*, both originally published in 1683. Successive editions of Pastorius's *Beschreibung* in 1702 and 1704 even increased the composite and transnational textual enterprise of promotion. For both editions, the publisher Andreas Otto appended a translation of the English settler Gabriel Thomas's *Historical and Geographical Account* (published 1698) and, published for the first time, Daniel Falckner's (1666–1744) report about early Pennsylvania, *Curieuse Nachricht von Pensylvania in Norden-America (Curious News from Pennsylvania in North America).* As in earlier adaptations of Penn's tracts, these composite editions of German and English promotional texts increased the impression among German readers that the transnational discursive representation of Pennsylvania signified a similar negotiation of community in the province.[37]

36. Pastorius, *Circumstantial*, trans. Kimball, in Myers, ed., *Narratives of Early Pennsylvania*, 445. Penn's original letter to Pastorius's father is in Latin; *Umständige geographische Beschreibung* provides a German translation: "So viel mir wissend so ist dein Sohn noch im Leben, und hält sich anjetzo zu Philadelphia auff. Er ist dieses Jahr der Stadt Friedens-Richter, oder hat jüngst das Ampt abgelegt. Er ist sonst ein Mann mässig und nüchtern, fromm, verständig und gottsfürchtig, von deme ein gutes untadelhafftes Gerüchte aller Orten erschallet" (97).

37. Thomas Paskell, *An Abstract of a Letter from Thomas Paskell of Pennsilvania to His Friend J. J. Chippenham* (London, 1683); Gabriel Thomas, *An Historical and Geographical Account of the Province and Country of Pensilvania; and of West-New-Jersey in America* . . . (London, 1698); Daniel

Bound together and sold with Pastorius's *Umständige geographische Beschreibung,* Daniel Falckner's *Curieuse Nachricht von Pensylvania* was a collaboration between Falckner and his most important sponsor and spiritual adviser, August Hermann Francke. Daniel Falckner and his brother Justus were the sons of a Lutheran pastor in Saxony, and both were slated for the ministry. When Daniel began his studies in theology at the University of Erfurt in 1690, he met Francke, who was teaching there but would soon be expelled by orthodox church authorities for his Pietist views, specifically Spener's notion that personal rebirth of each Christian would lead to institutional rebirth in the church and all branches of society. Falckner led a peripatetic life throughout northern Germany, all the while maintaining an active correspondence with Francke. In Hamburg, Falckner probably met Johannes Kelpius and the first leader of the "Chapter of Perfection," Johann Jakob Zimmermann, who had settled there after he had been removed from a position in the Lutheran Church in his Württemberg home and had traveled widely throughout Germany. In 1693, Zimmermann, Kelpius, Falckner, and a total of roughly forty mystical seekers (supposedly constituting a symbolic number and mystical order) left Germany for Rotterdam with the goal of establishing their Chapter of Perfection in Pennsylvania and awaiting the advent of the millennium. After Zimmermann passed away in Rotterdam, the rest of the group continued on to London, where they met with the members of the Philadelphian Society. They eventually arrived in Pennsylvania in 1694.[38]

Falckner, *Curieuse Nachricht von Pensylvania in Norden-America . . .* (Frankfurt and Leipzig, 1702). The Library Company of Philadelphia, for example, houses several German-language composite editions of Pastorius's *Umständige geographische Beschreibung,* Thomas's *Historical and Geographical Account* (translated in German as *Continuatio der Beschreibung der Landschafft Pensylvaniae en den End-Gräntzen Americae*), and Falckner's *Curieuse Nachricht,* published between 1702 and 1704. In these German compilations, the translation of Thomas's account appeared after Pastorius's account and was cast as its "continuation," thus reversing their actual order of publication.

38. For details on Daniel Falckner's life, see Julius Friedrich Sachse, "Introduction," in Sachse, trans. and ed., *Daniel Falckner's Curieuse Nachricht from Pennsylvania . . .* (Lancaster, Pa., 1905), 31–38; Sachse, *German Pietists,* 299–334. For Falckner's later work as minister to a small Lutheran congregation in the area later named "Falckner swamp," see Charles Henry Glatfelter, *Pastors and People: German Lutheran and Reformed Churches in the Pennsylvania Field, 1717–1793,* II (Breinigsville, Pa., 1981), 517–521. For Falckner's involvement in Johannes Kelpius's "Hermits," see Elizabeth Fisher, "'Prophesies and Revelations': German Cabbalists in Early Pennsylvania," *PMHB,* CIX (1985), 299–333. For Falckner's role in promoting various immigration schemes to Pennsylvania, see Beiler, "Bridging the Gap," in Finzsch and Lehmkuhl, eds., *Atlantic Communications,* 56–58. For Spener's influence on Francke, see Fisher, "'Prophesies and Revelations,'" *PMHB,* CIX (1985), 304.

After establishing a type of hermitage consisting of (mostly) celibate men on the Wissahickon Creek outside Philadelphia, some among Kelpius's Chapter of Perfection, particularly Heinrich Bernhard Köster, became involved in the Keithian controversy (see Chapter 3, below). Others married and moved to Germantown or other nearby settlements. Presumably, Falckner returned to Germany in 1698 in order to recruit additional members to replenish the shrinking group of hermits and maintain the mystical number of forty. Falckner then visited Halle, where Francke drew up a manuscript list of seventy-three questions regarding the state of religion, the land, civics, and native peoples of Pennsylvania. Falckner's answers were eventually published as *Curieuse Nachricht von Pennsylvania* and distributed throughout Germany. On his return journey, Falckner apparently visited the Frankfurt Pietists and received from them—along with Johannes Kelpius (in absentia) and Johannes Jawert—a letter of attorney to administer the holdings of the Frankfurt Land Company in Pennsylvania, thus replacing Pastorius. Falckner's answers to Francke's questions were printed in 1702, while Falckner was back in Pennsylvania.[39]

The promotional tract for which Falckner became known in early-eighteenth-century Germany created the image of Pennsylvania as a delicate, fragile, and in many ways flawed religious experiment that was nevertheless Europe's best hope for spiritual renewal. Tuning into the Babel criticism pursued by virtually all radical Protestant groups in Europe, Falckner specifically pinned his hopes for Pennsylvania to a brand of Philadelphianism that dissolved linguistic and religious differences by allowing human beings to read, once again, the book of nature. By standing in closer communion

---

For Daniel Falckner's correspondence with Francke, see Falckner, "Schreiben an August Hermann Francke, Lübeck, August 28, 1691," Tüb. Kapsel 32. Fasc. 12, 1108–1109, "Schreiben an August Hermann Francke, Lüneburg, 8. 2. 1692," Tüb. Kapsel 32. Fasc. 12, 1110–1111, and "Schreiben an August Hermann Francke, Hamburg, 1-27-1693," Tüb. Kapsel 32. Fasc. 12, 1106–1107, all part of the Francke-Nachlass Staatsbibliothek Berlin—Preußischer Kulturbesitz, microfilm at the Archives of the Franckesche Stiftungen, Halle. See also Johannes Kelpius, Journal, MS Am. 0880, photostat copy MS Am 08801, HSP. Kelpius's journal is bound together with his letterbook. For a published version, see Julius Friedrich Sachse, ed., *The Diarium of Magister Johannes Kelpius* (Lancaster, Pa., 1917). A letter reporting on the journey was written by another associate of the group, Johann Gotfried Seelig, and it was published in Halle as *Copia eines Send-Schreibens auß der neuen Welt . . . Germandon in Pennsylvania Americae d. 7. Aug. 1694* ([Halle and Frankfurt?], 1695).

39. For the manuscript version of Falckner's account, see Daniel Falckner, "Curiose Nachrichten von Pennsylvenien, 73 Fragen und Antworten über das Verhalten bei einer Reise nach Amerika und über die dortigen Verhältnisse von Daniel Falckner," MS AFSt/H D85, 469–597, Franckesche Stiftungen, Halle.

with and thus learning the divine meanings inscribed in nature, settlers in America could come closer to God and, if they gave up their doctrinal differences, closer to each other.

Falckner actually heightened Pastorius's chiliastic warnings of an impending cataclysm that would potentially wipe out Europe for its wickedness and pride. Falckner specifically located the corruption of religion in an empty and formulaic use of scriptural language: "At the present time God's word is frequently and abundantly preached to the world, it is proclaimed in the churches, it is found in books, it is piped to us; it is sung to us; it is painted upon the walls. Yet what happens? The majority pay no heed to it, and the kings and nobles persecute it most deplorably, revile and destroy it." Like at Babel, Protestantism was divorcing language from its spiritual essence. In particular, Christians in Germany, the homeland of the Protestant Reformation, were squandering their inheritance. As a result, Falckner threatened to disassociate himself from his German heritage and language: "If this is to be the rule in Germany, I shall regret that I am born a German, or ever spoke or wrote German."[40]

Falckner's fear that scriptural language was being corrupted extended to Pennsylvania, which was being infected by the European quarreling over dead letters. In this regard, Falckner diverged from his sponsor, August Hermann Francke. For Francke, education and conversion relied on the reading and spread of Protestant literature, and he thus asked Falckner "how to introduce good devout literature in the English and French languages for an energetic edification of such nationalities as have settled in Pennsylvania, Virginia and New England." Falckner, however, rebuffed Francke's emphasis on print dissemination:

---

40. German-American scholar Julius F. Sachse's *Daniel Falckner's Curieuse Nachricht* is a bilingual edition of Falckner's *Curieuse Nachricht,* with the German on the left side and the English on the right. In the German text, Sachse reproduced Falckner's published version in Gothic type, supplemented by passages that are exclusive to the manuscript version in roman type. Below, I am citing Falckner's account from Sachse's edition, with page references to the English translation first and those to the original following the respective German quotations. Moreover, I am adding "MS" or "print" after the page numbers to indicate which version of Falckner's account is quoted. Sache's English translation usually follows the fuller manuscript version.

See Sachse, trans. and ed., *Daniel Falckner's Curieuse Nachricht,* 69, MS ("Jetzt wird Gottes Wort der Welt häufig und mit Menge vorgetragen, man predigt es in den Kirchen, man findet es in denen Büchern, man pfeiffts uns, man singts uns, man mahlet es an die Wände, aber was geschieht, der meiste Theil achtet es nicht, und die Fürsten und Könige verfolgen es aufs jämmerlichste, schelten und vernichten es" [68, MS]), 73, MS ("Wann es so soll in Teutschland gehen, so ist mirs Leyd, daß ich ein Teutscher gebohren bin, oder je teutsch geredet oder geschrieben habe [72, MS]).

Here, we consider at the moment the Holy Scriptures next to the church history and Arndt's books as sufficient for those who are in need of guidance. Considering this seducing, skeptical, and satirical age, I fear the establishment of a printing business will only cause more misery and confusion here. But one has already been established at Philadelphia.

Similar to the Quaker concept of a guarded education, Falckner's response emphasizes a few central spiritual guidebooks—including the Bible and Johann Arndt's *True Christianity* (1605–1610)—and fears that printing will contribute to the proliferation of doctrinal strife in Pennsylvania. With a poignant ambiguity, Falckner's last sentence—stating elusively that "one has already been established at Philadelphia"—refers both to the printing press (William Bradford) and the confusion known as the Keithian controversy. For Falckner, the printing press and the spiritual confusion experienced at Philadelphia are identical: both proliferated false or inadequate human signifiers, which lead human beings farther and farther away from the true spiritual language.[41]

In classifying factional debates about faith as an alienation from God, Falckner recalled the Neoplatonic notion of the isomorphism between language and creation in paradise, encapsulated in Boehme's *Natursprache:* "America holds man under an external training. Adam tills his land and tends his cattle, all of which are letters and books, wherein his creator personally instructs him in thanksgiving, and asks him to remember what he has learned." Believing this original relationship between words and things, language and creation, to continue in America, Falckner went beyond most seventeenth-century Neoplatonists. In America, human beings regained insights into the spiritual significance of creation. European immigrants in America, therefore, could read the book of nature once again. With a jibe at Francke's emphasis on book learning, Falckner insisted that, through the "letters and books" of nature, the "creator himself" instructed man in praising and thanking God. Not surprisingly, Francke received this rejoinder the

41. Falckner, *Curieuse Nachricht,* 157, print (with MS insertions) ("Wie gute [Erbauliche] Schrifften hinein zu bringen [in Englischer und Französischer Sprachen, die *Nationes* so in Pennsylvanien, Virginia und New Engelland sind, dadurch kräftig zu erbauen.] die Landes Inwohner zu erbauen?" [156]), 159, print (translation mine) ("Bey uns halten wir der Zeit die H. Schrifft nebst der Kirchen-Histori, und Arndii Büchern Buches genug, für solche, die einer Anleitung vonnothen haben. Zur Buchdruckerey-Anordnung traue ich allhier nicht bey unserm verführischen, Seoptischen und Satyrischen Zanck-Seculo dadurch nur mehr Unglück und diffidenz angerichtet wird. Doch ist bereits eine zu Philadelphia angerichtet" [158]).

way it was meant. For the Lutheran Pietist who had established one of the most respected institutions of Protestant education in Europe, Falckner's image of a restoration of the *lingua Adamica* in America was too esoteric: he did not allow it to be included in the printed version of the tract.[42]

The Delaware Chief

In projecting Neoplatonist and Philadelphian ideals onto the spiritual landscape of Pennsylvania, English and German readers were curious about the moral disposition and the language of the indigenous inhabitants of the region. Of course, readers all across Europe had received a variety of theories on the origin and nature as well as widely differing descriptions of native Americans. Representations ranged from innocent children of nature living in a version of the classical concept of the Golden Age to bloodthirsty, savage heathens who were the descendants of the biblical people of Gog and Magog. Promotional accounts of early Pennsylvania, therefore, had to accomplish a dual task: they had to insert representations of native American life into existing discourses of the New World; at the same time, they needed to bring images of Indians encountered by early European settlers in line with spiritual, even utopian ideals that radical Protestants projected onto the colony. News about native Americans appearing in publications and private letters on Pennsylvania thus became a function of the discourse of spiritual promotionalism.[43]

The promotional literature on early Pennsylvania expanded the familiar concept of peaceful coexistence and just treaty making between Penn and the Delaware people to a broad delineation of native American spirituality, morality, and customs as compatible with the sensibilities of radical Protestant immigrants such as English Quakers and German Pietists. Judging primarily from observing the Lenni Lenape people of the Delaware Valley and New Jersey, writers elaborated on a set of supposedly innate native American qualities that could serve as proof of Pennsylvania's potential

---

42. Falckner, *Curieuse Nachricht,* 159, MS (*"America* hält den Menschen unter äusserlicher Übung: Adam bauet das Land und wartet seines Viehes, *welches lauter Buchstaben und Bücher sind,* dabei ihn sein Schöpfer selbst in der Danksagung *ex tempore* lehret und aufsagen heisset" [158]).

43. For overviews of early representations of the New World and its native American inhabitants in European print media, see Wayne Franklin, *Discoverers, Explorers, Settlers: The Diligent Writers of Early America* (Chicago, 1979); Anthony Grafton, *New World, Ancient Texts: The Power of Tradition and the Shock of Discovery* (Cambridge, Mass., 1992); Stephen Greenblatt, ed., *New World Encounters* (Berkeley, Calif., 1993).

as the location of a Philadelphian community characterized by brotherly love and transcultural and interdenominational cooperation as well as the anti-Babylonian sentiments shared by Quakers and Pietists. Descriptions of native American life and manners in these promotional accounts thus emphasized stock features of radical Protestant writings of the late seventeenth century such as simplicity, innate human spirituality free from the jarring influences of doctrinal theology and secular traditions, and brotherly love. Rather than predicating native American shortcomings on racial or cultural differences, promotional accounts blamed those vices—such as alcoholism—that Quakers and Pietists already lambasted as "Babylonian" in European society. Such accounts also took a keen interest in the Delaware language; writers compared it to the presumed *Ur*-language, Hebrew, and ascribed to it ideal qualities, such as full signification and sweetness, which were usually considered prerequisites of a perfect or universal language. English and German promotional accounts alike thus articulated the hope that spiritual and linguistic compatibility with the original inhabitants of Pennsylvania promised the perfect seed-plot for a Philadelphian community.

A comparison of English and German accounts demonstrates the translingual and transnational adaptation of this idealized concept of Delaware spirituality and language; specifically, English and German versions of a popular account of the so-called dying words of the Delaware chief Ockanickon show that promotionalism created ideas of spiritual community by wedding esoteric and radical Protestant sensibilities to an idealized Indian counterpart. At a moment when European encroachment on native American land began to make actual communal interaction less likely, the account legitimized European settlement and idealized the transfer of spiritual authority to the Christian witnesses of the chief's death and, implicitly, to the readers of the promotional accounts.

FOLLOWING THE LINGUISTIC speculations that had informed a variety of utopian and esoteric programs for spiritual reform during the seventeenth century, William Penn and Francis Daniel Pastorius focused on Indian (particularly Delaware) language—its supposed origin, alleged proximity to certain European languages, and presumed spiritual qualities—as evidence of the compatibility between native and immigrant spiritual sensibilities and ultimately as a vindication of the Philadelphian hopes informing the founding of Pennsylvania. Of course, a crucial part of familiarizing a Protestant audience with the Delaware people was to insert them into a Judeo-Christian framework of descent. Following frequent assertions of native American origins among the Ten Lost Tribes of Israel, Penn wrote in his *Letter to the Free Society of Traders:* "For their *Original,* I am ready to believe them of the *Jewish Race,* I mean, of the stock of the *Ten Tribes.*" As "evidence," Penn combined commonly cited scriptural sources, the land-bridge hypothesis of migration, and pseudo-ethnographic comparisons of physical features, customs, and beliefs. Yet Penn placed even more weight upon supposed linguistic similarities between the Lenni Lenape language and Hebrew. Building on the contemporary currency of Hebrew as the potential original language, Penn simultaneously hinted at the common linguistic *and* spiritual origins of the European and Delaware people.[44]

Penn further ascribed to the Delaware language specific characteristics such as "full signification" and a "sweetness" of sound that Neoplatonist linguists regarded as essential qualities of potentially universal or perfect languages:

Their *Language* is lofty, yet narrow, but like the *Hebrew;* in Signification full, like *Short-hand* in writing; *one* word serveth in the place of

44. Penn, *Letter,* 7. For an overview of the Ten Lost Tribes theory, see Andrea Mombauer, "The Myth of the American Indians as Descendants of the Ten Lost Tribes" (master's thesis, Johannes Gutenberg-Universität Mainz, 1998). Also see Gustav H. Blanke, "Early Theories about the Nature and Origin of the Indians, and the Advent of Mormonism," *Amerikastudien/American Studies,* XXV (1980), 243–268; John Canup, *Out of the Wilderness: The Emergence of an American Identity in Colonial New England* (Middletown, Conn., 1990); Lee Eldridge Huddleston, *Origins of the American Indians: European Concepts, 1492–1729* (Austin, Tex., 1967); Richard H. Popkin, "The Rise and Fall of the Jewish Indian Theory," in Yosef Kaplan et al., eds., *Menasseh Ben Israel and His World* (Leiden, 1989), 63–82.

Before Penn, the Swedish minister and missionary Johann(es) Campanius (Holm) (1601–1683) had studied the Delaware language of the lower Delaware Valley and come to the conclusion that it was based on and originated from Hebrew. During his work in the colony of New Sweden between 1642 and 1648, Campanius assembled a vocabulary of Delaware words and phrases arranged according to topics, and he translated Martin Luther's *Little Catechism* from Swedish into the Delaware language, which he identified as the "American-Virginian" or part of the Algonquian language. Campanius circulated both works in manuscript while working in New Sweden. Upon his return to Sweden, Campanius was unable to find a publisher for his works. His grandson Thomas Campanius Holm (1670–1702) had the catechism with an appendix consisting of the vocabulary published in 1696; both were subsequently sent to Swedish Lutheran ministers working with Swedish congregations in Pennsylvania. It is thus highly unlikely that Penn knew of Campanius's work or at least that he had seen his manuscript at the time he composed his *Letter to the Free Society of Traders.* See Isak Collijn, "The Swedish-Indian Catechism: Some Notes," *Martin Luther's Little Catechism, Translated into Algonquian Indian by Johannes Campanius* (Stockholm, 1696; facs. rpt. Uppsala, 1937), 1–21. Thomas Campanius Holm elaborated on his grandfather's missionary and linguistic activities among the Delaware in his *Description of the Province of New Sweden, Now Called by the English, Pennsylvania in America: Compiled from the Relations and Writings of Persons Worthy of Credit, and Adorned with Maps and Plates,* trans. Peter S. Du Ponceau (1834; rpt. Millwood, N.Y., 1975).

three, and the rest are supplied by the Understanding of the Hearer: Imperfect in their *Tenses,* wanting in their *Moods, Participles, Adverbs, Conjunctions, Interjections:* I have made it my business to understand it, that I might not want an Interpreter on any occasion: And I must say, that I know not a Language spoken in *Europe,* that hath words of more sweetness or greatness, in *Accent* and *Emphasis,* than theirs.

More important than its connection to Hebrew were the Delaware language's intrinsic qualities. By granting it to be "in Signification full," Penn allotted the Lenni Lenape language an intellectual and spiritual status comparable to European languages in being capable of expressing a "full" range of ideas and concepts. Nevertheless, his claim that the language is "Imperfect in their *Tenses,* wanting in their *Moods, Participles, Adverbs, Conjunctions, Interjections"* still ascribed it a lower grammatical complexity and developmental status.[45]

With Penn's Quaker sensibilities coming to the fore, his evaluation of the Delaware language turned toward its affective features. Penn provided several examples of Delaware words that he felt have "Grandeur in them" or that he considered "words of Sweetness." Citing *"Accent* and *Emphasis"* as support for his subjective impressions, he clearly revealed his Quaker bias in favor of oral communication. For Penn, the greatest strength of the Delaware Indian language, in other words, resided in its ability to convey emotional and spiritual states. For "Grandeur," Penn listed words such as "Octorockon, Rancocas, Oricton, Shakamacon, Poquessin, all of which are names of places." For "words of Sweetness," Penn cited "Anna, is Mother, Issimus, *a Brother,* Netap, *Friend,* usque orret, *very good;* pone, *Bread,* metse, *eat,* matta, *no,* hatta, *to have,* payo, *to come"* as well as a number of personal names and place-names. Penn did not explain what qualities gave certain words "Grandeur" or "Sweetness," but he clearly listed in the latter category semantically positive words as well as words he simply would have encountered frequently and thus might have considered more melodious than others.[46]

Penn's assumptions about the Delaware language reflected his still rudimentary knowledge of the language's complexity. In fact, Penn had not come in contact with the complete Delaware language but rather the Unami jargon, which was a pidgin language that had developed in the Delaware

45. Penn, *Letter,* 5.
46. Ibid. For an identification of these place-names, see *Penn Papers,* II, 458 nn. 25–30.

Valley during Swedish and Dutch colonization. It "featured only a limited vocabulary and virtually all of the grammatical inflections of Delaware were dispensed with in the jargon, impoverishing its communicative potential but also making it much easier to learn." Yet Penn's limited linguistic knowledge makes his eagerness to grant Delaware full signification all the more remarkable. Rather than linguistic study, the foundation for Penn's judgment was the utopian vision of uniting people of different faiths, languages, and nationalities in a single spiritual community. In evoking the affective qualities of the Delaware language, Penn translated the sensibilities he had promoted among other groups he was trying to win for his spiritual community — the Pietists, Quakers, Mennonites, and Labadists in Germany and the Netherlands. There, Penn had spoken of living a "sweet life" in Jesus Christ, found new friends "sweetly visited" by the spirit, and attempted to communicate a "sweet sense and feeling of the holy presence of god." For Quaker and Pietist readers in Germany, therefore, the Delaware language and people would be both strange and familiar; in spite of a strange lexicon and grammar, the "sweetness" of their words promised the spiritual familiarity desired by those contemplating immigration to Pennsylvania and subscribing to its Philadelphian vision.[47]

ALTHOUGH FRANCIS DANIEL PASTORIUS'S reports leaned on the structural elements of Penn's *Letter* — such as native Americans' language, customs, religion, and relationship to the Quaker immigrants — he elaborated and expanded on Penn's idealization of the Delaware Indians as a spiritual model and as a foil for European vices. Pastorius's discussions of native American language and spirituality often responded to inquiries from friends and family in Germany. Reviews of Pastorius's writings in German periodicals usually highlighted his descriptions of native Americans above other themes. Presumed similarities between radical Pietist and native American spirituality served to confirm and propagate the radical Protestant emphasis on an inwardly experienced religion expressed through outward piety, Christian love toward one's fellow human beings, and the rejection of orthodox rituals and doctrinal wrangling practiced among institutionalized Christian churches.

---

47. Claudio R. Salvucci, "Preface," *A Vocabulary of the Unami Jargon, by Thomas Campanius Holm, Translated by Peter Stephen Duponceau, with a Word-List of the Pennsylvania Indians by William Penn* (Southhampton, Pa., 1997), 1–6 (quotation on 1).

Immediately after settling into his first home in Philadelphia, Pastorius created the image of a transethnic community characterized by mutual affection, symbolically including the leaders of the three groups Pastorius considered the most important components of the new society—the English proprietor Penn, an Indian chief, and himself, the leader of German immigration:

> I was once dining with William Penn where one of their kings sat at table with us. William Penn, who can speak their language fairly fluently, said to him that I was a German, etc. He came accordingly on the third of October, and on the twelfth of December another kind and queen came to my house. Also many common persons over-run me very often, to whom however I almost always show my love with a piece of bread and a drink of beer, whereby an answering affection is awakened in them and they commonly call me "Teutschmann," also "Carissimo" (that is, brother).

No matter how self-glorifying, Pastorius's idealized tableaux linked the communion at the dinner table to tentative but amicable attempts at communicating. Penn and Pastorius used their narrow linguistic faculties to participate in the Augustinian mission of uniting all peoples in a common spiritual community. Pastorius buttressed this image of linguistic and spiritual mutuality with an image of affection facilitated by the symbolic exchange of bread and beer. The German terms "Lieb" and "Gegen-Lieb" (that is, "love" and "corresponding love" or "affection") perfectly expressed the Philadelphian ideal Pastorius and other Protestant immigrants desired to establish among one another; thus, the existence of such affections among European and native American residents served as an effective and *affective* confirmation of cherished ideals.[48]

Understanding the power of language to replicate fear of difference, Pastorius inverted the nomenclature Europeans had used to debase native Americans. He introduced the Delaware Indians in his *Sichere Nachricht* as the "erroneously-called savages" and modified stereotypical terminology in order to reveal its racially, culturally, and spiritually exclusive construction.

---

48. Pastorius, *Circumstantial,* trans. Kimball, in Myers, ed., *Narratives of Early Pennsylvania,* 400–401; Pastorius, *Sichere Nachricht,* 4: "Ich speiste einsten bey W. Penn, da einer von ihren Königen mit an der Tafel saß, diesem nun sagte W. Penn (welcher ihre Sprach ziemlich prompt reden kan) daß ich ein Teutscher, etc."

His word choice reached from "so-genannten Indianern oder Wilden" (so-called Indians or savages) to witty oxymorons such as "unwilden Wilden" (un-savage savages) to the familiarizing expression "meine jetztmahligen West-Indischen Landsleute" (my current West-Indian country-people). European Christians remaining in a Babylonian state as well as Christian immigrants living impiously or failing to share their Christian faith with native Americans, on the other hand, were derided as "nominal Christians." In the German original, Pastorius used far more pejorative-sounding terms such as "Schein-Christen," "Maul-Christen," and "Mund-Christen," representing not only a mere outward, verbal testimony of Christian faith devoid of practical piety and an actively Christian life but also the superficiality of a faith professed only with the mouth or, worse, a "snout" ("Maul"). Pastorius's description of Delaware Indian customs, spirituality, character, and language was thus designed as a rhetorical foil for the moral inadequacy of European morals, religion, and society. Though in need of conversion, Delaware Indians already embodied the ideals of Quaker and Pietist reformers, thus validating the reformers' challenge against the orthodox churches and European society, offering a fertile mission field for Christian immigrants, and sanctifying the Pennsylvania landscape and its spiritual influences.[49]

In describing native religion, worship, and spirituality, therefore, Pastorius claimed a fundamental translatability and deep spiritual connections between the radical Protestant emphasis on an inward, intuitive faith and the native American spiritual landscape. The Quaker ideal of a universally present Inward Light ennobled Indian spirituality and turned the Delaware people into a Christian community in waiting. In fact, Pastorius started to develop a phenomenology of spiritual responsiveness that would be much expanded by Moravian and other Pietist missionaries among the Delaware in the late eighteenth century (see Coda, below). His descriptions of Indian responses to the core doctrines of Protestant religion confirmed simultaneously the eligibility of Delaware Indians for receiving the divine Word and the validity of the Pietist-Quaker emphasis on the universal presence of the saving light of God:

49. Francis Daniel Pastorius, "Copia, eines von einem Sohn an seine Eltern auss America, abgelassenen Brieffes, sub dato Philadelphia, den 7. Martii 1684" (photostat copy of printed version), in Julius Friedrich Sachse, ed., *Letters Relating to the Settlement of Germantown in Pennsylvania 1683–4 from the Könneken Manuscript in the Ministerial-Archiv of Lübeck* (Lübeck and Philadelphia, 1903), 2; Pastorius, *Umständige geographische Beschreibung*, 58, 59; Pastorius, *Circumstantial*, trans. Kimball, in Myers, ed., *Narratives of Early Pennsylvania*, 419–420; Pastorius, *Sichere Nachricht*, 4.

They listen very willingly, and not without perceptible emotion, to discourse concerning the Creator of Heaven and earth, and His divine Light, which enlightens all men who have come into the world, and who are yet to be born, and concerning the wisdom and love of God, because of which he gave his only-begotten and most dearly-beloved Son to die for us.

Delaware Indians became test cases for the evolving Protestant ideal of a personal and emotional relationship to the savior manifested in sensory and physical responses; in accounts of the Moravian missions among the Indians, tears, in particular, served as a measure of the individual's responsiveness and state on the journey to salvation. While validating the Delaware Indians' potential for being saved, Pastorius's description also uses their emotional response—a type of universal language—to confirm radical Protestant doctrines of universal salvation. In short, Pastorius combined common beliefs among Quaker and Pietist immigrants with observations of Delaware Indians (whether they were authentic eyewitness reports or merely secondhand information mattered little for his purpose) in order to promote the idealized vision of a transcultural, transethnic, and translingual Philadelphian community in Pennsylvania.[50]

As a linguist trained in several classical and modern European languages, Pastorius was acutely concerned with the language spoken by the people he lionized in spiritual and moral terms. Similar to Penn, Pastorius familiarized the Delaware language by linking it to a European tongue: "Their native language is very dignified, and in its pronunciation much resembles the Italian, although the words are entirely different and strange." Considering native American and European languages to be completely different in their lexicon yet affectively similar, Pastorius retained the early modern mystical beliefs in underlying, hidden correspondences between languages that linked them to a common origin and their speakers to one another. Rather than merely appreciating the challenge of learning a non-European language or, like Penn, linking the Delaware language to Hebrew and the Ten Lost Tribes, Pastorius furthermore emphasized the Augustinian ideal

---

50. Pastorius, *Circumstantial,* trans. Kimball, in Myers, ed., *Narratives of Early Pennsylvania,* 385; Pastorius, *Umständige geographische Beschreibung,* 29: "Sie hören sehr gerne, und nicht ohne mercklliche Gemüts-Bewegung reden von dem Schöpffer Himmels und der Erden, und von seinem Göttlichen Liechte, welches alle Menschen erleuchtet die in diese Welt kommen sind, und noch kommen werden, und von GOttes Weisheit und Liebe, aus welcher er seinen eingebohrnen allerliebsten Sohn für uns in den Tod gegeben hat."

of learning other languages for the sake of building a spiritual community. The primary purpose of learning the Delaware language, therefore, was the transfer of articles of the Christian faith: "It is only to be regretted that we can not yet speak their language readily, and therefore cannot set forth to them the thoughts and intent of our own hearts, namely, how great a power and salvation lies concealed in Christ Jesus." But Pastorius went beyond trying to learn the language for an easier conveyance of Christian doctrine; his expression emphasized the ideal at the heart of Christian community propagated by Quakers and Pietists: communication in religious matters was the transfer of innermost, emotional matters — "the thoughts and intent of our own hearts."[51]

Yet Pastorius also knew that readers in Germany — especially academic circles — received his writings about native Americans in general and their language in particular not necessarily within the context of religious renewal in which he tried to couch them. For academic readers at universities in particular, Pastorius's account was merely another contribution to an already vast body of writings on the nature of the native inhabitants of the New World. Such readers were not interested in immigration and converting the Indians; rather, they probed whether any new contribution to the subject contradicted or agreed with existing accounts and whether it added any new information. As opposed to Pastorius's interest in native American languages, this audience's interest was divorced from any personal or higher spiritual relevance and had no consequences for their lives or experiences. Pastorius's letter to his old German friend Georg Leonhard Model most likely responded to an inquiry about Pastorius's experience with and knowledge of the Indians.

Pastorius had known Model from his time at the University of Altdorf, where he was still teaching in 1688 when Pastorius wrote the letter. Model subsequently assumed a position as principal at the "Gymnasium" at the imperial city of Windsheim, where Pastorius's father was mayor. According to Pastorius's letter, Model had asked him for an extensive relation on Pennsylvania at the behest of Johann Christoph Wagenseil (1633–1705), a

---

51. Pastorius, *Circumstantial,* trans. Kimball, in Myers, ed., *Narratives of Early Pennsylvania,* 385; Pastorius, *Umständige geographische Beschreibung,* 29–30 ("Nur ist zu betauren, daß wir ihre Sprache noch nicht recht können, und dahero ihnen unsere eigentliche Hertzens Gedancken und Intention nicht beybringen können, was nemlich in Christo JEsu für eine Krafft und grosses Heyl verborgen lige"), 30 ("Ihre National-Sprache ist sehr gravitätisch, und kommt in der Pronunciation der Italiänischen fast gleich, doch sind es gantz andere unbekannte Wörter").

prominent professor of law and oriental languages at Altdorf. Model, in other words, served as the interlocutor in a larger conversation between academic circles in Germany and one of the first German immigrants in the New World. Printed in Latin in a pseudo-academic periodical appealing to an educated middle- and upper-class audience, Pastorius's letter assumed a superior posture of teaching the European intellectual elite about material that only immigrants in America could know. Instead of acting the part of the gatherer of information on the colonial periphery, however, Pastorius referred his readers to previously published accounts for basic information and instead took Model on an imaginary journey from Germany to America, to Philadelphia, into Pastorius's humble dwelling, and, most important, to an Indian village situated, in typically German fashion, right outside the "city gates." He thus called attention to his learned readers' distance from the actual experience of life in America and their inattention to the spiritual implications of contact with the Delaware Indians as human beings.[52]

In an ironic fashion, Pastorius cast this trip as a quick stroll he and Model would take right before returning home for supper. In spite of his protest against providing redundant information from previous publications, Pastorius here copied unabashedly large portions from Penn's *Letter to the Free Society of Traders.* Instead of following Penn in linking the Indians to the Ten Lost Tribes of Israel, however, Pastorius concluded that he had not "found anything in any book about this and does not want to start an academic dispute about the issue." Further departing from Penn's account, Pastorius included a brief conversation in Delaware (probably the Unami jargon) and German; the dialogue included standard greetings and simple phrases about practical subjects such as coming and going, eating, sleeping, and so forth. Reflecting his characterization of the Delaware Indians as hospitable and welcoming, Pastorius depicted an unnamed "Indian" inviting himself and Model into his dwelling. In this conversation, both German men have sufficient command of Delaware to cement further the amicable

52. Julius Goebel, ed., "Zwei unbekannte Briefe von Pastorius," *German American Annals,* n.s., II, 492–503 (Pastorius quoted on 498). Goebel found the printed letters in Wilhelm Ernst Tentzel's *Monatliche Unterredungen einiger guten Freunde von allerhand Büchern und anderen annehmlichen Geschichten; allen Liebhabern der Curiositäten zur Ergetzlichkeit und Nachsinnen heraus gegeben* (1689–1706) (Monthly reviews of all kinds of books and other edifying stories by several good friends; published for all lovers of curiosities for edification and contemplation). Pastorius's letter to Model is dated Dec. 1, 1688.

relations between the Christian settlers and the native peoples of Pennsylvania generally praised in the promotional literature.[53]

Rhetorically, Pastorius reveled in his ability to baffle the academic elite by shrouding widely debated questions about the Indians, such as their origin and their language, in a sense of mystery that eluded book learning and elite European theorizing. Refusing to answer the question of the Indians' origin, he cheekily refered Model to "your Altdorf Polyhistor"—that is, Wagenseil, the professor of oriental languages—for further illumination. At the end of his Delaware-German dialogue, Pastorius jokingly commented that Model (or, implicitly, Wagenseil) would be "a good philologist" if he could use the language to deduce the origin of the Indians. Pastorius relished that he could place in front of his German friends a conundrum they would be unable to solve. He also implied that he no longer concerned himself with needless academic or intellectual speculation; his life instead was characterized by direct interaction with a people who were simple and benevolent. Pastorius cast himself as living with the Indians in an idyllic, neighborly relationship reminiscent of the pastoral mode prominent in classical and early modern European literature. He left the town just long enough to commune with nature and its original inhabitants and then returned refreshed and rejuvenated to his dwelling. While presenting little firsthand information and most likely nothing that would be new to his learned readers in Germany, Pastorius distanced himself from their expectations. Of course, his relationship with the Delaware Indians was hardly authentic. Rhetorically, this portrayal served to elaborate the contrast between Europe and America, between intellectualism and simplicity, between action and passivity. Although this letter—written to an academic rather than a personal or religious audience—lacked the overt sermonizing against the European Babel emphasized in his promotional tracts, Pastorius deployed the same tropes of contrasting Europe and America, dismissing the motivation of his correspondents for even writing to him to gain information—other than his own genuine perception of the place—and finally championing, although in a cliché and overdrawn fashion, the Philadelphian ideal of living in harmony with diverse religious, linguistic, and ethnic communities.[54]

Pastorius's letter was reprinted in summary in his 1700 promotional tract *Umständige geographische Beschreibung.* The summary—most likely pro-

53. Pastorius, quoted in Goebel, "Zwei unbekannte Briefe von Pastorius," *German American Annals,* n.s., II, 498.

54. Ibid., 498, 501.

duced by Pastorius's father or the publisher—cut out the first-person address to Model, the trope of the afternoon stroll to the Indians, and all of the satirical elements. Remaining is a straight repetition of "factual" information about the Indians as well as the Delaware-German dialogue. That the dialogue was also reprinted in its entirety in a brief summary of Pastorius's 1700 account in a German reader's digest demonstrates the immense interest in Indian languages among European elites. In the context of the 1700 reprint and its review, however, Pastorius's satirical call for European philologists to rack their brains over the origin of the Indian people and language lost its ironic tone and sounded like an honest call for more linguistic study *removed* from the experience of interacting with the Indians. Of course, Pastorius—fluent in seven European languages—was himself highly curious about native languages; far more than studying the Delaware language for the self-aggrandizement of European philologists, however, Pastorius wished for a harmonious communal interaction between Indians and Europeans. That his accounts reflected little actual interaction or detailed knowledge of Indian life and languages only reinforced the utopian, idealized foundation of Pastorius's writings.[55]

Like theologians and linguists before him, Pastorius was highly interested in finding correspondences among European and non-European peoples and striving for a universal brotherhood championed by Jan Amos Comenius, the Philadelphians, and radical Protestants throughout late-seventeenth-century Europe. Distinguishing and distancing himself from

55. "Contenta Literarum Francisci Danielis Pastorii, an Herrn Georg Leonhard Modeln, Rectorem Scholae Windsheimensis," in Pastorius, *Umständige geographische Beschreibung,* 77–81; "The Contents of a Letter of Francis Daniel Pastorius to Mr. George Leonhard Model, Rector of the School of Windsheim," in Pastorius, *Circumstantial,* trans. Kimball, in Myers, ed., *Narratives of Early Pennsylvania,* 433–435. Model was principal at the Windsheim school when the tract was printed, but not when Pastorius wrote him the letter.

See Pastorius, *Umständige geographische Beschreibung,* 80–81: "Ihre Sprache ist aus folgenden Dialogo abzunehmen: Eithanithap, seyd gegrüsset gut Freund. A eitha, seyd auch gegrüsset / tankomi, wo kommt ihr her / past ni unda qui, nicht weit von hier; gecho luensi, wie heisset er? Resp. Franciscus. O letto, es ist gut; Noha matappi, setz er sich her zu uns; gecho ki Wengkinum, was beliebt ihm? Husko lallaculla, mich hungert sehr / langund agboon, gebt mir Brod / lamess, Fisch / acothita, Obs / hittuck nipa, da ist ein Baum voll / Chingo metschi, wann reiset ihr wieder von hinnen? alappo, morgen/ nacha kuin, übermorgen/ etc. Sonst heisset ana, Mutter / Squaa, das Eheweib / hexis, eine alte Frau / Menitto, der Teufel / Murs, eine Kuhe/ Kuschkusch, ein Schwein / Wicco, das Haus / Hockihockon, ein Landgut / Pocksuckan, das Messer. Welcher Professor nun diese Indianische Wörter und Sprache originem und radicem hervor grüblet, dem will ich loben." For the review, see *Monatlicher Auszug aus allerhand neu-herausgegebenen, nützlichen und artigen Büchern* (Monthly digest of diverse newly published, useful, and modest books) (Hanover, 1700), 895–901.

the esoteric debates about universal languages and pansophism in Europe, however, Pastorius tried to focus on concrete, personal interactions founded on intimacy and affection. Although his early experiences in Pennsylvania corroborated these hopes, he eventually had to acknowledge that reality—the quick removal of the Delaware Indians from lands sold or ceded to William Penn and his agents—no longer allowed for a practical translation of such Philadelphian aspirations. For both English and German writers deeply invested in the extension of Philadelphian ideals to native Americans, the practical dispossession of the Indians necessitated the troping of land cessions and the power transfer to the colonists as a type of spiritual bequest that lionized the new owners as legitimate heirs to the Delaware. For this purpose, the accounts of "dying Indians" like the Delaware chief Ockanickon became widely circulated and translated tools of spiritual promotionalism; in their translingual distribution among English and German colonists, such narratives renewed the utopian promise of spiritual community—in spite of the loss of true community with the original inhabitants of Pennsylvania.

THE ACCOUNT OF OCKANICKON's "dying words" was first sent as a letter to England, where it was printed and distributed as part of the promotional effort in Europe. Typical for the multivocal and translingual transmission of information on early Pennsylvania, the story was retold in German promotional publications such as Pastorius's *Kurtze geographische Beschreibung (Brief Geographical Description)*. The narrative epitomized what promotional writers such as Penn and Pastorius suggested about the correspondence between the Delaware Indians and the new Christian immigrants: Delaware spirituality agreed with the radical Protestant ideals of a universal, indwelling spirit of God, simplicity, and brotherly love. In appealing to his successor to live in peace with the Europeans, Ockanickon not only legitimized Penn's settlement policy but also validated the idealization of Pennsylvania as a space where spiritual and linguistic congruencies could be harnessed to build a peaceful society. In fact, the transmission of spiritual authority through Ockanickon's dying words appealed to the mystical sensibilities of radical Protestant readers in Germany and England; much like Christian Rosenkreuz's esoteric knowledge was passed on to a suffering world through a magical text and a select group of followers, Ockanickon's parting wisdom was initially bequeathed only to a deserving few among both the Delaware and English people. Esoteric expectations pinned to

Pennsylvania were thus answered and validated through the mystical transfer of spiritual power through a dying chief.[56]

The first known fact about Ockanickon is that he sold land to the English in New Jersey in 1677. He was then involved in a deed of land made by several Delaware chiefs or "Sachamakers" to William Penn, dated July 15, 1682. According to the published account, however, Ockanickon passed away before July 12, 1682, the date when the New Jersey Quaker John Cripps sent a letter including the chief's dying words to publisher and bookseller Benjamin Clark in London. Clark printed Cripps's letter as well as the witnessed and certified version of Ockanickon's dying words as *A True Account of the Dying Words of Ockanickon, an Indian King, Spoken to Jahkursoe, His Brother's Son, Whom He Appointed King after Him*. According to Cripps, Ockanickon *"died in Burlington, and was Buried amongst Friends according to his desire."* Not only did Ockanickon choose to be inducted into the Quaker-Christian community by being buried in the Friends' cemetery, but also at his burial itself *"many Tears were shed both by the* Indians *and* English." Even before reading Ockanickon's dying words, the reader of the account was thus cued to the message that Delaware Indian spirituality corresponded with and would eventually be superseded by the Quaker faith and community. The tableau of Indian and English people mixing tears and emotions signaled through outward evidence their inward compatibility and the melding of their spiritual sensibilities.[57]

Ockanickon's words—represented as a first-person speech to his nephew and appointed successor—were followed at the end of the printed tract by a two-column list of the names and signatures of English Quaker and Delaware Indian witnesses, which created an idealized audience symbolizing transcultural and translingual mutuality. It is unclear what exactly the event and the act of signing the transcript of Ockanickon's dying words meant to Indian witnesses accustomed to an oral mediation of communal affairs and their fixing in a collective memory. For the English Quakers present and the readers in Europe, however, the dying words and their printing signified not only an orderly transfer of power from one Indian "king" to another but also a transfer of spiritual authority to the Christians.

56. Variant spellings in English are "Ockanichon" and "Ockanikon."

57. "Deed from the Delaware Indians," July 15, 1682, *Penn Papers*, II, 261–269; *A True Account of the Dying Words of Ockanickon, an Indian King, Spoken to Jahkursoe, His Brother's Son, Whom He Appointed King after Him* (London, 1682), 2.

The "imitation of the *Indian* Marks"—that is, an approximation of their signatures—on the last page not only authenticated the printed document as a truthful transcription of the words spoken by Ockanickon, but also it visually and textually represented various levels of translation that presumably occurred when the events of Ockanickon's death and dying words took place: visually and linguistically, these "Marks" represented the compatibility of seemingly alien languages and cultures (Figure 5). In arranging the names of both the English and the Indian witnesses in parallel columns, the tract signaled a mutual agreement on the fundamental concept of certifying the veracity of a document or account—even if in actuality making their marks did not signify the same thing to the Delaware as to the English people present. Though the English were dealing with an oral culture, the painstaking reproduction of the Indian signatures reassured European readers that such marks could be used to identify specific individuals among the Delaware and, as in later treaties and land sales, to hold them accountable for the texts they signed. The transcription and transliteration of their names on the right, therefore, tried to establish for the Delaware the same link between the mark as signifier and the person as signified as do the written or printed names for the English. Though the Delaware people did not subscribe to the same meaning of literacy as the English, the account of Ockanickon's dying words symbolically bound them to a community and a culture heavily invested in writing as an arbiter of "truth." In that sense, translation served to make Indian language and epistemology more intelligible and familiar to the English. In a communal sense, this form of translation conceptualized mutual understanding between two peoples and cultures that seemed exclusive and foreign. The name of the interpreter, Henry Jacob Falckinburg, listed in the middle between the English and Delaware Indian columns of names, represented the dual cultural and linguistic mediation and translation occurring both during the event witnessed and in the printing of the account.[58]

Certifying in writing and even in print Ockanickon's transfer of power on his deathbed to his nephew Jahkursoe further represented an appropriation of native American communal practices into a European perspective. Such a written authentication was necessary because the usual transfer

58. See Andrew Newman's forthcoming book, *On Records: Delaware Indians, Colonists, and the Media of History and Memory,* which is a study of a series of controversies in the shared histories of native Americans and settlers in the colonial mid-Atlantic region, specifically concerning differing concepts of literacy and memory.

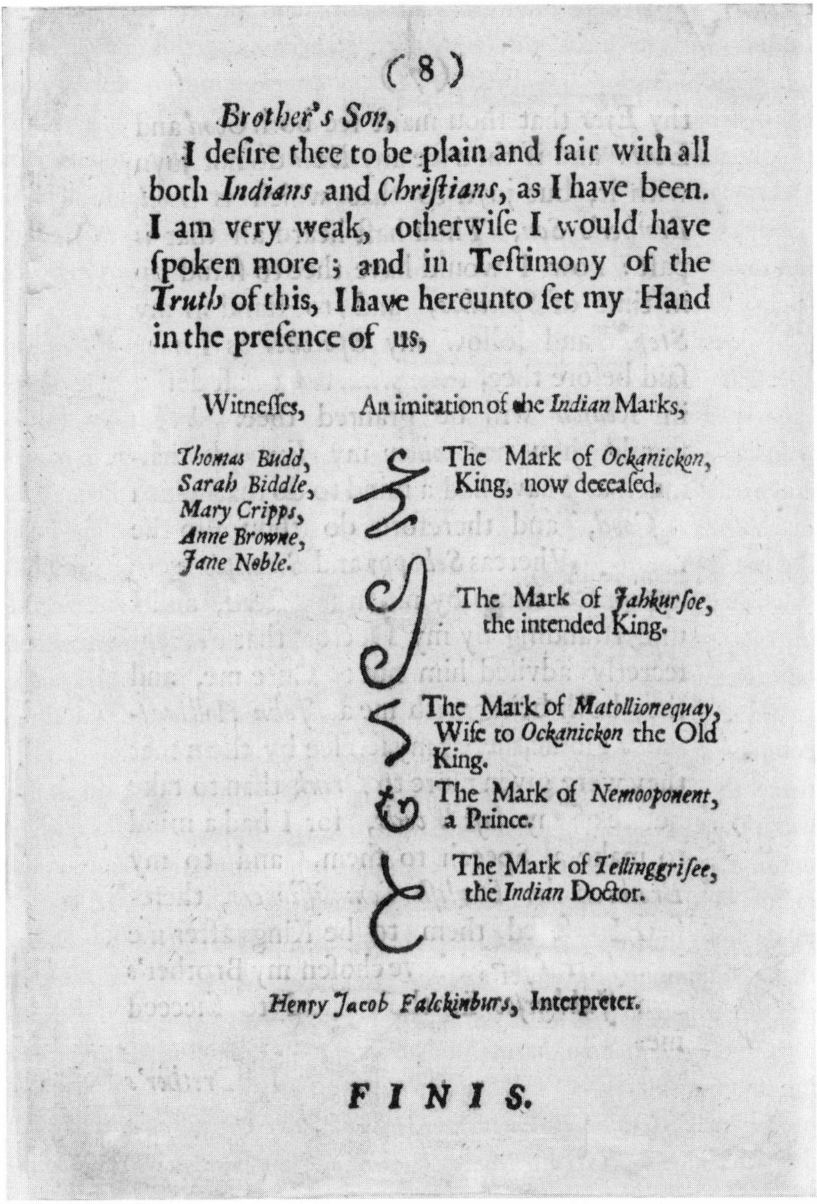

Brother's Son,

I defire thee to be plain and fair with all both *Indians* and *Chriftians*, as I have been. I am very weak, otherwife I would have fpoken more ; and in Teftimony of the *Truth* of this, I have hereunto fet my Hand in the prefence of us,

Witneffes,	An imitation of the *Indian* Marks,
Thomas Budd, *Sarah Biddle,* *Mary Cripps,* *Anne Browne,* *Jane Noble.*	The Mark of *Ockanickon,* King, now deceafed.
	The Mark of *Jahkurfoe,* the intended King.
	The Mark of *Matollionequay,* Wife to *Ockanickon* the Old King.
	The Mark of *Nemooponent,* a Prince.
	The Mark of *Tellinggrifee,* the *Indian* Doctor.

Henry Jacob Falckinburs, Interpreter.

F I N I S.

Figure 5. *Final Page from* A True Account of the Dying Words of Ockanickon, an Indian King, Spoken to Jahkursoe, His Brother's Son, Whom He Appointed King after Him *(London, 1682). This item is reproduced by permission of The Huntington Library, San Marino, California*

of power in Delaware culture was matrilineal and the account represents this event as patrilineal, with Ockanickon giving power to his *brother's* son. Yet the account does not clarify whether Ockanickon indeed broke protocol or whether the text merely adjusted to European gendered sensibilities the reason for Jahkursoe's selection—that he was also the grandson of Ockanickon's mother. Regardless, the message sent by the publication of his dying words to readers in Europe was clear: the spirituality of a moral but unconverted people would come to its greatest fruition in a *Christian* society.[59]

A closer analysis of Ockanickon's dying words in the context of mystical speculations about the correspondences between different languages and their speakers, moreover, suggests an even more utopian purpose to the painstaking reproduction of the Indian marks opposite the English names and explains the popularity of this story among immigrants in Pennsylvania and readers in Europe alike. While appropriating the Indian marks on the last page for a European system of authentication, the listing of both English and Indian signatures in parallel columns created a mystical sense of cohesion between both groups and the individual members represented here. Reminiscent of Comenius's bilingual and trilingual dictionaries popular in mid- to late-seventeenth-century Germany and England, the three columns at the end of this account suggested an internal coherence between the English and Indian signatures *and* the signers. This coherence was intimated, not so much by any similarity between both systems of signing, but rather by the notion of a supralinguistic connection between the members of both groups (and thus between both columns) reverberating throughout the entire account. The tract appealed to a Quaker sensibility that a community of Friends bound together by truth and mutual affection should be mediated orally or completely without language. Thus, the beginning of the account emphasized the physical presence of the witnesses and the oral transmission of Ockanickon's dying words, which were "Spoken in the Presence of several, who were Eye and Ear Witnesses to the Truth thereof." Already cast in a Quaker context and pitched to a Quaker audi-

59. James O'Neil Spady, "Colonialism and the Discursive Antecedents of *Penn's Treaty with the Indians*," in William A. Pencak and Daniel K. Richter, eds., *Friends and Enemies in Penn's Woods: Indians, Colonists, and the Racial Construction of Pennsylvania* (University Park, Pa., 2004), 29–30. Spady suggests that Ockanickon indeed broke protocol by alleging that his previously designated successors Sehoppe and Swampisse might have been absent at the event in order to protest this irregularity. However, the sources corroborate neither this reading nor Spady's speculation that Ockanickon might have ridiculed the Quakers from his deathbed.

ence, the text's evocation of "Truth" did not merely refer to documentary authenticity but also to the idea that the sentiments related were spiritually in accordance with divine truth.[60]

Ockanickon's recorded words sounded like a sermon instructing his successor — as well as his people — in religious and moral principles closely resembling Christian, specifically Quaker, ideals. His short speech confirmed the grandeur of his own sentiments, the compatibility of Indian and Christian moral principles, and, finally, the validity of the entire project of settling and founding a utopian community in Pennsylvania. In other words, the people assembled were "Eye and Ear Witnesses to the Truth" of Ockanickon himself witnessing to the truth. Ockanickon's words making Jahkursoe "KING" thus had relatively little to do with the political or civic role of a ruler; rather, they delineated the qualities and meanings of spiritual and moral leadership. Ockanickon began with a basic metaphor describing the transfer of emotional and ethical qualities: *"My Brother's Son,* This day I deliver my Heart into thy Bosom, and would have thee love that which is *Good,* and to keep *good Company,* and to refuse that which is *Evil;* and to avoid *bad Company."* The printed text thus not only presented a translation of Ockanickon's words from Delaware into English but specifically into the peculiar speechways of the Quakers, abounding in "thee's" and "thy's." English readers encountered an Indian "King" who thought and spoke like a Quaker. Specifying how his successor should reign as "King," Ockanickon placed most emphasis on the peaceful coexistence of *"Indians"* and *"Christians."* Ockanickon specifically believed that equanimity between Indians and colonists would be achieved through peaceful language:

> And if any *Indians* should speak any evil of *Indians* or *Christians,* do not joyn with it, but to look to that which is *Good,* and to joyn with the same alwaies. . . . In Speeches that shall be made between the *Indians* and the *Christians,* if any thing be spoke that is evil, do not joyn with that, but joyn with that which is good; and when Speeches are made, do not thou speak first, but let all speak before thee, and take good notice what each man speaks, and when thou hast heard all, joyn to that which is good.

Granted, Ockanickon might have been transmitting a traditional Delaware code of oral conduct to Jahkursoe. Yet the elder chief's deathbed was a poor occasion for shaping a potentially unprepared successor for a role he

60. *True Account,* 5.

should have become acquainted with long before. Thus, it is much more likely that Ockanickon's dying words—*as they were printed*—were calibrated more for the Quakers or Christians present than Jahkursoe himself. The text presents in a nutshell the *Quaker* ethics of communication that was designed to turn all members of the community into *Friends*. Un-*friendly*, un-Christian language in dealing with one another destroyed a fellowship based on mutuality and love. Speech received such attention among Quakers—and in Ockanickon's proto-Quaker address—because of the radical Protestant subscription to the Augustinian concept of spoken language reverberating with the *locutio cordis*, an inner language remaining in contact with the Word of God. Ockanickon's speech represented to Quakers in England and America the ideal state: a community consisting of disparate parts (*"Indian"* and *"Christian"*) joined together by an outward language that was a close approximation of the workings of the spirit within. Ockanickon's words to Jahkursoe were balm for the anxious Quaker heart: if a savage ignorant of the Christian faith spoke the language of love and peace, then the Quakers themselves could do so as well.[61]

After continuing with his instructions to Jahkursoe to "joyn with that which is *Good*, and refuse the *Evil*," Ockanickon finally explained why he renounced his earlier decision to appoint *"Sehoppy* and *Swanpis"*—two Delaware sachems who signed a land deed on July 15, 1682—as his successors. Besides a vague reference that Sehoppy had apparently conspired against Ockanickon by advising his doctor "not to Cure [him]," Ockanickon primarily cited the two successors' drunkenness at a public function involving representatives of the English settlers at the house of an Englishman named John Hollingshead, explaining that "there I my self see by them that they were given more to *Drink* than to take notice of my *last Words*, for I had a mind to make a Speech to them, and to my *Brethren* the *English Commissioners*, therefore I refused them to be Kings after me in my stead, and have chosen my Brother's Son *Jahkursoe* in their stead to succeed me." Owing to their drunkenness, Sehoppy and Swanpis had failed to pay the dying chief the proper respect by listening to his last speech; thus, they had not only broken the social bonds provided through an oral transfer of power and values, but they also denied the chief the ability to deploy his last words as a means to forge friendships between his successors and the English commissioners. Although the drunkenness of Sehoppy and Swanpis at an event that Ockanickon might have intended as a moment of transcultural bonding

61. Ibid., 5–6.

was technically a reproach to the Europeans who had introduced liquor to the New World, the Quaker witnesses and Quaker readers more likely recognized Ockanickon's words as a familiar call for temperance. Ockanickon emerged as a wise ruler who demoted those who violated Quaker beliefs and advanced another who abided by them. After various acts of translation emerged a community consisting of Indian and English people who subscribed to common linguistic and spiritual ideals and were thus separated from those who did not—both among the Indians and the Europeans. Just as Ockanickon asked Jahkursoe (and, by extension, his people) to "walk in a *good Path*," English Quakers (as well as German Pietists) asked readers in Europe and Pennsylvania to leave behind Babel/Babylon and forge a Philadelphian community in America. The dying words of Ockanickon, in a European publication following a promotional formula, served primarily a self-reflective purpose.[62]

In the adaptation of Ockanickon's dying words in Quaker Thomas Budd's *Good Order Established*, the author turned the idea of a unified spiritual purpose into a clear promotional selling point. Budd reproduced the account, framing it with several accounts of Indian speeches to the English settlers, all of which he claimed to have witnessed himself. Immediately preceding Ockanickon's dying words, Budd recounted a conference between eight Indian "Kings" (one of whom, Budd says, was Ockanickon) and several English colonial representatives during which an unnamed chief gave a speech blaming the Swedes and Dutch for the introduction of liquor. According to the speaker, the ability of the English settlers—presumably Quakers—to see the destructive influences of liquor distinguished them from the previous colonists and made them friends of the Indians. The Indian "King" compared both sides through an elaborate metaphor: "Those People that sell it [liquor], they are blind, they have no Eyes, but now there is a People come to live amongst us, that have Eyes, they see it to be for our Hurt, and we know it to be for our Hurt: They are willing to deny themselves the Profit of it for our good; these People have Eyes; we are glad such a People are come amongst us." The practice of selling liquor, the speaker demanded, must be stopped "by mutual consent; the Cask must be sealed up." This episode idealized the newly established colony and its European settlers as colonists of a higher moral and spiritual order. Immediately following his reproduction of Ockanickon's dying words, Budd recounted a speech given by an unnamed Indian at *"a Conference held with the* Indians *at* Burlington,

62. Ibid., 6, 7. On Sehoppy (Sahoppe) and Swanpis (Swanpisse), see *Penn Papers*, II, 266–267.

shortly after we came into the Country." This speech balanced the previous speech about alcoholism by discussing the origin of smallpox among the Indians. Similarly, the Indian speaker exculpated the English Quakers, because the disease supposedly arrived two generations before the establishment of Pennsylvania as an English province. Couched between these two narratives, Ockanickon's dying words clearly appeared in an accommodating rhetorical context. Audiences in America and Europe would read Ockanickon's words even more strongly as a deferral to the higher spiritual and moral attainments of the newly arrived English Quakers than a universal exhortation to speak and do good that applied equally to both sides represented in the colony. No matter how self-serving, Budd deployed an image of transcultural harmony as a promotional device; the ideal of a spiritual language facilitating a community of brotherly love could be harnessed to promote worldly goals and even to whitewash the dispossession of native American peoples.[63]

In translating and adopting the evocative story of Ockanickon and his dying words for a German audience, Francis Daniel Pastorius established yet another rhetorical and literary context. Pastorius reproduced a selection of Ockanickon's words in his 1692 tract *Kurtze geographische Beschreibung.* Pastorius might have taken Ockanickon's dying words either from the 1682 London publication or from Budd's *Good Order Established.* The latter may be more likely, as Pastorius erroneously dated Ockanickon's dying words as 1685, the year Budd's tract was published. Rather than establishing a context that exculpated English (and, by extension, German) settlers from the introduction of disease and alcoholism among native Pennsylvanians, Pastorius first returned to the well-established contrast between a European Babel/Babylon that corrupted an America that elevated its inhabitants spiritually. In contrast to the European Babylon he had left behind, Pastorius ironically cast himself in company with Indian royalty by retelling from his earlier account *Sichere Nachricht* his story of dining with Governor William Penn and an "Indian king," who later came to visit Pastorius with his wife in Germantown. Rhetorically, Pastorius thus expanded the peaceful society Penn cultivated with the Indians to newly arrived German settlers as well as prospective immigrants from Germany.[64]

63. Thomas Budd, *Good Order Established in Pennsilvania and New Jersey in America* . . . ([Philadelphia], 1685), 29, 32–33.

64. Francis Daniel Pastorius, *Kurtze geographische Beschreibung der letztmahls erfundenen Americanischen Landschafft Pensylvania,* in Melchior Adam Pastorius, *Kurtze Beschreibung der Reichs-*

Next, Pastorius inserted a shortened version of Ockanickon's dying words, claiming—unlike the original tract and Budd's tract—that the Indian chief (whom he calls "Colkanicha") fell ill and delivered his speech during a visit to the governor. Although Pastorius does not directly name Penn as the governor visited by Ockanickon (Penn had already returned to England in 1684), he certainly tried to insert this event into a master narrative that placed himself and Penn at the center of the early history of Pennsylvania. Pastorius presented Ockanickon / Colkanicha's speech even more explicitly than the previous versions as evidence of the Indian chief's "great inclination toward the Christian Religion" and "great desire for the light of truth in his heart." Whereas the 1682 publication implied Ockanickon's spiritual agreement with Quaker principles, Pastorius placed his "Colkanicha" squarely in line with the Friends' belief in the Inward Light. In paraphrasing Colkanicha's speech, Pastorius emphasized the command for following good and living a harmonious existence with both the Indian and the Christian inhabitants of Pennsylvania. Instead of finishing his account on this conciliatory note, however, Pastorius retold an episode from *Sichere Nachricht* about a "cunning savage" who tried to cheat him by selling him a hawk or eagle instead of a turkey and slyly commented that he did not think a newly arrived German knew the difference. Pastorius used this anecdote to moralize that vice had also taken hold on "this side of the ocean in the New World among those who were not one in spirit with God." Thus, Pastorius again returned to the trope of a fallen human world in the midst of the utopian ideal of a regenerate Pennsylvania.[65]

But Pastorius's linking of the vices of the Old and the New World did not turn his promotional tracts into self-consuming artifacts. Rather than building up the possibility for spiritual renewal and then tearing it down, Pastorius placed the recurring seventeenth-century desire for the linguistic and spiritual reconciliation of mankind on an evolving, more mature foundation. Disappointed by the lackluster fervor among his Pietist friends in Frankfurt and the beginning corruption of Pennsylvania's original inhabitants, Pastorius came to understand that the physical removal from Babylon alone could not create a Philadelphian community solely dedicated

stadt Windsheim (Nürnberg, 1692), 30: "Weme aber die jetzt-erzehlte Puncten nicht zu hart fallen, der mag in dem Namen des Herren aus dem Europäischen Babylon ausgehen."

65. Pastorius, *Kurtze geographische Beschreibung*, 31: "In dem Winter Anno 1685, besuchte der König Colkanicha unsern Gouverneur, und bezeugte eine grosse Inclination zu der Christen Religion, und hatte eine grosse Begierde zu dem Liechte der Warheit in seinem Hertzen."

to principles of practical piety, brotherly love, and a unified language of the spirit. The acerbic debates of the Keithian controversy throughout the 1690s, moreover, shook to the core the faith in such an ideal among Quakers and radical Pietists. In this period, endless quarrels about the quality and authenticity of speech used by the contending parties in the controversy seemed to deny the possibility of a community bound together by a spiritual language reverberating with Christian love and religious truth. As before at Babel, human pride once again seemed to take control of human language and disperse a people who had congregated for a unified effort.

Debating Pennsylvania

RELIGIOUS AND LINGUISTIC DIVERSITY
AND DIFFERENCE

wo cities occupied prominent places in the imagination of colonial Pennsylvania: Philadelphia and Babel / Babylon. The first was the City of Brotherly Love, founded by Quakers and other European dissenters as a holy experiment to be governed by Christian affection, religious tolerance, and moral integrity. The second city was not only the place where—according to the book of Genesis—human pride had built a tower reaching to heaven and had thus induced God to separate human language from its divine roots; it was also— reincarnated as the Babylon of the book of Revelation—the allegorical "mother of harlots" (Rev. 17:5). The frequent conflation of Babel / Babylon reveals that Pennsylvanians or writings about Pennsylvania folded linguistic confusion and moral degeneration into a pervasive fear that Philadelphia might devolve into Babel. Throughout the colonial period, Pennsylvanians of various religious, ethnic, linguistic, cultural, and national backgrounds asked how they could build a city or community founded on the dual principles of individual religious freedom and Christian love without falling into a state of linguistic, moral, and civic dissolution.

As the first justice of the peace of Germantown, Francis Daniel Pastorius wondered how he could establish "Love and Peace and Unity" / "Liebe, Fried u. Einigkeit"—symbolically expressed in a bilingual poem—when the acerbic doctrinal debates among the Pennsylvania Quakers known as the "Keithian controversy" seemed to turn Philadelphia into its evil twin. Weighing the tools of linguistic and civic power against the ideal of brotherly love, Pastorius declared the suppression of someone's testimony—no matter how misguided or wrong in his own eyes—to be "Committing fratricide" / "Ein art des bruder-Mords." The paradox Pastorius struggled with became paradigmatic for Pennsylvania: unchecked, religious and linguistic division, resulting from an excess of freedom and differences, might drive the "holy experiment" into becoming a new Babel / Babylon. Yet if power, in the form of oppression, limited dissent in order to enforce "Peace and Unity," it might destroy the principal ideal of "Love." Which city Pennsylvanians would build always depended on the type of language they used.[1]

The spiritual and social utopianism that undergirded the founding of Pennsylvania soon seemed to yield to a spirit of contentiousness that rivaled the denominational strife of Europe. Communal, religious, and political partisanship in early Pennsylvania first climaxed in the Keithian controversy, which historians have variously interpreted as a dispute over religious doctrine, ministerial authority, or political power among Pennsylvania Quakers during the 1690s and early 1700s. In spite of considerable differences among scholars regarding its causes, most seem to agree that the Keithian controversy constituted a conflagration virtually consuming the bonds that tied together civil and religious community in the nascent province. Suddenly, the cultural and linguistic diversity of early Pennsylvania touted in early promotional tracts seemed to cause or at least fan the dissolution of community. An analysis of the English and German writings participating in and responding to the Keithian controversy, however, calls into question facile assumptions about a mutually compounding effect of religious heterodoxy and other types of diversity, particularly multilingualism, in the development of community in early Pennsylvania. The confrontation with and frequent embrace of linguistic difference allowed individuals and groups to see past seemingly insurmountable religious differences. At least in part, German- and English-speaking Pennsylvanians counteracted communal divisiveness by exploring linguistic and spiritual correspondences through translation and multilingual writing in poetry and prose.[2]

1. Francis Daniel Pastorius, "Silvula Rhytmorum Germanopolitanorum," in "Bee-Hive," #38, MS Codex 726, Rare Book and Manuscript Library, University of Pennsylvania. Pastorius entitled his poetic miscellany within the larger "Bee-Hive" manuscript "Silvula Rhytmorum Germanopolitanorum," that is, "A Little Forest of Verse from Germantown." All entries within this section are numbered consecutively.

2. Jon Butler, "'Gospel Order Improved': The Keithian Schism and the Exercise of Quaker Ministerial Authority in Pennsylvania," *William and Mary Quarterly*, 3d Ser., XXXI (1974), 431–452; Butler, "Into Pennsylvania's Spiritual Abyss: The Rise and Fall of the Later Keithians, 1693–1703," *Pennsylvania Magazine of History and Biography*, CI (1977), 151–170; Butler, "Power, Authority, and the Origins of American Denominational Order: The English Churches in the Delaware Valley, 1680–1730," American Philosophical Society, *Transactions*, LXVIII (1978), 32–39; Butler, "The Records of the First 'American' Denomination: The Keithians of Pennsylvania, 1694–1700," *PMHB*, CXX (1996), 89–105; Edward J. Cody, "The Price of Perfection: The Irony of George Keith," *Pennsylvania History*, XXXIX (1972), 1–19; J. William Frost, ed., *The Keithian Controversy in Early Pennsylvania* (Norwood, Pa., 1980); Frost, "Unlikely Controversialists: Caleb Pusey and George Keith," *Quaker History*, LXIV (1975), 16–36; David L. Johns, "Convincement and Disillusionment: Printer William

The disputes of the Keithian controversy did not result from the clash of different religious, ethnic, or linguistic groups aggregating under the umbrella of Penn's policy of toleration; rather it originated from a split within the Society of Friends. Although the Quaker faith sprang from the belief that a common knowledge of truth or Inward Light permeates all believers and produces a spirit of "Love and Unity" among the faithful, Pennsylvania Friends suddenly found that on religious issues they did not speak the same language. Each side alleged that the religious error of the opposing camp manifested itself in the ranting or babbling of individual Friends, particularly George Keith, the main critic of Quakerism in Pennsylvania. Conflating spiritual and linguistic confusion, writers abandoned any substantive discussion of doctrinal matters and delved into textual disputes that valued the letter of religious testimony higher than its spirit. Errors were not so much found in the religious tenets of the opposing camp but in the way individuals had heard, read, and interpreted professions of faith. Keithians and orthodox Quakers confronted one another like two groups lacking a common linguistic system, an impartial go-between, or an adequate translator. The controversy appeared as a relapse into the linguistic confusion of Babel.[3]

On the surface, the influx of German immigrants seemed to enhance the religious wrangling among English Quakers. Some of Johannes Kelpius's followers joined the Keithians in their critique of orthodox Quakers, whereas Pastorius rushed to their defense. To a certain degree, German immigrants reenacted the linguistic and spiritual confusion of the Keithian controversy. Rather than causing the sudden disappearance of the Philadelphian desire for linguistic and religious reformation and unification, however, the intense debates over doctrinal differences among related religious groups in Pennsylvania confirmed the passionate search for a common spiritual language. Whether agreeing or disagreeing in religious terms,

Bradford and the Keithian Controversy in Colonial Pennsylvania," *Journal of the Friends' Historical Society*, LVII (1994), 21–32; Clare J. L. Martin, "Controversy and Division in Post-Restoration Quakerism: The Hat, Wilkinson-Story, and Keithian Controversies and Comparisons with the Internal Divisions of Other Seventeenth-Century Non-Conformist Groups" (Ph.D. diss., Open University, 2004); Andrew R. Murphy, *Conscience and Community: Revisiting Toleration and Religious Dissent in Early Modern England and America* (University Park, Pa., 2001); Gary B. Nash, *Quakers and Politics, Pennsylvania, 1681–1726* (Boston, 1993); John Smolenski, *Friends and Strangers: The Making of a Creole Culture in Colonial Pennsylvania* (Philadelphia, 2010), 149–177.

3. See Hermann Wellenreuther, "The Quest for Harmony in a Turbulent World: The Principle of 'Love and Unity' in Colonial Pennsylvania Politics," *PMHB*, CVII (1983), 537–576.

German- and English-speaking neighbors inevitably had to confront and overcome linguistic differences in order to communicate with one another. Even for a dispute to take place across these linguistic divisions, at least one side had to be capable and willing to transpose religious testimony from one language into another. Translation and multilingual composition highlighted linguistic correspondences and, in doing so, frequently established new spiritual alliances. In the wake of the Keithian controversy, linguistic multiplicity did not spur the disintegrating forces of religious controversy; it strengthened communal cooperation.

"Brat of Babylon": George Keith and the Crisis of Spiritual Communication

Scholarly opinion about the causes of the Keithian controversy is almost as divided as Pennsylvania Quakerism was in the late seventeenth century. Historians variously stress Keith's public rebellion against the overlapping of church and state, his denunciation of doctrinal ignorance and theological error among fellow Friends, or his haughty manners in dealing with highly respected members of the community. My purpose in rereading the Keithian controversy through the lens of linguistic confusion and multilingual cooperation is not to refute any existing scholarly opinions about the causes of this religious and communal upheaval. Understanding the controversy as a dispute about the communal agency of language, instead, helps to explain the largely unaccounted fact that the textual debates surrounding the controversy continued for years after doctrinal matters had been dissected into the minutest details, after Keith had left the province, and even after Thomas Lloyd, the Keithians' principal political target, had died.[4]

---

4. According to Frost ("Unlikely Controversialists," *Quaker History*, LXIV [1975], 20–23), a group of scholars including Keith's biographer Ethyn Williams Kirby believes that the controversy was caused and spurred by Keith's obnoxious personality and his violation of personal bonds with other members of the community, especially prominent ministers such as Samuel Jennings and William Stockdale as well as Penn's lieutenant governor Thomas Lloyd. Another group, represented by Gary Nash, argues that existing political animosities between opponents and supporters of the proprietor William Penn spread to the religious realm, where accusations of religious heresy intensified earlier partisanship. Jon Butler, among others, argues that Keith's attacks sprang from his discontent over the magisterial rule of Quaker ministers. Thus, the controversy was largely an expression of disagreement over church polity and the power of the ministry. Frost himself argues that the central issue sparking the Keithian controversy was doctrinal. Specifically, the debate raged over the dual nature of Christ, with Keith alleging that most Quakers in Pennsylvania denied the physical return of Christ after the resurrection. See Butler, "'Gospel Order Improved,'" *WMQ*, 3d Ser., XXXI

My interpretation of the Keithian controversy focuses on the ways in which communal confrontation with religious dissent and linguistic differences reshaped the original vision of establishing Pennsylvania as an experiment simultaneously repairing the linguistic and spiritual causes of Babel and Babylon. A steady erosion of trust in the ability of oral and written language to mediate truthfully religious testimony and to bind individuals together in a common experience and awareness of faith lay at the heart of the controversy. The shift from the oral culture of the Quaker meeting system to the widespread dissemination of opposing arguments in print encapsulates a communal groping for a trustworthy medium and mode of communication. After oral exchanges had devolved into the hissing of linguistic and spiritual dissonance, print discourse quickly gained a similarly derisive reputation of falsifying personal testimony for the manipulation of public opinion.

Even a cursory outline of the Keithian controversy reveals a preoccupation with the ability of language to give voice to an acceptable and trustworthy representation of religious truth and thus establish a foundation for a coherent community of the faithful. George Keith—one of the leading figures of late-seventeenth-century Quakerism and one of the most astute theologians in early Pennsylvania—differed widely from the ruling Quaker ministers in defining what constituted an acceptable religious testimony. Valuing a personalized faith over a set of doctrines establishing church discipline, Quakers traditionally regarded religious testimonies as an extension of individuals' experience of the Inward Light or indwelling spirit of God. Keith, however, was appalled at the supposed ignorance of his fellow Quakers in scriptural knowledge and the most basic tenets of Christianity. During the late 1680s and early 1690s, he called for a set of doctrines to which prospective and existing members of the Society of Friends in Pennsylvania would have to consent in a public statement of faith. Keith, in other words, tried to install a normative linguistic performance as an effective platform for judging an individual's faith and access to religious truth.[5]

Orthodox Quakers initially refused to comment on the doctrinal issues

---

(1974), 431–452; Butler, "Into Pennsylvania's Spiritual Abyss," *PMHB*, CI (1977), 151–170; "American Denominational Order," APS, *Trans.*, LXVIII (1978), 32–39; Butler, "Records of the First 'American' Denomination," *PMHB*, CXX (1996), 89–105; Ethyn Williams Kirby, *George Keith (1638–1716)* (New York, 1942); Nash, *Quakers and Politics*, 144–180. On Lloyd, see David Haugaard, "Thomas Lloyd," in Craig W. Horle et al., eds., *Lawmaking and Legislators in Pennsylvania: A Biographical Dictionary*, I, *1682–1709* (Philadelphia, 1991), 505–516.

5. Frost, *Keithian Controversy*, 27.

raised by Keith. When several Quaker ministers, however, accused Keith of heresy for denying the sufficiency of the Inward Light and preaching two different Christs — one within and one without — he increased the pitch of his attacks. He personally denounced the most prominent Pennsylvania Quakers and public officeholders, including the deputy governor Thomas Lloyd and the minister Samuel Jennings. Ostensibly disagreeing over a change of venue in the spring of 1692, Keith and his followers established a separate meeting and dubbed themselves Christian Quakers. The Quaker establishment rejected the new meeting and disowned Keith. With the support of William Bradford, the only printer in Pennsylvania at the time, Keith blamed the orthodox Quakers for the controversy and publicly ridiculed the Quaker ministry for their ignorance in doctrinal matters and refusal to accept his demands for reform.[6]

To curb Keith's denunciations, the Quakers brought a libel suit against him and Bradford for publicly attacking those ministers who were also provincial magistrates. Although Keith, Bradford, and several others were convicted and fined, the temporary suspension of Quaker rule with the arrival of royal governor Benjamin Fletcher prevented further action against them. The climax of the controversy occurred in 1693, when Keith and his followers rudely disrupted an orthodox meeting. In early 1694, Keith left Pennsylvania for London to present his grievances at London Yearly Meeting. He eventually leveled similar charges at the London Friends, who concluded that "George Keith is Gone from the blessed unity of the peaceable spirit of our Lord . . . and hath separated himself from the holy fellowship of the Church of Christ." Keith became an Anglican minister in 1700 and returned to Pennsylvania for a two-year visit in 1702.[7]

---

6. The term "orthodox" for the Quakers who did not follow Keith is very misleading. The *Oxford English Dictionary (OED)* defines "orthodox," with regard to opinion or doctrine, as something "right, correct, in accordance with what is accepted or authoritatively established." Following this definition, Keith intended to make the Quakers *more* orthodox, and his camp should be, strictly speaking, designated as "orthodox" because they tried to revive Quaker adherence to established Christian doctrine. Ultimately, the designation "orthodox Quakers" emphasizes Keith's actions as a form of apostasy from standard Quakerism, even if that standard was perceived to be unorthodox by many, including Keith. I continue to use the term "orthodox Quakers" for consistency with most existing scholarship.

William Bradford had originally been employed by Pennsylvania Friends to print their officially sanctioned publications. During the controversy, Bradford emphasized that he would publish the positions of both camps. Orthodox Quakers, however, demanded that he desist completely from publishing anything critical of their position.

7. Quoted in Butler, "American Denominational Order," APS, *Trans.*, LXVIII (1978), 39.

A closer examination of the terminology both sides used to characterize their opponents illuminates the central debate over language that propelled the controversy for more than a decade. According to George Keith and Thomas Budd's *Account of the Great Divisions* (1692), orthodox Quakers added to the list of epithets describing Keith—which already included "heretic," "schismatic," and "apostate"—the appellation "Brat of Babylon." If Keith's opponents had indeed used this term, they probably meant to evince the ominous conflation of spiritual dispersion epitomized by Babel and the moral corruption represented by Babylon. Yet both sides believed that their opponents had fallen prey to a religious heresy or error that manifested itself in a confusion of language, witnessed in such characteristic acts as "railing" and "babbling." Orthodox Friends, in particular, feared that the distortion of religious truth through unfriendly public uses of language turned their holy experiment into a new Babel, doomed to linguistic and spiritual dispersion. Upon his arrival in Pennsylvania, the German mystic Johann Gotfried Seelig believed to have found the Quakers in a post-Babel state of confusion, claiming that the "pieces of their established Meetings lie scattered all over." Seelig's trope recalled the ruined Tower of Babel and signified the breakdown of the Quaker attempt to build a new community on the premise of a universal spiritual truth imparted on all people by the Inward Light. During the controversy, any deployment of oral or written language to cement this truth against dissolution provided further evidence of spiritual error, resulting in a spiral of accusation and counteraccusation.[8]

As a member of a religious community relying largely on the mediation of faith through oral testimony representative of the operations of an inward language or Inward Light, Keith faced a fundamental dilemma. In trying to address the heresy he claimed to be prevalent among Quakers, Keith could not rely on any written statements that would have espoused such false beliefs. In his tract "Gospel Order Improved," he called for a written confession of faith, which would reveal doctrinal errors to the entire community. When the Philadelphia Yearly Meeting refused to act upon Keith's demands, he decided to reveal heresies among the Friends himself. Keith interpreted oral testimonies delivered in meeting and subsequently repre-

8. George Keith [and Thomas Budd], *An Account of the Great Divisions amongst the Quakers in Pensilvania* . . . (London, 1692), 5, 6; Johann Gotfried Seelig, *Copia eines Send-Schreibens auß der neuen Welt . . . Germandon in Pennsylvania Americae d. 7. Aug. 1694* ([Halle and Frankfurt?], 1695), 9.

sented supposed errors to the aggregate members of the church. The discrepancy between what these individuals *thought* they believed and what Keith *told* them they had confessed sparked the verbal battles of the Keithian controversy.[9]

Keith leveled his accusations both within the oral culture of the meetings and, more subversively, in unauthorized print publications. Orthodox Friends particularly objected to Keith's haughty public use of language in confronting others. Samuel Jennings believed that the "General Cause" for Keith's actions was "an *Unbounded Ambition* . . . which had blown him up into such *Towering Thoughts* of himself, as made him a very uneasie Member of any *Society,* either *Civil,* or *Religious.*" Sharing a *"Towering"* pride with the builders of the Tower of Babel, Keith allegedly caused a similar linguistic and spiritual confusion. In a letter to London Yearly Meeting, orthodox ministers complained about "the disorder and distraction occasioned . . . by George Keith, and our time being much gone by hearing and suffering his Clamours against us from which he by no means of perswasion be reclaim'd."[10]

Keith, in turn, detected the same linguistic derangement among his opponents and blamed them for "railing." In *An Account of the Great Divisions,* Keith and his follower Thomas Budd described a scene of physical, spiritual, and linguistic confusion resembling Babel:

> Was it therefore any matter of Wonder or Crime, that G.K. being zealous and fervent for the true Faith, and Doctrine of Christ . . . was stirred in spirit to use sharp words against them, which yet were all true, and therefore no Railing, nor yet blameworthy. . . . Is it not great Hypocrisie and Partiality of these men so severely to judge him, and wholly to conceal, not only their own Ignorance, Error and Blasphemy, but the extream Passion, the rude, uncivil and unmannerly Speeches they uttered against him, both in these Meetings, and often since, calling him, *Reviler of his Brethren, Accuser of the Brethren, Brat*

9. The manuscript "Gospel Order Improved" was first published as "Gospel Order and Discipline," *Journal of the Friends' Historical Society,* X (1913), 70–76. See also Butler, "'Gospel Order Improved,'" *WMQ,* 3d Ser., XXXII (1974), 435 n. 14.

10. Samuel Jennings, *The State of the Case, Briefly but Impartially Given betwixt the People Called Quakers, in Pensilvania, etc. in America, Who Remain in Unity; and George Keith* . . . (London, 1694), 13 (emphasis added); Frost, *Keithian Controversy,* 138. On the Quakers' use of and relationship to print culture in seventeenth-century England, see Kate Peters, *Print Culture and the Early Quakers* (Cambridge, 2005).

of Babylon, One that always endeavoured to keep down the power of Truth, drawing from the Gift of God; calling him also, *Pope, Primate of* Pensilvania, *Father Confessor,* accusing him of *Railing, Envy, extream Passion, and a Turbulent and Unsubdued Spirit,* and not only so, but most uncivily and unchristianly, yea, inhumanely, otherwise treating him in these Meetings, often six or ten, all at once, speaking to him, and some pulling him by one sleeve, and others by the skirts of his Coat, more like Mad men than Sober; and some bidding him go out, and when he essayed to go out, and prayed them to let him go, others pulling him back, and detaining him; so that greater Confusion was scarce ever seen in any Meetings pretending to *Christianity.*

Keith and Budd's account revealed a complete breakdown of proper communication and Christian fellowship. Apparently, both sides traded the principles of "Love and Unity" and the rhetorical means of "perswasion" for name-calling and physical attacks. The central accusation of "Railing" not only implied an uncivil deportment but also a cacophony of voices that degraded language from a system of intelligible utterances to a nonsensical "babbling." The threat of a Babylonian confusion had become a reality, with the separation or scattering of the Quaker community following the inability of Friends to speak with one voice or one language.[11]

Although Keith could not feasibly deny his own yelling, name-calling, or even passion, he claimed superiority over the orthodox Quakers by redefining the language acceptable within the meeting system (and in the community at large). His emphasis on a discourse of truth supposedly validated any utterance delivered in any manner as long as it communicated divine will or the fundamental tenets of Christianity. Elsewhere in the same tract, Keith even admitted to having called his opponents *"Fools, ignorant Heathens, Infidels, silly Souls, Lyars, Hereticks, Rotten Ranters, Muggletonians";* yet he claimed that "he never gave such Names to any of them, but to such as he can prove did deserve them, and for which he can appeal to all impartial men that profess Christianity." For the orthodox Quakers, any linguistic utterance that did not abide by their principle of communal affect and unity

11. Keith [and Budd], *Account of the Great Divisions,* 5-6. The *OED* defines "babbling" as a "a confused murmur or noise, as of many voices heard at once." Already guilty of "babbling," the Quaker meeting would have deserved the related name "Babel" in three ways: as "a lofty structure; a visionary project" (Friends tried to build a perfect society), as "a scene of confusion; a noisy assembly," and, finally, as "a confused medley of sounds; meaningless noise" *(Shorter Oxford English Dictionary).*

was unintelligible and constituted "Railing"; for Keith, any utterance complying with his standard of truth deserved to be heard.[12]

Keithians and orthodox Quakers further entrenched their positions by waging a relentless pamphlet war. Yet the increasing reliance on print did not open up the forum of public debate to a wider spectrum of individuals; the extreme literalism of the discourse narrowed the number of those who could legitimately write about the issue. For example, William Davis's single publication, *Jesus the Crucified Man* (1700), attacked the elitism of the discourse on both sides and tried to return to the Quaker reliance on the individual access to truth unmediated by education or social distinction. The "thirst after Truth," he wrote, "doth illustrate a mans Name more than the Trophies of his Ancestors, or the Success of his indisputable Courage and Bravery, or what ever other brave Qualifications in famous humane Arts and Sciences, as well as Tongues and Languages he may or hath attained unto." Seemingly rejecting the theological and linguistic acumen necessary to follow the debate, Davis's tract itself practiced the endless refutation of the opposing side's writings that became the hallmark of the controversy.[13]

Both sides soon discovered that the spirit of contention equally infiltrated print discourse. Readers and writers complained that their opponents twisted their words, cited their statements out of context, and generally manipulated language for sheer demagoguery. Writers such as Caleb Pusey (for the orthodox Quakers) and Daniel Leeds (for the Keithians) deployed print discourse as a representation of truth all the while using a pedantic metadiscourse over the misrepresentation of one another's statements. Falsification of written testimony had apparently become so rampant that Pusey introduced his pamphlet *The Bomb Search'd* (a refutation of Leeds's tract "call'd a BOMB") with lengthy instructions on proper reading:

> And now we shall desire the Candid Reader, that in reading the following charges against these men and our observation on them that he read and consider them very impartially; but before we recite them, we also request the Reader that he would be Pleased to take the advice given by these eminent persons following concerning the reading of books. The first is the famous John Lock *[sic]*, who saith thus 'To have one's words exactly quoted, and their meaning interpreted by the plain and visible *design* of the Author in his whole discourse being a

12. Keith [and Budd], *Account of the Great Divisions*, 8.
13. William Davis, *Jesus the Crucified Man* . . . ([Philadelphia], 1700), preface.

right that every writer hath a just claim to, and such as a lover of truth will be wary of violating.'

Pusey's anxious attempt to mold the ideal reader fleshed out what he believed had been going wrong in the exchanges surrounding the controversy. Pamphleteers quoted passages from orthodox Quaker or Keithian writings out of context and even twisted quotations to serve their own purpose. Specifically, Pusey blamed Leeds for *"miscitations, Clipping of sentences, and perverting of our friends writings."* Much of Pusey's tract, therefore, was bogged down in quoting passages from Quaker writers such as William Penn and demonstrating how Leeds and others falsified them in word and spirit.[14]

Leeds rebutted Pusey's accusation of twisting evidence by making his sources physically accessible to the reader. In his pamphlet *The Great Mistery of Fox-craft Discovered,* Leeds encouraged his readers to inspect "two letter[s] written by G. Fox to Coll. *Lewis Morris,* deceased, exactly Spell'd and Pointed as in the Originals, which are now to be seen in the Library at *Burlington* in *New Jersey,* and will be proved (by the likeness of the Hand, etc.) to be the Hand-Writing of the *Quakers* learned *Fox,* if denied." Reading had devolved into a subcategory of forensics, with readers cross-checking handwriting samples to determine the identity of the author and exclude the possibility of forgery.[15]

Again, orthodox Quakers went along with such an exacerbation of distrust and assembled an entire library of reference works serving as the seemingly incorruptible evidence for Leeds's deception and Pusey's honesty. Pusey wrote:

We have procured the books out of which their quotations are pretended to be taken to be lodged one whole year, commencing the first of the ninth month 1705 at the house of *Robert Burrow in Chesnut Street in Philadelphia,* where any person may seasonably and soberly

14. [Caleb Pusey], *The Bomb Search'd and Found Stuff'd with False Ingredients* . . . (Philadelphia, 1705), 13, 75. Also see [Pusey], *Daniel Leeds, Justly Rebuked* . . . (Philadelphia, 1702); [Pusey], *Satan's Harbinger Encountered* . . . (Philadelphia, 1700). For one of the first scholarly efforts to recover the importance of Caleb Pusey as Quaker writer and community leader, see John Smolenski, *Friends and Strangers,* 286–296.

15. D[aniel] L[eeds], *The Great Mistery of Fox-craft Discovered* . . . ([New York, 1705]), 1. Also see Leeds's earlier tract, *News of a Trumpet Sounding in the Wilderness* . . . (New York, 1697). The following tract has been attributed to Leeds: [J.B. A Protestant], *News of a Strumpet Co-habiting in the Wilderness* . . . ([New York?], 1701).

come and view any of the said passages in order to satisfy himself, whether what we have here transcribed out of their books, and our observations on them *be not genuine.*

This erosion of the Quaker belief in an essential link between religious testimony and the inward language of the soul thus disrupted the bonds that tied members of the community to one another. The endless transcribing, excerpting, quoting, and disputing of passages removed testimony so far from the author that only the return to a library of disembodied but ostensibly original sources could presumably ensure genuineness. Both Leeds and Pusey tried to replace a community of Friends who trusted that one another's speech was filled with spiritual truth with a meeting of books that spoke in its stead.[16]

In their effort to construct Pennsylvania as an antidote to the linguistic and moral corruption of Europe, Quakers had restaged the confusion of Babel. For Keith, the Quaker emphasis on individual inspiration—the Inward Light—sanctioning and sanctifying individual religious testimony undermined the authority of the Bible as the original and direct Word of God and the authority of Christ, the Word made flesh. For the orthodox Quakers, Keith's demand for doctrinal soundness and the primacy of the scriptures denied the primacy of individual inspiration; his vociferousness and wild accusations, more importantly, perverted the desire to turn the language of the community into a direct expression of the mutual love and affection that held the Society of Friends together. Eventually, both sides pushed their respective truth claims so far that only a return to the original, physical handwriting of people like George Fox and William Penn could, presumably, authenticate the relationship between language—in speech, writing, or print—and the individual believer. Ironically, therefore, Quakers on both sides had descended into a Babylonian confusion precisely through their efforts to tie the language of individual believers and the community ever closer to the divine Word.

SIMILAR TO THE EARLIER promotional discourse, the Keithian controversy soon involved German immigrants and thus developed transnational and translingual dimensions. Although several Germantown residents joined the Keithians early on, the German immigrant community became thoroughly embroiled in the dispute with the arrival of the mystical Pietist group

16. [Pusey], *Bomb Search'd*, 76.

under Johannes Kelpius in 1694. Kelpius and his followers championed a mystical union of the individual believer with Christ, metaphorically revered as the heavenly bridegroom or the "Beloved" of the Song of Songs. The strongly physical, even erotic dimension of the mystics' concept of Christ clashed with the Quakers' rather disembodied Inward Light theology. Although Kelpius and most of his followers avoided open doctrinal disputes, a more quarrelsome member of the group, Heinrich Bernhard (Henry Bernhard) Köster, tried to direct German and English Pennsylvanians back to orthodox Protestantism and reinstate the rites of baptism and the Lord's Supper shunned by the Quakers. Köster joined with English Keithians, such as William Davis, Thomas Rutter, and Thomas Boyer, to form an independent religious community close to the Baptists. On September 22, 1696, the group violently disturbed the Philadelphia Yearly Meeting held at Burlington. Pastorius witnessed the intrusion and broke his public silence on the issue by printing—with the Meeting's approval—the anti-Keithian pamphlet *Four Boasting Disputers of This World Briefly Rebuked,* a vehement condemnation of Köster, Davis, Rutter, and Boyer.[17]

In responding to Köster's accusations in general and the tone of his tirades in particular, Pastorius himself slipped from language mindful of brotherly love into a vitriolic condemnation of opposing viewpoints. Falling prey to the same rage he detected in his four culprits, Pastorius named Babel / Babylon as the allegorical origin of an earlier publication issued by his opponents without an imprint:

> Though this their said Pamphlet doth not set forth the place where it was printed, yet mentioning so many things of Babylon; for Example, *The Councils, and Clergies, and Universities of Babylon,* page 2. *The Babylonian Churches,* page 4. *The Babylonian Beasts,* page 7. *The four chief Quarters of Babylon,* page 8. And being it self thoroughly full of Babel, or Confusion, it thereby plainly discloseth, that it was hatched in the very Center of that great City, whose wise and learned men most able (in their own Conceit) to advise others, can not write but thus sinisterly, even with their right hands. . . . They stile themselves, *The Brethren in America* page 7. *The true Church of Philadelphia or*

---

17. For a list of Quakers associated with the Keithians, see Frost, *Keithian Controversy,* 371–375. The records of the Pennepek Baptist Church state: "William Davis, with one Henry Bernard Koster a Germane, and some more made up a kinde of Society, did Break bread, Lay on hands, washed one anothers feet, and were about having A Community of Goods. But in a little time they disagreed, and broke to pieces" (quoted in Butler, "Into Pennsylvania's Spiritual Abyss," *PMHB,* CI [1977], 160).

Brotherly Love, etc. . . . He the said H. B. *Koster* arriving here in *Pen-silvania,* . . . was as cunning as to intice and induce four or five to a Commonalty of goods, and so settled a Plantation near *German Town,* upon a Tract of Land given unto them, calling the same IRENIA, that is to say, The House of Peace, which not long after became ERINNIA, The House of raging Contention, and now returned to the Donour, the Brethren in *America* being gone and dispersed, and the Church of *Philadelphia* (falsly so called) proving momentary, and of no moment, *Mark* 3, 25.

In using Greek (the etymological source of "Philadelphia"), Pastorius described the fate of the group as a fall from "IRENIA" into "ERINNIA," a fall from a place of peace to a place of error or confusion. The homonymic proximity of the Greek words "IRENIA" and "ERINNIA" symbolized how dangerously close the opposite spiritual states they designate in fact were. Further parading his own superior linguistic acumen (and thus a vain use of language), Pastorius also punned on the Latin meaning of the word "sinister," that is, left or left-handed. Even when writing with the "right" side, the Keithians (according to Pastorius) only achieved "left-handed" or "sinister," that is, false, results.[18]

With his two double entendres, Pastorius tried to illustrate that spiritual and linguistic confusion were the ultimate enemy of community in Pennsylvania. Lacking the self-reflective scrutiny Pastorius later used in his multilingual poetry on the Keithian controversy, however, the pamphlet also demonstrated that the slippery slope from spiritual unity to dissolution was paved with the prideful use of the human power over language. Further emphasizing the rift between the testimony of the orthodox Quakers and their opponents, Pastorius likened the Keithians' speech to the falseness of theatrical performance, a practice reviled by all Friends: "But ours being in God, and the members thereof chosen out of the world, and redeemed from the Contentiousness and other vain Customs of the same, will never engage in such a stage play or Theatrical Jangling and Wrangling with these Bablers [*sic*] and Mountebanks of Babylon." The Keithians, Pastorius alleged, had

18. Francis Daniel Pastorius, *Henry Bernhard Koster, William Davis, Thomas Rutter, and Thomas Bowyer, Four Boasting Disputers of This World Briefly Rebuked, and Answered according to Their Folly, Which They Themselves Have Manifested in a Late Pamphlet, Entituled, Advice for All Professors and Writers* ([New York, 1697]), 1–3. No copy of the pamphlet published by Köster et al. is extant; according to Pastorius, it was published in both English and German.

disqualified themselves as a true church and distinguished themselves as *"Babylonians* . . . because of the confusedness of their Language, some not understanding the Speech of the others, who cryed for Water to be plunged in; so that they were scattered before they finish't the Tower of their imaginary Church." Pastorius might have recognized that his tract helped to usher the community further along in their plunge into the waters of spiritual and linguistic confusion, for he never published any tracts on the Keithian controversy again. Köster and Pastorius thus reenacted the confusion of Babel by battling over language, especially the linguistic representation of Quaker principles of faith. During the Keithian controversy, English and German writers alike ironically fostered confusion through their very endeavor to unite the people in true "Philadelphia."[19]

Even while participating in the pamphlet war against the Keithians in Pennsylvania, Pastorius attempted to salvage the image of Philadelphianism in his representation of the province to readers in Germany, particularly his Pietist sponsors. Pastorius wrote a lengthy letter to the Pietists in Frankfurt, who promptly published it as a tract. In his letter, Pastorius presented his own view of the Keithian controversy, refuted Köster's specific allegations (which, he alleged, had been published in Germany for political reasons), and vindicated his newly adopted religious community—the orthodox Pennsylvania Quakers. Although the printed tract was entitled "A Letter of Open-Hearted Affection to the So-Called Pietists in Germany," its purpose was ironically to declare Pastorius's affection for the "so-called" Quakers in America.[20]

Pastorius's specific refutation of Köster and the Keithians was of a kind with other orthodox Quaker writings on the subject; his strategically placed references to his own conversion and embrace of his new community, however, are all the more significant for demonstrating the multiple acts of translation and transformation Pastorius accomplished in mediating between different languages and faiths. Pastorius distanced himself from the Pietists and aligned himself with the Quakers. For instance, he referred to Lutheranism as "the Religion in which [he] was born and raised," rather than his

19. Ibid., 5, 13–14. Pastorius is referring to the disputes over the legitimacy of water baptism among Davis and Köster's group. See Butler, "Into Pennsylvania's Spiritual Abyss," *PMHB*, CI (1977), 161–166.

20. Pastorius, *Ein Send-Brieff offenhertziger Liebsbezeugung an die so genannte Pietisten in Hoch-Teutschland* (Amsterdam, 1697).

current religion. Moreover, Pastorius cast himself as an authority in Quaker writings and a personal witness to Quaker preaching. In order to mediate between his old and new allegiances, Pastorius recommended to the German Pietists specific Quaker books (most prominently, Robert Barclay's *Apology for the True Christian Divinity* [1678]) that had been translated into German and would place the Friends (and his new faith) in the correct light.[21]

Instead of overemphasizing the authority of written texts and even translations, Pastorius referred his readers "primarily to the indwelling Word of God, from which originate and come forth all good words and salvific teachings, as well as sufficient strength to sanctify our souls. If people would only listen properly to and follow *the word hovering in their heart and in their mouth,* then all academic quarreling, war of words, and blasphemy would soon come to an end." Pastorius thus distanced himself and his readers from the perceived pitfalls of contemporary European and, more recently, Pennsylvanian society: the rancorous fighting over words and doctrines. In the act of mediating or translating between two faiths, two languages, and his past and present community, Pastorius asked Pennsylvanians and Europeans alike to return to a goal of the highest order—to reform human society by rooting out, as Jacob Boehme had put it, the quarrelling "over the spirit of the letters" and to put in its place a mutually accessible, inward language.[22]

In his later manuscript reflections on the Keithian controversy, Pastorius regretted its effects on the language and feeling of Christian affection and thus its erosion of the possibilities for the establishment of a Philadelphian

21. Pastorius, *Ein Send-Brieff,* 10 ("Dann ob schon dieses von vielen Lutheranern, [als in welcher Religion ich gebohren und erzogen worden], vor unmüglich gehalten wird, so wissen jedennoch die so genannte Quäker, daß sonder diß es nicht müglich, ein rechtschaffener Jünger Christi zu seyn"), 11 ("Und wünschte ich hertzlich, daß ihr und alle meine geliebte, umb ihre Seligkeit bekümmerte Landsleut dero Bücher in unserer Mutter Sprach haben und lesen möchtet").

22. Pastorius, *Ein Send-Brieff,* 11-12 (emphasis added). The complete passage in the German original reads: "Weilen aber dieselbe in Englisch, und (so viel mir bewust ist) nur einige wenige Tractätlein ins Teutsche übersetzet sind, weise ich euch vors erste dahin, und unter solchen zu ged. Robert Barclays Catechism und so intitulirter Apologia; haubtsächlich aber zu dem eingepflantzten Wort Gottes, von welchem beedes alle gute Wörter und heilsame Lehren, als auch gnugsame Krafft unsere Seelen seelig zu machen entspringen und herrühren. Wolten die Menschen diesem ihnen so nah, in dero Hertzen und Mund schwebenden Wort einst gebührlich Gehör geben und folgen, würde alles Schuhlgezänck, Wortkrieg, und Lästerung bald ein End gewinnen." See also Jacob Boehme, *Sämtliche Schriften* (1730), ed. Will-Erich Peuckert, 11 vols. (Stuttgart, 1955-1960), VII, 261.

community. In an anniversary poem written to the daughters of his late friend Thomas Lloyd in 1714, Pastorius combined religious allegory with political satire, ridicule over the fate of an enemy with lament over the suffering of a friend: "It seem'd to me, he [Lloyd] would his Master [Christ] equalize, / And suffer wretched fools his Station to despise, / Especially George Keith, well nigh devour'd by Lice." Suffering for his faith, Thomas Lloyd earned the honor to follow Christ. Pastorius and his friends were joined through a deep congeniality in personal affairs and through common bonds in civic and religious matters. Severing the bonds of political and doctrinal allegiance, contentious Friends / friends such as George Keith also severed the ties of personal relationships. In an encomium commemorating Penn's return to Pennsylvania, Pastorius deployed even stronger satire to condemn the Keithian "Apostacy" and the concomitant abuse of language:

We understood what things in Pensilvania were
Of good or evil use, to follow, or t'avoid,
The wisest of us all was honest Thomas Lloid.
Some lent their itching Ears to Kuster, Keith and Budd,
And miserably fell into the Ditch of Mud,
Where they may stick and stink; For as a sightless whelp,
So stark-blind Apostates do grin at profer'd help:
They spend their Mouths, and fain with words would ensnare,
Or if this will not do, scold, back-bite, bug-bear, scare;
Hereof, brave William Penn, me thinks, thou hadst thy share.

Pastorius described the deterioration from deceptive language slyly tempting individuals toward apostacy (a betrayal of mutual beliefs) to full-blown verbal violence. The trauma of such vituperative language lingered: nowhere else in his manuscript poetry did Pastorius resort to crude figures of speech such as "Ditch of Mud" or "stick and stink." The most fundamental threats to community in Pennsylvania, in other words, lay in the disruption of personal bonds mediated by a common language of love or affinity.[23]

23. Pastorius, "Ship-Mate-Ship: An Omer Full of Manna, for Mary, Rachel, Hannah, the Daughters of Brave Lloyd, by Brave Men Now Enjoy'd," composition book, 5, Pastorius Papers, Historical Society of Pennsylvania, Philadelphia; Pastorius, "Bee-Hive," 108.

"In These Seven Languages I This My Book Do Own": Linguistic Multiplicity and Spiritual Unity in Francis Daniel Pastorius's Manuscript Writings

In order to overcome the contentious literalism of the Keithian controversy, writers and readers had to abandon their fear that any deviation from their own representation of religious truth constituted a malicious deception. Relinquishing the acrimony of his earlier writings on the subject, Pastorius's manuscript poetry deployed translation and multilingualism to undermine the literal-mindedness at the heart of the controversy by pairing an implicit acceptance of linguistic incongruence with the desire to establish mutual understanding. Pastorius realized that the encounter with actual linguistic difference allowed individuals and groups to explore spiritual affinities in spite of the inaccuracy inherent in any act of translation. He fashioned himself as a linguistic and cultural mediator between the German and English sections of the community. Although he conceived the multilingual poetry collected in manuscript volumes such as the "Bee-Hive" and *Deliciae Hortenses* as a direct reflection of his work as teacher and court scribe in a multilingual community, he understood his polyglot poetics as symbolic of the spiritual unity possible across multiple linguistic systems.

Pastorius's poetics inscribed the actual and the metaphorical relationships between the multilingual self and a multilingual community. For the combatants of the Keithian controversy, even the slightest variation in the written representation of truth constituted complete error or deliberate falsification. Multilingualism, however, enabled Pastorius to write out a single spiritual or moral precept in up to seven languages while preserving the same core meaning or spiritual content. Where monolingual speakers would have encountered utter difference and the absence of meaning outside their own version of truth, Pastorius found harmony and unity. The reproducing of religious and moral truth in different languages allowed Pastorius and like-minded Pennsylvanians to envision a multiplying of community, that is, a diversification of the religious, linguistic, and ethnic composition of community without the disintegration of community itself. Pastorius understood the Keithian controversy as a fundamental threat to the linguistic and spiritual utopia he had hoped for. Yet he came to regard multilingualism, not as a sign of a fallen humanity, but as an antidote to spiritual confusion or a means for reversing Babel.

Clearly, Pastorius's multilingualism embodied the elitist, humanistic ideal of education with its emphasis on a polyglot training, particularly in the classical languages Latin and Greek. He had studied law for seven years at various European universities, and his Latin-language dissertation conformed to the requirements of his discipline. During a two-year grand tour through Holland, England, France, Switzerland, and Italy, Pastorius perfected his knowledge in modern philology, particularly in the vogue languages French and Italian. This background has tempted scholars to interpret the multilingual choices of Pastorius's Pennsylvanian poetry primarily through the lens of European literary aesthetics. Even if these aesthetics and literary traditions match Pastorius's poetry, their motivations, however, had changed. Rather than a sign of elite distinction, Pastorius flaunted his multilingualism both as a practical tool for the advancement of community and as a poetic antidote to the spiritual and linguistic dispersal of community in the province.[24]

Through his work of translating court documents from English to German (and vice versa), keeping multilingual court records, and translating the English laws of Pennsylvania into German, Pastorius mediated between two linguistically and culturally different groups. An entry in Pastorius's "Bee-Hive" manuscript, his monumental commonplace book and encyclopedia, for instance, reflected on the cultural implications of translating English legal terms for the sake of the German immigrant community. Pastorius recounted annotating an English legal manual for his fellow German settlers: "By adding [a] few lines I do expect No Briths [sic] by birth to teach, but

24. For a discussion of Pastorius's elite European education, see Marion Dexter Learned, *The Life of Francis Daniel Pastorius, the Founder of Germantown* (Philadelphia, 1908), 50–115; DeElla Victoria Toms, "The Intellectual and Literary Background of Francis Daniel Pastorius" (Ph.D diss., Northwestern University, 1953), 32–65; John David Weaver, "Franz Daniel Pastorius (1651–c.1720): Early Life in Germany with Glimpses of His Removal to Pennsylvania" (Ph.D. diss., University of California, Davis, 1985), 184–264. For references to Pastorius's travels and education in his own work, see *Circumstantial Geographical Description of Pennsylvania*, trans. Gertrude Selwyn Kimball, in Albert Cook Myers, *Narratives of Early Pennsylvania, West New Jersey, and Delaware* (New York, 1912), 361–363 ("Preface"), 429–430 (letter to his father, Mar. 1, 1697); "Genealogia Pastoriana," in "Bee-Hive," 221–226; "Kurtzer Lebens Lauff," in "Res Propriae," 5–12, Pastorius Papers. For Pastorius's thesis, see Pastorius, *Disputatio Inauguralis . . .* (Altdorf, 1676). For various interpretations of Pastorius's multilingual poetics, especially within a baroque aesthetics, see Christoph E. Schweitzer, "Introduction," in Francis Daniel Pastorius, *Deliciae Hortenses; or, Garden-Recreations and Voluptates Apianae*, ed. Schweitzer (Columbia, S.C., 1982), 5; Schweitzer, "Excursus: German Baroque Literature in Colonial America," in Gerhart Hoffmeister, ed., *German Baroque Literature: The European Perspective* (New York, 1983), 178–193; Schweitzer, "Francis Daniel Pastorius, the German-American Poet," *Yearbook of German-American Studies*, XVIII (1983), 21–28. For a general study on the literary aesthetics of the time, see Robert M. Browning, *German Baroque Poetry, 1618–1723* (University Park, Pa., 1971).

to direct / My loving Countrymans (:the Dutch's:) defect." The "defect" Pastorius hoped to correct with his annotations was the Germans' lack of familiarity with the English language and with English jurisprudence. As a multilingual individual *and* a lawyer by trade, Pastorius helped German immigrants to bridge both divides. The annotated legal volume resulting from his dual capacities became a textual emblem for Pastorius's multiple communal roles and ability to mediate between identities and languages; he thus described himself as someone "Who English'd does himself to them [his fellow Germans] Connect." By acquiring the English language, the German immigrant Pastorius assumed an English cultural subjectivity and connected both groups. His use of the term "Dutch"—an English moniker for *German* immigrants—translated his personal and communal identity into an English cultural system and made it intelligible for an English audience.[25]

By his own account, Pastorius did not speak any English when he arrived in Pennsylvania, using Latin or French in conversing with elite residents such as William Penn and Thomas Lloyd. Quite possibly, a Latin-English version of Jan Amos Comenius's *Janua Linguarum Reserata* helped him with the acquisition of the predominant language of his new home. Although Comenius was certainly not the only influence on Pastorius's ideas about multilingualism, his multilingual poetics visually and spiritually reflected Comenius's bilingual and trilingual works and the spiritual coherence between languages they tried to establish; Pastorius's ethos of creating spiritual unity from multiple linguistic and religious voices also echoed Comenius's ideal of harnessing language learning for "the conversion of all non-Christians and the unification of all Christian sects."[26]

Overall, Pastorius's acquisition of English seemed to suggest that a speedy assimilation of German and Dutch immigrants into an English linguistic, legal, civic, and religious system would ensure greater communal

25. Pastorius, "Silvula Rhytmorum," in "Bee-Hive," #48.

26. Pastorius's library in Pennsylvania included three volumes by Comenius, including John Robotham's English translation of the *Janua Linguarum Reserata.* See Pastorius, "Res Propriae," Pastorius Papers; Learned, *Life of Pastorius,* 280. In the "Bee-Hive," Pastorius included lengthy lists of Quaker and non-Quaker writers he had consulted in assembling the manuscript. The bibliography for "non-Quakers" lists several references to Comenius's linguistic work. See Lyman W. Riley, "Books from the 'Beehive' Manuscript of Francis Daniel Pastorius," *Quaker History,* LXXXIII (1994), 116–129. Also see Alfred L. Brophy, "The Quaker Bibliographic World of Francis Daniel Pastorius," *PMHB,* CXXII (1998), 241–291; Walter W. Woodward, *Prospero's America: John Winthrop, Jr., Alchemy, and the Creation of New England Culture, 1606–1676* (Chapel Hill, N.C., 2010), 58.

harmony. Pastorius's observation of and participation in the Keithian controversy, however, must have taught him that a shared linguistic system did not ensure spiritual compatibility. The poetry collected in Pastorius's manuscript volumes visually and poetically argued that linguistic difference presented no obstacle to spiritual coherence. If, according to Quaker doctrine, an Inward Light permeated all human beings, all languages equally gave voice to this indwelling sense of divine truth. The simultaneous deployment of different languages in Pastorius's poetry thus proclaimed that different representational systems or languages signified a unified idea, moral precept, or religious truth. Visually, the many title pages of Pastorius's "Bee-Hive" manuscript declared the volume's goal of presenting universal moral or spiritual precepts in a multiplicity of languages. Pastorius designed these title pages not only to outline the "Bee-Hive's" different stages of composition and functions as commonplace book, encyclopedia, and collection of original poetry but also to address specific ideological and philosophical issues. Thus, he felt the need to justify and explain his use of up to seven languages as a means to enhance spiritual unity rather than—as readers then and now might suspect—to parade his elite education. Paradigmatically, Pastorius asserted that writing the date of the "Bee-Hive's" commencement (1696) in three different numerals "plainly shews, that we may word a thing many ways to the same intent." On another title page, Pastorius wrote his name and the title of his book in seven different languages: Greek, Latin, English, Dutch, German, Italian, and French (Figure 6).[27]

Such a linguistic profusion certainly was not within the reach of every Pennsylvanian immigrant; nevertheless, the poem following the title rushed to undermine any impression of superiority or class distinction:

27. Pastorius, "Bee-Hive," 7 (n.b. variant pagination of title pages). The most frequent languages Pastorius used in his "Bee-Hive" are English and German, followed by Dutch and Latin. English, German, and Dutch were the three main languages used in Pastorius's late-seventeenth- and early-eighteenth-century Pennsylvania. Latin and French were used as learned or genteel languages for communication among scholars and social elites in late humanistic Europe, and Pastorius's use of these languages reflects this status to a certain degree (for example, in his communication with William Penn in French). Pastorius used all seven languages for the kind of multilingual or bilingual meditations on similar spiritual or intellectual points throughout his "Bee-Hive"; my analysis focuses on English and German because they are the most frequent and because they parallel my discussions of translingual relationships between speakers of both languages throughout this book. This focus is not designed to privilege these two languages in any way from a present-day perspective. See below for Pastorius's own favoring of English as the lingua franca of Pennsylvania.

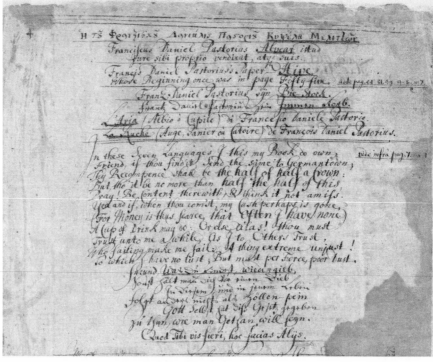

Figure 6. Detail of Title Page from Francis Daniel Pastorius's "Bee-Hive" in Seven Languages. MS Codex 726. By permission of the Rare Book and Manuscript Library, University of Pennsylvania

In these Seven Languages I this my Book do own, . . .
Friend, if thou find it, Send the same to Germantown;
Thy Recompence shall be the half of half a Crown:
But, tho' it be no more than half the half of this,
Pray! Be Content therewith, and think it not amiss.
Yea and if, when thou com'st, my Cash perhaps is gone,
(For Money is thus scarce, that Often I have none.)
A Cup of Drink may do.

Pastorius did not belong to the economically struggling members of early Pennsylvanian society, but this passage demonstrated his wish to inscribe his personal and communal ideology of simplicity and communal harmony within the first lines of his manuscript writings. Subsequently, these German and Latin lines emphasize a strict adherence to the principle of brotherly love or the Golden Rule:

Freünd, *Was Du findest,* *wiedergieb,*	[Friend, whatever you find, return,
Sonst hält man dich vor einen Dieb	otherwise people will call you a thief
In diesem; und in jenem Leben	and in this life and the next
folgt anders nichts als Höllen- pein.	follows nothing but the pains of hell.
Gott Selbst hat diß Gesetz gegeben	God Himself gave us this law
Zu thun, wie man Gethan will seÿn.	do unto others, as you
Quod Tibi vis fieri, hoc facias Alÿs.	would have them do unto you.]

The multilingual title and the trilingual (English, German, Latin) reflection on simplicity and brotherly love encapsulated the significance of linguistic multiplicity in Pastorius's poetic works and commonplace collections: moral and spiritual truth remained the same no matter what language or system of representation was used. In a similar fashion, the multiple selves visualized in the many versions of Pastorius's name (from the Latin Franciscus Daniel Pastorius to the Italian Francesco Daniele Pastorio) and the multiplying of the volume's title (from the English "Paper-Hive" to the Dutch "Bie-Stock") ultimately shared the same referents. Whereas the pamphleteers of the Keithian controversy suspected a spiritual aberration in the slightest deviation in language, Pastorius rejoiced that seven different languages described the same person, the same work, and the same moral or spiritual insight.[28]

Given the universalizing possibilities offered by the spiritual unison of different languages, Pastorius rejected the manipulation of language for the sake of spiritual division during the Keithian controversy. In a poem descriptively titled "Zur Zeit der Anno 1692 in Pennsilvanien entstandenen Trennung" (During the schism that arose in Pennsylvania in 1692), he revealed his inner conflict over taking a partisan position. Pastorius recognized the conflicting demands of protecting the sanctity of individual testimony and preventing the community from fracturing under the pressure of religious schism. He apparently paid utmost attention to weighing the equally frightening specters of communal dissolution and spiritual repression, for he wrote the entire poem in both German and English, appealing

28. Pastorius, "Bee-Hive," 3 (the English text in brackets is my translation). See Matt. 7:12.

to all members of the community. In both languages, Pastorius began by presenting the infighting of the Keithian controversy as a violation of the fundamental laws of nature:

Jedes schonet seiner Art,	None deal with his own hard;
Tÿger, Wolff, u. Leopard.	Tyger, Bear, Wolf, Lion, Pard.
Eÿ wie kommts dann daß ein Christ	What provok's so harshly than *[sic]*
wider seines gleichen ist?	Christian against Christian?
Da ihm doch sein Herr gebeüt	When Christ command's constantly
Liebe, Fried u. Einigkeit.	Love and Peace and Unity.
Joh. 13:34.	Joh. 13:34.

Not even the fiercest predators destroy their own kind, but Christians can be their own worst enemies. The linguistic unison between the German and English versions, however, envisions cooperation not only within one's own group or kind but also across divisions of language and culture. Significantly, the core values of "Liebe, Fried u. Einigkeit" / "Love and Peace and Unity" run exactly parallel in both versions, whereas other sections show significant syntactic differences.[29]

Pastorius's reflection on the dilemma between his civic obligation to preserve peace and his faith in the divine nature of personal testimony among Friends reveals some crucial differences in both languages. Pastorius did not literally translate from German to English but geared both toward the specific concerns of each community and his own role within it:

Die fehler meiner brüder	Sound Doctrine I approve
sind mir zwar gantz zu wider: 1. Tim. 5:22.	As much as men behoove;
Doch wegen eines Worts Jac. 3:2. 2. Tim. 2:14.	Yet talking is but foul
Ihr Zeügniß zu vernichten,	And merely idle Noise,
u. freventlich sie richten, Röm. 14:13. 1. Cor. 4:5.	If I to Wisdom's Voice
befind ich meines Orts	Not hearken in my soul.
Zu seÿn ein luft-streich kämpfen, 1. Cor. 9:26.	Pray! what can me availe high knowledge?

29. Pastorius, "Silvula Rhytmorum," in "Bee-Hive," #38.

Ein Gottlos Geistes-Dämpfen,	When I deale most spitefully
1. Thes. 5:19.	with most,
Ein art des bruder-Mords,	And by my learned Pride
1. Joh. 3:15.	Committing fratricide,
	Do quench the holy ghost.

In a community joined by brotherly love, a judgment based on linguistic disagreement — "wegen eines Worts" (because of one word) — would destroy this spiritual bond and thus dissolve the relationships that tie them together as Friends. In the German version, the suppression of the testimony of others implicitly evoked Pastorius's power as justice of the peace in Germantown to judge ("richten") his neighbors and resolve the controversy politically. In the English version, however, he noticeably shifted the locus of authority in judging over others from political power to intellectual acumen. For English readers, Pastorius's position in Germantown would have been less meaningful, but Quakers throughout the colony were familiar with his learnedness. Thus, Pastorius feared that "high knowledge" degenerated into "learned Pride" and, in turn, led to the suppression of the testimony of fellow Friends, a form of "fratricide." Clearly, Pastorius regarded his own intellectual ability as a dubious tool in dealing with other Christians. Yet, unlike the German version, the English part of the poem simultaneously implicated Keith, who, unlike Pastorius, never refrained from harnessing his superior education to condemn others and thus committed "fratricide."[30]

In poetic practice, Pastorius thus preserved cultural and linguistic differences while seeking out spiritual harmony. Following the epigrammatic style characteristic of the seventeenth century, he encapsulated the desire for peace and unity in the following English and German lines from the "Bee-Hive":

How happy could men be in all their Course of life,
If they did Strive to love, as they do love to Strive.
= Wie klüglich könnten wir Ja glücklich allhier leben,
Wann Lieben uns so lieb wolt seÿn als widerstreben!

This bilingual epigram doubly counteracted division, both through its sentiment and the unison of languages expressing the same thought. In these four parallel lines, Pastorius strategically placed key words representing key values or actions in the same position in both languages. Thus, "life" and

30. Ibid.

"leben" as well as "strive" and "widerstreben" at the end of the English and German lines shared the same meaning and syntactic position. Yet the German version is not a literal translation of the English. Both are original verses, for both employ a verbal witticism specific to each language. In English, Pastorius played on the double meaning of the verb "strive" if combined in different syntactical combinations with "love." "Strive to love" designates a laudable eagerness to love others, whereas "love to strive" means the desire to struggle. In the first German line, Pastorius punned on the phonetic similarity of the words "klüglich" (wisely) and "glücklich" (happily). The near equal sound of the two words referred to their semantic closeness, for those who live wisely would also live happily. The key to love and a happy life—in English or German—was the avoidance of unnecessary strife. Pastorius's multilingual poetics, therefore, created multiple originals that highlighted the idiosyncratic qualities of each language while conveying the idea of spiritual and moral unity.[31]

Pastorius acknowledged that multilingual individuals occupied a privileged position in exploring such spiritual correspondences across linguistic divisions. In the "Bee-Hive," he explained having read and excerpted books in "my Mother-Tongue, but likewise in the Low-Dutch, French, Italian and Latin," but he concluded that his two sons (Johann Samuel and Heinrich or, in English, John Samuel and Henry), to whom he dedicated the manuscript, "will never attain to the Understanding of the said Languages." Perhaps Pastorius did not make any attempts to teach them these languages because he did not see any practical use for them in the community where they were growing up. Ultimately, Pastorius believed that the project of discerning truth among a multiplicity of voices could also proceed in a single language. Thus, the "Bee-Hive" declares as its goal "the better learning of the ENGLISH [tongue], and that my two Sons . . . might hereafter have some of their Fathers Steps, thereby to be guided to the same Diligence and Assiduity of *Picking the BEST* out of GOOD Writings."[32]

It would be easy to categorize Pastorius's embrace of English—the language of choice for his sons and the *exclusive* language of the "Alphabetical Hive," an encyclopedia of terms attached to the "Bee-Hive"—as a resignation to the powerful forces of acculturation and the dissolution of a minority subjectivity under the pressure of English dominance. However, Pas-

31. Ibid., #9.
32. Pastorius, "Bee-Hive," 55.

torius's choice of English was not a decision made under cultural duress; it was primarily a continuation of his endeavor to find spiritual unity within a multiplicity of voices. For Pastorius, English was multilingual in itself, for it united influences from a plethora of other languages. The "English Tongue," he explained in an entry in his "Alphabetical Hive," is "a hotch-potch of many languages." On a title page to the "Bee-Hive," Pastorius at length described English as a linguistic mosaic, allowing the observer insights into the many languages contributing to its development:

> *The Language now a days spoken in England* and Colonies thereunto belonging is not the ancient Britan-Tongue; No, not the least Off-spring thereof; But a Mingle-mangle of Latin, Dutch and French: Relicks or Remains of the Roman, Saxon and Norman Conquests. Most Mono Syllables are of a Dutch Origin, ax, ox . . . Words of Many Syllables are either brought by the Romans . . . Or by the Normans . . . And besides those there are also Hebrew, Arabick, Greek, Italian, Spanish, Danish and Welch words in the said English Tongue. . . . Hence it is, that when other Europians can not deliver their minds but by expressing one thing by one word, the English may do it Commonly by two; Oftentimes by three or four.

As a microcosm of human linguistic diversity, English offered various choices in expressing a single thought. Pastorius's embrace of the English language might thus have been a compromise between the continuation of the form of linguistic diversity that requires a mediator or translator and a crystallization of this diversity in a single language. In English, speakers of other languages could still find a representation of their own heritage.[33]

Above all, Pastorius was so fascinated by the etymological multiplicity of the English language because it presented the best medium for his quest to express a single spiritual idea or concept in a variety of ways. His use of English allowed him to construct a polyphonic poetics and simultaneously advance a common, spoken language for the Pennsylvanian experiment. English was akin to multilingualism and the wealth of nature in capturing the central paradox of spiritual unity from external diversity. In a poem from his book of gardening emblems, *Deliciae Hortenses,* he conjoins the multiplicity of language with the diversity of nature in a poetic whole extolling God:

33. Ibid., 50; Francis Daniel Pastorius, "Alphabetical Hive" (encyclopedic commonplace book), in "Bee-Hive," #1382.

Non levis est Cespes, quin probet esse Deum.
In all wat groeyt
Godts Eere bloeyt.
Der bunten Blumen-pracht
Zeigt Gottes Wunder-macht.
Laudat et extollit quaelibet herba Deum.
Jedes Kraut sammt seinem Samen,
Lobt und preiset Gottes Nahmen.
[There is no grass so insignificant that it does not prove the existence
   of God.
In all that grows God's honor flourishes.
The colorful magnificence of the flowers shows God's wonderful
   power.
Every plant praises and extols God.
Every herb and all its seeds laud and praise the name of God.]

All languages and all of nature, Pastorius asserts, praise in unison the name of God. If God epitomized the unity of all things, then true faith could unify language. Pastorius found no difference between using multiple languages or a single language like English that still made visible its multiple linguistic origins. Either way, the apparent dualism between the many and the one collapsed entirely through faith in God and the evocation of nature as God's visible manifestation.[34]

The back and forth between actual linguistic multiplicity and the polyphonic variety of English in Pastorius's poetry ultimately climaxed in the device of listing the seemingly limitless number of names for Jesus—the Word of God:

My Wisdom, way, Truth, righteousness, my Blessing, Strength and
   Peace. . . .
Ye word, ye good and perfect Gift, ye true Light alone
Sufficient and marvellous, which does in all that blossom
Discern the very hidden Thoughts and Intents in their bosom.
The Lord, ye Prince, ye Govr. ye Prophet, head and Preacher,
Ye godly Shepherd of his Church, Guide, Counsellor and Teacher,
My high-Priest truely merciful, harmless and undefiled,
Melchisedec, by whom I am through bloodshed reconciled.
The Lamb of God and Passover for my sins sacrificed,

34. Pastorius, *Deliciae Hortenses,* ed. Schweitzer, 58 (translations by Schweitzer).

A full Propitiation and Ransom greatly priced;
My Mediatour, Advocate and Intercessor there,
Where I with Zions Children once expect to have a Share.
Yea with ye well beloved Son and Image of the Father,
The brightness of his Majesty, the heir of all, or rather
JEHOVAH and Emmanuel, God Self for ever blessed,
Professed by the hypocrites, by Upright-ones possessed.
Thus much of ye Messias now, whom in good Confidence
(—who cleanses and who purifies my Soul and Conscience)
I call my dear and choicest Friend, my Bridegroom and my Brother,
My First and Last, mine All in All, JESUS and not another.
  DEUS meus et OMNIA!

Pastorius arranged this catalog of names to climax in the single name that comprises all the others: Jesus Christ. The diversity of all languages — whether expressed through one or many tongues — was always subsumed in Christ, the word made flesh, as the center of all faith and the end of all language.[35]

I DO NOT MEAN to fashion Pastorius as a proto-multiculturalist who presaged English as a common medium for an ethnically diverse nation. Yet the questions he addressed more than three hundred years ago are no less topical today. As Pastorius's example demonstrates, the relationship between personal identity and language always had broad communal implications. For Pastorius, languages were at once an object of study, a plaything, and a means to insert himself into different communal and cultural settings. Of course, his often whimsical use of multilingualism hinted at the baroque love for excessive intellectualism. Yet, in the context of early Pennsylvania and his search for spiritual cohesion, the expression of the same thing or idea in several languages was also a yardstick for the development of a concrete communal ethics. If different linguistic versions existed of the same concept, there had to be a common spiritual language that expressed all things perfectly.

In many ways, Pastorius's approach to the multiplicity of languages made the long-standing debate between the naturalist and conventionalist

---

35. Pastorius, "Canticum, or an Hymn of the Beloved of My Soul," in "Silvula Rhytmorum," in "Bee-Hive." See August Hermann Francke's list of seventy-five "names" or titles the Bible gives Christ in his *Christus der Kern heiliger Schrifft* (Francke, *Schriften zur Biblischen Hermeneutik I*, ed. Erhard Peschke [Berlin, 2003], 313–322).

theories of language irrelevant. Whether human languages indeed carried vestiges of an original, divinely inspired tongue or merely represented social and cultural constructs mattered little in the concrete, multilingual environment of early Pennsylvania. Pastorius thus submerged theological and linguistic debates over linguistic multiplicity, perfect or universal languages, and linguistic reform in the encyclopedic portion of his manuscripts. In his poetry, he foregrounded the practical desire for spiritual unity and brotherly love that had motivated him to settle in Pennsylvania. A common spiritual language, above all, emerged when disparate members of a community accepted differences and explored interpersonal, supralinguistic relationships and affinities. Instead of making a single, unified language a prerequisite for communal cohesion, Pastorius demonstrated that different linguistic approaches provided access to the same spiritual knowledge.

In light of the Keithian controversy and other political, social, and religious debates, English and German immigrants wondered how to apply the colony's original vision — the Philadelphian concept of a unified spiritual language and society — to concrete communal interaction. Pennsylvania seemed to have fallen prey to the same ills as Europe, particularly the incessant arguing over the dead letter of doctrine. Unfortunately, scholarship has too narrowly followed those commentators in colonial Pennsylvania and across the Atlantic who declared Penn's holy experiment a failure. Nevertheless, Pennsylvania has also been stereotyped as the birthplace of pluralism in America. This disconnect stems from a failure to recognize and describe the ways in which Pennsylvanians adapted the ideals of seventeenth-century radical Protestantism to communal interaction in a fractured society. Historians have largely missed the continuation and adaptation of the original dream of a common spiritual language as the foundation for a renovation of human society in the province because they have dismissed the spaces, moments, relationships, and practices where it continued to thrive the most — in the transfer and translation of religious, communal, intellectual, and personal ideals *across* differences in language, denomination, gender, and class.

In colonial Pennsylvania, the central means for creating community from disparate parts were translation and other tools of translingual and transcultural communication. The remaining chapters describe iconic moments and spheres of translation and translingualism that reapplied earlier visions of linguistic and spiritual unity to concrete communal relationships and crises in colonial Pennsylvania. The search for a common spiritual language did not thrive in spite of or next to political and religious divisiveness; rather, translation and multilingualism expressed the desire to mend factionalism, partisanship, and communal acrimony. Though the on-the-ground effects of translation and multilingualism are difficult or impossible to measure, schemes for discovering or building a common spiritual idiom and thus a more harmonious community continued to flourish throughout the colonial period.

"Honey-Combs" and "Paper-Hives"

FRANCIS DANIEL PASTORIUS AND THE GATHERING OF A
TRANSLINGUAL COMMUNITY OF LETTERS

My Rare and Real Friend, as I at present may Justly Stile thee according
to the Old and true Saying, A Friend In Need is a Friend IN deed. The Letter,
which I joyfully received from thy hands the Night before yesterday,
abounding in extraordinary Cherishing and refreshing Terms, Seemed little
Inferior to me, than if thou hadst Personally Visited thy poor Friend.
— Francis Daniel Pastorius to Isaac Norris, Mar. 15, 1717

uring the Keithian controversy, Francis Daniel Pastorius began to
deploy his multilingual manuscript writings to construct a common spiritual vision in various languages and thus to counteract
the communal divisions precipitated by the schism. The following chapter argues that Pennsylvania Quakers fashioned manuscript writing and exchange as an alternative form of literacy that was in-
extricably tied to nontextual bonds such as personal friendship as well as
intellectual and spiritual affinity. The exchange of manuscripts—letters,
commonplace books, poetic miscellanies, and inscriptions in printed volumes—wed textuality to nontextual relationships. These forms of literary
transmission not only functioned as reflections of existing friendships or
affection, but they actively cultivated personal and communal bonding. The
focus on Pastorius's personal and literary circle will show a cross section
of literary and communal exchanges—primarily in manuscript but accompanied by the intimate circulation of print—among prominent Quakers in
early Pennsylvania.

For Pastorius, the crucial question was how to translate the largely symbolic and visual unison of languages and voices unfolding on the pages of
his manuscript books to actual communal relationships and interactions.
Ultimately, he followed the principles of his multilingual poetics and at-

tempted to distill from a multiplicity of voices and individuals a community of literary and spiritual exchange. Pastorius understood that community needed above all else an apt translator, someone who could mediate between Pennsylvania's different languages and spiritual vocabularies. In the aftermath of the Keithian controversy, Pastorius cultivated personal and literary relationships that encapsulated the simultaneity of difference (such as language and gender) and deep-seated, supralinguistic affinities that were based on friendship, love, and a shared history. While finding little common ground with former opponents, Pastorius attempted to fashion the Pennsylvania Quakers into a harmonious community fortified against future factiousness. He cultivated these relationships through literary exchanges that functioned as microcosms of a larger communal ideal.

Rather than negating differences and thus creating a false sense of unity, Pastorius highlighted how spiritual and intellectual consanguinity could render those differences acceptable or even welcome. In communicating with prominent Quakers such as William Penn, Thomas Lloyd, and Samuel Carpenter, for example, Pastorius recalled and celebrated moments of translingual spiritual unity. His exchange of letters, printed books, and manuscript poetry with Lloyd's daughters long after their father's death built on the acceptance Pastorius had found as a "foreigner" among English and Welsh Quakers and cast the developing Quaker society as a multigenerational and translingual community. Gender differences, moreover, could be bridged or rendered negligible by cultivating common spiritual and intellectual sensibilities. Rather than affecting a patriarchal and intellectual superiority in his exchange with young women like Elizabeth Hill or the indentured servant Jane Fenn, Pastorius underscored the reciprocity engendered by spiritual and intellectual community.

Certainly, Pastorius's literary circle often took shared social class, elite intellectual training, and religious beliefs for granted. Indeed, Pastorius espoused no particularly radical concepts of female emancipation, linguistic diversity, cultural relativism, or religious universalism. His ideas—as on female education, for example—were neither particularly progressive nor controversial; in seventeenth- and early-eighteenth-century Quakerism (in England as well as America), women played an increasingly forward role in areas of ministry, literary production, and education. Also, Pastorius's translingual literary exchanges primarily relied on his facility in English rather than his Quaker correspondents' acquisition of the German language. His cultivation of scribal publication, manuscript transmission, and personal exchange of printed matter, moreover, shared important similarities with practices in colonial New England as well as the humanistic and scholarly circles of Renaissance Europe.[1]

Nevertheless, Pastorius's literary community was not merely based on European humanism, social privilege, religious exclusivity, and linguistic assimilation. A more nuanced picture of the ways in which difference and unity were negotiated in early America emerges when seeing early Pennsylvania through his eyes and through the lens of his literary community. Pastorius—when regarded as a central rather than marginal figure in understanding early Pennsylvanian society—transcends the simplistic dualism of assimilation and ethnicization that has dominated immigration history. He neither insisted on a German linguistic or ethnic separatism, nor did he simply yield his language and perspective to English Quaker dominance. The subtle, witty, and at times tender bonds Pastorius described, established, and celebrated in his writings highlight an almost entirely unknown dimension of linguistic and cultural multiplicity in early America.

Pastorius and the Quakers were certainly not unique in their practices of literary exchange and scribal production, and Pastorius's translingual literary community represents a common yet neglected phenomenon in early America. In line with scholarship that has applied an increasingly common trope to communities of literary and intellectual exchange, Pastorius's world represented a translingual "Republic of Letters." Indeed, Pastorius's literary community shared the flexible negotiation of private and public as well as political and personal spheres that is implicit in this critical paradigm. Yet in describing the multiplicity of voices represented in his manuscripts and literary exchanges, Pastorius used a more homely and natural trope—the bee-

---

1. Margaret Hope Bacon, *Mothers of Feminism: The Story of Quaker Women in America* (San Francisco, 1986); Mary Garman et al., eds., *Hidden in Plain Sight: Quaker Women's Writings, 1650–1700* (Wallingford, Pa., 1996); Rebecca Larson, *Daughters of Light: Quaker Women Preaching and Prophesying in the Colonies and Abroad, 1700–1775* (Chapel Hill, N.C., 1999); Cristine Levenduski, *Peculiar Power: A Quaker Woman Preacher in Eighteenth-Century America* (Washington, D.C., 1996); Michele Lise Tarter, "Quaking in the Light: The Politics of Quaker Women's Corporeal Prophecy in the Seventeenth-Century Transatlantic World," in Janet Moore Lindman and Michele Lise Tarter, eds., *A Centre of Wonders: The Body in Early America* (Ithaca, N.Y., 2001), 145–162; Tarter, "Sites of Performance: Theorizing the History of Sexuality in the Lives and Writings of Quaker Women, 1650–1800" (Ph.D. diss., University of Colorado at Boulder, 1993); Tarter, "Varied Trials, Dippings, and Strippings": Quaker Women's Irresistible Call to the Early South," in Mary C. Carruth, ed., *Feminist Interventions in Early American Studies* (Tuscaloosa, Ala., 2006), 80–93.

On scribal publication and the role of manuscript circulation in the early modern age, see David D. Hall, *Ways of Writing: The Practice and Politics of Text-Making in Seventeenth-Century New England* (Philadelphia, 2008); Anthony Grafton, *Worlds Made by Words: Scholarship and Community in the Modern West* (Cambridge, Mass., 2009).

hive. Himself an avid beekeeper, Pastorius fashioned the idea of the beehive to describe the collection and selection of the best and spiritually most profitable writings and thus the distillation of spiritual essences from manifold books, opinions, and ideas. For Pastorius, the metaphor of the beehive not only signified the collection and storage of the essence of his wide-ranging readings—the honey—in commonplace books and manuscript encyclopedias but also the creation of an orderly and peaceful community united by a common spiritual language and purpose. In emulating the beehive, Pennsylvanians would find and cultivate the sweet rewards of communal love.[2]

Pastorius thus mapped supralinguistic bonds of affection, mutual suffering, shared experiences, and common spiritual ideals onto textual representation and literary exchange. As Pastorius's response to a letter from Isaac Norris demonstrates, literary exchanges that were suffused with mutual affection attempted to connect human language to an interiorized, spiritual meaning. Old age and various ailments had increasingly prohibited Pastorius and Norris from visiting each other, yet the letter Pastorius received from Norris was apparently imbued with his spiritual presence. Although the acrostic on Norris's initials ("A Friend In Need is a Friend IN deed") reflected a common practice in Baroque poetics, Pastorius here insisted that language—down to the letters of a friend's name—could once more reverberate with spiritual meaning if it was infused with mutual affection or a common pursuit of truth.[3]

2. Michael Warner applied the term "Republic of Letters," which formerly referred to the community of scholars in Renaissance and early modern Europe, to the Revolutionary and early Republican period in America. See Warner, *The Letters of the Republic: Publication and the Public Sphere in Eighteenth-Century America* (Cambridge, Mass., 1990), xi. The paradigm of the "Republic of Letters" has more recently been applied to transatlantic conversations throughout the colonial period, yet the focus in early Americanist scholarship has frequently remained on exchanges between English-speaking individuals in England and the English-speaking colonies in North America. For example, see Alison Searle, " 'Though I am a Stranger to You by Face, Yet in Neere Bonds by Faith': A Transatlantic Puritan Republic of Letters," *Early American Literature,* XLIII (2008), 277-308. Nevertheless, Searle describes similar bonds of affection and spiritual community facilitated through letter writing.

For assessments of the role letter writing played in the early modern period in mediating human and communal relationships, especially personal affection in transatlantic contexts, see Eve Tavor Bannet, *Empire of Letters: Letter Manuals and Transatlantic Correspondence, 1680–1820* (Cambridge, 2005); Konstantin Dierks, *In My Power: Letter Writing and Communications in Early America* (Philadelphia, 2009); Sarah M. S. Pearsall, *Atlantic Families: Lives and Letters in the Later Eighteenth Century* (Oxford, 2009). I specifically refer to Bannet's critique of the Habermasian division between public and private spheres, which this chapter develops in more detail.

3. Francis Daniel Pastorius to Isaac Norris, George W. Norris Papers, Historical Society of Pennsylvania, Philadelphia. For textual exchanges as tokens of amicability, see David S. Shields, *Civil*

"A Token of Love and Gratitude":
Translingual Friendships and the Language of Affect

On August 20, 1714, Pastorius began a series of anniversary poems commemorating the day thirty-one years earlier when he and his late friend Thomas Lloyd (1640–1694) arrived in Philadelphia. Addressing Lloyd's daughters Hannah Hill, Rachel Preston, and Mary Norris, Pastorius praised the role of friendship in his personal life in Pennsylvania and in the life of the province as a whole. As both title and controlling metaphor of Pastorius's collection of anniversary poems, the idea of "ship-mate-ship" described literally the companion*ship* between Pastorius, Lloyd, and his family on board the ship *America,* and, on a larger, figurative level, it encompassed religious and civic community in Pennsylvania. In a passage from the first anniversary poem, entitled "A Token of Love and Gratitude" (1714), Pastorius used the familiar literary technique of likening the passengers and crew of a ship to a social body by translating the events of his own journey to the larger scale of communal interaction in the province:

I'm far from Flattering! and hope, ye read my Mind,
Who can't, nor dare forget a Ship-mate true and kind,
As he your Father was to me, (an Alien,)
My Lot being newly cast among such English men,
Whose Speech I thought was Welsh, their Words a Canting Tune,
Alone with him I could in Latin then commune:
Which Tongue he did pronounce right in our German way,
Hence presently we knew, what he or I would say.
Moreover to the best of my Rememberance,
We never disagreed, or were at Variance;
Because God's sacred Truth, (whereat we both did aim,)
To her indeared Friends is ev'ry where the same.

The passage begins with Pastorius's paying homage to the kindness of his erstwhile "Ship-mate" and then develops the particular reasons for his gratefulness. Notably, Pastorius's company on the *America* was characterized by national and linguistic differences or even dissonances; it thus fore-

Tongues and Polite Letters in British America (Chapel Hill, N.C., 1997), xxxi. Texts as material objects became tools of translation between different linguistic and religious groups. This interpretation expands on Matthew P. Brown's "phenomenology of the book"; see Brown, *The Pilgrim and the Bee: Reading Rituals and Book Culture in Early New England* (Philadelphia, 2007), xi.

shadows diversity *in* America and simultaneously evokes the larger human condition of separation, displacement, and dispersion encapsulated in the Babel story.[4]

The predominantly English shipmates made Pastorius feel nationally and linguistically alien. His use of the term "Welsh" for the English shipmates was a double pun enforcing the idea of linguistic confusion. Pastorius alluded to the German "Kauderwelsch," an umbrella term for a confused manner of speaking, an unintelligible mixture of languages, or simply a foreign language. Etymologically, it referred to the Welsh language, which was considered strange and alien even by English speakers. Pastorius self-mockingly reflected in hindsight on the degree of his linguistic confusion: he mistook the English people on board for speaking "Welsh" or, worse, "Kauderwelsch." Even individual words for Pastorius become "a Canting Tune," which, following late-seventeenth-century English usage, referred either to a "Diabolical Inspiration" or the "peculiar phraseology of a religious sect or class." Certainly, by the time of the poem's composition (1714), Pastorius was familiar enough with pro- and anti-Quaker literature to know that the term "cant" had particularly been applied in a derogatory manner to the peculiar speechways of the Society of Friends.[5]

Pastorius thus constructed a series of confusions about the language of his shipmates that ironically highlighted his own misunderstanding or even prejudices, undermining or questioning his obvious fear of differences. Pastorius himself adopted the Quaker faith and speechways—their "Canting Tune"—after only a few years in Pennsylvania. The supreme irony for Pastorius was that Thomas Lloyd, the Welsh Quaker who, from a German point of view, spoke a doubly confused or confusing language, became the individual who made him feel most welcome. Pastorius thus might have felt grateful to Lloyd not the least because he taught him that a common language was no prerequisite for understanding and friendship. The lesson was

---

4. Francis Daniel Pastorius, "Ship-Mate-Ship: An Omer Full of Manna, for Mary, Rachel, Hannah, the Daughters of Brave Lloyd, by Brave Men Now Enjoy'd," composition book, 4–5, Pastorius Papers, HSP. For a genealogy of the Lloyd family, see Karin A. Wulf, *"Milcah Martha Moore's Book:* Documenting Culture and Connection in the Revolutionary Era," in Catherine La Courreye Blecki and Wulf, eds., *Milcah Martha Moore's Book: A Commonplace Book from Revolutionary America* (University Park, Pa., 1997), 17; Frederick B. Tolles, *Meeting House and Counting House: The Quaker Merchants of Colonial Philadelphia, 1682–1763* (Chapel Hill, N.C., 1948), 119–122.

5. Though now obsolete, the *Oxford English Dictionary (OED)* lists several usages of the noun "cant" in the late seventeenth century that Pastorius might have been familiar with.

clear: what seemed most strange and alienating becomes most familiar and dear once hearts and minds open to true understanding.

How, then, did Lloyd and Pastorius communicate and develop a deeper, spiritual affinity? Comenius and Fox would have been pleased to see that, in this instance, Latin served, not as a vain language of elite distinction, but rather as a lingua franca for two "alien" men to communicate, transcend their differences, and eventually establish a greater understanding of their common faith. Yet Pastorius quickly undermined the use of Latin as the gold standard of translingual communication with another ironic, self-reflective pun. Just as his judgment of his shipmates' language was inflected through a limited, German perception, even Latin is intelligible only because it is pronounced "right in our German way." Whether, in 1714, Pastorius still believed this was the "right" way to pronounce Latin is beside the point or lesson he was driving at in the passage: precise linguistic correspondence mattered only as long as ("presently") both men had not yet established a deeper, spiritual understanding. Similar to a musical sequence that dissolves a series of dissonant chords in a pleasant harmony, Pastorius's poem led the reader to a common spiritual language, "God's sacred Truth," that resolved all linguistic confusion or insistence on linguistic particularity.

Pastorius's anachronistic application of the terms "Truth" and "Friends" to both himself and Lloyd linked the timeframe of their Atlantic passage with the historical development up to the point of composition and concomitantly reinforced a major point of Quaker doctrine. When Lloyd and Pastorius met on the *America,* the former was already a prominent Quaker, and the latter was a Pietist. In spite of certain doctrinal differences, Pastorius alleged that they "never disagreed, nor were at Variance; / Because God's sacred Truth, (whereat we both did aim,) / To her indeared Friends is ev'ry where the same." Though describing a point in time when he was not yet a Quaker, Pastorius infused the scene with a double meaning that brought him retroactively into the fold of the Society of Friends. The upper-case spelling of "Truth" implied that Pastorius and Lloyd already shared the Inward Light. In other words, Pastorius and Lloyd *became* friends on the *America* because they already *were* Friends, that is, they shared the Quaker belief in the universality of divine "Truth" inside every human being. The final irony, therefore, was that, in spite of seemingly insurmountable linguistic differences, Lloyd and Pastorius spoke the same language all along.

The bridging of linguistic and cultural differences and the forging of friendships through a common language of spiritual and linguistic affinity was a recurring theme in poems or other manuscript writings Pastorius sent to or exchanged with friends. For instance, he connected his experiences on the *America* to a similar moment in Pennsylvania—his conversations in French with William Penn. In a poem written and sent to Penn on the occasion of his return to Pennsylvania in 1699, Pastorius interwove his native German with French and Latin, which he and the proprietor used during their initial encounters, as well as English. The poem celebrated Penn's second—which Pastorius mistakes for his third—arrival in Pennsylvania, "for which good Patriots these sev'ral years did long, / And which Occasions this his German's English Song, / Who'f old could talk with him but in the Gallic Tongue." Although their common education and knowledge of French and Latin had originally united the two men, the situation had changed upon Penn's return to the province. Pastorius had learned Penn's native tongue through his involvement in the community. Instead of eclipsing their linguistic differences for a common *(English)* Quaker idiom, however, Pastorius emphasized his desire to mediate between different languages and, in doing so, gain a higher spiritual awareness. Apparently, even Penn needed to be reminded that neither French nor English but a common pursuit of friendship and communal harmony was to become the ideal language of the province.[6]

Thus, Pastorius concluded the poem with a German section asking that the addressee meet the writer on *his* own native ground. After an English introduction, Pastorius used German to play on different meanings of the name "Penn":

Whereas, Loving and dearly Esteemed Friend, in thy Travails in Holland and Germany thou hast heard and learned somewhat of my Mother-tongue; I hereby make bold to subjoyn a few lines in the same, as followeth:

Penn heißt auf Welsch ein Haubt, auf Nieder Teutsch ein Feder,
[Penn means in Welsh a head, in Low German a feather,]
Die man zum schreiben braucht; das Haubt ersinn't entweder

---

6. Francis Daniel Pastorius, "Epibaterium; or, A Hearty Congratulation to William Penn, Chief Proprietary of the Province of Pennsilvania etc. upon His Third Arrival into the Same," in "Silvula Rhytmorum Germanopolitanorum," in "Bee-Hive," #372, MS Codex 726, Rare Book and Manuscript Library, University of Pennsylvania. For a published transcription, see Marion Dexter Learned, *The Life of Francis Daniel Pastorius, the Founder of Germantown* (Philadelphia, 1908), 210–215.

[which one uses for writing; the head devises either]
Gut oder Bös, womit die Königin paar Geldt,
[good or evil, and with it the Queen]
Durch Hülff der Feder Zwingt, die Gross und kleine Welt.
[forces both rich and poor to pay her money]
Nein, wanns hier Wünschens gält, so wolt ich, daß mein Feder
[No, if I had one wish, I would that my feather]
Ein solchen Nach-druck hätt, damit sich Ja Ein jeder
[had such an impact that everyone would become]
Als ein gehorsam Glied ergäbe Jesu Christ,
[A submissive part of Jesus Christ,]
Der da das Eintzig Haubt der wahren Kirchen ist;
[who is the only head of the true church.]
So wäre weder Heid, noch Jud; auch kein Papist.
[Then, there would be no heathen, no Jew, and no Papist.]

The prefatory line returned to an earlier time—during his travels in Germany—when Penn had to adjust linguistically to Pastorius's native language and culture. In concluding an otherwise laudatory poem, Pastorius not only switched from English to German but also adopted a much more critical tone. He thus reminded Penn that their friendship necessarily relied on a mutual adoption of each other's subjectivity rather than a one-sided deference.[7]

The poem, moreover, critically examined the word "Penn" as a multivalent term referring to an object that could be applied for good or bad, thus highlighting the proprietor's own need for self-examination. Pastorius ingeniously interwove the Welsh and Low German (as well as the English) meanings of the word "Penn"—"head" or "feather"—to demonstrate that any concept or person can assume different, frequently opposite meanings. Linguistic diversity thus complicated the existing layers of meaning, asking the reader (Penn) to penetrate to a deeper level of self-awareness and understanding. First, Pastorius reminded Penn—the *head* of government in Pennsylvania—that he could think and produce things good or evil, but also that the true *head* of the church was Jesus Christ. Since the name of his friend could also signify quill *(feather)* or pen, Pastorius reflected on the arbitrary power of a king or queen to sign laws oppressing the people. With the power implicit in both *head* and quill *(feather)*, Penn could oppress the citizens of

7. Pastorius, "Epibaterium," in "Silvula Rhytmorum," in "Bee-Hive," #372.

his province or lead them toward greater good. At the same time, Pastorius hoped that his own *feather* or pen could influence unruly or unfaithful members of the community — such as George Keith — toward a greater deference to William Penn, the *head* of government in Pennsylvania, and, ultimately, to Jesus Christ, the *head* of the church. Closing the circle, Penn might also be the *feather* in the hand of his friend and writer Pastorius.[8]

In this web of signification, William Penn is cast in multiple roles, and he has to choose which meaning and position to embrace, which to discard. Pastorius's wordplay, therefore, asserted that all people play multiple roles in their public and private lives that depend on their social status, language, cultural or national heritage, and maybe even their name. The encounter with linguistic multiplicity became a training ground for leaders like Penn and by extension all citizens in Pennsylvania in negotiating the difficult moral and political choices they faced in the new community. Ultimately, Pastorius hoped to employ writing to unite separate elements in the pursuit of spiritual perfection. By urging Penn to peruse this subtle poetic meditation on his own name in German rather than English, Pastorius imagined a community that gained insight into one another's cultural and linguistic position for the sake of a common religious vision. In confronting, learning, and eventually accepting different languages, leaders and members of the community could find a common spiritual idiom. To put it differently, Pastorius gave Penn a lesson in the work of the translator: from the potential indeterminacy of language and the discrepancy between languages and peoples, they had to distill a mutually intelligible meaning. Building community in Pennsylvania was an exercise in translation.

Ultimately, Pastorius regarded mutual love as the glue that held disparate voices and languages together. If love helped to mediate or transcend differences in language, nationality, or even political opinion, how, in turn, could individuals and communities preserve existing ties of affection and create new ones? Having left behind family and friends in Germany and mourning the loss of new friends (like Lloyd) through his years in Pennsylvania, the aging Pastorius (he was sixty-two when he began his anniversary poems in 1714) knew all too well that time and distance were cruel enemies to the fragile bonds of human affection. Though concerned with the efficaciousness

8. The use of "pen," meaning "head," is the more rare of the two, of course. The *OED* cites the origin of this meaning as "Brittonic," "a promontory, a head . . . chiefly in place names." Pastorius's use of "pen" for the body part, of course, works much better to establish the connection to the writing instrument and the act of writing.

of his poetry and literary exchanges to bridge a variety of differences, his anniversary poems were most interested in the ability of written language to refresh, continue, and increase emotional bonds. While harnessing his friendship with Lloyd to link himself to Lloyd's daughters, Hannah Hill, Rachel Preston, and Mary Norris, Pastorius engaged with the way mere language could do justice to, recreate, and even revive an old and potentially faded connection. In his first poem, written in 1714, Pastorius approached the Lloyd daughters in the obsequious and somewhat hesitating manner of someone who is anxious about how his attempt to revive and celebrate a former friendship would be received.

Bridging differences in time, generation, and even gender, Pastorius was careful to translate his friendship with Lloyd to his daughters while simultaneously valuing a relationship with the three women for their own sake. In the preface to the first poem, Pastorius praised the three women as the proponents of their father's civic and religious heritage. Yet he also imagined the reversal of the father-daughter relationship, all the while thanking the Lloyd family for valuing friendship over national or linguistic differences:

> I . . . heartily Love you and every one of yours for his sake, who was so extreme kind and obliging towards me, (an unknown Stranger,) whereas some others have Reason to Love (and no question do love) him even for your Sake, because you are his own (Fatherlike) Daughters, Filiae Patrissantes, as I might stile you to him, if he still were with us, etc. I herewith make bold to declare mine unfeigned affection and Respect to Both, giving you the Trouble of perusing a whole Sheet of paper, which I intend to fill up with Prose and Rime, though but a Stammerer of the English Tongue; However I hope, and beg of you, that you will be pleased to receive it with that Sincerity of ♥ , as it was written in.

Even though the three Lloyd daughters had married influential Quaker men, Pastorius did not transfer the status of paterfamilias from father to husbands but to the daughters themselves. By perpetuating their father's ideal of brotherly (or sisterly) love after his death, the three daughters became the standards on which the family—including their father—was judged. After his death, therefore, Lloyd's reputation or communal afterlife entered a childlike dependency on his daughters, who—"Fatherlike"—established a reputation for their deceased parent.[9]

---

9. Pastorius, "Ship-Mate-Ship," 1, Pastorius Papers.

As the recipients of Pastorius's homage to their father, the Lloyd daughters also gained the "affection" of their father's friend; in the absence of his old friend, a poem to his daughters was simultaneously addressed to both. The relationship between Pastorius and the Lloyd daughters, therefore, would become one of reciprocity. Like their father, Mary, Rachel, and Hannah crossed national divisions by including their German correspondent in the community of "Friends." In turn, Pastorius submitted to their scrutiny some of his most sustained poetic endeavors as a "Token of Love and Gratitude." The poems thus gave thanks for kindness and affection past and present, even soliciting the daughters' *future* kindness by desiring their appreciation and love for the gift received. Self-consciously calling attention to the inadequacy of human language per se and specifically to his newly acquired language English, Pastorius asked the sisters' approval of his words *and* his friendship. One could not make the codependency between language and communal love any clearer: supralinguistic feelings of affection overcame differences or deficiencies in human language; in turn, language—especially in the form of a handwritten, tangible poem—could echo, refresh, and even create personal bonds.

Pastorius's first poem evidently received the desired approbation. In his second anniversary poem, dated August 20, 1715, he wrote:

Your kindness, wherewithal my Last Years Meeters met,
Does this new **Monument of Ship-mate-ship** beget,
Which, if received with the same Benevolence,
May rise as **high** again, and shew a Twelve month hence
Some matters as I hope, of greater Consequence . . .

The affection and approval Pastorius received from his friends triggered the writing of another poem, or, metaphorically, the construction of a "new **Monument.**" This architectural metaphor explained that textuality did not exist within the isolated world of the author's mind, thus representing a separation of language from feeling; rather, it was created and recreated through the reception and response of the readers. In the ideal community of readers and writers that Pastorius wished to build, textuality and meaning developed through communal affection and cooperation. Pastorius, in other words, did not wish his faith and his fellow believers to relate to one another altogether subtextually but to do so intertextually and interpersonally. His "**Monument** . . . May rise as **high** again"—instead of crumbling—because of the affection and probably the writings returned by the addressees (we have no evidence of the sisters' written response). Although

Pastorius did not make the allusion to the Tower of Babel explicit, his poetic monument to friendship was in many ways an anti-Tower. As the prideful edifice constructed at Babel had confused human languages and thus separated humans from one another and from God, Pastorius's humble and affectionate poetry was a monument built to reconstitute and strengthen those ties.[10]

Yet a different scriptural monument appeared directly in Pastorius's anniversary poems: the pillar Jacob erected on the grave of his wife Rachel (Gen. 35: 20). After the death of Rachel Preston, Pastorius continued his architectural metaphor, describing the friendship with the Lloyd daughters with a textual *and* visual grave marker for his deceased friend that simultaneously evoked the pillar for the Old Testament Rachel. Pastorius thus began the anniversary poem for the year 1717 by drawing a pillar on paper—complete with the mortar between each brick (Figure 7). Across this construction, he wrote a poem, beginning with the lines, "A Pillar upon Rachel's Grave / Brave Jacob once would set, / That he a Monument might have / so as not to forget." Assuring that Rachel Preston—just as her biblical namesake—would not be forgotten, Pastorius sent his poem "in form of a Letter to [his] Loving Friend Samuel Preston" as well as her sisters Hannah and Mary.[11]

The paper pillar and "engraved" poem Pastorius erected in Rachel's memory, therefore, elaborated and heightened the tripartite link between text (and, by extension, language), physical object, and love. Of course, grave markers always wedded textuality to physicality in order to memorialize the affection and lasting bonds between the deceased and those who remained. Pastorius explained his particular reason for sending a *paper* memorial: Rachel was

> buried at Philadelphia the 15th [of the VI.th month, 1716] when [my] Son John Samuel married with Hannah, (the youngest Daughter of John) Lucken, at Germantown, By which [I] was hind'red to Accompany the Body of so dear a Friend (as the sd. Rachel has been unto me,) to its Requietorium, or Resting-Place, And so could not perform to her the last Office of Love and Respect, to my great Sorrow.

Pastorius's paper memorial, therefore, attempted several remarkable feats of translation. He had missed Rachel's funeral and thus the opportunity to

10. Ibid., 5 (emphasis in the original).
11. Ibid., 36.

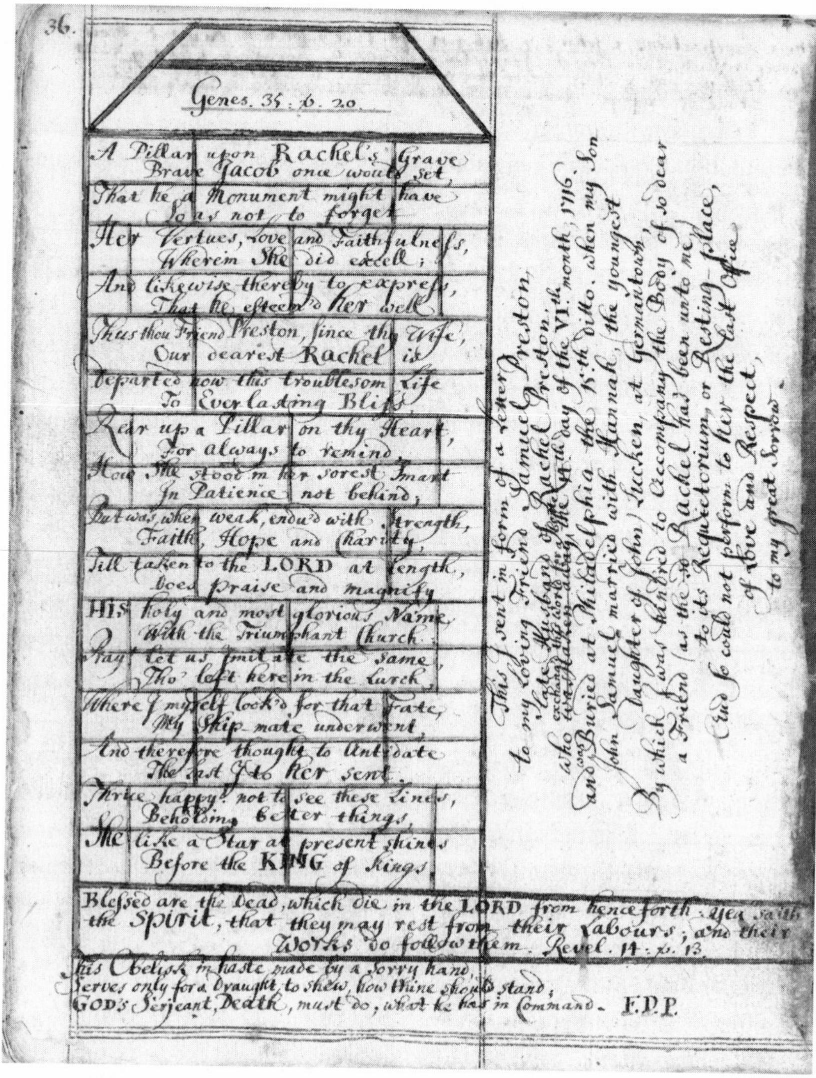

Genes. 35. 6. 20.

A Pillar upon Rachel's Grave
 Brave Jacob once would set
That he a Monument might have
 Sons not to forget

Her Vertues, Love and Faithfulness,
 Wherein She did excell;
And likewise thereby to express,
 That he esteem'd her well

Thus thou Friend Preston, since thy Wife,
 Our dearest Rachel is
Departed now this troublesom life
 To Everlasting Bliss

Rear up a Pillar on thy Heart,
 For always to remind
How She stood in her sorest Smart
 In Patience not behind;

But was, when weak, endu'd with strength,
 Faith, Hope and Charity,
Till taken to the LORD at length,
 Does praise and magnify

HIS holy and most glorious Name,
 With the Triumphant Church.
Nay let us imitate the same,
 Tho' left here in the lurch

Where I myself look'd for that rate,
 My Ship-mate underwent
And therefore thought to Antidate
 The last to her sent

Thrice happy! not to see these lines,
 Beholding better things
She like a Star at present shines
 Before the KING of Kings

Blessed are the dead, which die in the LORD from henceforth yea saith
the Spirit, that they may rest from their labours, and their
 Works do follow them. Revel. 14. v. 13

His Obelisk in haste made by a sorry hand,
Serves only for a Draught to shew, how thine should stand;
GOD's Serjeant, Death, must do, what he has in Command. F.D.P.

This I sent in form of a Letter Preston.
To my loving Friend Samuel Preston,
who Master Walter ... that his Rachel Preston,
exchang'd this mortal Life ... the 6th day of the VI. month, 1716.
and Buried at Philadelphia the 8th ditto. when my Son
John Samuel married with Hannah, the youngest
Daughter of John Jacken at Germantown.
By which I was hindred to accompany the Body of so dear
a Friend (as the sd Rachel has been unto me)
to its Requietorium or Resting-place,
of Love and Respect,
 to my great Sorrow.

*Figure 7. Francis Daniel Pastorius, "Ship-Mate-Ship: An Omer Full of
Manna, for Mary, Rachel, Hannah, the Daughters of Brave Lloyd, by
Brave Men Now Enjoy'd," composition book, 36, Pastorius Papers,
Historical Society of Pennsylvania, Philadelphia. By permission
of The Historical Society of Pennsylvania (HSP)*

express personally and physically his grief and affection for her family. His note of regret for missing the funeral and his poetic pillar, therefore, simultaneously attempted to translate several emotions into language and to cement a friendship that his earlier efforts had tried to continue and strengthen. Just as his previous anniversary poems hoped to rebuild the bonds of affection between Pastorius and Lloyd by extending them to his daughters, his visual and poetic marker for Rachel sought to translate the text-object-emotion connection implicit in a gravestone to a similar triad, merely replacing stone with paper. Understanding that neither words nor paper make a lasting monument, Pastorius lifted Rachel up as a witness to the ultimate Word. Rachel is taken to heaven, where she "Does praise and magnify / His holy and most glorious Name, / with the Triumphant Church." Pastorius knew that poetic monuments and paper pillars had to suffice until, in heaven, humanity was once again unified with God and one another in a common language and spirit. His footnote at the bottom of Rachel's pillar, therefore, summed up Pastorius's overall concept toward the fallibility of human languages and image making: "This Obelisk in haste made by a Sorry hand, / Serves only for a Draught, to shew, how thine should stand; / GOD's Serjeant, Death, must do, what he has in Command." Until humans were once again unified by God, their attempts to make permanent images would be foiled by death. Nonetheless, on the plane of human imperfection, the "Draught" or textual attempt at memorializing Rachel and simultaneously consoling her family had to suffice.[12]

Pastorius's literary circle soon encompassed the children of Lloyd's daughters, for whom Pastorius played the role of educator and friend. For instance, Pastorius exchanged personal poetry as well as books on a wide spectrum of topics with Elizabeth Hill, the granddaughter of Thomas Lloyd and daughter of Hannah Hill. In this exchange, Pastorius frequently bridged the borders between manuscript and print by inscribing poems or short reflections in the books he received or circulated. On May 3, 1717, for instance, Pastorius copied into the "Bee-Hive" a poem he had first inscribed in a printed book that Elizabeth had sent him, entitled *A Legacy for Children, Being Some of the Last Expressions and Dying Sayings of Hannah Hill Junr.* Elizabeth's older sister Hannah had died on August 2, 1714, of a "violent Feaver and Flux," and her conversations with and testimonies to her family and other Friends were recorded and subsequently circulated in manuscript form as *Expressions and Dying Sayings of Hannah Hill Junr.*

12. Ibid.

(1714). By sending him the printed book, Elizabeth gestured that Pastorius was included, by extension, in the list of mourners inside the book; in returning the book with a personal inscription (which encouraged Elizabeth to continue the intellectual pursuits of her deceased, elder sister), Pastorius, in turn, gave a personal token of gratitude and simultaneously signaled his interest in Elizabeth's development.[13]

Rather than standing in for physical, communal displays of affection, textual exchange in this instance mirrored and reinforced previous personal interaction. The book recorded that Hannah had requested, shortly before her death, that "Friends and others might generally be invited to her Burial, and mentioned divers Persons particularly *by Name,* that were Non-Residents and some *Strangers, that but lately came into the Country,* lest they should be omitted."[14] The distinction between "Non-Residents" and "Strangers" showed that the latter were recent and probably non-English immigrants. Whether such reaching out to other nationalities or ethnicities in their midst was actually the sentiment of the dying Hannah or not, it certainly characterized the general spirit that pervaded the circle witnessing her death. Though not mentioned by name in the manuscript or print version of the *Expressions, and Dying Sayings,* Pastorius had been present at her burial. In the prose introduction to his first anniversary poem, he specifically referred to young Hannah, who had died

> but lately, to wit in this selfsame Sixth Month [August 1714], at whose Burial I was greatly refreshed both in the Meeting-house and Graveyard; but much more, when (before we came thither, and after we went thence,) I in the Face and Countenance of the deceased Young Maidens loving Parents *very legibly and Intelligibly* could read the Resignation of their own Selves into the unalterable good Will of Our God.

Just as Hannah's sentiments before passing had been captured in writing, her parents' submission to God's will had been inscribed in their features "very legibly and Intelligibly," ready to be read by a community of mourners. In reading Hannah's *Expressions, and Dying Sayings* as well as

13. Hannah Hill, *A Legacy for Children, Being Some of the Last Expressions, and Dying Sayings of Hannah Hill, Junr. of the City of Philadelphia, in the Province of Pensilvania, in America, Aged. Eleven Years and Near Three Months* (Philadelphia, [1717]), 5; "Expressions and Dying Sayings of Hannah Hill Junr. Together with Griffith Owen's and Thomas Chalkey's Testimony Concerning Her," transcribed by G. Nathan Cox, 1714, MS, Cox-Parrish-Wharton Papers, HSP.

14. Hill, *A Legacy for Children,* 11 (emphasis added).

the expressions on her parents' faces, Pastorius fathomed the imbrication of spirituality, communal affection, and textuality. The personal encounter at the funeral and the textually mediated encounter with her last words interchangeably allowed Friends to participate in the personal tragedy of a child's death and the drama of Quaker humility and intimate experience of God's dealings. The universal language written on the faces of Hannah's grieving yet resigned parents as well as the specific textual transmission of her dying expressions together spread the girl's faith and undying desire for a community of love (represented by a *translingual* and *transnational* community of mourners at her funeral). Inserted into a web of personal relationships, texts allowed Pennsylvania Quakers—including recent immigrants and "Strangers"—to bridge the supposed chasm between inward and outward language, between the fallen word and the divine Word. In conjunction, nonverbal gestures and texts tapped into and created a common spiritual language.[15]

In joining spiritual and personal infinities to textual expression, Pastorius was also able to expand his literary community to Friends with whom he had no previous, communal interaction or, to put it differently, Quakers who were not part of the civic elite of early Pennsylvania. In particular, women still held somewhat tenuous positions in early American Quaker society. Although the Society of Friends far exceeded other religious denominations in allowing women to hold public positions and become writers, the two examples discussed here—traveling minister Lydia Norton and indentured servant Jane Fenn—reveal Pastorius's key role in seriously probing and encouraging each woman's craft and tying her intellectually, spiritually, and textually into the Quaker religious and literary community. Just as English or Welsh Quakers like the Lloyds had traversed linguistic differences to include Pastorius in the Quaker body, Pastorius looked across lines of gender and class to forge community.

During a missionary journey from New England to Barbados, Norton spent some time preaching among the Friends' meetings in the Philadelphia area. Pastorius admired her gift as a minister and borrowed her journal. During "4 days, (taking the Nights with it)," Pastorius "Copied 44 Quart-Leaves" of Norton's journal before she left for the Caribbean. As usual when returning a borrowed book, Pastorius attached a few verses of his own composition:

15. Pastorius, "Ship-Mate-Ship," 3 (emphasis added), Pastorius Papers.

Friend Lydia Norton,   Go and Set forth on
Thy Journey, and the Lord   Be pleased to afford
His Presence so to be   for Ever-more with thee,
As he has to this day   Been thy sure Staff and Stay
That many may Believe,   On him, and never grieve
That holy Spirit who   Will teach him what to Do.

In Norton, Pastorius saw a model case of the workings of Quaker communal cohesion through the sharing of God's indwelling light. God communicated his will and support to Lydia Norton, who, as his spokesperson, shared the Holy Spirit with others so that "many may Believe."[16]

That Pastorius took such haste to transcribe the journal of a traveling woman minister confirms his admiration for her accomplishments and acceptance of preaching women. Journals and autobiographies of Quaker ministers in general represented one of the most respected forms of religious and literary expression among Quakers throughout the late seventeenth and the eighteenth centuries. Pastorius's encouragement of Norton's public preaching becomes more remarkable when considering that the role of women preachers was still contested among early-eighteenth-century Quakers. Norton herself had been publicly rejected by Quaker meetings elsewhere in the American colonies. Quaker minister Thomas Story recorded an incident at a Friends' meeting in Haverhill, Massachusetts, in 1704: "Soon after, *Lydia Norton* stood up, and several of the People went out in contempt of her Sex, (though she had a Ministry as affecting and satisfactory as most Women or Men either) and, when she had done, I concluded the Meeting in Prayer. . . . Another of those Opposers raised some fresh Cavils about Womens' Preaching." Pastorius's recognition of Norton's gift, therefore, counteracted the "Cavils" against women's public ministry and strengthened her place within the Society of Friends.[17]

---

16. Pastorius, "Silvula Rhytmorum," in "Bee-Hive," #486. According to the "Quaker Dictionary of Biography," typescript, Quaker Collection, Haverford College, Haverford, Pa., Norton lived at Salem, Massachusetts, and was a member of the monthly meeting there. She was apparently an "able minister" and went on several missionary journeys along the eastern seaboard, including "a religious visit to Southern and Western provinces" in 1717. Also see Larson, *Daughters of Light*, 101, 278, 285, 347 n. 7. Norton's journal was not printed, and I have not been able to locate the original or Pastorius's transcription.

17. Tarter, "Sites of Performance," 15; Thomas Story, *A Journal of the Life of Thomas Story . . .* (Newcastle upon Tyne, 1747), 327–328. The Quaker preacher Samuel Bownas recounted in his autobiography, *An Account of the Life, Travels, and Christian Experiences in the Work of the Ministry of*

Pastorius's poetic response, recorded in the "Bee-Hive," indicates his appreciation of Norton's journal primarily as "divine testament." Norton's experiences allowed insight into the dealings of God with humankind in general and with those chosen to profess their indwelling spirituality in particular. The journal, in that sense, served to mediate a supralinguistic knowledge derived, not through the study of books, but—as Pastorius says in his poem—through attention to "That holy Spirit who / Will teach [them] what to Do." Yet a letter Pastorius sent to Norton when returning her journal (recorded in his letter book) bespoke a simultaneous appreciation of such autobiographical writings for the sake of aesthetic pleasure and intellectual stimulation. Pastorius's response to Norton's writings, in other words, far exceeded his agreement with the spiritual notions of a fellow Quaker. That he did not refrain from criticizing Norton's journal for lacking a rigorous organization and structural conciseness demonstrates that Pastorius regarded his work as a contribution to improving her writing, not just her spiritual state. Moreover, Pastorius would not have voiced such criticism if he had expected Norton's journal to remain exclusively in private use. His comments would have helped Norton if she had wanted to submit her writing to the public eye. Pastorius wrote:

> Not withstanding I was almost wearied with the frequent Repetitions of (:after Meeting went to such or such a house, dined there, lodged there that Night, and Stayed there the next day, etc.) which being not very Material or Edifiable, takes up a [?] of Paper as well as time, which both might (as I think,) be more profitably bestowed else where. . . . Journals, that contain only remarkable Passages, (in mine Eyes) are the best, seeing we can the sooner peruse 'em and the things therein related will stick the more firmly in our Memory. I do not hint this to thee, as if I was any ways displeased with Thine; but Simply, because now a days most Readers loath superfluities in all Sorts of Writings, and much more those, to whose Task it falls to Copy or tran-

---

Samuel Bownas (London, 1761), a similar incident involving Lydia Norton that reveals the general resentment against women preachers (100): "And in some convenient Time a young Woman stood up who had a pretty Gift, but the People behaved very rudely, so that it put the poor Girl out of Countenance, and she sat down. Then stood up one *Lydia Norton,* a famous Minister, none more so of that Country, and indeed she had an excellent Gift, and knew how to conduct herself in it; but all this did not avail, the People grew worse and worse in their Behaviour; and *Lydia* having a very strong manly Voice, extended it very loud, but all to no purpose, for the People were as loud as she, calling for a Dram, and sporting themselves in their Folly, so she sat down."

scribe them. Thou seest hereby, (and as I hope, wilt not take it amiss,) that I deal plainly, being by Birth a Franconian, and measurably by Regeneration a Free-man of the Lord.

Pastorius here emphasized the relationship between text and audience in order to raise Norton's awareness of the public nature and communal significance of her writing. Her journal should not—as a diary might do— merely chronicle the minutiae of the writer's life; it should consider the readers' expectations and appeal to their sense of aesthetic pleasure. Pastorius argued that Norton's journal could not effectively complete its public ministerial agenda if it lacked literary accomplishment. Pastorius acted as a literary critic representing the tastes of a reading public—specifically the Society of Friends—to a writer of a popular Quaker genre. Pastorius by no means disparaged Norton's more mundane experiences and daily routine as inconsequential, but, by trying to make her writing adhere to the conventions of a genre, he actively improved her reception and participation within a community of Friends.[18]

Whereas Pastorius's reaction to Norton's writings harnessed literary criticism to enhance the ministerial purpose of her work, his response to the poetry sent to him by Jane Fenn Hoskens scrutinized poetic principles and, moreover, inserted her into a community of biblical and historical women poets. At the time when Jane Fenn (later Hoskens) corresponded with Pastorius, she was going through an intense period of spiritual turmoil that ultimately resulted in her embrace of the ministry and numerous missionary journeys throughout North America, the Caribbean, and the British Isles. Her published spiritual autobiography reported that Fenn had come to Philadelphia in 1712 after she perceived a divine communication during a near-fatal illness, telling her, "If I restore thee, 'go to *Pennsylvania.*'" For several years, she wrestled with another divine communication that virtually ordained her as a preacher for the Society of Friends. Similar to other women preachers such as Elizabeth Ashbridge, Fenn struggled to reconcile

18. Tarter, "Sites of Performance," 15; Francis Daniel Pastorius, "Copies of Letters" (letter book), 113, Pastorius Papers. In the line, ". . . I deal plainly, being by Birth a Franconian . . . ," Pastorius was probably punning on the English adjective "frank" being phonetically included in "Franconian." The German phrase "frank und frei" means "frankly" or "straight out." The effect of this pun clearly derives from Pastorius's interest in correspondences between the English and German language. He most likely did not mean to imply that all Franconians (that is, the people of the German region of Franconia) were plain dealers.

this commandment to work as an instrument or "captive maid" of the Lord with her socially determined aversion to women's speaking in public, particularly of spiritual matters.[19]

Pastorius's response did not react to Fenn's struggle with cultural norms and personal prophecy. The poetry he received from Fenn seemed to have been of a religious character, and he commended her on the sentiments expressed. Yet he was more interested in instructing her in poetic composition:

> *Jane Fenn* sent me the 5th of the 11th mo: 1717/8 a Sheet full of Rimes of her own Make; Upon which I answered her the next ensuing day etc.

> Loving Friend.
> Thy Rimes I read, and like them pretty well;
> For they do run, but run not parallel:
> One wants some Feet, the other does abound,
> which matters not, the Matter being Sound.
> Go thou but on! thou wilst <u>most of</u> thy Sex surpass,
> And be a Poëtress, as <u>famous</u> Sappho was.

> Mind, that each of these my two last Verses having two feet more than the former, are of a different race or species; But leave out the underlined words, and they'll be of due length.

Pastorius takes metric irregularities in Fenn's poetry as an occasion to demonstrate with a few of his own rhymes how to vary and adjust the number of metric units ("Feet") in a line and thus change the sound of the poem. His instruction exhibits a linguistic playfulness that does not seem to agree with his avowed emphasis on the spiritual soundness of her poetry. Clearly, Fenn's and Pastorius's interest in poetry goes beyond its ability to express

19. Jane [Fenn] Hoskens, *The Life and Spiritual Sufferings of That Faithful Servant of Christ Jane Hoskens, a Public Preacher among the People called Quakers* . . . (Philadelphia, 1771), 4, 23. For manuscript versions of her journal, see Hoskens, "Journal, 1727–1729," Friends Historical Library, Swarthmore College, Swarthmore, Pa.; "A Short Narrative of the Life of Jane Hoskins, Who Departed This Life in the 11th Month 1764," MS 975B, Quaker Collection. Excerpts from her spiritual autobiography can be found in Carolyn A. Barros and Johanna M. Smith, eds., *Life-Writings by British Women, 1660–1850: An Anthology* (Boston, 2000). Also see, Larson, *Daughters of Light;* Michele Lise Tarter, "Jane Fenn Hoskens, (1693–1770?)," in Carla Mulford et al., eds., *American Women Prose Writers to 1820,* Dictionary of Literary Biography, CC (Detroit, 1999), 187–194.

religious or moral sentiments; both relish its aesthetic and literary qualities.[20]

Though his claim that she might *"most of* her Sex surpass" could be
interpreted as a somewhat chauvinistic remark about the literary superiority of men, he nevertheless went on to supply a multiplicity of precedents
that are all designed to encourage Fenn to continue her poetic endeavors.
Pastorius found that she "has a vertuous Inclination to Poëtry" and consequently enumerated women in the Bible who also demonstrated poetic
talent, including Deborah, Hannah, Mary, and Elizabeth. He further supplemented this list of spiritual precedents with an enumeration of the nine
most famous women poets of England as well as the most recent American
example of female poetic talent:

> Finally I here shall set down the Names of some English and Scotch
> women, who well skill'd in Versifying left us divers good works behind,
> to wit 1. Jane Gray./. 2. Anne Askew./. 3. Mary Wroth./. 4. Catherine
> Philips./. 5. Margaret, Duchess of New-Castle./. 6. Mary, Countess of
> Pembroke./. 7. Elizabeth Carew./. 8. Mary Morpeth./. 9. Mary Moli-
> neux./. To these Nine Muses of Great Britain I shall add the Tenth,
> sprung up in New-England, viz. Anne Broadstreet *[sic]*, etc.

Given this impressive list of biblical as well as English poetic talent among
women, Fenn must have felt encouraged to pursue her literary aspirations.
Yet the end of Pastorius's entry seemed to recant this forceful support of her
work. He recounted inserting into his response to Fenn a note of caution
that he had already issued to his sons in another section of the "Bee-Hive."
Pastorius had advised his sons not to attempt poetry as their primary occupation. Professional poets, he argued, were bound to live in isolation and
misery. Thus, poetry should rather be practiced following his own example,
that is, as an expression of spiritual and intellectual congeniality exchanged
between friends. Pastorius, in other words, reflected in his comments on
Fenn's poetry the sensibility of an age that still measured literature—and
poetry in particular—according to its social or communal functions. Even
though his remarks upon meter testify to his interest in aesthetics independent from spiritual or social value, his listing of female poets asserted that
poetry required community.[21]

---

20. Pastorius, "Silvula Rhytmorum," in "Bee-Hive," #475. I have not found any surviving poetry
by Fenn.

21. Ibid. (emphasis in the original).

Commonplace Writing and the Problem of Discernment

Pastorius's literary circle also subjected reading and writing to communal scrutiny and the mediation of communal affection in order to avoid the cacophony of voices created by the Keithian schism. Mediation between multiple languages and ideas—especially through an able translator like Pastorius—could benefit the community by fleshing out joint religious, intellectual, and social ideals, especially if they were undergirded by supralinguistic feelings of love and trust. On the flip side, a proliferation of opinions, ideas, and texts became disruptive to such a communal ethics if each voice or party considered its testimony mutually exclusive or a sole arbiter of truth. In reading, exchanging, and discussing a multiplicity of books and voices with his trusted friends, Pastorius sought to create a sphere and a method that engaged with a broad spectrum of knowledge while preventing debates over doctrine or dead letters. Similar to other early modern societies, early Pennsylvania confronted an explosion of knowledge facilitated by print, travel, imperial expansions, and international trade; more than any of the authoritarian, even feudal, states of Europe and more than other North American colonies ruled by the tandem powers of magistrates and a state-sponsored church (such as Massachusetts and Virginia), Pennsylvania allowed a hitherto unknown diversification of opinions, religious groups, languages, political factions, and reading materials.

In this environment, Pastorius attempted to render acceptable the reading and circulation of widely divergent books and ideas by emphasizing the key role a community of readers played in interpreting texts and determining their meaning. Pastorius best explained his system to his young friend Lloyd Zachary in a letter dated December 20, 1718. In spite of his role as a mentor, Pastorius revealed his own dependency on a larger circle of friends willing to part with their books. In turn, he hoped that the much younger Zachary would enrich his wisdom:

> Thou further addest . . . that of any edifying Book or books thou wilt take all possible Care; To this I say, that those few I have thou art free and welcome to borrow. I in deed did read, press and cull several hundreds, whilst in this Countrey, and yet bought none, but they were lent me by lo: friends as ex. gr. by W. Penn, S. Carpenter, I. Norris, R. Preston, Gr. Owen, etc. to whom (tho' most of 'em deceased,) I still am Obliged for their kindness. However I here with send and lend thee 1st the Writing Scholar's Companion, wherein

thou wilt meet with a world of my Manuscript Remarks, and some thereof not altogether useless or unpleasant, 2d a Merry piece of Edw. Blount's, Inscribed Micro-Cosmographie in Essays and Characters. 3d my Melliorum Sententiarum, a hasty and uncompleat Treatise by me begun, (yea and only begun,) these 20 years since, when I was teaching School in Town. Thou mayst run this soon over, and if there be any Sentence therein yet unknown to thee, receive it as from thy best friend's hand, and if thou art acquainted already with 'em all, remember, quod Lectio lecta placet, decies repetita placebis. In case thou wilt be so good as to augment the so defective Manuscript with some that occur unto thy Memory, those that henceforth shall see ye same, Nunq. cessabant Loidio benedicere docto.

Through his correspondence with Pastorius, Zachary became part of a select group of Pennsylvania Quakers, including some of the most prominent leaders of the province. Pastorius revealed a list of people who had lent books and enabled the expansion of his knowledge, and he continued this system by lending books to his latest friend and correspondent. In asking for specific recommendations, Zachary solicited the assistance of his experienced and well-read friend in choosing appropriate readings from the unwieldy sphere of print. Thus, he could rest assured that the three pieces Pastorius sent along with the letter had already passed the discerning eye of a trusted friend. One of these books, *The Writing Scholar's Companion,* even contained Pastorius's personal reading notes and thus allowed the borrower additional insight into the mind and scrutiny of his friend. Significantly, not all three items were printed books; Pastorius also sent along his "Melliorum Sententiarum" (that is, his "Bee-Hive"), the product of collecting wise or insightful sentences for twenty years.[22]

Accompanied by manuscript commentary and a compendium carrying the results of a friend's endeavor to collect knowledge, books lost their potential as deterrents from personal meditation or diluents of the Inward Light. In perusing Pastorius's "Bee-Hive" or other commonplace collections such as the earlier "Alvearialia," Zachary not only had the opportunity to encounter a wealth of quotations but also his friend's commentary on a

22. Pastorius, "Copies of Letters," 63–64, Pastorius Papers. Lloyd Zachary (1701–1756), a nephew of Richard and Hannah Hill, later studied medicine at Saint Thomas's Hospital in London under Dr. William Cheselden, established a successful medical practice in Philadelphia, and became one of the original trustees of the Philadelphia Academy. See Tolles, *Meeting House and Counting House,* 226–227.

wide range of books—both Quaker and non-Quaker. The reading interests of Pastorius's literary circle displayed not only the vigorous international book trade but also the cosmopolitan attitude of its members.

In a letter to his influential friend Samuel Carpenter, for instance, Pastorius referred to borrowing a book from Carpenter entitled *The Historical Relation of the Charity Schools and Orphan-House etc. at Glaucha before Hall in Saxony.* Clearly, the English Quaker Carpenter displayed an interest in the religious and social affairs of Germany, specifically the charitable movement of the Halle Pietists under August Hermann Francke. In manuscript, Pastorius augmented the content of the book with some of his own observations on various charity schools and orphanages he had visited. In joining his own diverse and broad reading interests with his German correspondent's international experience, Carpenter participated in and contributed to a cosmopolitan and intellectually open-minded spirit of inquiry among Quakers in early Pennsylvania.[23]

Crucially, the exchange between Pastorius and Carpenter by no means remained limited to topics of literary, scholarly, or spiritual significance. Pastorius candidly applied the subject of the borrowed book to the public realm of communal life in Pennsylvania, thus widening the import of a correspondence between friends to a form of social activism, in this case the plea for public education:

> For, that public Schools are of an absolute Necessity, (: to have the Children of the poor taught as well as those of the rich,) thou thyself are most sensible, otherwise thou wouldst not have taken that care about your Philadelphian 7 years School, wherein I was concerned as Pedagogue, as thou hast done. To speak true, without flattery, (which would be Madness itself between us, who Intimately have been acquainted almost 26. years, from the very Infancy of this Province) thou approvedst thyself unto Philad.a, what that faithful Centurion Luke 7. was to the Jews of Capernaun, in building a Schoolhouse, etc. But to pass by all what's past, Schools, Orphanotrophies and Bridwells are still a wanting in Pensilvania and it lies at the door of you Common-wealth men, to erect and establish as many as you can; I, who as yet go twice to School every day . . . can contribute no more to your Endeavours than mine earnest prayers for the speedy Success thereof, wherewith I ever remain.

23. Pastorius to Samuel Carpenter, n.d., in Pastorius, "Copies of Letters," 7–8.

Pastorius interwove several layers of personal affection, communal history, biblical precedent, and common sense reasoning. Most important, he evoked the bonds of a long-lasting friendship ("almost 26. years") in order to make a plea of social relevance. By tying their mutual friendship to the communal beginnings of Pennsylvania, Pastorius exalted personal bonding as the foundation of any social endeavor. The trope of the province as a young child that had to be nourished to adulthood and strength established both men as parent figures for the community as such. The rest of the passage, therefore, outlined how Pastorius would like to distribute the "parental" responsibilities between himself and Carpenter. In the past, Carpenter contributed to this endeavor by petitioning for the chartering of the Friends' Public School and providing sufficient funds for its operation. Pastorius, in turn, proffered his work as a pedagogue.[24]

Rhetorically swinging from a consideration of the past to an evaluation of the present, Pastorius simultaneously moved from praise to polite criticism. Bearing upon the bonds of friendship and communal activism, he created a sense of failure in terms of the educational development of Pennsylvania and charged Carpenter, the politician (or "commonwealth man"), with public action. In a sly rhetorical move, Pastorius asserted that—as a former teacher at the Quaker school in Philadelphia and current instructor at the Germantown school—he had done and was still doing his part in advancing education. In terms of their mutual parenting of a province that was now in its twenties but apparently lacking in refinement, Pastorius asked his partner to complete his portion of the educational responsibilities. Along with his letter, Pastorius returned both the book he had borrowed and the responsibility for social activism to his friend Samuel Carpenter. At the center of this coupling of personal and communal significance, thus, stood the books and the letters exchanged between Carpenter and Pastorius and the personal affection between the two friends. Instead of creating volatility among a people bound together by a personal faith or Inward Light, books functioned as agents of communal renewal and cohesion. Reading could bridge or erase those divisions or differences that jeopardized the harmony and the advancement of community.

In his manuscripts, particularly his commonplace collections, as well as his literary circles, Pastorius endeavored to bridge the ostensible split

24. Ibid. The *OED* provides "bridewell," meaning a prison or reformatory, a term derived from Bride's Well in the City of London, near which such a building stood.

between his scholarly pursuits and his practical communal challenges as well as the potential tension between book learning and communal affection. Pastorius hoped that the process of reading, selecting, excerpting, and composing that generated his manuscript writings could also produce a precedent for civic conduct. Just as his commonplace books, volumes of law, and schoolbooks required the skill of making critical or moral choices, the success of the Pennsylvanian experiment depended upon the ability of individual citizens to form personal judgments based on the ethical or spiritual foundation of the entire community. By endowing readers with the responsibility for making critical choices, the manuscripts Pastorius circulated among his friends — such as the "Bee-Hive" or "Melliorum Sententiarum" mentioned in his letter to Zachary — introduced crucial changes in the relationship between writers, readers, and the authority of texts.

Pastorius's manuscript writings demonstrated that the integration of intellectual and experiential worlds did not exclusively take place in a textual sphere but also in the material world of his manuscript volumes. For instance, he called attention to the physical nature of his "Bee-Hive" manuscript by noting his ownership, reminding other residents to return the volume if lost, and stipulating his sons as the book's physical heirs and custodians. His manuscript volumes abound with references to the collecting, entering, and arranging of passages as well as the binding of his manuscript pages. By highlighting the parallelism between the material and mental processes of collecting and selecting materials, Pastorius illustrated the participatory and continuous nature of both the production of the text and the construction of the community. Like the development of spiritual community in early Pennsylvania, each manuscript volume, for Pastorius, was not a static, finished text; it was a tangible and dynamic compilation of entries that invited readers to join in the project of intellectual, cultural, and material ordering and thus to fashion a coherent whole from the multiplicity of languages and opinions.

A number of scholars have called attention to the apparent disjunction between the intellectual accomplishment of Pastorius's manuscripts and the cultural reality of early colonial Pennsylvania. Accordingly, Pastorius privately preserved the elitist notions of the European intelligentsia in the erudite aphorisms of his commonplace books while publicly advancing the civic and educational life of the fledgling German settlement. Instead of merely transporting European learning to Pennsylvania, Pastorius adapted the intellectual principles of his reading and writing in the cultural context of his new home. On one of the "Bee-Hive's" numerous title pages, he announced his book's role in mediating between Old World sensibilities and New World contingencies:

> After I had collected Two Volums of delightful Proverbs, witty Sentences, wise and godly Sayings; Comprizing for the most part necessary and profitable Caveats, Advises, Doctrines and Instructions; out of many Authors of many minds and different Opinions, not only in my Mother-Tongue, but likewise in the Low-Dutch, French, Italian and Latin which both Books in 4° are still with me. For the better learning of the ENGLISH *[sic]*, and that my two Sons (who probably will never attain to the Understanding of the said Languages) might hereafter have some of their Fathers Steps, thereby to be guided to the same Diligence and Assiduity of *Picking the Best* out of good Writings, I endeavoured at Spare-times to make this present Hive on a Quire of fine Paper, which a Friend of mine *[Jacob Tellner]* departing for Europe did give me; And when allover filled up with honey-combs, I was Constrained to enlarge my Hive with more courser, homely or home-spun Stuff of this Country-Product. Thus I leave it for the Perusing of those for whom it was contrived in the first beginning thereof; Nevertheless If any other besides them should happen to be benefitted by these Miscellanies, It will not sad, but glad my heart.

In this complex passage, Pastorius connected the intellectual and material strata of his writing and, by extension, the literary and cultural traditions of Europe with his concrete experience in Pennsylvania. One thread linked the subject, the process, and the goal of Pastorius's writing. He explained that the activity of culling edifying material from his reading did not result directly in the "Bee-Hive" itself but in two previous "Books in 4° [quarto]." In partially compiling his "Bee-Hive" manuscript from these sources, Pastorius not only continued to refine his own critical skills but also he explained and demonstrated the principles that would enable his sons to profit from their own reading and writing.[25]

25. Christoph E. Schweitzer, "Francis Daniel Pastorius, the German-American poet," *Yearbook of German-American Studies*, XVIII (1983), 22; John David Weaver, "Franz Daniel Pastorius (1651–c.1720): Early Life in Germany with Glimpses of His Removal to Pennsylvania" (Ph.D. diss., University of California, Davis, 1985), 383; Marianne S. Wokeck, "Francis Daniel Pastorius," in Craig W. Horle et al., eds., *Lawmaking and Legislators in Pennsylvania: A Biographical Dictionary*, I, *1682–1709* (Philadelphia, 1991), 589; Pastorius, "Bee-Hive," 55. Pastorius is referring to his "Alvearialia, or Such Phrases and Sentences Which in Haste Were Booked Down Here, Before I Had Time to

He also addressed the seeming discrepancy between his scholarly endeavors—which comprise reading and writing in multiple languages—and the linguistic, social, and intellectual circumstances of the American colonies. Instead of separating his scholarly achievement from its communal context, Pastorius conceives of the "Bee-Hive" and his other manuscript writings as the material, textual, and cultural link between both realms, and he fashioned them as agents of transition from a European to a North American subjectivity. Pastorius's reading in his "Mother-Tongue, but likewise in the Low-Dutch, French, Italian and Latin," reflected the seventeenth-century European movement toward an equal position of different vernaculars beside the classical languages. As a product of Pastorius's studies in Pennsylvania, however, the "Bee-Hive" incorporated English into its linguistic multiplicity. Pastorius, in other words, acknowledges the changed parameters of his sons' education away from European institutions of learning, and he adapted his instruction accordingly. His polyglot abilities no longer reflected only the elite education of his childhood and adolescence but also the multiple ethnic and linguistic traditions of his adult life in Pennsylvania. He further abandoned any exclusionist notions by widening the "Bee-Hive's" audience from his sons to other readers in the community who "happen to be benefitted by these Miscellanies." Following the "Bee-Hive's" literal and symbolic transition from the "fine Paper" of Europe to the "home-spun Stuff" of Pennsylvania, Pastorius's manuscript volumes served as the material and textual nodal points in a web that began with the traditions of his European learning but knitted together the ideological, social, political, religious, linguistic, and ethnic strands of late-seventeenth- and early-eighteenth-century Pennsylvania.[26]

In his "Bee-Hive" manuscript, therefore, Pastorius continually elaborated on the interconnected structure of his world of reading and writing, in which intellectual properties were intricately tied to both the material realm of the book and the experiential world outside the text. Pastorius

---

Carry Them to Their Respective Proper Places in My English-Folio Bee-Hive," Pastorius Papers, and "F.D.P. Francis Daniel Pastorius," Commonplace Book, Pastorius Papers. Learned provides further evidence for the preliminary status of these two manuscripts as predecessors of the "Bee-Hive" (237).

26. For the development of a vernacular tradition in seventeenth-century European literature and culture, see Leonard Forster, "Neo-Latin Tradition and Vernacular Poetry," 87–108, and Peter Schaeffer, "Baroque Philology: The Position of German in the European Family of Languages," 72–84, both in Gerhart Hoffmeister, ed., *German Baroque Literature: The European Perspective* (New York, 1983); and Forster, *The Poet's Tongues: Multilingualism in Literature* (Dunedin, N.Z., 1970), 26–50.

often illustrated this relationship with the title itself. First, he drew the more conventional analogy between the selection of memorable and useful material from one's reading and the collection of honey by bees. On one title page, he carried on the analogy with the wry humor characteristic of much of his writing: "I am a Bee, (no Drone) tho' without Sting, / Here you may see, what Honey-Combs I bring." The work of collecting knowledge here paralleled the activity of bees' selecting flowers and carrying nectar to their hive. At the same time, Pastorius enlarged the analogy between gathering knowledge and gathering honey by extending the metaphor into the material world of the book. He repeatedly named his manuscript "Paper-Hive" and thus yoked the intellectual realm of reading and writing to both the natural world and the book's specific material conditions. Instead of composing a contiguous text for publication, Pastorius gradually filled an existing, empty volume of pages with his "honey" or the products of his studies.[27]

As the designation "Paper-Hive" demonstrated, Pastorius's manuscripts integrated both the material and the intellectual phenomena that constitute collecting and writing, culminating in the text and pages of his books. The title pages not only provided such cohesion within each volume, but also they distinguished individual manuscripts as steps within a larger project of compilation and composition, beginning with a more indiscriminate style of excerpting in a volume such as "Alvearialia" and culminating in the "Bee-Hive" as the ostensible end product. The second title page of the smaller commonplace book "Alvearialia" highlighted the convergence of the material and textual properties of this manuscript. Pastorius described the material process of screening and filtering the results of his studies by binding the worthy elements in a book and dignifying the result with a title page. This description mirrors the mental activity that goes hand in hand with the material selection process as well as the social and emotional activity of gathering friends into a literary and spiritual community:

> Looking over of late my Rejectanea or Waste papers, among a great heaps of others I met also with these here partly Inclosed, and partly Stitch'd together, which making (as you see) a pretty Little Book, deserve (me thinks,) a Frontispice *[sic]* or Title-page; And forasmuch as all what's Cancell'd is Inserted in mine English Bee-Hive in folio, I thought Convenient to call them

27. Pastorius, "Bee-Hive," 1.

Tantum Quantum Lac Infantum. Or
Talia Qualia Alvearialia,
   What others did Contrive, I carry to my Hive.

The material process Pastorius followed on this title page reinscribed the mental activity of separating the metaphorical "Waste papers" that he encountered in his reading from those pages that would deserve the honor of a title page. Hence, the volume at hand physically manifested Pastorius's initial attempts to select ideas and concepts from other writers that seemed worthy to be bound and introduced formally. Instead of discarding these preliminary steps, Pastorius deemed them necessary for the reader's contemplation. The Latin title "Tantum Quantum Lac Infantum" or "Just as Great [a Thing] as Milk to an Infant" perfectly expressed the dual significance of these first stages. Although milk is the first nourishment for an infant and more substantial fare will follow, it is also the essential food for a developing human being. Pastorius regarded the excerpts in this volume as evidence of his initial and possibly immature readings and selections, yet they are also essential for the development of his subsequent, more refined work in the "Bee-Hive." "Talia Qualia Alverialia" or "Such [Things] as Pertain to Beehives" further indicates the role of this volume as a precursor of the actual "Bee-Hive" manuscript. The value of the present material, then, depended on its function within the larger project. By themselves, these excerpts may be immature or preliminary. Yet in the larger context of Pastorius's reading and writing, they emphasized the need for continual critical evaluation and revision.[28]

28. Pastorius, "Alvearialia," 2, Pastorius Papers. On early modern practices of commonplacing, see Anthony Grafton, "The Humanist as Reader," in Guglielmo Cavallo and Roger Chartier, eds., *A History of Reading in the West*, trans. Lydia G. Cochrane (Amherst, Mass., 1999), 179–212; Catherine La Courreye Blecki, "Reading *Moore's Book:* Manuscripts vs. Print Culture and the Development of Early American Literature," in Blecki and Wulf, eds., *Milcah Martha Moore's Book*, 59–106; R. R. Bolgar, *The Classical Heritage and Its Beneficiaries* (Cambridge, 1954), 265–275; Mary Thomas Crane, *Framing Authority: Sayings, Self, and Society in Sixteenth-Century England* (Princeton, N.J., 1993), 3–38; Peter Mack, "Humanist Rhetoric and Dialectic," in Jill Kraye, ed., *The Cambridge Companion to Renaissance Humanism* (Cambridge, 1996), 82–99; Susan Miller, *Assuming the Positions: Cultural Pedagogy and the Politics of Commonplace Writing* (Pittsburgh, 1998), 1–49; Ruth Mohl, *John Milton and His Commonplace Book* (New York, 1969), 11–30; Ann Moss, "Commonplace-Rhetoric and Thought-Patterns in Early Modern Culture," in R. H. Roberts and J. M. M. Good, eds., *The Recovery of Rhetoric: Persuasive Discourse and Disciplinarity in the Human Sciences* (Charlottesville, Va., 1993), 49–60. For the role of commonplace writing in a specifically early American context, see Kevin Berland, Jan Kirsten Gilliam, and Kenneth A. Lockridge, eds., *The Commonplace Book of William Byrd II of Westover* (Chapel Hill, N.C., 2001).

On one level, Pastorius valued the commonplace book as a tool that would allow him to retain much of the memorable material he had encountered in his reading, particularly from the books he would not be able to collect in his personal library. On the first of the "Bee-Hive's" title pages, he described this function of keeping a commonplace book: "For as much as our Memory is not Capable to retain all remarkable words, Phrases, Sentences or Matters of moment, which we do hear and read, It becomes every good Scholar to have a *Common-Place-Book,* and therein to Treasure up whatever deserves his Notice, etc." Beyond an attempt to hold on to a quickly deteriorating system of education in an isolated wilderness, however, Pastorius understood his commonplace books as the tools that would allow himself and his readers to develop a propensity for critical and personal judgment in an increasingly diverse communal environment. Whereas the classical tradition aimed at solidifying preconceived patterns, Pastorius's manuscripts resisted the imposition of permanent structures. On the title page of his "Alvearialia," he immediately began to dissolve the order he had imposed on his papers. As much as this volume testified to his desire to make sense of the profusion of knowledge, Pastorius referred his readers to another marker in the operations of critical scrutiny, his "English Bee-Hive," in which he inserted "all what's Cancell'd" in "Alvearialia." The title page reminds the reader that this particular manuscript formed a single step within a continuing process of compilation.[29]

In this process, readers and writers had to take on the perpetual role of translator—making judgments about the correlation between different languages, ideas, or books and deciding on a meaning that distilled correspondences among differences. While imposing his own order on the knowledge of the time and infusing it with his commentary, he advised his readers to continue this project by judging his work with critical discernment. In doing so, Pastorius muddled the separation between writer and reader, which traditionally served to lodge authority within the former. Thus, he proposed an intellectual and physical world of reading, collecting, and composing in which writers and readers perpetually assume the role of the apparent opposite. If readers and writers could work like translators—that

---

An emerging field of cultural history, the history of information, fruitfully studies the social roles of commonplace writing. See Ann M. Blair, *Too Much to Know: Managing Scholarly Information before the Modern Age* (New Haven, Conn., 2010); John Seely Brown and Paul Duguid, *The Social Life of Information* (Cambridge, Mass., 2000); Peter Burke, *A Social History of Knowledge: From Gutenberg to Diderot* (London, 2000).

29. Pastorius, "Bee-Hive," 1; Pastorius, "Alvearialia," 2, Pastorius Papers.

is, continually consider the commensurability of meaning between different languages or opinions—they would develop into more proficient members of the community.

On the same title page from "Alvearialia," Pastorius set up a theory of reading and writing relying on the personal scrutiny and negotiation between different options germane to translation. He advises his readers to apply their own rational powers in perusing and evaluating his book, instead of trusting the judgment of the compiler:

> Read, Reader, read Judiciously,
> Shun Implicit Credulity:
> Prove first and then Approve what's Good;
> Judge not of things not understood.

Pastorius bolstered this principle with a slight variation of a scriptural motto in Latin from 1 Thess. 5:21: "Omnia explorantes Bonum tenete," or "Prove all things: hold fast that which is good." Like the translator evaluating and determining a common meaning between different linguistic systems, readers and writers confronted with a profusion of knowledge had to apply the same system of testing everything and holding on to "that which is good." Like translation, the reader's judgment needed to be based on scrutiny, which in turn should rest on a solid spiritual and moral foundation rather than the ignorance, flippancy, or pride he encountered during his European course of studies. While rebuking many seventeenth-century intellectuals for abandoning the pursuit of truth for personal advantage, Pastorius acknowledged others whose critical principles agreed with his own tenets. On a title page in the "Bee-Hive," he referred to Francis Bacon, founder of the "New Science," and the English theologian Henry Ainsworth as champions of careful critical evaluation. Paraphrasing a passage from Bacon's essay "Of Studies," Pastorius wrote: "Read not to Contradict, nor to Believe; But to weigh and Consider." The ideal reader of Bacon's *Essays* and Pastorius's "Bee-Hive" was neither judgmental nor gullible. Expressing a similar theory of critical inquiry, Pastorius rehearsed Henry Ainsworth and added his own maxim: "Let not anything which I have written be accepted without Trial, or further than it agreeth with the Truth, saith Henry Ainsworth in an appendix to his Annots. upon the 5 books of Moses. / And so say I, Come Reader; try, What Words and things ensue: / Hold fast that wch is true." As his expertise in different languages had enabled him to become a judicious translator and communal mediator, Pastorius asked readers to weigh different ideas or linguistic expressions and "Hold fast that wch is true," that is, penetrate to a deeper, spiritual meaning.[30]

Pondering what distinguished the New World from the Old, Pastorius wished to establish the activity of critical reading or translating between different ideas and languages as precedent for communal formation and as the means for finding a common spiritual language. Like Walter Benjamin's ideal translator, Pastorius struggled throughout his life to create a unified world from the broken parts of the old and the many different elements of the new. He thus concluded his "Alvearialia" manuscript, turning the responsibility back over to the reader: "If any would have me Dedicate it to some Body, I herewith Complementally consecrate the same *To himself*, of what Quality soever, provided nevertheless he be One of the Excellent-Spirited in this New English World." Translation, as well as the regimes of critical reading and discernment Pastorius tried to propagate in his commonplace writings, relied upon astute readers and writers who continually searched for correspondences between different spiritual and intellectual models. Just as translation asked translators and readers to search for and reveal deep connections and common spiritual understanding underlying seemingly divergent linguistic representations, commonplace writing demanded that readers and writers distill coherent ethical and social principles from the proliferation of knowledge.[31]

THE RAPID EXPANSION of knowledge in the early modern age—spurred by imperial conquest and explorations in America—thus presented a problem similar to the multiplicity of languages. In spite of persistent dreams to discover the original language or to create a universal one, Pastorius and other immigrants in early Pennsylvania knew they had to face and even embrace the multitudinous voices, opinions, and ideas aggregating in the New World. On the one hand, Pastorius and his English Quaker friends adapted Renaissance and late humanistic regimes of ordering knowledge such as the commonplace book as well as the European "Republic of Letters" to New World circumstances. On the other hand, newly arrived groups representing the radical Protestant and Neoplatonist dream of a common spiritual language renewed mystical and esoteric approaches to linguistic and religious diversity in early Pennsylvania. Both approaches were equally utopian in their ethical motivation. As the next chapter demonstrates, mystical

30. Pastorius, "Alvearialia," 2, Pastorius Papers; Pastorius, "Bee-Hive," 5.
31. Pastorius, "Alvearialia," 2, Pastorius Papers.

seekers such as Johannes Kelpius, Conrad Beissel, Peter Miller, and Count Nikolas Ludwig von Zinzendorf (who arrived from the 1690s to the 1740s) established settlements and utopian experiments that applied the Augustinian and Neoplatonist search for translingual religious community to particularly American circumstances. For example, they harnessed multilingual singing to bind together divergent members of the community, such as the representatives of the Moravians' global missions. Seemingly waning epistemological models — such as the continuing search for hidden links between languages and human beings — gained new relevance in the bafflingly diverse environment of colonial Pennsylvania. Peter Miller's communication with Benjamin Franklin in the 1770s (Chapter 5) and David Zeisberger's and John Heckewelder's translation work well into the early nineteenth century (Coda) demonstrate the continued purchase of early modern, esoteric ideas of language, translation, and community in early America.

A Hidden Voice Amplified

MUSIC, MYSTICISM, AND TRANSLATION

ometime in late 1771 or early 1772, Benjamin Franklin—during one of his extended visits to England—received an unusual gift. Probably "absent in Ireland," Franklin said he did not actually encounter the person who had delivered the "Box and Letter." "If," as he reported in a note to his wife Deborah, "Enoch Davenport brought it, I did not see him." Franklin never learned the identity of the messenger, but the sender of the package was Franklin's longtime correspondent Peter Miller ("Brother Jaebez") of Ephrata, prior of the Pennsylvanian celibate community known as the Ephrata "cloister" and successor of the deceased Conrad Beissel, the founder and spiritual father ("Father Friedsam") of the community. Upon opening the box, Franklin found something he described elusively as "a most valuable Curiosity."[1]

Miller's letter to Franklin accompanying his "Present" detailed the contents of the package and mentioned several individuals involved in its transmission. Miller expressed his intention that "the whole will be forwarded by the Care of your Lady, with which and her Family we have in your Absence cultivated the same Friendship, which was established for many Years." In addition, Miller "gave Mr. Christ. Marshal Liberty, to peruse said Writings, and even to copy of for his Friends, if he would, which have inquired for such Things." The box contained a manuscript "Collection,"

---

1. [Georg] Conrad Beissel was born Mar. 1, 1691, in Eberbach, in the Electoral Palatinate, and died July 6, 1768, in Ephrata, Pennsylvania. [John] Peter Miller (Johann Peter Müller)—known at Ephrata as Brother Jaebez and later as Brother Agrippa—was born in Zweikirchen, Germany, on Dec. 25, 1709, and died at Ephrata, Pennsylvania, on Sept. 25, 1796. Beissel and Miller are buried next to one another at the Ephrata cemetery. For biographical information on Miller, see Jeff Bach, *Voices of the Turtledoves: The Sacred World of Ephrata* (University Park, Pa., 2003), 8; Whitfield J. Bell, Jr., "Peter Miller," *Patriot-Improvers: Biographical Sketches of Members of the American Philosophical Society* (Philadelphia, 1999), 82–91; Benjamin Franklin to Deborah Franklin, Jan. 28. 1772, in Leonard W. Labaree et al., eds., *The Papers of Benjamin Franklin*, XIX (New Haven, Conn., 1975), 42–45 (quotation on 42).

which included Miller's commentary on Beissel's *Dissertation on Man's Fall* (translated and published by Miller in 1765) as well as his translations of Beissel's *Mystische und sehr geheyme Sprueche* — "Ninety and Nine Mystical Sentences" (originally published in German by Franklin in 1730) — and fifty-seven "apothegms" collected from Beissel's writings. The object Miller actually called the "Present . . . was the Father's musical Book, wherein are contained the most part of the musical Concerts, by himself composed. It did cost three Brethren three Quarters of a Year Work to write the same."[2]

Impressing the value of this volume on Franklin, Miller projected its significance further into the future than he could have imagined. The manuscript book, entitled "Die Bittre Gute Oder Das Gesäng der einsamen Turtel-Taube" (The bitter good, or the songs of the lonely turtledove), an illustrated score of hymn tunes composed by Beissel and other Ephrata residents, is today known as the "Ephrata Codex" and located in the Library of Congress, where it has become part of the "American Treasures" exhibition. Twenty-first-century librarians, historians, art historians, and other scholars are still involved in fully assessing the importance of the "Codex" — along with other Ephrata manuscripts, publications, artifacts, and architecture. Miller's "Present" and his accompanying exposition showcase the integral role played by hymn culture and manuscript illustration among mystical Pietist communities — Johannes Kelpius's "Hermits of the Wissahickon," the Ephrata cloister, and Moravian Bethlehem — in transplanting and translating the seventeenth-century Neoplatonist ideal of a common spiritual language to eighteenth-century America.[3]

Miller's "Collection" and "Present" highlight the interwoven disciplines of music, translation, and manuscript illustration and their combined sig-

2. [John] Peter Miller to Franklin, June 12, 1771, in Labaree et al., eds., *Papers of Benjamin Franklin*, XVIII (New Haven, Conn., 1974), 130–132 (quotations on 130 and 131). Julius Friedrich Sachse published selections from Miller's "Collection," including his letter and his translations of Beissel's *Mystische und sehr geheyme Sprueche* [Mystical and very secret sayings] and fifty-seven apothegms, but not Miller's commentary on *Dissertation on Man's Fall*; see Julius F. Sachse, ed., "A Unique Manuscript by Rev. Peter Miller . . . ," *Proceedings and Addresses at York, PA, October 14, 1910*, Pennsylvania-German Society, *Publications*, XXI (1912). Beissel's *Dissertation*, a tract explaining his concept of an androgynous Adam and his division into male and female entities, was originally written in German but first published in English (1765). The first German publication is an untitled version in *Deliciae Ephratenses, pars I . . . geistliche Reden* (Ephrata, Pa., 1773), and the first separate German publication is entitled *Göttliche Wunderschrift* (Ephrata, Pa., 1789).

3. For an online glimpse of the "Ephrata Codex" or "Ephrata Community Songbook," see http://www.loc.gov/exhibits/treasures/trm005.

nificance in tying these mystical groups to the transatlantic exchange of ideas and to the cultural composition of Penn's province. Even in a material sense, Miller's gift to Franklin made tangible two of Ephrata's practical activities designed to lead the community toward spiritual perfection. The hymn score tied together singing and manuscript illustration as the most highly acclaimed pursuits of the cloister. Miller's translation of Beissel's writings and his monumental translation of the Mennonite *Martyrs' Mirror* also reveal a long-standing occupation with linguistic difference and the attempt to render mystical thought and expression in other languages. Both music and translation represented efforts to heighten the receptiveness of individuals and the community for divine wisdom or "the heavenly Sophia," which, according to Jacob Boehme, had become disunited from humankind as a result of the fall but was attainable through disciplined spiritualization of body and mind. Music and translation collaborated in attempting to leave behind the effects of Babel, that is, the tainting of language by human self-will or pride, confusion, and contention. Although language was originally tied to divine creation and constituted one of the fundamental principles of a harmonious universe, human corruption had turned it into an instrument of doctrines, arguments, and laws serving the superiority of one religious group or opinion over another. In singing, language could be reattached to another divine principle — music — that had somehow escaped the corrupting influence of the fall and of Babel.[4]

For Protestant mystics in America and Europe, language diversity per se was not the problem. The potent example of Pentecost demonstrated that a unity of spirit allowed representatives of various languages to understand one another as if speaking in and listening to one tongue. Rather, in singing, mystics aspired to the "original" language spoken by Adam before the fall, or, as Boehme put it, a "natural language" *(Natursprache)* unaffected by Babel. In translating mystical writings, translators — particularly within the multilingual environment of colonial Pennsylvania — repeatedly stressed that they did not attempt to reproduce a perfect linguistic analogue but rather the spirit of mystical experience or divine knowledge. In essence, mystical literature (including mystically inspired hymnody) thus constitutes an exceptional case in the general discipline of translation. Since a mystic does not express any thoughts originally conceived in the human mind but

4. On Beissel's notion of the androgynous Adam and the "heavenly Sophia," see Bach, *Voices,* 33–35, 102–107.

claims to record divine visions or illuminations, the task of the translator is not to transpose an author's individual thoughts into a different linguistic and cultural system; rather, it is to create another rendering of the divine wisdom that—at least theoretically—speakers of any language can attain. Among the Hermits of the Wissahickon and the Brothers and Sisters at Ephrata, both music and translation were part of the same effort to create harmonious communities of the spirit that the "heavenly bridegroom" would recognize upon his return.

Writing in the late eighteenth century, Miller followed a line of thought with roots in the works of the German mystic Jacob Boehme in the early seventeenth century as well as "Behmenist" groups such as the Philadelphian Society around Jane Leade in the 1680s and 1690s. Miller presumed a persistence of a pre-Babel language or knowledge that is at least contiguous to the divine spirit. Writers and composers of music—such as Beissel—who allowed the spirit to dictate their work thus tapped into the common pool of a higher language still accessible to certain human beings, especially in singing. Miller wrote to Franklin:

> In the Composition the Father had the same Way as in his Writings, viz: he suspended his considering Faculty, and putting his Spirit on the Pen, followed its Dictates strictly, also were all the Melodies flown from the Mystery of Singing, that was opened within him, therefore have they that Simplicity, which was required, to raise Edification. It is certain, that the Confusion of Languages, which began at Babel, never did affect Singing: and therefore is in the Substance of the Matter in the whole World but one Way of Singing; altho' in particulars there may be Differences.

While certainly trying to apotheosize Beissel, Miller located agency, not within the "Father" (Beissel), but with a higher authority that literally used him as an outlet or dispensed parts of its mysteries upon the composer. Beissel's contribution thus represented a passive opening of the self rather than a self-contained creative process. The question of origin was so important for Miller (and Beissel) because it linked both the music and the words to a realm unaffected by the human pride commonly associated with Babel (and human nature per se). Miller's unabashed universalism of course reverberates with Christ's injunction of being the sole "Way" to salvation. But the passage also suggests a soteriological purpose for human language. In spite of being debased in "the Confusion . . . which began at Babel," language could still be put to a spiritual use in its association with music. Notably, it was the wedding of language and music in "Singing" that enjoyed global unity.[5]

Although singing might provide human language with a lifeline to its divine origins, human language should never be confused with divine wisdom itself. Miller introduced this important caveat in a section concluding his commentary on Beissel's *Dissertation:*

> These Sheets were by no means written with an Intention, to sell them for infallible Truths: but to stir up the capacity of the Reader, and therefore is every line submitted to Judgment[.] Supernatural Things, if proposed even in the best method in Words, carry not with them that Impression, which they had, before they were uttered: *and therefore are the Words of the h. Scripture defective.* . . . I hope therefore the Reader will use in Reading those Lines the same Freedom, which I have used in writing the same. For altho' the Substance of the matter stands firmly, yet am I a Foreigner to the Language, and have not sufficiently Words at Command to express clearly the Ideas *[sic]* of the Mind. And if any Expression should seem offensive, or destroy any Article of our common Faith: I shall not refuse to acknowledge my Fault, knowing well that our own self is nothing else, but a concatenated Series of Errors.

Miller's remark that *"the Words of the h. Scripture [are] defective"* would have stood out like a sore thumb to orthodox Christian readers. Quoted out of context, this phrase may indeed sound incendiary, but Miller's notion followed from a specific attitude toward the relationship between divine knowledge and human language. Miller denied neither the divine inspiration of scriptures nor a faith in absolute truth. But, in examining the outpouring of the divine spirit where such truth resided through its pinning down in human language, Miller found a gap between "Supernatural Things" and "Words." Any divine or mystical vision thus became subject to the fallacies of language at the moment it was "uttered."[6]

5. Miller to Franklin, June 12, 1771, in Labaree et al., eds., *Papers of Benjamin Franklin,* XVIII, 131–132.

6. Sachse, ed., "A Unique Manuscript by Rev. Peter Miller," *Proceedings and Addresses,* Pennylvania-German Society, *Publications,* XXI (1912), 4–5 (emphasis added); "Original Manuscript Prepared by Rev. Peter Miller for Benjamin Franklin," MSS 974.8/P387, American Philosophical Society, Philadelphia.

Miller himself was intimately acquainted with the difficulty in transferring meaning from one language into another because he was not a native speaker of English and thus struggled to verbalize ideas with the same clarity or intensity with which they existed in his mind. In concluding that we are all "but a concatenated Series of Errors," he expanded the predicament of the translator or multilingual writer to the plane of human language and even human nature. Any use of language—not just in a situation of linguistic difference—inherently presupposed a loss of meaning, especially when the speaker or writer attempted to harness language to express divine truths. The humility he brought to the translation of Beissel's words, Miller implied, should to a larger degree apply to the verbalization of the divine spirit. Thus, he identified two stages to translation: a first step occurred every time writers attempted to bridge the discrepancy between a higher plane of knowledge—such as a mystical experience or the prophetic inspirations of the biblical writers—and human language. The second and more familiar step of translating from one language into another thus became part of a dilemma human beings face when attempting to communicate their experience of the divine.

Miller therefore moved translation into a realm of spiritual significance similar to that of singing. For the so-called Solitary Brothers and Sisters at Ephrata, as well as Kelpius's Hermits and the Moravians at Bethlehem, hymn singing transformed human expression into an approximation of a spiritual or angelic sound—a process Jan Stryz calls "The Alchemy of the Voice at Ephrata Cloister." In singing, language was transformed into a medium that carried a purer representation of divine wisdom or the heavenly Sophia. The translator shared with the hymn composer the task to convey a spiritual essence that would shine forth despite the limitations of human language. Both endeavors distracted the listener / reader from the inadequacies of the sign or signifier and directed attention to the plenitude of the divine referent or signified. Translators of mystical writings had to believe in this plenitude—that is, the notion of the inherent completeness and continuity of the divine spirit—in order to pursue their trade at all. If divine wisdom or inspiration were in any way tied to a specific human language, the spirit would literally disappear during the transposition into another linguistic system. As a prolific translator, Miller clearly believed that translation did not diminish or disrupt spiritual plenitude. Although all human languages provided equally flawed paths to representing divine knowledge, each language, in turn, also contained the potential to reveal a glimpse of that wisdom. In music as in translation, therefore, human beings consciously confronted the shortcomings of their worldly selves in order to gain access to a constant and more complete spiritual potential.[7]

Because the pursuits of the hymn writer and the translator served the same goal of understanding God's hidden principles and the divine meaning of the universe, Miller emerged, not merely as Beissel's successor as "Vorsteher" or prior of the community, but rather as a second intellectual and spiritual head. In other words, Miller played a significant role for both the inner coherence and the outward representation of the cloister. By the same token, Johannes Kelpius's work as a multilingual correspondent with other Pietist mystics on both sides of the Atlantic as well as his efforts toward a bilingual representation of the mystic writings of the community deserve recognition. Though it remains unclear whether Kelpius himself or Christopher Witt (an English immigrant and convert to the Hermits) was responsible for most of the translation work, multilingualism certainly constituted a structural principle of the group and established important external relationships.

Extending the spiritual, even mystic dimension of hymn singing toward translation allows for a fuller understanding of the spiritual impact of the Ephrata community—as well as the earlier "Hermits on the Ridge" and the Moravians at Bethlehem—on different religious and ethnic groups across the province. Mysticism in the New World contained a seemingly paradoxical impetus for an inward spiritualization prone to inner-worldly withdrawal along with an evangelical desire to share experiences of and pathways to the divine with outsiders. Miller's emphasis on the community's friendship with Franklin and his family as well as his explicit mention of Christopher Marshall and "his Friends" (that is, his Quaker community), who had actively "inquired" for translations of Beissel's writings, by no means stand alone in linking translation to a wider dissemination of mystical thought in early Pennsylvania. Radical Protestant groups passed on much of their heritage by placing a decidedly mystical stamp on the hymnody of the German and English inhabitants of the Middle Colonies, especially Pennsylvania. In translation, they disseminated not only the thought of their own leaders such as Kelpius, Beissel, and Zinzendorf, but they also helped to popularize German and English mystical literature from Europe in early America.

7. Jan Stryz, "The Alchemy of the Voice at Ephrata Cloister," *Esoterica*, I (1999), 133–159, http://www.Esoteric.msu.edu/Alchemy.html.

On the Wissahickon: Johannes Kelpius
and the "Chapter of Perfection"

The writings of early-seventeenth-century mystic philosopher Jacob Boehme held a central position in the religious thought of both Johannes Kelpius and Conrad Beissel. In the case of Kelpius and the Hermits, Boehme extended a twofold influence: Kelpius imbibed his ideas through direct study of his works (through Johann Georg Gichtel's comprehensive edition of 1682) and through contact with members of the Philadelphian Society during Kelpius's extended stay in London on his journey from Germany to America and his correspondence with them from Pennsylvania. Beissel, in turn, stood in contact with Boehme's editor Gichtel through a common acquaintance. During his peripatetic life before emigrating, Beissel also encountered various Philadelphian groups throughout Germany. Scholars continue to argue over the extent of the influence of the philosophy of the Rosicrucians on Kelpius and Beissel. Whether Kelpius and Beissel considered themselves Rosicrucians ultimately does not matter, since seventeenth-century publications of the elusive "Order of the Rose Cross" (such as the *Confessio* and *Fama*) were in turn influenced by Boehme's thought.[8]

To the surprise of many Pietist immigrants, Pennsylvania displayed many of the same characteristics Boehme had ascribed to the Babel-churches of Europe. Johannes Kelpius and his followers arrived in the province during the height of the Keithian controversy in 1694. Some members of Kelpius's group—especially Heinrich Bernhard Köster—became involved in the schism. While trying to remain impartial in public in order to avoid a further escalation of the disputes, Kelpius did not disguise his loathing for both parties in the controversy in a personal letter to another German immi-

---

8. For Boehme's influence on Kelpius and his associates, see Willard M. Martin, "Johannes Kelpius and Johann Gottfried Seelig: Mystics and Hymnists on the Wissahickon" (Ph.D. diss., Pennsylvania State University, 1973), 3–9. For Boehme's influence on Beissel, see Bach, *Voices*, 26–47; Stryz, "Alchemy," *Esoterica*, I (1999), 141–142; E. G. Alderfer, *The Ephrata Commune: An Early American Counterculture* (Pittsburgh, 1985), 19–20. The *Chronicon Ephratense*, the chronicle of the Ephrata community, mentions that Beissel "met a learned scholar named Haller, a strong suitor of the virgin Sophia, and also a correspondent of Gichtel." See [Jacob Gast and Peter Miller], *Chronicon Ephratense; a History of the Community of Seventh Day Baptists at Ephrata, Lancaster County, Penn'a, by "Lamech and Agrippa,"* trans. J. Max Hark (Lancaster, Pa., 1889), 5; Bach, *Voices*, 26; Stryz, "Alchemy," *Esoterica*, I (1999), 133–134. See also Julius Friedrich Sachse, *The German Sectarians of Pennsylvania, 1708–1742: A Critical and Legendary History of the Ephrata Cloister and the Dunkers* (1899) (New York, 1971); E. Ernest Stoeffler, *Mysticism in the German Devotional Literature of Colonial Pennsylvania* (Allentown, Pa., 1950).

grant, Maria Elisabeth Gerber in Virginia. Kelpius's description of the disputers harked back to Boehme's condemnations of denominational quarrels as the true Babel:

> They . . . contend among themselves, but not as did erstwhile the Disciples of Christ, as to who should be regarded chief in the Mystery of Grace (devotion), but which of them be most accomplished in the mystery of malice, the arch heretic, yea, even the Babylonian harlot herself: nor are they content with reviling, those that are in power use the sword, those lacking the sword make swords of their tongues, and with such blind rage, that it moves to pity.

The blame Kelpius placed upon the Pennsylvania Quakers as a whole mirrored the accusations that the contending parties in the controversy were flailing at each other, always abounding in the language and behavior of Babel and Babylon.[9]

Despite such discouragement, radical Pietist mystics also came equipped with certain tools to cope with these controversies or even to recognize the enduring spiritual potential of a fallen Pennsylvania. Boehme's work, as well as the radical Pietist thought influenced by him, sought to find mystical solutions to the paradox of a unified spirit of God and the multiplicity of languages, peoples, cultures, and natural phenomena. In *The Way to Christ*, Boehme provided several natural analogies for a reconciliation of unity and diversity in a common foundation of the spirit. Beginning with his characteristic raillery against the language of Babel, Boehme moved to a conciliatory, even serene image of unity:

> Therefore I say that all is Babel that bites and argues with the other over the letter. The letters all stand in one root, which is the Spirit of God, even as various flowers all stand and grow on the earth beside one another. None bites at the other because of colour, smell, and taste. They allow the earth and sun, the rain and wind and also heat and cold to do with them as they will. Each grows according to its own essence and characteristic. So it is with the children of God. They have many gifts and much knowledge, but all of one Spirit. They rejoice with one another in the great wonders of God and thank the

9. Julius Friedrich Sachse, ed., *The Diarium of Magister Johannes Kelpius* (Lancaster, Pa., 1917), 65. In manuscript, Kelpius's journal *(Diarium)* is bound together with his letter book. See Johannes Kelpius, "Briefbuch," bound with "Journal," MS Am. 0880, Historical Society of Pennsylvania, Philadelphia.

Highest in His wisdom. Why should they argue long about Him in whom they live and are, and of whose being they themselves are?

In nature, differences in "colour, smell, and taste" did not cause contention because they were all nourished by one spirit, or the elements and soil where they grow. As evident to anyone contemplating the beautiful manuscript illuminations of letters in the *Frakturschriften* of Ephrata, members of the community appeared to follow Boehme in recognizing the variety and magnificence of nature as an emblem for spiritual unity underlying human language.[10]

For Boehme, linguistic and religious differences only caused contention and strife if one valued the outward manifestation more than the spiritual root. If different languages were joined in a common "root" (the ultimate, divine referent or signified), then different signifiers are all manifestations of a divine unity. In another natural analogy, Boehme linked the music of nature to the spiritual harmony possible among the multiplicity of God's "children":

> If we now dwell beside one another in Christ's Spirit as humble children and each one enjoy the other's gifts and knowledge, then who will judge us? Who judges the birds in the forest who praise the Lord of all being with many voices, each one out of its essence? Does God's Spirit punish them for not bringing their voices into harmony? Does not all their sound come from His power, and do they not play before Him?

Contemplating a natural world pervaded literally and metaphorically by the sounds, smells, and images of the Holy Spirit, mystics remained hopeful that human beings, too, could regain a glimpse of that spirit by penetrating the enduring links between divinely created systems such as star constellations, music, mathematics, and even language. As literary critic George Steiner remarked, Boehme saw a return to or at least an approximation of the lost Natursprache in " 'sensualistic speech' — the speech of instinctual, untutored immediacy, the language of Nature and of natural man as it was bestowed on the Apostles, themselves humble folk, at Pentecost. God's grammar sounds through echoing Nature, if only we will listen." In

---

10. Jacob Boehme, *The Way to Christ*, trans. Peter Erb (New York, 1978), 165. On Ephrata's Frakturschriften, see Cynda L. Benson, *Early American Illuminated Manuscripts from the Ephrata Cloister* (Northampton, Mass., 1994); Bach, *Voices*, 141–170.

Boehme's mystical concept of human language, therefore, not all was lost: the divine meanings and sounds of creation still pervaded human language, especially in singing.[11]

Kelpius came into close contact with English "Behemenists" of the Philadelphian Society who championed music as a conduit to the hidden, divine mysteries of the universe. One of the foremost proponents of music among the Philadelphians was Francis Lee, whose "New Theory of Musick" was published in the Society's own journal, *Theosophical Transactions*. Kelpius's manuscript journal included a small list of European contacts, which conspicuously listed Lee's name and residence. Even though Lee did not publish his theory on music until 1697, three years after Kelpius's sojourn in London, the two mystics undoubtedly used their acquaintance to exchange common notions on language and music. Lee's ideas encapsulated the very spirit and enthusiasm that motivated German mystical communities in Pennsylvania such as the Hermits and Ephrata to produce an outpouring of spiritual music. Fueled by Boehme and Lee's theories, Pennsylvania German hymnists such as Johannes Kelpius and Conrad Beissel as well as Moravian missionaries like David Zeisberger who translated hymnody for native Americans tried to harness the "True and natural Harmony" of the human voice in singing to attain, if not a "perfect" language, then an approximation of the spiritual language purportedly spoken in Eden. Singing would allow human beings to rediscover the original language, Boehme's Natursprache, which was replete with the hidden meanings of the universe. In dipping into this common pool of divine inspiration, singers would reverse the effects of Babel, especially if members of different linguistic and ethnic origins would join their voices.[12]

Imbibing the mystical notions on language and music promulgated by Boehme and other European mystics, radical Pietist communities in Pennsylvania also possessed tools that allowed them to wield linguistic diversity

11. Boehme, *The Way to Christ*, trans. Erb, 166; George Steiner, *After Babel: Aspects of Language and Translation*, 2d ed. (Oxford, 1992), 62.

12. On Kelpius's sojourn in London and contact with the Philadelphians, see Julius Friedrich Sachse, *The German Pietists of Provincial Pennsylvania, 1694–1708* (1895; rpt. New York, 1970), 15–16. The entry in Kelpius's journal mentioning Lee is "Mr. Francis Lee in Hoisdon Town over against the Land of Promise." Sachse's edition of Kelpius's "Journal," *The Diarium of Magister Johannes Kelpius*, does not include these entries. See Johannes Kelpius, "Journal," MS Am. 0880, HSP; Francis Lee "A New Theory of Musick," *Theosophical Transactions: Consisting of Memoirs, Conferences, Letters, Dissertations, Inquiries, etc. for the Advancement of Piety, and Divine Philosophy*, I, no. 1 (March 1697), 65.

in the province to further spiritual perfection. In other words, the multi-lingual society of Pennsylvania might not be a nuisance following from the confusion of languages at Babel; it could be an opportunity that, in the right hands, allowed the exploration of the unified spiritual origins from which all languages spread. The polyphonic setting of early Pennsylvania seemed to resemble Boehme's metaphor of the "birds in the forest who praise the Lord of all being with many voices, each one out of its essence." Countering the degenerative effects of the Keithian "Babel" on the spiritual advancement of the province, Kelpius and his followers at the Wissahickon united hymn singing with translation and bilingualism to find a common or new language of the spirit that would speak equally to all Pennsylvanians.

Arriving in Philadelphia in 1694, Johannes Kelpius and his forty-odd followers chose their residence in the wilderness of Pennsylvania—on Wissahickon Creek outside Philadelphia—for two main reasons: to await the Second Coming of Christ and to enjoy natural seclusion as a shield to protect the soul against the distractions of a carnal life, thus initiating the "secret" or "hidden" courtship of the heavenly bridegroom. Having emerged from the larger Pietist movement, Kelpius's group included several Lutheran theologians officially dismissed by the church for their unortho-dox teachings, including Johann Jakob Zimmermann (the initial leader of the group who died before the group departed for America), Johann Gotfried Seelig, and Heinrich Bernhard Köster. Pietist hymnody in general and Kelpius's hymns, in particular, expressed the soul's longing for a union with Jesus Christ (metaphorically represented as the Beloved of the Song of Songs or the heavenly bridegroom).[13]

13. The original group was forty members strong (and believed in the mystical significance of this number). For further background reading on Kelpius, the "Hermits of the Wissahickon" (as his group came to be known), and their peculiar theology, see Edythe L. Brooks, "A Re-evaluation of the Significance of Johannes Kelpius and the 'Woman of the Wilderness'" (master's thesis, University of South Florida, 1996); Elizabeth W. Fisher, "'Prophesies and Revelations': German Cabbalists in Early Pennsylvania," *Pennsylvania Magazine of History and Biography,* CIX (1985), 299–333; Klaus Deppermann, "Pennsylvanien als Asyl des frühen deutschen Pietismus," *Pietismus und Neuzeit,* X (1984), 190–226; Sachse, *German Pietists of Provincial Pennsylvania.* For further background reading on Rosicrucianism in seventeenth-century German and American thought, see Reiner Smolinski and Kathleen B. Freels, "'Chymical Wedding': Rosicrucian Alchemy and Eucharistic Conversion Process in Edward Taylor's Preparatory Meditations and in Early-Seventeenth-Century German Tracts," in Udo J. Hebel and Karl Ortseifen, eds., *Transatlantic Encounters: Studies in European-American Relations* (Trier, 1995), 40–61. For biographical information on Kelpius, see Claus Bernet, "Kelpius, Johann," *Biographisch-bibliographisches Kirchenlexikon,* XXIII (2004), columns 778–786, www.bautz.de/bbkl/k/kelpius_j.shtml. See also Karl Kurt Klein, *Magister Johannes Transylvanus, der Heilige und Dichter vom Wissahickon in Pennsylvanien* (Hermannstadt, Rumania, 1931); Ernest

The two primary physical and mental dispositions the Hermits tried to further in their community and within the self were constant watchfulness and the perfection of the soul into a virginal state pleasing to Christ. In his letters to sympathizers in North America and Europe, including members of the Philadelphian Society, Kelpius bemoaned his own lack of perfection, or, in other words, the discrepancy between his worldly self and the spiritual, virginal self completely prepared for a mystical union with God. In a letter to Swedish Lutheran pastor Eric Bjorck in Christiana, Delaware, Kelpius exclaimed:

> How happeneth it, my Kelpius! That unto thy God, so love-worthy, so rich, so liberal and in endless ways transcending thine every desire, in these least things, in temporal affairs, in perishable things, in foreign things, in external and transitory affairs (not to say eternal and spiritual), I say, in these thou hast not hitherto shewn the acme of perfection and scarcely shewest it even now?[14]

Calling his group the "Chapter of Perfection," Kelpius considered the continual weakening of his personal health as a sign of the erosion of his carnal nature and his transformation into a virginal, spiritual state. In an epigrammatic sentence, he concluded: "And so the virtue of the Almighty is perfected in mine infirmity." The spiritual pursuit of both individual and community, he recommended, must therefore be, not to serve church doctrines, but "Christ, in whom there lie hidden all treasures of wisdom and understanding, yea the entire plenitude of the Deity dwelleth corporally in Him." A mystic union with Christ would grant human nature a renewed unity with the divine wisdom that created and still pervaded the universe. Important here is Kelpius's choice of the word "plenitude": a fullness and continuity of divine wisdom that had left humanity in the dual falls of Eden and Babel. Remarkably, the pursuit of spiritual renewal seemed to provide the Hermits with a twofold impetus of inward spiritualization and an outward gathering of a true church awaiting the arrival of Christ. Both endeavors required the development of a new language that distanced itself from the effects of Babel. This new linguistic and spiritual makeup would not only change the community within but also would trigger — similar to the

---

Schell, "Hermit of the Wissahickon: Johannes Kelpius and the Chapter of Perfection," *American History Illustrated*, XVI (1981), 24–28, 48.

14. Sachse, ed., *Diarium of Kelpius*, 60. The copy of the letter in Kelpius's "Journal" is undated, but it was written before 1704 and was translated from the original Latin by Sachse.

Moravian Church—a missionary impulse to advance such renewal in the broader population.[15]

In his letter to Germany, Seelig reported the bilingual missionary activities of Heinrich Bernhard Köster, another member of the Hermits: "Every week, three gatherings take place in [Jacob Isaac's] house, where Küster *[sic]* speaks publicly for the great edification of many. He also holds a meeting once a week in Philadelphia, where he speaks in English." Köster's later embroilment in the Keithian controversy, of course, demonstrated the slippages between using multilingualism to achieve transnational harmony across denominational differences and a restaging of linguistic and spiritual confusion. Less comfortable with public appearances, Kelpius entertained a regular correspondence with English settlers throughout the colonies, including the Quaker minister Esther Palmer on Long Island. The multilingual skills and cosmopolitan attitude of the Kelpius group apparently attracted English newcomers such as the physician Christopher Witt, who joined the mystics in 1704. The so-called Hermits shared an evangelical spirit that was expressed in public preaching in German and English, public ceremonies at their worship building called "Tabernacle," and the teaching of children from surrounding communities.[16]

15. Ibid., 60, 62, 66.

16. [Johann Gotfried Seelig], *Copia eines Send-Schreibens auß der neuen Welt . . . Germandon in Pennsylvania Americae d. 7. Aug. 1694* ([Halle and Frankfurt?], 1695), 10. Witt (also know as De Witt or deWitt) was born in Wiltshire, England, in 1675, came to Pennsylvania in 1704, and joined the Hermits at the Wissahickon the same year. Witt had been trained as a physician in England and practiced medicine in Pennsylvania after the dissolution of the Hermits around Kelpius's death in 1708. Witt lived a long life in Germantown in a house furnished by Christian Warner and, later on, by Warner's son Christian. Witt apparently gained fame in Pennsylvania and beyond as a physician, clockmaker, organ builder, and cultivator and trader in medicinal herbs and plants as well as a botanist (Sachse, *German Pietists,* 403–418). As a botanist, Witt became an intimate acquaintance of John Bartram, whose correspondence with Peter Collinson in London frequently mentioned Witt's work. In a letter from Pennsylvania botanist William Young to John Stuart, third Earl of Bute, in Great Britain (dated May 15, 1765), Young provided one of the most glowing accounts of the recently deceased Witt: "And as Doctor De Witt was my special good friend, and who was in deed a very wonderful man. He was the most Ingenious and greatest botanist and Doctor in all north America, and for his Skillfulness and wonderful cures he performed was often called the father and Doctor of all Doctors in America[.] He had practiced physic in germanton 6 miles from philad. 60 years died lately was old 90 years. He has been always a very healthy man was never married. A Separatist was his Religion, and by his particularly godly life and exemplary behalf [behavior?] was beloved by all. When he was 83 years old I did see him ride on his horse like a young man, when he went into the woods to the mountains for seeking plants. And when he was 85 visited me for the last time in my house and as he was well known in great britain, and a certain plant is called after his name in the catalicum or Description of plants viz. Dr. Witt's Snake root" (Society Miscellaneous Collection, HSP). Also see David S. Shields, ed.,

Among the Hermits, the primary medium for regaining knowledge of the harmony and wisdom of God was hymnody. Kelpius and his followers deployed hymn singing—in the words of Francis Lee—as an outward manifestation of the "Harmony of the Divine Powers and Properties in the nature of God," who exists "in infinite variety and multiplicity, all in perfect Concord and Unity." On one level, the Hermits gathered the many voices pointing toward a common spiritual foundation by compiling existing hymns by mystical German composers and poets including Angelus Silesius, Christian Knorr von Rosenroth, and Philipp Niccolai. On another level, the Hermits sought spiritual harmony in linking the two major European languages spoken within the community and in Pennsylvania at large—English and German.[17]

Multilingual hymnody among Kelpius and his followers did not merely satisfy the needs of a bilingual community. Hymns written and sung in multiple languages also represented the mystical notion of a multiplicity always hinting at an ultimate, hidden spiritual unity. Thus, in writing, reading, and singing hymns in different languages, the Hermits tried to sharpen and tune their senses beyond what was visible on the page or audible to human hearing, hoping to perceive a language and a sound resonating somewhere in the registers of divine fullness. In describing the transformation of human properties and senses into a being more perceptive of and pleasing to God, Kelpius frequently deployed the scriptural metaphor of the "turtledove," whose diminutive, mournful wooing stood in opposition to man's carnal desire or self-will:

> But as regards the actual state of a soul in the wilderness, I cannot at present describe. If She, dear soul! become rightly participant of the

American Poetry: The Seventeenth and Eighteenth Centuries (New York, 2007), 878. Shields also includes selections from the bilingual hymn book, "Die klägliche Stimme der verborgenen Liebe / The Lamenting Voice of the Hidden Love" (284–298), discussed below.

17. Lee, "A New Theory of Musick," *Theosophical Transactions,* I, no. 1 (March 1697), 60–65. For background on Pietist hymnists and hymnody, see Friedrich Blume, *Geschichte der Evangelischen Kirchenmusik* (Kassel, 1965), 186–250; Christian Bunners, "Gesangbuch," 121–142, and Bunners, "Musik," 428–455, both in Hartmut Lehmann, ed., *Glaubenswelt und Lebenswelten,* vol. IV of *Geschichte des Pietismus* (Göttingen, 2004); Wolfgang Miersemann, "Auf dem Wege zu einer Hochburg 'geist-reichen' Gesangs: Halle und die Ansätze einer pietistischen Liedkultur im Deutschland des ausgehenden 17. Jahrhunderts," in Gudrun Busch und Wolfgang Miersemann, eds., *"Geist-reicher" Gesang: Halle und das pietistische Lied,* Hallesche Forschungen, III (Tübingen, 1997), 11–80; Miersemann, ed., *Johann Anastasius Freylinghausen (1670 Gandersheim-1739 Halle): Lebens-Lauf eines pietistischen Theologen und Gesangbuchherausgebers* (Halle, 2004).

dove-kind, she will, as aforesaid, also obtain eagle's wings to fly there-into. Then will she *experience,* what it be, to chatter (coo) as a lonely turtle-dove, day and night for the longed for loved one, how, mean-while, the loved one feed her with the hidden manna, Apoc. 2, 7. . . . How He will teach her to know the hidden God and Saviour.

The dove embodied characteristics that could not be completely described. The insufficiency of language to grasp and express the fullness of the hid-den meanings lead to the reliance on a nonhuman language—the dove's "chatter" or cooing—as a more appropriate medium for approaching God, or the Beloved.[18]

Kelpius and Witt compiled, composed, and translated a bilingual manu-script hymnal that proclaimed the group's mystical longings for Christ as the "loving moan" of a "disconsolate soul" secluded in a literal and spiri-tual wilderness. Reflecting the group's eremitism, the volume was entitled "Die klägliche Stimme der verborgenen Liebe / The Lamenting Voice of the Hidden Love." The volume's most notable quality was its dialogic design, with the German hymns on the left and the English translations on the right (Figure 8). This design mirrored the bilingual composition of the Kel-pius group and its translingual pursuit of spiritual perfection. Spiritually, it epitomized the union arising from the joining of seemingly dissonant or disunited voices. Not only do the German and English hymn texts differ linguistically, but the obvious discrepancy between German and English scripts appears to disunite visually what the writers and composers tried to bring together on corresponding pages of the same hymnal. In a mystical fashion, the volume displayed "hidden" clues that signified how the multi-plicity of languages was linked to a single spiritual language sought after by the hymns and their singers.[19]

Scholars have generally credited Christopher Witt, the most educated English member of the group, with the English translation. The manuscript

18. Sachse, ed., *Diarium of Kelpius,* 75.

19. Johannes Kelpius, "The Hymn Book of Magister Johannes Kelpius," trans. Christopher Witt, *Church Music and Musical Life in Pennsylvania in the Eighteenth Century,* Publications of the Penn-sylvania Society of the Colonial Dames of America, IV (Philadelphia, 1926), I, 19–165 (facsimile re-production of the manuscript). For the original manuscript, see Johannes Kelpius, "Die klägliche Stimme der verborgenen Liebe / The Lamenting Voice of the Hidden Love," [trans. Christopher Witt] (HSP catalogue: "Hymnal; Collection of Songs, Chiefly Composed and All Arranged by John Kel-pius; Copied German and English; English by Dr. De Witt"), MS Ac 189, HSP. For a musicological perspective, see Albert G. Hess, "Observations on *The Lamenting Voice of the Hidden Love," Journal of the American Musicological Society,* LIII (1952), 211–223 (esp. 212).

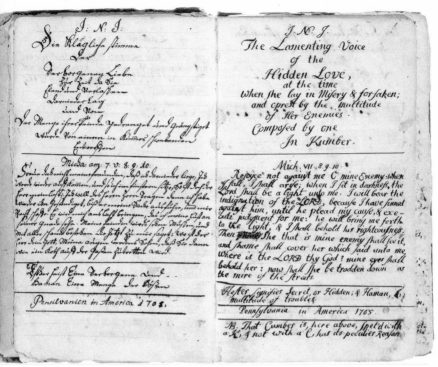

Figure 8. Title Page from Johannes Kelpius, "Die klägliche Stimme der verborgenen Liebe/The Lamenting Voice of the Hidden Love," [trans. Christopher Witt], MS Ac 189, Historical Society of Pennsylvania, Philadelphia. By permission of The Historical Society of Pennsylvania (HSP)

itself, however, does not contain any explicit reference corroborating this assumption. Although Kelpius did not sign the hymnal, the manuscript provides a definite clue to his authorship. A footnote inserted only in the English version states "That Cumber," an archaic word for distress, "is, here above, spel'd with a K and not with a C, has its peculiar Reason." The first letters of "In Kumber," of course, hint at the initials of Johannes Kelpius (with the "J" Latinized as "I") and thus identify the author in a mystical manner. The insertion of this reference to the author *exclusively* in the English version supports the assumption that the composers of the German and English hymn texts were not the same person. By creating a connection between English translation and German original, the hymnal hinted at a deeper, spiritual interpenetration of both. In placing a hidden significance on individual letters, the hymnal also harked back to Boehme's observations and speculations on the spiritual meanings and sounds of letters in

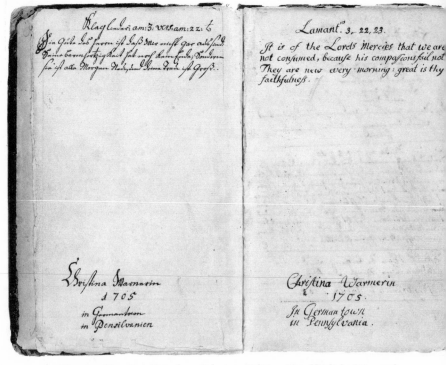

Figure 9. Signature Page from Johannes Kelpius, "Die klägliche Stimme der verborgenen Liebe / The Lamenting Voice of the Hidden Love," [trans. Christopher Witt], MS Ac 189, Historical Society of Pennsylvania, Philadelphia. By permission of The Historical Society of Pennsylvania (HSP)

the Natursprache. Dominating the entire page are the letters "I.N.I." or "Im Namen Jesu / In the Name of Jesus," signifying the godhead that subsumes all mystical knowledge. Notably, the letters referring to the name of Jesus are the same in both German and English, thus corroborating the belief that words and letters referring to God are the same in all languages.[20]

The play on mystical connections between expressions of multiplicity was also continued by the scribe who copied "Die klägliche Stimme / The Lamenting Voice." Though composed by Kelpius and most likely translated by Witt, the hymns in this volume were probably compiled from earlier drafts by Christina Warner and transcribed by her into the extant volume (Figure 9). Christina Warner and her husband Christian were associated with the celibate Hermits but lived in nearby Germantown. During his

20. Kelpius, "Lamenting Voice," [trans. Witt], MS Ac 189, ii, HSP.

frequent illnesses, Kelpius often recovered in the Warner household. On a page preceding the title page, Warner signed both the German and the English versions with her name, date, and place. Warner's signature lines, complete with the difference in spelling "Pennsylvania" in German and English, thus relate the different languages and scripts to the hidden or mystic unity signified by the entire volume. Ultimately, Warner's dual act of linguistic translation (into a different language and into a different script) symbolized the entire group's multilingual pursuit of a single spiritual goal.[21]

The most apparent and most potent device accomplishing the mystical union of different languages in "Die klägliche Stimme / The Lamenting Voice" was the hymn tunes, which physically span the left and right sides of the manuscript volume, thus crossing or bridging linguistic differences (Figure 10). This arching of both linguistic versions underscored the translingual quality of music and epitomized the desire for spiritual unity through multilingual cooperation. The hymn score accomplished visually, musically, and spiritually the uniting of human language with divine sounds that provided the link between words and things in Boehme's Natursprache. The knowledge Kelpius and his associates were seeking in the wilderness lay hidden beneath the German and English language as well as the system of notes representing divine harmony.

Finally, the German and English hymns in this volume are united by the Christocentrism of the Hermits and their constant pursuit of the soul's union with the heavenly bridegroom. The following hymn demonstrates the translingual emphasis on Christ in this hymnal. Here, the speaker assumed the characteristically submissive stance of the soul longing for the arrival of the bridegroom and desiring the consummation of their spiritual union. The hymn is entitled "Ein verliebtes Girren der trostlosen Seele in der Morgen Demmerung / A Loving Moan of the Disconsolate Soul in the Morning Dawn." The hymn has a strongly autobiographical dimension, as Kelpius wrote it as he "lay in Christian Warners House very weak, in a small bed, not unlike a Coffin, in May 1706." This personal situation explains much of the deathbed imagery in the hymn. In a religious paradox, however, Kelpius equated this near-death experience with an approach to the spiritual marriage with Christ. The physical weakness of the earthly body, in other words, beckoned the spiritual (as well as erotic) fulfillment of the soul's union with Christ:

21. Ibid., i. Christina (also known as "Christiana") signed her last name with the now obsolete German "-in" suffix signifying a married woman, both in the German and the English version.

Figure 10. Musical Score from Johannes Kelpius, "Die klägliche Stimme der verborgenen Liebe / The Lamenting Voice of the Hidden Love," [trans. Christopher Witt], MS Ac 189, Historical Society of Pennsylvania, Philadelphia. By permission of The Historical Society of Pennsylvania (HSP)

Die Seele begehret
    die früchte der Eh
doch da sie Sich kehret
    zu frühe zur höh'
Entweichet der bräutigam und läst sie allein
Sie wünschet Vollkommen Gelassen Zu sein
So findet man endlich das Seelige ein.

The Soul does desire
    To have nuptial fruit
But as she rose hier
    To soon in pursute,
The Bridgroom slipt from her, and left her alone
She wish's to be perfect Resigned, in moan,
So finds she then lastly that most blessed one.

The soul's sudden longing for the union with the bridegroom allows it to rise from its misery and, ironically, prevents the "nuptial fruit." Only when the soul entirely resigns herself to her weakness can she accomplish the desired union.[22]

Other extant manuscript hymnals also signal an investment in the translation and multilingual dissemination of Kelpius's hymns in early Pennsylvania. The identical handwriting in Kelpius's journal and in the hymnal "The Voice of the Thirsty-Ones or Some Songs of Sion" reveals that he wrote — and most likely translated — this volume himself. Kelpius apparently prepared the manuscript for Henry Batcock (usually Babcock), a Philadelphia brewer and member of the Philadelphia Yearly Meeting of Friends. In spite of doctrinal differences between the Quakers and the Hermits, Kelpius cultivated an intensive exchange in spiritual matters with Friends in Pennsylvania and other American colonies. "The Voice of the Thirsty Ones" contains English translations of hymns original with the Kelpius group as well as traditional German hymns. Another manuscript volume, containing hymns in either English or German, is entitled "The Hymnal of the Pietists of the Wissahickon." It was compiled by an individual named Benjamin Lehman, who autographed the volume in 1700. Lehman apparently copied this hymnal from other manuscripts written by the Hermits themselves, such as "The Lamenting Voice" and a monolingual German hymnal entitled "The Hermits of the Wissahickon," since it contains several hymns appearing in one or the other. Finally, an untitled manuscript containing hymns in English and German is today located in the Schwenkfelder Library in Pennsylvania. The anonymous scribe claims to have copied the hymns from the handwriting of Johannes Kelpius in June 1755. The date of the transcription not only demonstrates the continued circulation of manuscript hymnals associated with the Hermits throughout colonial Pennsylvania but also connects the hymnody of the Hermits chronologically to the most prolific period of singing and hymn writing at Ephrata in the mid-eighteenth century. The association of the hymnal with the Schwenkfelder community indicates that Kelpius's hymns also influenced the rich hymn tradition of this radical Pietist group from Germany.[23]

---

22. Kelpius, "Lamenting Voice," [trans. Witt], 57, HSP.

23. Johannes Kelpius, "The Voice of the Thirsty-Ones or Some Songs of Sion Speaking of Its Instant Introduction and Appearance among the Nations, after So Many Troublesome Days of Israel Caused by the Hard Gouvernements and Smoaky Influences of Sanai, Translated for the Most Part Out of the High German-Tongue for Henry Batcock [or Babcock] Anno 1695–1703," Bassler Collection, Franklin and Marshall College, Lancaster, Pa.; Johannes Kelpius and Benjamin Lehman, "The

The first time any of Kelpius's hymns appeared in print was in a collection printed by the Germantown printer Peter Leibert in 1788. The title page announces the addition of "several, never before printed, and very edifying hymns by Joh. Kelpius, who already passed away 80 years ago in his blessed savior." Further, the edition claims to have been compiled "upon the request of many admirers." Peter Leibert also appended two hymns by Kelpius to an 1800 edition of a canonical Pietist tract, the *Glaubens-Bekänntniss* by Ernst Christoph Hochmann von Hochenau. The inclusion of Kelpius's hymns in a German tract published in 1800 bespeaks the persistent cultural currency of his hymns well into the early national period. The continued influence of these hymns, however, did not rely on print dissemination but rather on the vibrant circulation of literary and religious writings in manuscript and, thus, on a widespread interest in German hymn traditions throughout the colonial period.[24]

In fact, Kelpius and his followers introduced German hymnody to Pennsylvania before it became widely known in England. The introduction of German hymns to England coincided with the efflorescence of English hymnody itself, commonly associated with the first publication of Isaac Watt's hymns in 1706. In 1708, an anonymous edition of translated German hymns appeared as *Lyra Davidica; or, A Collection of Divine Songs and Hymns, Partly New Composed, Partly Translated from the High German and Latin Hymns,* which included such Pietist favorites as Philipp Nicolai's "Wie schön leuchtet der Morgenstern" ("How Fairly Shines the Morning Star") and "Wachet auf, ruft uns die Stimme" ("Awake, the Voice Is Crying"). The latter hymn was the favorite hymn of Philipp Jakob Spener, the patriarch of Pietism in Germany. After the 1708 appearance of *Lyra Davidica,* German hymnody did not gain true currency in England until Johann Christian Jacobi's publication of *Psalmodia Germanica* in 1722. Jacobi, keeper of the Royal German Chapel at the court of the Hanoverian

Hymnal of the Pietists of the Wissahickon," Borneman Collection, MS 1, Rare Book Department, The Free Library of Philadelphia; Johannes Kelpius, Schwenkfelder MS, VS 13-13, Schwenkfelder Library, Pennsburg, Pa.

24. Peter Leibert, ed., *Etliche liebliche und erbaulichen Lieder . . . nebst etliche noch niemal im Druck erschienene sehr erbaulichen Liedern, von Joh. Kelpius . . . auf Begehren etlicher Liebhaber, und in Hoffnung der Erbauung gedruckt, und heraus gegeben, von Peter Leibert; Germantaun Gedruckt* (Germantown, Pa., 1788), 1; Ernst Christoph Hochmann von Hochenau, *Ernst Christoph Hochmanns von Hochenau Glaubens-Bekänntniss . . .* (Germantown, Pa., 1800), "Anhang zweyer Lieder, von Johannes Kelpius," 45-48.

king George I, enlarged and reissued this volume several times during the next decades. The first American edition appeared in New York in 1756.[25]

By this time, Kelpius and his followers had already established their vibrant tradition of hymn singing in the American colonies and triggered or encouraged other religious communities — such as the Swedish Lutheran community at Wicacoa — to practice congregational singing. In fact, Conrad Beissel was originally inspired to come to Pennsylvania by news of Kelpius's community and experiments in hymnody; Beissel's hymnody as well as Ephrata Fraktur writing (a type of manuscript calligraphy) centrally incorporated the trope and image of the turtledove wooing the heavenly bridegroom from its hidden perch in the wilderness. Subsequent waves of German immigration — consisting increasingly of members of the orthodox Lutheran and Reformed faith — further spread Pietist hymnody in Pennsylvania, Virginia, and other colonies with strong German communities. Count Nikolaus Ludwig von Zinzendorf, leader of the Moravians, moreover, contributed many original hymns to the efflorescence of hymnody in America and garnered the admiration of Charles Wesley. These later developments seem like well-established facts today; yet Kelpius's contributions remain shrouded in obscurity.[26]

A brief look at Kelpius's efforts of disseminating traditional German hymnody — such as the hymns of Philipp Nicolai — in English translation already provides a sense of the crucial cultural and aesthetic agency of Kelpius's manuscript hymnals. Nicolai's most well-known hymns — "Wie schön leuchtet der Morgenstern" and "Wachet Auf" — first appeared in

25. Garold N. Davis, *German Thought and Culture in England, 1700–1770: A Preliminary Survey Including a Chronological Bibliography of German Literature in English Translation* (Chapel Hill, N.C., 1969), 17; *Lyra Davidica; or, A Collection of Divine Songs and Hymns, Partly New Composed, Partly Translated from the High-German, and Latin Hymns; and Set to Easy and Pleasant Tunes, for More General Use; the Musick Engrav'd on Copper Plates* (London, 1708), esp. 40, 73.

26. On the spread of Pietist hymnody among orthodox Lutheran and Reformed immigrants in America, see A. Gregg Roeber, "Lutheran Hymnody and Networks in the Eighteenth Century," in Philip V. Bohlman and Otto Holzapfel, eds., *Land without Nightingales: Music in the Making of German-America* (Madison, Wis., 2002). For the orthodox Pietist influence in North America beyond the sectarian, radical Pietist groups discussed here, see Aaron Spencer Fogleman, "Hallische Pietisten und Herrnhuter in Nordamerika," *Pietismus und Neuzeit,* XXIX (2003), 148–178; A. Gregg Roeber, "The Migration of the Pious: Methodists, Pietists, and the Antinomian Character of North American Religious History," in Hermann Wellenreuther and Norbert Finzsch, eds., *Visions of the Future in Germany and America* (Oxford, 2001), 25–47; Roeber, "Der Pietismus in Nordamerika im 18. Jahrhundert," in Martin Brecht and Klaus Deppermann, eds., *Der Pietismus im achtzehnten Jahrhundert,* vol. II of *Geschichte des Pietismus* (Göttingen, 1995), 666–699.

Germany in 1599. Both hymns espouse the theme of the soul's courtship with the heavenly bridegroom (see Rev. 19:7, 21:2–9, 22:17; Eph. 5:22–24) and spiritual marriage with Jesus Christ, which soon made them favorites with mystically inclined Pietists in Germany. Not surprisingly, both hymns feature prominently in Kelpius's manuscript hymnals. Kelpius's English translation of these hymns reveals the interest of English residents in German hymnody and the role of the Kelpius group in facilitating this interest. The aforementioned hymnal "The Voice of the Thirsty-Ones" includes translations—in Kelpius's handwriting—of both hymns by Nicolai. Kelpius translated "Wachet auf" as "Awake! Resounds the Voice" and "Wie schön leuchtet der Morgenstern" as "How Brightly Shines the Morning Star." The latter seems to have been the more popular of the two hymns, since the English translation was also included in the volume "The Hymnal of the Pietists of the Wissahickon" and the later "Schwenkfelder Manuscript." Both translations, except for some obvious transcription errors, exactly match the translations in "The Voice of the Thirsty-Ones." An inspection of the rhythmic quality and refined imagery of the English translations underscores the absurdity of any attempt to exclude them from literary and cultural investigations and champion the German originals. A comparison of Kelpius's translation of "Wie schön leuchtet der Morgenstern" as "How Brightly Shines the Morning Star" with Jacobi's translation as "How Bright Appears the Morning Star" in *Psalmodia Germanica* furthermore reveals significant discrepancies between the two. Therefore, Kelpius and Jacobi did not work from a common source translation, and the Kelpius manuscript is not a later transcription of the translation in *Psalmodia Germanica*. The Kelpius translation, in other words, already circulated in Pennsylvania before Jacobi's version was published in London. Cultural transmission, in this case, did not proceed primarily from the English imperial metropolis to its North American colonies, but rather through multinational and multilingual European immigration to Pennsylvania and the adaptation of religious and aesthetic traditions to the cultural and social conditions in the New World.[27]

27. Philipp Nicolai, "Awake! Resounds the Voice," 43–44, and Nicolai, "How Brightly Shines the Morning Star," 9–10, both in Kelpius, "The Voice of the Thirsty-Ones," Bassler Collection; Nicolai, "How Bright Appears the Morning Star," in Johann Christian Jacobi, trans. and ed., *Psalmodia Germanica; or, A Specimen of Divine Hymns, Translated from the High Dutch; Together with Their Proper Tunes and Thorough Bass* (London, 1722), 90–92.

Kelpius's letter book (bound with his journal) demonstrates his wide-ranging circle of German and English correspondents. For instance, Kelpius communicated with the Quaker minister Esther (or Hester) Palmer in Flushing, Long Island. The single extant letter to Palmer hints toward a personal meeting between Kelpius and Palmer as well as a more extensive correspondence. In the letter, Kelpius explained what he calls the "threefold wilderness states." Following the flight of the woman into the wilderness described in Revelation 12, the church as well as each individual believer had to follow this desertion of the carnal world. The actual wilderness of Pennsylvania was the physical environment best suited for the spiritual withdrawal from the world and the pursuit of mystical perfection. Each "wilderness state" represented a step in the approach toward a perfect union with God. The movement from the first, the "Barren Wilderness," to the second, or "Fruitfull Wilderness," could be accomplished by human beings who strove to dedicate themselves to spiritual perfection. The third, or "wilderness of the elect of God," however, could only be reached by the chosen few.[28]

Though written in a letter to a Quaker preacher, Kelpius's three-tiered process established a theological dictum conflicting with the doctrines of the Society of Friends. Kelpius criticized the supposed self-delusion of gaining access to divine communications without a gradual preparation and approach to the mystery of God as well:

And what a great presumption it is . . . to go forth without being thus duly prepared beforehand. For though such many have inspirations, Revelations, Motions and the like Extraordinary Favours . . . yet they will effect and build nothing, but only . . . destroy. . . . Yea, there is no small Danger of loosing themselves and to bruise and grind that good seed, which was not designed for Meat but for increase, not for to be sent forth but to be kept in an honest and Good Heart.

It is unclear whether Kelpius implied that Hester Palmer was not spiritually ready to spread God's word and first needed to work—in seclusion—on approaching a spiritual union. Kelpius himself championed eremitism and a mystical pursuit of divine knowledge. Nevertheless, the letter seems to have struck a nerve among American Quakers, for it continued to circulate

28. For detailed information on Esther Palmer (married name "Champion"), see Rebecca Larson, *Daughters of Light: Quaker Women Preaching and Prophesying in the Colonies and Abroad, 1700–1775* (Chapel Hill, N.C., 1999), 9–11, 115–118.

in manuscript and was finally published in a collection of Quaker writings in 1886.[29]

The letter appeared in a commonplace book Anthony Benezet gave to Ann Emlen, who later became the wife of Warner Mifflin of Philadelphia. Benezet began the transcription of Kelpius's letter, but Ann Emlen completed the work. Here, Kelpius's letter was in the company of a transcription of "The Foregoing Account of the Life of Elizabeth Ashbridge" as well as the journal of Margaret Ellis. Apparently, Kelpius had entered the realm of instructional writings circulated among elite Friends throughout the colonial and early national periods. Emlen's commonplace book containing the works by Ashbridge, Ellis, and Kelpius was finally published in a single volume in Philadelphia in 1886, entitled *The Life of Elizabeth Ashbridge, Wife of Aaron Ashbridge, of Goshen, Chester County, Pa.* The title does not mention Kelpius's letter; his communication with the late-seventeenth-century Quaker minister Esther Palmer was thoroughly assimilated into the corpus of Quaker devotional writings.[30]

The seamless incorporation of Kelpius's letter in one of the most popular Quaker autobiographies, *The Life of Elizabeth Ashbridge,* at least symbolically erased the divisions created by the Keithian schism. When Kelpius's associate Johann Gotfried Seelig wrote about the state of Quakerism in Pennsylvania, he claimed that he and his religious associates could convert the scattered Friends back to a more orthodox faith. Yet the multilingual representation of the group's religious thoughts contributed to a common spiritual idiom that was spoken, adopted, and spread by Quakers and German Pietists alike. The bridging of linguistic differences on the pages of Kelpius's hymnals and their dissemination through intersecting modes of publication (manuscript and print) counteracted the acerbic literalism in the doctrinal debates of both Europe and Pennsylvania. The mystical voice of the "Hidden Love" echoing through the Pennsylvania wilderness shifted attention away from the letter and back to the spirit of the word.

29. Sachse, ed., *Diarium of Kelpius,* 94.

30. *The Life of Elizabeth Ashbridge: Wife of Aaron Ashbridge, of Goshen, Chester County, Pa. . . .* (Philadelphia, 1886). The original manuscript book by Emlen could not be located; however, the 1886 publication describes in detail the features of the manuscript, such as Benezet's dedication to Emlen, "Anthony Benezet to his friend Ann Emlen, 1784" (in the hand of Anthony Benezet), and Emlen's note, "This Present is gratefully received 4th mo. 30th, 1784, it being on my birth Day, and 3 days before his Decease.—A. Emlen, Jr" (30).

On the Cocalico: Ephrata, or the Camp of the Solitary

Though a product of the late-seventeenth-century Pietist movement emerging from within the Lutheran and Reformed faiths under the leadership of Philipp Jakob Spener and August Hermann Francke, Beissel and other members of the so-called Ephrata cloister—like Kelpius's Hermits before them—took a more radical route in keeping with the teachings of Jacob Boehme and his early-eighteenth-century publisher Johann Georg Gichtel. Building a monastic communal settlement on the Cocalico Creek in Lancaster County in the early 1730s, Beissel and his followers adopted Boehme's worship of the virgin Sophia, the supposedly female aspect of God, which had once been wedded to Adam and had become disunited with mankind and God during the fall. All human beings—but men in particular—had to overcome their supposedly male self-will and attempt to reunite with the virgin Sophia or divine wisdom. The path to this mystical reunion at Ephrata led through a variety of activities aimed at self-denial: the adoption of a monastic way of life and dress, self-mortification (including celibacy and denying oneself food, drink, and sleep), continuous hard work, the establishment of rigorous singing schools designed to purify the human voice, the practice of Fraktur writing, and, beginning in the mid-1740s, the operation of a printing press that incorporated the production of paper, ink, and type. Though complemented and induced by such outward forms, suffering and martyrdom at Ephrata were understood as evidence of an internalized and spiritualized struggle with the anti-Christ in every individual.[31]

Whereas Kelpius's ability to approach the heavenly bridegroom in a state of heightened spiritual awareness was precipitated by his physical infirmities, Conrad Beissel—the spiritual leader of the Ephrata community, hymn writer, and head of the community's famous singing school—actively

31. Bach, *Voices,* 33–35. For the role of music, especially hymnody, at Ephrata, see Lucy Ellen Carroll, "Three Centuries of Song: Pennsylvania's Choral Composers, 1681 to 1981" (D.M.A. diss., Coombs College of Music, 1982); Betty Jean Martin, "The Ephrata Cloister and Its Music, 1732–1785: The Cultural, Religious, and Bibliographical Background" (Ph.D. diss., University of Maryland, 1974); Martin, "Johannes Kelpius and Johann Gottfried Seelig"; Julius Friedrich Sachse, *The German Sectarians of Pennsylvania, 1742–1800: A Critical and Legendary History of the Ephrata Cloister and the Dunkers* (New York, 1971); Julius Friedrich Sachse, *The Music of the Ephrata Cloister, Also Conrad Beissel's Treatise on Music as Set Forth in a Preface to the "Turtel Taube" of 1747, Amplified with Fac-Simile Reproductions of Parts of the Text and Some Original Ephrata Music of the Weyrauchs Hügel, 1739; Rosen und Lilien, 1745; Turtel Taube, 1747; Choral Buch, 1745, etc.* (New York, 1971); David W. Stowe, *How Sweet the Sound: Music in the Spiritual Lives of Americans* (Cambridge, Mass., 2004), 220–247; Stryz, "Alchemy," *Esoterica,* I (1999), 133–159.

ensured that his singers approached God in a humble and purified state. According to the *Chronicon Ephratense,* the community's chronicle and largely a product of Peter Miller's pen, "the Superintendent conducted the [singing] school with great sternness, so that whoever did not know him, might have thought him to be a man of unchecked passions. At times he scolded for one or two hours in succession." Along with Beissel's prescriptions regarding the diet of his singers, such active humiliation was meant to erode all personal or individual features that would obstruct the decidedly communal enterprise of giving expression to a mystical desire for a union with God. In his paradigmatic preface to one of Ephrata's hymnals, *Das Gesäng der einsamen und verlassenen Turtel-Taube* (The songs of the lonesome and deserted turtle-dove [1747]), Beissel wrote:

Thus the community has taken possession of us and has taken away all of our jewels, ornaments, riches, and beauties; yes, it has even placed us in mental poverty and nakedness, in which alone the praise of God may be brought forth. . . . On the contrary, as much as we carry creatural comforts in our heart, we lose the community, the spirit of singing, for the pure dove withdraws, and the praise of God is no longer heard. Thus, the practice of community is important beyond all measure.

Beissel turned the call for a communal search for a spiritual language implicit in Kelpius's bilingual hymnal into an explicit prescription. But community among the Ephrata singers did not merely serve to enforce a spiritual stripping of the individual of all worldly attachments and thus a prepping of voice and soul for what Beissel called the "angelic art of singing."[32]

---

32. [Gast and Miller], *Chronicon Ephratense,* trans. Hark, 162; *Chronicon Ephratense; enthaltend den Lebens-Lauf des ehrwürdigen Vaters in Christo Friedsam Gottrecht, Weyland Stiffters und Vorstehers des geistl. Ordens der Einsamen in Ephrata in der Graffschaft Lancaster in Pennsylvania; zusammen getragen von Br. Lamech u. Agrippa* (Ephrata, Pa., 1786); [Conrad Beissel], *Das Gesäng der einsamen und verlassenen Turtel-Taube nemlich der christlichen Kirche . . .* (Ephrata, Pa., 1747), iii ("Also hat die Gemeinschafft sich unserer bemächtigt und uns allen Schmuck, Zierrath, Reichthum und Schönheit benommen, mithin uns in die Geistliche Armuth und Entblösung gesetzt, worinnen allein das Lob Gottes ausgebohren wird. . . . Und im Gegentheil so viel als der Trost der Creaturen noch wird zu Hertzen genommen, so viel verlieret man die Gemeinschafft, der Geist des Singens, als die reine Taube entziehet sich, und das Lob Gottes wird nicht mehr gehöret. Darum ist es eine über alle massen wichtige Sache, stets Gemeinschafft zu pflegen"). The German term "englische Sing-Kunst" refers to angelic, not Anglophone, singing. One of Ephrata's most vocal critics and erstwhile "Brother," Ezechiel Sangmeister, interpreted singing in the community exclusively as a policing tool that allowed Beissel to squelch all opposition to his authority. In the autobiographical *Das Leben*

Explaining not only the art of singing at Ephrata but also the flourishing of translation at the cloister, Beissel championed community as the locus of the mystical paradox of unity from multiplicity. The submission of individuals to the community was necessary, Beissel explained, if a "well-established harmony and concord of all minds shall be brought forth." On this journey, Beissel traveled on a road virtually paved with Boehme's words and metaphors. Beissel thus described the collection of hymns in the *Turtel-Taube* in terms directly reminiscent of Boehme's similes comparing the multiplicity of human languages and voices to the unity of spirit in nature:

> We must consider this collection of spiritual poems and songs as roses that have grown forth from among the coarse thorns of the cross and which are, therefore, not without a pleasing color and scent. . . . To note something else of this collection of spiritual labor, the same *is* a spiritual field of flowers, in which flowers of various colors and scent have grown forth, *just as the same* [the collection] has been wrought from the mystery of God through the spirit of the community.

Collective singing produced a mutually reinforcing or even dialectical opening of divine mysteries and a musical invitation to divine knowledge. Ephrata's angelic voices would either attempt to regain the Adamic language or a new language of the spirit that would restore the plenitude of divine wisdom within humankind: "The matter of which we speak, is the holy dove, which has . . . unsealed the gates of the secret and hidden wisdom and has come forth to us [and] opened us a glimpse of the secret of Paradise, while enticing us to a holy eagerness to be occupied with such things as will occur in that other world." In Europe, Beissel argued, "the Babel church has lost the third witness from heaven, the holy ghost, who unifies all language." Singing at Ephrata would transform the language of the community, for the time being, into an approximation or anticipation of the spiritual plenitude between human language and divine creation purportedly

---

und Wandel des in Gott ruhenten und seligen Br. Ezechiel Sangmeisters; Weiland ein Einwohner von Ephrata . . . , 3 vols. (Ephrata, Pa., 1825–1827), Sangmeister wrote: "[Beissel's] foremost motive was to bring the souls that much closer and under him through this school, for generally he made the souls believe that his quarrels and squabbles, which were often more tyrannical than Christian, were divine trials and passions for them, which then was also generally believed. If someone spoke a word against it, it was as if he had committed a sin against the Holy Spirit which was unforgivable. It was alleged that this singing was the very one which the angels sang at the coming of Christ and whoever did not learn it in this world, he would have to learn it in eternity" (*Life and Conduct of the Late Brother Ezechiel Sangmeister . . . ,* trans. Barbara M. Schindler [Ephrata, Pa., 1986], 72).

found in the Adamic language. The community at Ephrata thus prepared for the end of time, when the Holy Spirit would gather the true church that "speaks the unified mother tongue." Beissel thus imagined hymn singing — and the broader reformation of language at Ephrata — explicitly as an instrument for reversing the heritage at Babel. The voices of the Ephrata hymn singers were inviting the spirit to reenter and unify all human language.[33]

Whereas Kelpius's Hermits had used their hymnals to wed musical harmony with the unison of different languages, Ephrata hymns — maybe predictably — remained untranslated. After all, the above-quoted passage already links the spirit of singing in the community intimately to the spirit of the divine; any further translation would have seemed redundant or even a distraction from an already purified language. Hubris or not, Beissel claimed that singing at Ephrata was already translating human speech into a new language similar to the voices of the angels. Yet actual linguistic translation still took on a prominent place within the spiritual economy of Ephrata. Ephrata residents used the monumental translation of the Mennonite *Martyrs' Mirror* to produce a state of spiritual martyrdom while pursuing an evangelical outreach to a broader community (see Chapter 6).[34]

In addition to a wealth of hymn compositions, the Ephrata community created a rich archive of Fraktur or Frakturschriften — writings in broken, or "fractured," Gothic letters — that they illustrated or illuminated with elaborate nature motifs. Most of Ephrata's Frakturschriften were illustrations of the musical score composed by Beissel and copied by the hands of the Sisters employed in the writing school. Whereas Fraktur in early modern Germany referred primarily to a specific style of printed letters, Pennsylvania German Frakturschriften are predominantly manuscript calligraphy illuminated with abstract, stylized, or representational images. Some of

33. [Beissel], *Das Gesäng der einsamen und verlassenen Turtel-Taube*, iii and unpaginated section: "Der Himmel, der sich schon vor langen Zeiten auf uns hernieder gelassen, bleibe auf uns beruhen mit der Heiligen Taube die bishero unsere Vorsteherin und Rathgeberin gewesen in allen unsern Wegen, da sie uns dann unter viel Gedult und Leidenschafft kein Geheimnuß der Liebe unsers Gottes verhelet, sondern die Pforten der heimlichen und verborgenen Weißheit aufgesiegelt und zu uns heraus getreten, uns im Vorblick das Geheimnuß des Paradieses geöffnet, und so gleich im H. Schauen uns angreitzet, um mit dergleichen Sachen beschäfftigt zu seyn, welche alldorten in jener Welt werden vorkommen, von dem reden wir." See also Beissel, "Conrad Beissel Letterbook," Borneman Collection, B. MS 22, Free Library of Philadelphia, 75 ("Die Babel-Kirche hat den dritten Zeugen vom Himmel, den Heiligen Geist, der alle Sprache vereint, verloren"), 170 ("wo man die einige Mutter Sprache redet").

34. [Gast and Miller], *Chronicon Ephratense*, trans. Hark, 214.

the hand-drawn Fraktur letters were also engraved and reproduced in print, thus effectively interlocking both manuscript and print in the production of text and art. Stock images of Pennsylvania Fraktur writing, such as the lily, the carnation, and the turtledove, have been interpreted by scholars as imbued with Christian symbolism referring to theological concepts, such as the spiritual bride's (the church's or individual believer's) yearning for Jesus Christ. From the illumination of manuscript hymnals among the radical Pietist members of the communitarian settlement or cloister at Ephrata in the mid-eighteenth century to the decoration of family documents such as birth and marriage certificates among broad sections of Pennsylvania Germans well into the nineteenth century, Fraktur is broadly regarded as the artistic and material evidence of the flourishing and persistence of German immigrant culture in Pennsylvania and adjacent colonies. The nature illustrations are seen as semiotic systems that point, not at environmental realities, but at theological ideals or ethnically distinct aesthetics.

Of course, the stylized tulips, trees, vines, pomegranates, and turtledoves typical of the Ephrata Fraktur are not naturalistic representations of the Pennsylvania environment, and, as scholars have shown, they closely resemble similar images in European folk art traditions. Yet, does this mean that they are exclusively emblematic, symbolic, or ornamental? Missing from most scholarly as well as popular treatments of these illustrations is an integrated understanding of the relationship among the natural, linguistic, and spiritual worlds joined in these Fraktur writings, following the mystical, radical Pietist ideal of discovering within nature a hidden alphabet leading humankind once more to the divine script of the universe or the divine Word of God. Only the recognition that language and environment shared (at least in the mind of the artist) an underlying, essential, and spiritual connection explains why a Fraktur artist would take such pains to join letters with natural images.[35]

35. My analysis and argument here are specifically focused on the spiritual significance of Frakturschriften at Ephrata but does not necessarily extend to Pennsylvania German Fraktur writings in general. The scholarship on Pennsylvania German Fraktur writing is broad; in my work, especially my understanding of Ephrata Fraktur, I have relied on Benson, *Early American Illuminated Manuscripts;* Henry S. Borneman, *Pennsylvania German Illuminated Manuscripts: A Classification of Fraktur-Schriften and an Inquiry into Their History and Art* (Norristown, Pa., 1937); Kari M. Main, "From the Archives: Illuminated Hymnals of the Ephrata Cloister," *Winterthur Portfolio,* XXXII (1997), 65–78; Paul Conner and Jill Roberts, eds., *Pennsylvania German Fraktur and Printed Broadsides: A Guide to the Collections in the Library of Congress* (Washington D.C., 1988); Donald A. Shelley, *The*

Indeed, Ephrata Fraktur writing must be understood as a unified vision and practice with the communal ideal of hymn singing produced at the cloister. As Miller claimed in his letter to Franklin, the hymns Beissel composed at Ephrata and taught at the singing school were a direct dictate of the Holy Spirit, thus overcoming the separation between language and creation wrought at Babel. In his preface to the *Turtel-Taube,* Beissel seconded Boehme by arguing that the hymns in that collection became an emanation of the divine text of creation. Though Beissel phrased the link between the hymns collected in the *Turtel-Taube* and a "field of flowers" as a literary metaphor, the connection he wished to establish between both is not literary or metaphorical; it is entirely spiritual and mystical. As emanations of the spirit that has entered the community, the hymns are equated with the flowers as divinely inspired texts.

That hymns possess "scent" and "color" was then translated by the community's artists onto the pages of the manuscript hymnals in the form of Fraktur illuminations. Far from being mere ornaments or symbols, therefore, the flowers emanating from the letters and the music of the Ephrata manuscript hymnals were part of a mystical restoration of human insight into the divine language of all creation. As the pages of the 1754 hymnal *Paradisisches Wunderspiel* demonstrate, Ephrata nature illuminations added another "universal" text or "signature" to the divine language of sound (Figure 11).

Before the *Wunderspiel,* manuscript hymnals such as the "Ephrata Codex" accompanied printed hymn text published in separate volumes. In the *Wunderspiel,* Ephrata Brethren for the first time printed the hymn titles, the first lines of each hymn, and the bars; the notes and illuminations were to be filled in by individual artists. The chronicle of the Ephrata cloister, or *Chronicon Ephratense,* describes the production of Frakturschriften in the Scriptorium,

> where the writing in ornamental Gothic text was done, and which was chiefly instituted for the *benefit of those who had no musical talents.* The outlines of the letters [Beissel] himself designed, but the

Fraktur-Writings or Illuminated Manuscripts of the Pennsylvania Germans (Allentown, Pa., 1961); John Joseph Stoudt, *Early Pennsylvania Arts and Crafts* (New York, 1964); Frederick S. Weiser, "Fraktur," in Scott T. Swank, ed., *Arts of the Pennsylvania Germans* (New York, 1983), 230–263; Weiser, "Piety and Protocol in Folk Art: Pennsylvania German Fraktur Birth and Baptismal Certificates," *Winterthur Portfolio,* VIII (1973), 19–43; Don Yoder, "A Fraktur Primer," American Folklife Center at the Library of Congress, *Folklife Annual* (1988–1989), 100–111.

20. Und die Kelter ward ausser der Stadt gekeltert, und das Blut ging von der Kelter, bis an die

2.Chor

Zäume der Pferde, durch Tausend 600. Feld weges.

beyde Chor

2.Chor

Das hohe Lied Salomons Mögte Er mich nur küssen mit einigen von den Küs-

sen seines Mundes, dann seine Liebe ist lieblicher dann Wein.

3. Daß man deine gute Salbe rieche 2.Chor

Figure 11. [Conrad Beissel], Paradisisches Wunderspiel . . . *(Ephrata, Pa., 1754).*
Printed hymnal with calligraphy illustrations in color. Courtesy, The Winterthur
Library: Joseph Downs Collection of Manuscripts and Printed Ephemera

shading of them was left to the scholar, in order to exercise himself in it. But none was permitted to borrow a design anywhere, for he said: "We dare not borrow from each other, because the power to produce rests within everybody." Many Solitary spent days and years in these schools, which also served them as a means of sanctification to crucify their flesh. The writings were hung up in the chapels as ornaments, or distributed to admirers.

Although the letters of human language might be static or given, mystical inspiration allowed the individual to fill the letters and words with the "scents and colors" or divine signatures belonging to the divine text of creation. Music and nature illustrations, therefore, revealed the knowledge hidden from he who, as Boehme said, "bites and argues with the other over the letter." Rather than pointing like symbols or emblems toward a truth beyond themselves—that is, something on a higher spiritual plane—the music and the nature illustrations in the Ephrata hymnals were themselves parts of a divine text or immanent mystery of God. That those who had no talent for singing could find a suitable occupation in manuscript illumination proves that both were regarded as the outpouring of the divine spirit. In other words, the union of music and nature illustrations in the Ephrata hymnals constituted an attempt to approximate the original union between human language and the divine essence of all things. The purpose of singing, writing, and illustrating at Ephrata was to collapse the gap between signifier and signified, between signs and their meanings. What the illustrators beautifully revealed on the manuscript page was nothing less than the interpenetration of all forms of existence as a common, spiritual text. Language and nature in this work had become indistinguishable, for both were already part of a single divine language (Figure 12).[36]

On the Lehigh: Bethlehem and the Moravians

In the 1740s, the leader of the Renewed Unitas Fratrum or Moravian Church, Count Nikolas Ludwig von Zinzendorf, articulated the idea of a "natural language" or "central language" that joined Augustine's Pentecostal desire for a global church with a Neoplatonist concept of a mystical system of signification. In a 1746 speech, Zinzendorf expressed his expec-

36. [Gast and Miller], *Chronicon Ephratense*, trans. Hark, 168–169 (emphasis added).

Figure 12: Ephrata Community, Title Page from Manuscript Hymnal "Die bittre Gute oder das Gesäng der einsamen Turtel-Taube. . . ." Courtesy, Library of Congress

tation that the Moravian Church would ultimately build a language that combined the spiritual elements of all languages represented in the community—German, Dutch, Latin, French, Greek, and others—in a single, spoken tongue that would be understood by everyone within, but by nobody outside, the *Gemeine*. Concretely, two strategies for overcoming linguistic and spiritual differences emerged in the Moravian Church, specifically in so-called pilgrim congregations like Bethlehem, which were both centers of Moravian spiritual and communal life as well as launching pads for missionaries among indigenous and migrating European peoples. First, Moravians cultivated an intense focus on Christ's body and wounds as a supralinguistic system of spiritual signification. Secondly, Zinzendorf's call for linguistic and spiritual universalism triggered wide-ranging and intensive linguistic work, especially translation. Zinzendorf and the Moravians who carried his ideas abroad understood fully that linguistic multiplicity was not the enemy; rather, it was the gate or key to achieving spiritual community. In communal practice, the ideal of a common spiritual language derived from a multiplicity of voices represented in the global Moravian Church was encapsulated in the practice of multilingual hymn singing, which celebrated the simultaneous joining of different languages in a mystical moment of Pentecostal unity of word and spirit.[37]

The primary locus for the project of building a "natural language" that would approximate the "spiritual language" was hymnody. The Moravian belief that any tunes and texts were in some way divinely inspired explains why their 1735 hymnal, *Herrnhuter Gesangbuch*, grew to such epic proportions—it contained, after twelve appendixes and several additions, 2,357 entries. Moravians regarded an individual relationship to the savior as the foundation of Christian faith; an expression of an individual's knowledge of the divine through musical compositions, therefore, could not simply be erased. Many hymns were retained that in literary or theological terms were considered substandard; the measure of value was clearly spiritual, not aesthetic. As John Gambold wrote in his preface to the cumulative 1754 *London Hymnal*—itself an expression of the Moravian Church's expansion into a multilingual and transnational community—the collection even included hymns that were not

> regularly authorized, nor always passably review'd; yet Thousands in different Parts of this Land will testify, that they have drawn from them many a holy and seasonable Direction or Consolation for their

37. On Zinzendorf's concept of a "natural language," see Chapter 1. For general histories of the Moravian Church and its worldwide expansion, especially in America, see Adelaide L. Fries, *The Moravians in Georgia, 1735–1740* (Raleigh, N.C., 1905); Michele Gillespie and Robert Beachy, eds., *Pious Pursuits: German Moravians in the Atlantic World* (New York, 2007); J. Taylor Hamilton, *A History of the Church Known as the Moravian Church, or the Unitas Fratrum, or the Unity of the Brethren, during the Eighteenth and Nineteenth Centuries* (Bethlehem, Pa., 1900); Hamilton and Kenneth G. Hamilton, *History of the Moravian Church: The Renewed Unitas Fratrum, 1722–1957* (Bethlehem, Pa., 1967); Vernon Nelson, "The Moravian Church in America," in Mari P. van Buijtenen, Cornelis Dekker, and Huib Leeuwenberg, eds., *Unitas Fratrum: Herrnhuter Studien / Moravian Studies* (Utrecht, 1975), 145–176; Jon F. Sensbach, *A Separate Canaan: The Making of an Afro-Moravian World in North Carolina, 1763–1840* (Chapel Hill, N.C., 1998); Daniel B. Thorp, *The Moravian Community in Colonial North Carolina* (Knoxville, Tenn., 1989).

There is a broad range of scholarship on Moravian Christology and its role for a unified communal identity, especially through the famous or infamous "blood and wounds" theology. See Craig D. Atwood, *Community of the Cross: Moravian Piety in Colonial Bethlehem* (University Park, Pa., 2004); Katherine Carté Engel, *Religion and Profit: Moravians in Early America* (Philadelphia, 2009); Aaron Spencer Fogleman, *Jesus Is Female: Moravians and the Challenge of Radical Religion in Early America* (Philadelphia, 2007); Paul Peucker, "Inspired by Flames of Love": Homosexuality, Mysticism, and Moravian Brothers around 1750," *Journal of the History of Sexuality*, XV (2006), 30–64; Peucker, "The Songs of the Sifting: Understanding the Role of Bridal Mysticism in Moravian Piety in the Late 1740s," *Journal of Moravian History*, III (2007), 51–87.

Heart. And this is the Reason why, as those former Materials in general were to be retained as far as was possible without swelling this Book too much, the Reader will meet with some Compositions here, (by Hands either unlearned, or when their Acquaintance with the Brethren was young) which he may think do but express the same Truths more slightly, that have, on the next Pages, fuller Justice done them over and over. He must consider that even these little Hymns have got their Lovers, who would be sorry to lose them all at once.

Gambold here encapsulated the communal meaning of hymn composition for the Moravians. As evidence for the continuity and plenitude of the Holy Spirit—from the divine source, to hymn writers, to the audience whose heart is touched—the hymns conveyed ultimate truths rather than a specific linguistic rendering of church doctrine.[38]

This use of hymnody for transferring or translating religious truths and their emotional realization in the hearts of individuals within the community became crucial in the context of the global expansion of the Moravian Church. During the 1740s, the Moravian Church found a particularly active following in England. The theoretical and practical implications of translating the vast body of Moravian hymns into English set the stage for later non-

---

38. [John Gambold], "Preface," *A Collection of Hymns of the Children of God in All Ages, from the Beginning till Now; in Two Parts; Designed Chiefly for the Use of the Congregations in Union with the Brethren's Church* (London, 1754), unpaginated. On the establishment of Moravian communities in England, especially the Fetterley Lane Church where John and Charles Wesley first encountered the Moravians, see Colin Podmore, *The Moravian Church in England, 1728–1760* (Oxford, 1998); Podmore, "Zinzendorf und die englischen Brüdergemeinen," in Martin Brecht and Paul Peucker, eds., *Neue Aspekte der Zinzendorf-Forschung* (Göttingen, 2006), 188–206; Edward Wilson, "The Moravian Church in England and Ireland," in van Buijtenen, Dekker, and Leeuwenberg, eds., *Unitas Fratrum,* 119–143.
  Surprisingly few scholarly treatments of Moravian hymnody remark on its multilingual spread through translation, although there are numerous works on Moravian music and hymnody in general. See Charles B. Adams, *Our Moravian Hymn Heritage: Chronological Listing of Hymns and Tunes of Moravian Origin in the American Moravian Hymnal of 1969* (Bethlehem, Pa., 1984); Walter Blankenburg, "Die Musik der Brüdergemeine in Europa," 351–385, and Karl Kroeger, "Moravian Music in America: A Survey," 387–400, both in van Buijtenen, Dekker, and Leeuwenberg, eds., *Unitas Fratrum;* Rufus A. Grider, *Historical Notes on Music in Bethlehem, PA, from 1741–1871,* Moravian Music Foundation Publications No. 4 (Winston-Salem, N.C., 1957); Jeannine S. Ingram, "Music in American Moravian Communities: Transplanted Traditions in Indigenous Practices," *Communal Societies,* II (1982), 39–51; Henry Llewellyn Williams, *The Development of the Moravian Hymnal* (Bethlehem, Pa., 1962); Erich Beyreuther, Gerhard Meyer, and Gudrun Meyer-Hickel, eds., *Herrnhuter Gesangbuch: Christliches Gesang-Buch der evangelischen Brüder-Gemeinen von 1735,* 3 vols. (Hildesheim, 1981).

European manifestations of Moravian hymn singing. In detail, Gambold's preface laid out the specific Moravian use of hymnody as an antidote against the spiritual and linguistic splintering of Babel. Like Miller, Gambold considered singing an uncorrupted medium for the soul to express itself:

> The practice of cloathing divine Thoughts in Metre, is perhaps as universal as Speech itself; and has two Grounds for it. First, that when our Affections are strongly moved, which surely Religion may be allow'd to do, singing or a sort of Modulation of the Voice is what the Heart naturally chooses to vent itself by. Secondly, that the comprizing of important Truths or Counsels in Verse, is a Help to their being remember'd, and a Kind of *Memoria technica.*

Singing was a universal impulse triggered by the desire to express "divine Thoughts." The hymns in Gambold's compilation, therefore, were considered emanations of a language unencumbered by conventional, historical, or doctrinal strictures. Following Augustinian concepts of a *locutio cordis* or inner language, Gambold suggested that singing was a more spiritually fulfilled language because it "is what the Heart naturally chooses to vent itself by." Singing was apparently the natural expression of the Moravian ideal—a faith of the heart. Secondly, Gambold mentioned the important use of hymnody as a mnemonic device for inscribing principles of faith within the individual.[39]

Even more consequential for the missionaries' encounter with linguistic difference were Gambold's remarks on translation. The Moravian hymnal itself followed in a tradition of German hymnody translated into English popularized by Johann Christian Jacobi, the German chaplain to George I. In his *Psalmodia Germanica*—large portions of which were included in Gambold's Moravian hymnal—Jacobi reflected on the linguistic and spiritual problems inherent in the translation of "divinely" inspired language; yet he already provided part of the solution to his own dilemma:

> A Version of this Kind lies under various Disadvantages, known only to those, who in any Degree are acquainted, with any Poetical Translations of this Kind. A great Deal is lost of the Life and Spirit of an Hymn, when it appears in another Language. I have, with the Leave of the Reverend Mr. Watts, transcrib'd one entire Hymn out of his *Horae Lyricae,* upon the Nativity of Christ, and the 127 Psalm, out of his new

39. [Gambold], "Preface," *Collection of Hymns,* [i].

Translation; both which agree so well with our German Composures on those Subjects, that I made bold to try, how a good English Verse, set to a German Tune, might be relish'd by a British Singer.

Hymn translation had to contend with the fundamental problem of translating poetic language; expressions of spiritual truths, in particular, might be inextricable from the language in which they first were conceived. Driven by his desire to carry the "Life and Spirit" of the originals into the English hymn book, Jacobi conducted an experiment ("I made bold to try . . ."). In combining a hymn text on a specific subject written in English by Isaac Watts with German musical compositions treating the same subject, Jacobi produced a hybrid of English text and German tune that, ultimately, pulled out the rug from under the division of Babel. As the translator or bilingual individual, Jacobi himself could see and feel the spiritual congeniality between religious expressions in both German and English. Hymn tunes on both sides *already* spoke the same spiritual language; the translation of that expression from one human language into another, however, might simply lose that spirit. Yet, if the music that accompanied the original German text was an expression of the same spiritual truth, it could carry—without an attendant loss of spiritual force—the same in conjunction with English words.[40]

In his preface to the *London Hymnal*, Gambold also reflected on the dilemma Jacobi had outlined, and he developed another remedy particularly suited for the Moravian faith. First, Gambold identified German as a type of *original tongue* of the Moravian Church:

Concerning the *High-Dutch* Language, one Observation is necessary. It is indeed a living one, and spoken in a Country not very remote: this will disincline the Reader to believe, what I must nevertheless say of it, that it has a good deal of the old Oriental Genius. As to the Brethren in particular, they have not damp'd, but rather pursued, these ingenuous Sparks they found in their Mother-Tongue. For which, no good Critic will blame them: but their Translators, it must be own'd, are hereby put to some Difficulties, and render'd obnoxious to just Criticism sometimes. We don't doubt however, but it is in the Compass of the *English* Tongue, to afford one time or other the fully corre-

40. [Johann Christian Jacobi], trans. and ed., *Psalmodia Germanica; or, a Specimen of Divine Hymns, Translated from the High Dutch; Together with Their Proper Tunes and Thorough Bass* (London, 1722), ii–iii.

sponding Phrases: And indeed the Cause of some less happy, too flat or obscure Translations hitherto, has been not only that intrinsic Obstacle now mention'd, but withal a Care to translate literally, carried to a needless Excess.

Gambold's rendering of the German language was replete with early modern, particularly Neoplatonist theories about the original language. In the footsteps of Boehme, German linguists and theologians, in particular, had championed the German language as closest to the Edenic—hence "oriental"—tongue and thus most filled with divine inspiration. Gambold gestured toward this status of German within the Moravian faith to deflect criticism of his translations. The "ingenuous Sparks" to be found in the German hymn texts of the Moravian Church confounded the translator; but Gambold also hinted at linguistic universalism in defending the ability of English to express adequately similar spiritual ideas. Finally, Gambold rejected a slavish attendance to literal correspondences in translating spiritual texts, especially hymns. In dealing with the hymns as expressions of a "heart religion" (a faith championing an emotional relationship to the savior), translators must find and reveal spiritual correspondences between the German and English languages. The translation of German Moravian hymn texts, therefore, made the larger spiritual community between German and English members of the church possible.[41]

Gambold did not hit his stride in defending the spiritual probity of the Moravian hymns and their translations until he discussed the actual center of Moravian hymnody in any given language—Jesus Christ. Christocentrism transformed the religious ideals displayed in Moravian hymns from objects to be represented into subjects possessing spiritual agency regardless of the vehicle in which they were put forth. Reminiscent of Comenius's concept of thought as "internalized action," hymns focusing on Christ actively promoted community formation. Gambold's explanation particularly stands out through its reliance on active verbs revealing the work hymns ("they") performed within the Gemeine or church community:

The Brethren's grand Topic in their Hymns, as every one may see, is the Person and Propitiation of *Jesus Christ:* they collect, as in the *Focus* of a Burning glass, what has descended to them from past Ages, or properly from the Bible itself, upon this Head; and that it may

41. [Gambold], "Preface," *Collection of Hymns*, [iii].

not be evaded under the Notion of *dicta ardentia* they present it in a System, and apply that System to Practice. They affirm our free Acceptance with God as Sinners, and thro' pure Grace; and yet, the Necessity of, and powerful Assistances for, a most real Holiness of Life afterwards: with such a Warmth upon each of these Subjects successively, that many a Reader runs away with a Supposition of their over-doing on that side he happen'd first to take notice of, for want of waiting the Balance. They cherish, as an hereditary Platform from their Ancestors, a very high Persuasion of, and very strict Rules concerning, a New-Testament Church. To mention but one Peculiarity more, they continually betray a burning Propensity to the Work of propagating the Gospel of Peace.

In focusing solely on Christ, Moravian hymnody escaped the predicament of the translator and established, without further mediation, the pillars of the Moravian faith and communal order. Notably, hymns combined church tradition with divine authority derived from scriptures. Hymnody, in other words, constituted the spiritual language of the community on which its structure, harmony, and traditions relied. Most important—appearing at the end of Gambold's list—Moravian hymns were the missionary tool par excellence because of their fiery ("burning"), transforming nature.[42]

Gambold thus evoked the early modern alchemical notion of the transformative power of music. Indeed, Moravians believed that human beings could be sanctified in their earthly lives. In following alchemical concepts of transforming substances from a lower to a higher level of purity, Moravian hymnists hoped to enlist their divinely inspired compositions to lift themselves and the community onto a higher spiritual level. In radical Pietism and Baroque mysticism more broadly, alchemy was considered a model of universal purification and renovation. Christian alchemy sought after an earthly and cosmic renovation, which was in part to be reached through the sublimating powers of music. Hymn singing, in particular, would modify and transform human beings and their affect by connecting body and mind. The alchemical or mystical transformation into a higher spiritual form presumably made human beings capable of a higher spiritual language that

---

42. Ibid., [vi–vii]. For a sustained treatment of the role Moravian hymnody played in facilitating spiritual and social harmony while inculcating theological probity, see Anja Wehrend, *Musikanschauung, Musikpraxis, Kantatenkompositionen in der Herrnhuter Brüdergemeine: Ihre musikalische und theologische Bedeutung für das Gemeinleben von 1727 bis 1760* (Frankfurt am Main, 1995), esp. chap. 3.

was, once more, capable of expressing fully the divine meanings of the universe. Moravian missionaries applied this ideal of the transforming power of hymnody to their wide-ranging activities of converting indigenous peoples around the world, specifically in North America. Hymn singing and translation into various native American languages thus constituted the core strategy among missionaries such as David Zeisberger, Johann Christoph Pyrlaeus, Abraham Luckenbach, and John Heckewelder (see the Coda).[43]

Before serving as a concrete missionary tool in the field, multilingual hymnody symbolized the linguistic and spiritual unity of a worldwide Moravian Church community. In creating multiethnic and translingual communal settlements in Europe and abroad (such as Herrnhut, Herrnhaag, and Bethlehem), polyglot singing encapsulated the development of a common spiritual idiom and the transforming power of the Moravian Christology across all borders. Multilingual hymn singing, in other words, took the power of hymnody to a universal communal level and transformed separate national, racial, and linguistic constituencies into a "community of the cross." Whereas the universalizing appeal of the emphasis on Christ's suffering and sacrifice (celebrated in the "blood and wounds" imagery) has been thoroughly studied, an in-depth investigation of polyglot singing and hymn translation has been absent.[44]

In the 1740s, polyglot singing became a special means to celebrate missionary occasions in Bethlehem and other communal settlements around the world. All individuals present sang a specific hymn simultaneously in their native language; if the hymn had not yet been translated, multilingual individuals, especially missionaries, would prepare translations for that specific purpose. In reflecting in hindsight on the spiritual life and practices of the Moravian communal settlement of Herrnhaag in the German region of Wachovia in 1750, Zinzendorf pointed out the frequent use of multilingual hymn singing: "We have here sung to our savior in 25 languages at once

---

43. Burkhard Dohm, "Heiligkeit im Diesseits: Hermetische Konzepte im halleschen und im herrnhutischen Lied," in Wolfgang Miersemann and Gudrun Busch, eds., *Pietismus und Liedkultur* (Tübingen, 2002), 309. Dohm explains the connections between alchemy and the religious poetics of Pietism extensively in his book *Poetische Alchimie: Öffnung zur Sinnlichkeit in der Hohelied- und Bibeldichtung von der protestantischen Barockmystik bis zum Pietismus* (Tübingen, 2000). For the role of singing in Moravian mission communities, see Walter W. Woodward, "'Incline Your Second Ear This Way': Song as a Cultural Mediator in Moravian Mission Towns," in A. G. Roeber, ed., *Ethnographies and Exchanges: Native Americans, Moravians, and Catholics in Early North America* (University Park, Pa., 2008), 125–142.

44. For scholarship discussing the Moravian "blood and wounds" theology, see Note 37, above.

Figure 13. Johann Valentin Haidt, First Fruits. *1747. Oil on canvas.*
Courtesy, Moravian Archives, Bethlehem, Pennsylvania

more than once." Moravian communal settlements were called pilgrim communities that were charged with the preparation of missionaries across the world. Multilingual singing thus celebrated the translingual and multiethnic community missionaries would help build in the mission field.[45]

The interdependency of hymn singing and the advancement of a multilingual, multiethnic spiritual community in the Moravian Church was most visibly exemplified in the painting *First Fruits* by Moravian painter Johann Valentin Haidt (Figure 13). When, on March 15, 1747, Zinzendorf received news in Herrnhaag of the death of Johannes (formerly known as "Tschoop" or Job), the first Mahican Indian baptized in the Moravian mission community in Shekomeko, New York, he composed a hymn celebrating the first fruits—initial converts—in general and specifically eighteen individuals from among various Moravian mission communities who had passed away and were presumably in heaven with Christ. In his hymn, Zinzen-

45. Nicolas Ludwig Count Zinzendorf, "Zinzendorfs letzte Rede in Herrnhaag, aus dem Jüngerhaus-Diarium vom 9. August 1750," in Helmut Reichel, "Das Ende der Brüdergemeine in Herrnhaag, 1750," *Unitas Fratrum: Zeitschrift für Geschichte und Gegenwartsfragen der Brüdergemeine,* XVI (1989), 52–76 (esp. 74).

dorf mentioned each of the eighteen first fruits by name, thus uniting all representatives of the global church community in the universal language of hymnody. Haidt was then asked to translate this image of transnational and translingual unity into a painting. Adding three more first fruits, Haidt placed twenty-one individuals dressed in their native garb or Moravian dress and portrayed in their respective skin colors around the throne of Christ. Haidt's painting thus reflected the gathering of "a great multitude, which no man could number, of all nations, and kindreds, and people, and tongues, stood before the throne, and before the Lamb" shown in Revelation 7:9. Zinzendorf's hymn and Haidt's painting together represented the members of the Moravian Church in a linguistic and ethnic unity created through a common spiritual foundation in Christ.[46]

Along with the trek of Moravian missionaries across the Atlantic to North America, the practice of simultaneous multilingual hymn singing was transplanted as well, especially to pilgrim and mission communities like Bethlehem. Bethlehem was founded close to native American peoples such as the Delawares, Iroquois, Shawnees, and Mahicans, whom Moravian missionaries tried to convert. Multilingual singing in Bethlehem thus reflected not only the presence of native American converts and their languages but also the continual presence of travelers from Moravian mission communities around the world. For instance, the Bethlehem Diary mentioned a love feast on August 21, 1745, where "Indian, English, German, Swedish, Danish, and Jewish-German verses were sung, and we counted that we [as a church] are able to sing and speak of the Lamb and the wounds in 18 different languages." In advance of such a celebration on September 4, 1745, Johann Christoph Pyrlaeus, an Indian missionary and leader of the missionary school in Bethlehem, was charged with the translation of the famous hymn "In Dulci Jubilo" into Mahican. The entry in the Bethlehem Diary for the celebration notes that hymns were sung — simultaneously — in Ger-

46. [Paul Peucker], "Haidt's Painting of the *First Fruits, 1747*," *This Month in Moravian History: A Monthly Newsletter Published by the Moravian Archives in Bethlehem Commemorating Events from Moravian History*, XVII (March 2007), 1. For an excellent account of the Shekomeko community, see Rachel M. Wheeler, *To Live upon Hope: Mohicans and Missionaries in the Eighteenth-Century Northeast* (Ithaca, N.Y., 2008). The hymn was published in the third supplement to the Herrnhuter Gesangbuch as "#2298: Am 18. Merz 1747. occasione der Loosung: GOtt sey dir gnädig!" For the third supplement, see *Das Gesang-Buch der Gemeine in Herrn-Huth*, Zugabe 3 (n.p. [1747]); for the full hymnal, see *Das Gesang-Buch der Gemeine in Herrn-Huth* ([Herrnhut], 1735–1748). The hymns in the *Gesang-Buch*, including all appendixes and supplements published from 1735 through 1748, are numbered consecutively.

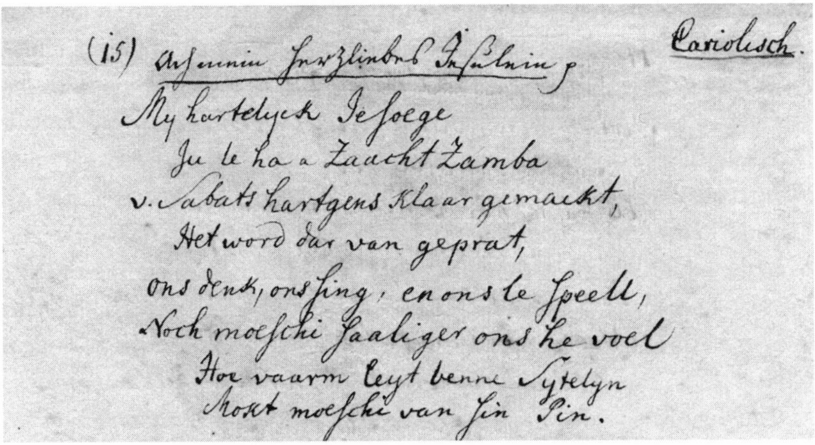

Figure 14. "Ach mein herzliebes Jesulein," in Dutch Creole. From "Three Moravian Hymns in Various Languages, ca. 1750 (reference # PP ND 27)," David Nitschmann Papers, Moravian Archives, Bethlehem, Pennsylvania

man, English, Latin, Greek, Mohawk, Mahican, French, Irish, Bohemian, Wendish (that is, Sorbian, the language of a Slavic group living in eastern Germany), Swedish, Welsh, and Dutch. The diary specifically noted that the Danish, Polish, and Hungarian Brothers present at the celebration failed to contribute their verses, which confirms that speakers of different languages were charged with translating hymns usually sung in the Moravian Church in German, English, or Latin into a multiplicity of other languages. The direct involvement of speakers of these languages in translating and making the hymns available for singing hours and love feasts thus made multilingual singing a truly collaborative effort, attesting to Zinzendorf's vision of a Moravian Natursprache that united all members in a common spiritual language.[47]

47. Bethlehem Diary, June 1745–February 1746, III, Moravian Archives, Bethlehem: "Den 21 Aug. [1745]: Bey unserem stillen Sabbaths Lmahl [that is, Liebesmahl] wurden Indianische, Engl. Deutsche, schwedische, dänische u. Jüdisch-deutsche Versel gesungen, u. 18 Sprachen nachgerechnet, darin wir aus unseren Mittel vom Lamme u. Wunden singen u. sagen können"; "September Den 1sten. . . . Dem Brud. Pyrlaeus wurde commitiert Mahikander Verßen zu machen in Forma des Liedes in dulci Jubilo"; "Den 4ten Sept. Zum Besuch beym Sabb. Lmahl [that is, Liebesmahl] wurden deutsche, Engl. Lateinische, Griechische, Maquaische [Mohawk], Mahikanderische, Frantzösiche, Eyrische, Böhmische, Wendische, Schwedische, Walisische 'Holländische' Verßen gesungen. Unser dänischer Bruder Matthew Beütz, der Polacke Hancke u. Christ. Bower der Ungar blieben noch die ihrigen schuldig."
On the founding and settlement of Bethlehem, see Joseph Mortimer Levering, *A History of Bethle-*

In addition to such notations in the Bethlehem Diary, the Moravian Archives hold textual and material evidence of multilingual singing, including a manuscript booklet containing translations of three hymns from the German into seventeen different languages: Hebrew, Greek, Latin, Danish, Swedish, English, Spanish, French, Italian, Bohemian (Czech), Hungarian, "Wallachian" (Romanian), Latvian, Estonian, Dutch Creole (Figure 14), "Amina," and "Acra." Particularly noteworthy is the range of languages, from the biblical languages Hebrew and Greek, to the lingua franca of early modern humanism, Latin, to western, central, and eastern European languages, to three tongues spoken in the Caribbean missions of the Moravian Church.[48]

The linguistic and textually congruous arrangement of these languages on the pages of this manuscript represented the physical coherence between the diverse parts of the Moravian community during the singing hours or love feasts when the hymns were sung. Based on the Bethlehem Diary, the late-nineteenth-century Moravian historian John W. Jordan described how representatives of various nationalities, ethnicities, and languages gathered for a love feast virtually as a single body and in this arrangement performed multilingual singing:

> At a Love-feast given in Bethlehem on June 9th [1749], the Greenlanders appeared in their native costume. In the center of the chapel sat the Greenlanders and aside of them two Arawacks, from the Berbice mission in South America; next some thirty converts from five or six Indian tribes, and back of them the "missionaries to the Heathen," then present in Bethlehem. All the hymns sung were in the languages of the nationalities present.

The multilingual hymn composition and the communal arrangements of the congregation at the love feast did not erase difference; instead, they explicitly recreated a post-Babel community that was united in a single language

---

hem, Pennsylvania, 1741–1892, with Some Account of Its Founders and Their Early Activity in America (Bethlehem, Pa., 1903). Though Levering's historical account is one of the few that mentions multilingual hymn singing in Bethlehem explicitly, Levering misses the spiritual and communal significance of the practice and instead belittles it as "a fanciful diversion that came into vogue" and attributes it merely to "the cosmopolitan population of the place" (204).

48. "Three Moravian Hymns in Various Languages, ca. 1750 (reference # PP ND 27)," David Nitschmann Papers, Moravian Archives. The hymns are: "Ach mein herzliebes Jesulein" (HG 2279:3), "Geschöpfen zur Geburt gebracht" (HG 2279:4), "So singt die seelge Assemblée" (HG 2188:16).

of the spirit. The communal and larger eschatological significance of this gesture cannot be overestimated: the Moravian Church used the spiritual coherence found in their intense Christocentrism to unite all languages; translation and multilingual singing, therefore, paradigmatically reversed the confusion of Babel by celebrating the multiplicity of voices.[49]

49. John W. Jordan, "Moravian Immigration to Pennsylvania, 1734-1767," Moravian Historical Society, *Transactions*, V (1896), 69-70.

"What Will Become of Pennsylvania?"

WAR, COMMUNITY, AND THE LANGUAGE OF
SUFFERING FOR PEACE

he vision of spiritual coherence celebrated in multilingual communal singing among the Kelpius Hermits, the Ephrata cloister, and the Moravians was, of course, not indicative of an all-encompassing reconciliation of linguistic, religious, ethnic, and political differences in colonial Pennsylvania. Scholarship has cemented the image of a turbulent society rife with divisive political controversies (especially between the Quaker Assembly and the Proprietors and the Proprietary party) as well as a chaotic religious landscape that presaged the end of organized, institutional religion. Debates over war and the defense of the province, in particular, seemed to lay bare insurmountable fault lines in this diverse society. Beginning with the War of Jenkins's Ear and King George's War in the 1740s, Pennsylvania's hitherto peaceful status was threatened by rising imperial tensions. In this situation, writers and commentators argued that an external threat required an internal consolidation of communal differences, oftentimes painting the opponents as traitors to a variety of causes—the religious ideals of the founders, the economic self-interest of the emerging middling people, and the cohesion of the British Empire and its expanding cultural and political sphere. The debates over war and defense seemed to herald the end of the ideal of spiritual community and exacerbate existing as well as perceived differences. However, scholarship emphasizing the role of controversy and divisiveness has overlooked the continuation and even resurgence of the ideal of building community around a common spiritual language in mid- to late-eighteenth-century Pennsylvania.[1]

1. A particularly scathing view of Pennsylvania's pluralistic society at midcentury is the account of the German immigrant Gottlieb Mittelberger, who returned to Germany and, in 1756, published an antipromotional tract (*Journey to Pennsylvania*, ed. and trans. Oscar Handlin and John Clive [Cambridge, Mass., 1960]). For scholarship on Pennsylvania's turbulent religious and political atmo-

Although debates over war, defense, and pacifism bespeak a significant departure from the ideal that a holy experiment could be created by harnessing underlying spiritual congruencies among diverse constituencies, they also marked a return to and rejuvenation of the hope for building spiritual community across linguistic, religious, and political divisions. In response to the first direct threat of war against Pennsylvania in 1747–1748 and the evolving debate over defense, Franklin and his rival German printer Christoph Saur advanced two competing and mutually exclusive visions of society. For Franklin, a rising ideology of self-interest, imperial expansion, and racial and ethnic exclusiveness defined a Pennsylvania that should break with a vision of community anchored in a common spirituality. Saur considered Franklin's call for defense in particular and his secular vision of society in general as a breach of the religious liberty promised by William Penn in his 1701 *Charter of Privileges* and a violation of the bonds established between the first generations of English Quaker and German Pietist and sectarian immigrants who founded Pennsylvania. In his various print publications (newspaper, almanac, pamphlets), Saur tried to recreate a common feeling and language of community among these groups. By lifting out the mutual ideal of suffering, especially that of the suffering "Quaker mother," Saur provided a rhetorical and spiritual center around which English Quakers and a variety of German pacifists could rally. He thus translated the transcultural and translingual appeal of seventeenth-century promotional literature on Pennsylvania into the mid-eighteenth-century debate over defense.[2]

sphere in the eighteenth century, see Patricia U. Bonomi, "The Middle Colonies: Embryo of the New Political Order," in Alden T. Vaughan and George Athan Billias, eds., *Perspectives on Early American History: Essays in Honor of Richard B. Morris* (New York, 1973); Bonomi, " 'Watchful against the Sects': Religious Renewal in Pennsylvania's German Congregations, 1720–1750," *Pennsylvania History*, L (1983), 273–283; Bonomi, *Under the Cope of Heaven: Religion, Society, and Politics in Colonial America* (New York, 1986); Donald F. Durnbaugh, "Pennsylvania's Crazy Quilt of German Religious Groups," *Pennsylvania History*, LXVIII (2001), 8–30; John B. Frantz, "The Awakening of Religion among the German Settlers in the Middle Colonies," *William and Mary Quarterly*, 3d Ser., XXXIII (1976), 266–288; Sally Schwartz, *"A Mixed Multitude": The Struggle for Toleration in Colonial Pennsylvania* (New York, 1987).

2. Franklin vented his anxieties over the cultural impact of German mass immigration in the 1740s and 1750s and notoriously called the new immigrants "the most stupid of their own nation" (Glenn Weaver, "Benjamin Franklin and the Pennsylvania Germans," *WMQ*, 3d Ser., XIV [1957], 539). On Franklin's attitude toward immigration in general and German immigrants in particular, see Stephen Fender, "Franklin and Emigration: The Trajectory of Use," in J. A. Leo Lemay, ed., *Reappraising Benjamin Franklin: A Bicentennial Perspective* (Newark, Del., 1993), 335–346; John B. Frantz, "Franklin and the Pennsylvania Germans," *Pennsylvania History*, LXV (1998), 21–34;

In addition to Saur's publications, two iconic instances of translingual and transcultural communication tried to recreate the ideal of a Philadelphian society joined by a common spiritual language. In the 1740s and 1750s, Pennsylvania German Mennonites (an Anabaptist denomination) and the radical Pietists at Ephrata transplanted and translated the language of suffering and the Dutch *Martyr's Mirror*—as the central text embodying the ideology of Anabaptist martyrdom—into the communal and political context of a province rife with fears of war and mandatory armament. The Dutch-German translation of the *Martyrs' Mirror* produced at Ephrata renewed the utopian ideal of preserving spiritual congruencies across linguistic and doctrinal divisions, which could counteract the language of militarization and invigorate the spirit of resistance among a variety of German peace sects, including Dunkers, Schwenkfelders, and Mennonites. Second, the joint English Quaker–German sectarian participation in the Friendly Association for Regaining and Preserving Peace with the Indians by Pacific Measures during the Seven Years' War precipitated a revitalization of a common spiritual foundation among both groups, especially by stressing their common history of persecution and suffering, and resulted in revitalizing the ideal of a common spiritual language in spite of increasing internal and external threats.

Beyond the political goals uniting Quaker and German voters usually described in scholarship, members of both groups fostered a knowledge of one another's spiritual ideals by exchanging writings—often in manuscript translations—that ranged from the works of medieval mystic Johannes Tauler, to the early Protestant reformer Caspar Schwenckfeld, to the Pennsylvania Charter, to testimonies of Christian Indians that helped dispel the vilification of native Americans during the war and after. Concretely, English Quakers such as Anthony Benezet and Israel Pemberton took up an avid correspondence with leaders among the German peace sects, such as Christopher Schultz among the Schwenkfelders, Benjamin Hershey among the Mennonites, and August Spangenberg among the Moravians. Standard

---

Weaver, "Benjamin Franklin and the Pennsylvania Germans," *WMQ*, 3d Ser., XIV (1957), 536–559. On Franklin's rivalry with Saur, see Ralph Frasca, "'To Rescue the Germans out of Sauer's Hands': Benjamin Franklin's German-Language Printing Partnerships," *Pennsylvania Magazine of History and Biography*, CXXI (1997), 329–350. Tellingly, the first German translations of the Charter appeared in the 1740s, precisely at a moment when its fundamental provisions seemed to be abridged for German immigrants in the province. See, *Der neue Charter oder schrifftliche Versicherung der Freyheiten, welche William Penn, Esq: den Einwohnern von Pennsylvanien und dessen Territorien gegeben; aus dem englischen Original übersetzt* (Germantown, Pa., 1743).

histories hold an internal renaissance of the ideals of suffering, persecution, and religious and civic activism among so-called religious Quakers as primarily responsible for the sudden shift in direction among the Society of Friends with regard to war, slavery, and the role of nonconformists in government office. Yet this scholarship has overlooked that the reciprocal translation and communication networks linking Quakers and German peace sects acted as a potent catalyst for this remarkable reorientation.[3]

Since eighteenth-century Quakers often did not have widespread access to the classical texts of seventeenth-century Quaker spirituality, the translation, manuscript circulation, and print publication of German mystical, esoteric, and radical Protestant writings infused American Quakerism with a renewed spiritual foundation. German immigrant groups such as the Schwenkfelders and Mennonites had experienced persecution much more recently and kept the memory of suffering alive through translations and publications such as the *Martyrs' Mirror* and the hymnal *Der Ausbund*. While large portions of Pennsylvania's political and religious establishment during the Seven Years' War called for widespread armament to defend the province against a French imperial and allied native American invasion, religious Quakers and German peace sects revived the late-seventeenth-century Philadelphian ideal and created a common spiritual language of suffering for peace.

3. For standard scholarship on the Pennsylvania German-Quaker interaction in eighteenth-century Pennsylvania politics as well as developing tensions between English and German groups, see Dietmar Rothermund, "The German Problem of Colonial Pennsylvania," *PMHB*, LXXXIV (1960), 3–21; Rothermund, *The Layman's Progress: Religious and Political Experience in Colonial Pennsylvania, 1740–1770* (Philadelphia, 1961); Alan Tully, "Englishmen and Germans: National-Group Contact in Colonial Pennsylvania, 1700–1755," *Pennsylvania History*, XLV (1978), 237–256; Tully, "Ethnicity, Religion, and Politics in Early America," *PMHB*, CVII (1983), 491–536; Tully, *Forming American Politics: Ideals, Interests, and Institutions in Colonial New York and Pennsylvania* (Baltimore, 1994); Tully, "King George's War and the Quakers: The Defense Crisis of 1739–1742 in Pennsylvania Politics," *Journal of the Lancaster County Historical Society*, LXXXII (1978), 174–198; Tully, "Politics and Peace Testimony in Mid-Eighteenth Century Pennsylvania," *Canadian Review of American Studies*, XIII (1982), 159–177; Tully, *William Penn's Legacy: Politics and Social Structure in Provincial Pennsylvania, 1726–1755* (Baltimore, 1977); Hermann Wellenreuther, "Image and Counterimage, Tradition and Expectation: The German Immigrants in English Colonial Society in Pennsylvania, 1700–1765," in Frank Trommler and Joseph McVeigh, eds., *America and the Germans: An Assessment of a Three-Hundred-Year History*, 2 vols. (Philadelphia, 1985), 85–105. For changes in Pennsylvania Quakerism during the second half of the eighteenth century, see, esp., Jack D. Marietta, *The Reformation of American Quakerism, 1748–1783* (Philadelphia, 1984).

"The Quaker Mother": Christoph Saur's Response to Benjamin Franklin's Voluntary Association

During the War of the Austrian Succession (1740–1748), known as King George's War in the colonies, hostilities for the first time threatened Pennsylvania. After New England militia forces had captured the French fortress Louisbourg on the mouth of the Saint Lawrence, French and Spanish privateers marauded up and down the eastern seaboard. In 1747, they put ashore a French raiding party only forty miles from Philadelphia and sailed up the Delaware, unopposed, to within twenty miles of the city. News of such incursions and the possible threat of an attack on a defenseless Philadelphia put many inhabitants of the city in a state of panic. Meanwhile, Quakers had won the elections of 1747, dominated the Assembly, and refused any contributions to the military defense of the colony. On the other hand, the proprietors had repeatedly refused to provide defense at their own expense, claiming that it was the responsibility of the legislature. In this apparent deadlock, Benjamin Franklin took matters into his own hands and established a voluntary militia, the Association. As the primary means to propagate his scheme, Franklin wrote, printed, and distributed the pamphlet *Plain Truth* in November 1747.[4]

Though Franklin's *voluntary* militia technically did not violate the religious liberties of Quaker and German sectarian pacifists, his campaign for the Association strongly insinuated that conscientious objectors would be guilty of disloyalty and cowardice. In *Plain Truth,* Franklin even doubted the ability or willingness of German pacifists to appreciate and defend their *"newly acquired* and most precious *Liberty* and *Property"* because they had formerly lived under the rule of despots and tyrants. In promoting the military organization, Franklin organized public parades in which the associa-

---

4. For the impact of these wars on Pennsylvania and the debate of military expenditures in the province, see Robert L. D. Davidson, *War Comes to Quaker Pennsylvania, 1682–1756* (New York, 1957), 25–48; and Nathaniel C. Hale, *The Colonial Wars in Pennsylvania* ([Philadelphia], 1967), 7–9. On the Association debate in particular, see Barbara A. Gannon, "The Lord Is a Man of War, the God of Love and Peace: The Association Debate, Philadelphia, 1747–1748," *Pennsylvania History,* LXV (1998), 46–61; Sally F. Griffith, "'Order, Discipline, and a Few Cannon': Benjamin Franklin, the Association, and the Rhetoric and Practice of Boosterism," *Pennsylvania History,* CXVI (1992), 131–155; and J. Bennett Nolan, *General Benjamin Franklin: The Military Career of a Philosopher* (Philadelphia, 1936). For details on the establishment of the Association, see, J. A. Leo Lemay and P. M. Zall, eds., *Benjamin Franklin's Autobiography: An Authoritative Text, Backgrounds, Criticism* (New York, 1986), 92–95; Davidson, *War,* 49–63; Hale, *Colonial Wars,* 9–13; and, esp., Gannon, "The Lord," *Pennsylvania History,* LXV (1998), 47–51.

tors flew banners with martial mottoes and images embroidered on them. His campaign thus insulted the sensibilities of English and German pacifists alike and flew in the face of the Quaker-dominated Assembly's efforts to make defense the responsibility of the proprietors. As a result, Germans (sectarian and orthodox alike) as well as Quakers boycotted the Association, an alliance that Franklin regarded with great misgivings.[5]

Although Franklin never openly acknowledged even the existence let alone the influence of his great rival, the German printer Christoph Saur, the Lutheran minister Henry Melchior Muhlenberg specifically credited Saur's pamphlets and newspaper with aligning the Germans and Quakers against the Association. In his own representation of the historical relationship between Quakers and non-English, non-Quaker groups, Saur stressed common pacifist sensibilities as well as Penn's promotional activities in Germany and Holland. Most important, Saur appealed to the sensibilities of German sectarians by emphasizing the Quakers' original suffering, their stance for liberty of conscience, and their renewed trials under the agitations of non-Quaker (and presumably nonpacifist) "children":

The honest and kind Quakers, *for the blood they have lost*, finally received from God a place in the world (Pennsylvania) where they can live in peace and freedom of conscience. In this place, many foreign children have joined the Quaker mother and, until now, have enjoyed their mother's peace, liberty and happiness. As the number of these foreign children grew above that of its mother, it seems as if the foreign

5. [Benjamin Franklin], *Plain Truth; or, Serious Consideration on the Present State of the City of Philadelphia and Province of Pennsylvania* . . . (Philadelphia, 1747), 20–21. In the *Pennsylvania Gazette* of Jan. 12, 1748, he printed a list of "Devices and Mottoes" painted on the banners of the various regiments of the Association, including the virile and patriotic "Lion erect, a naked Scymeter in one Paw, the other holding the *Pennsylvania* Scutcheon, Motto, PRO PATRIA [for the fatherland / country]" and "An Elephant, being the Emblem of a Warrior always on his Guard, as that Creature is said never to lie down, and hath his Arms ever in Readiness. Motto, SEMPER PARATUS." Whereas the men are bearing arms and banners exulting martial prowess and the defense of the country, the women have made this display possible: "Most of the above Colours, together with the Officers Half-Pikes and Spontons, and even the Halberts, Drums, etc. have been given by the good Ladies of the City, who raised Money by Subscription among themselves for that Purpose." In a letter to his friend Peter Collinson in England, Franklin recollects: "Indeed in the last war our Germans shewed a general disposition that seems to bode us no good; for when the English who were not Quakers, alarmed by the danger arising from the defenceless state of our Country entered unanimously into an Association within this Government and the lower Countries [Counties] raised armed and Disciplined [near] 10,000 men, the Germans except a very few in proportion to their numbers refused to engage in it" (May 8, 1753, in Leonard W. Labaree et al., eds., *The Papers of Benjamin Franklin*, IV [New Haven, Conn., 1961], 485).

children were tired of the mother's peaceful habitation and would like to put it in a state of unrest, yes, even as if they would like to abolish their freedom of conscience: wouldn't that be the greatest injustice?

Saur's argument goes beyond praising the Quakers' commitment to pacifism by inserting specifically Anabaptist ideals of suffering; the emphasis on blood directly relates to the Mennonite *Martyrs' Mirror*. In the 1740s, anyone in Pennsylvania—including Quakers themselves—probably needed reminding that Quakers, too, had once been persecuted and that they designed Pennsylvania specifically as a bulwark against such actions. The common suffering for truth in the past, therefore, created a sense of cohesion between German and English sectarians. The "foreign" children could, after all, be both immigrants from non-English countries *and* members of other denominations (or both). The agreement or disagreement with the "Quaker mother," therefore, relied entirely on the attitude of these "children" toward the central principle of freedom of conscience, especially in matters of war.[6]

That Saur pitched his argument against the Association by appealing particularly to common understandings of the spiritual significance of war among Quakers and Mennonites becomes clear through the apocalyptic language he uses in describing the author of *Plain Truth*. Saur allegorizes Franklin and his argument / pamphlet as "Unglaube" (unbelief), "Welt-Priester" (worldly

6. Henry Melchior Muhlenberg, *The Journals of Henry Melchior Muhlenberg*, 3 vols., trans. Theodore G. Tappert and John W. Doberstein (Philadelphia, 1942), I, 212. Muhlenberg writes: "During this year a great deal has been conjectured and said about a hostile attack by the Spanish and French. Consequently there are two chief parties here among the English and they have entered into a violent newspaper war before the Spaniards and the French have come. The Quakers, who are the foremost party in this province, have on their side the German book publisher Sauer, who controls the Mennonites, separatists, Anabaptists, and the like with his printed works and lines them up with the Quakers. All of these speak and write against the war and reject even the slightest defense as ungodly and contrary to the command of Jesus Christ. The church party has the English book publishers on its side, and they maintain in speech and printed word that defense is not contrary to God's command, but right and necessary and in accord with the laws of nature. This party makes use of the preachers of the Episcopal and Presbyterian churches on its side."

See also Christoph Saur, *Ein gründliches Zeugnüß gegen das kürtzlich herausgegebene Büchlein, Genandt: Plain Truth; Oder: Lautere Wahrheit; von einem teutschen Bauers-Mann, in Pensylvanien* (Germantown, Pa., 1748), 5–6 (emphasis added): "Die ehrlichen und liebenswürdige Quäcker, haben wegen ihrem verlohrnen Bluts, endlich von GOtt in der Welt einen Ort (Pensylvanien) alwo sie in Ruh und Gewissens-Freyheit leben können, überkommen, alwo sich viele fremde Kinder zu der Quäkerischen Mutter eingefunden haben, und haben bis dato der Mutter Ruhe, Freyheit und Glückseligkeit mit genossen, da sich aber nunmehro, die Zahl dieser fremden Kinder über die Zahl der Mutter ihrer Kinder vermehret hat, so scheint es, als wann die fremde Kinder der Mutter ruhige Wohnung müde wären, und dieselbe in Unruh setzen wollen, ja gar ihre Gewissens-Freyheit aufheben wollen: wäre solches nicht das gröste Unrecht?"

priest), and "Antichrist": "Further, the Antichrist has tempted in Pennsylvania with his monstrous speech many peace-loving and quiet spirits and moved them to participate in this arms association." Saur's logic depends entirely on a theology of suffering; if resistance to Franklin's Association equaled resistance against the forces of darkness, any negative consequences for *non-associators* would be elevated to the level of suffering or even martyrdom.[7]

Saur was joined in his discursive attacks on Franklin in particular and defense in general by several Quaker pamphleteers. As war had not directly entered Pennsylvania yet, these writers largely engaged in theological arguments over differences between defensive and offensive war with advocates of defense such as Franklin and Presbyterian preacher Gilbert Tennent. They also resembled Saur in tapping into a basic Christian dialectic between redeemed and unredeemed individuals, natural men and true Christians, good and evil. Benjamin Gilbert, for instance, sermonized that all war was "as opposite in its Nature and Tendency, as Light to Darkness, or Good to Evil." John Smith similarly juxtaposed justifications of war occasioned by the "degenerate fallen Light of Nature" with a complete adherence to Christian principles. All Quaker writers, finally, complained that the proponents of war tried to disparage and abuse pacifists in general but Quakers in particular. Samuel Smith, for instance, wrote that in response to their efforts toward peace "the People called *Quakers* are stigmatized and reproached for beginning a Work so generally acknowledged glorious in itself, and beneficient in its Tendency." Clearly, Quaker advocates of pacifism already felt on the defensive in the 1740s, and they confirmed Saur's metaphor of the mother beset on all sides by ungrateful children. Yet a sense that Quakers needed to accept and steel themselves for a return of persecution is still missing from these pamphlets.[8]

Both Saur and the Quaker pamphleteers shared an emphasis on peacefulness as the central doctrine of Pennsylvania history anchored in Penn's treaties with the Indians. The specter of war in mid-eighteenth-century Pennsylvania, in other words, generated a renewed interest among Quakers

7. Saur, *Ein gründliches Zeugnüß*, 5, 16, 20.

8. Benjamin Gilbert, *Truth Vindicated, and the Doctrine of Darkness Manifested: Occasioned by the Reading of Gilbert Tennent's Late Composure, Intituled, Defensive War Defended: Dedicated to the Service of the Christian Reader* (Philadelphia, 1748), 18; John Smith, *The Doctrine of Christianity, as Held by the People Called Quakers, Vindicated: In Answer to Gilbert Tennent's Sermon on the Lawfulness of War* (Philadelphia, 1748), 9; [Samuel Smith], *Necessary Truth; or, Seasonable Considerations for the Inhabitants of the City of Philadelphia, and Province of Pennsylvania; in Relation to the Pamphlet Call'd Plain Truth: And Two other Writers in the News-Paper* (Philadelphia, 1748), 14.

and German sectarians in the interpretation of the province's history. Saur, in particular, stressed the transnational and cross-denominational character of early Pennsylvania. Almost mythologizing the founder, Saur wrote:

> William Penn was a man who loved a quiet and godly life, he wanted to have this country settled only with pious and godly people. And since at that time there were a number of pious people who were serious about their life with God, this godly Penn traveled through England, Scotland, Ireland, and Germany and sought out such people who were being oppressed for Christ's sake and were not being tolerated. . . . Since among the first inhabitants most were pious, godly, cordial, faithful, loving, and brotherly, they named their city Philadelphia, that is brotherly love, and William Penn befriended the Indians and paid them for the land so that they voluntarily withdrew and it is still happening in the same manner. Those who remember this country 40, 30, or 20 years ago, will admit that it was a blessed land full of righteous people.

Saur's idealized version of the early history of colonial Pennsylvania specifically links the pious and pacifist principles of the first settlers—both English Quakers and German Pietists and sectarians—to the peaceful, diplomatic relationships with the Indians. Translated into the Pennsylvania of the 1740s, Saur is arguing that the same alliance should again be in charge of regaining peaceful conditions. In another tract, Saur recommended a course of action that virtually outlined the central program of the Friendly Association, founded in 1756: "One should praise God alone, respect his word and command, show love to one's enemies . . . , give plenty to the poor Indians in their need, so that they may live with us in peace and love." Quaker John Smith similarly evoked Christian virtues as the principles by which "the first Settlers of this Province cultivated a good Understanding and Harmony with numerous warlike savage Nations, which still subsists." In the 1740s, therefore, Saur as well as the Quaker defenders of pacifism could still insist on the continued practicality of negotiating with native Americans in a peaceful manner. When Indian attacks on the Pennsylvania frontier during the Seven Years' War made this argument less convincing to anyone other than Quakers and German sectarians, these groups knew that the old Pennsylvania had changed radically and that a time of renewed suffering for all nonresistant Christians had returned.[9]

9. Christoph Saur, *Christliche Wahrheiten, und kurtze Betrachtung über das kürtzlich herausgegebene Büchlein, genannt: Lautere Wahrheit; aufgesetzt zur Überlegung, von einem Handwercksmann*

"That the Truth Remain Unblemished by the Translation": The Ephrata "Martyrs' Mirror" and the Linguistic Transfer of Martyrdom

When the brutalities of the Seven Years' War first came upon Pennsylvania in 1755, Governor Denny indignantly reported the slaughter of frontier inhabitants to support his calls for a colonial defense:

> Four dead Bodies, one of which was a Woman with Child, were brought to Lancaster from the neighbouring Frontiers, scalped and butchered in a most horrid Manner, and laid before the Door of the Court House for a Spectacle of Reproach to every one there, as it must give the Indians a sovereign Contempt for the Province. . . . The poor Inhabitants where these daring Murders were committed, being without Militia or Association, and living among Menonists, a numerous Sett of German Quakers, came supplicating me for Protection.

Mennonites were suddenly implicated in the misery and death of fellow Pennsylvanians. In the face of frontier suffering, their stance of defenselessness was considered an atrocity. In Denny's rhetoric, the "poor Inhabitants" were surrounded by Indians and Mennonites, presumably needing "Protection" from both. The blame heaped upon Mennonites eerily recalled the public ostracism they had experienced since the beginning of the Anabaptist movement.[10]

---

in Germanton (Germantown, Pa., 1748), 14–16 (". . . und weil William Penn ein Mann war, der die Stille und wahre Gottseeligkeit sehr liebte, so hätte er gern gesehen daß dieses Land mit lauter Frommen und Gottseeligen Leuten bewohnet werden mögte! und weil zur selbigen Zeit hin und wieder viele Frommen Leute waren, denen es ein Ernst um GOtt war, so reißte dieser Gottseelige Penn in Engeland, Schottland, Eyerland und Teutschland, und suchte solche Leute auf, welche um Christi willen gedrückt wurden, und nicht selten geduldtet werden. . . . Weil dann im Anfang unter den ersten Einwohnern die meiste fromm, Gottseelig, hertzlich, einander getreu, liebreich und brüderlich waren, so nenneten sie ihre Stadt, Philadelphia [16], das ist Brüderliche-Liebe, und William Penn bezahlte, und befriedigte die Indianer vor das Land, so weit sie haben zurück weichen wollen, und so geschiehet ihnen noch. Wer sich zu besinnen weiß was es vor 40 30 auch 20 Jahren im Land gewesen, der muß bekennen, daß es ein recht gesegnetes Land gewesen von redlichen Menschen . . . ."); Saur, *Ein gründliches Zeugnüß,* 13; Smith, *Doctrine of Christianity,* 31.

10. Quoted in Richard K. MacMaster, Samuel L. Horst, and Robert F. Ulle, *Conscience in Crisis: Mennonites and Other Peace Churches in America, 1739–1789, Interpretation and Documents* (Scottdale, Pa., 1979), 121–122. On the theological foundations of suffering and martyrdom in the Mennonite and larger Anabaptist tradition, see Ethelbert Stauffer, "The Anabaptist Theology of Martyrdom," trans. and ed. Robert Friedmann, *Mennonite Quarterly Review,* XIX (1945), 179–214. Also see Cornelius J. Dyck, trans. and ed., *Spiritual Life in Anabaptism* (Scottsdale, Pa., 1995); Dyck, "The

How, one might ask, had Pennsylvania Mennonites preserved the spirit of suffering and martyrdom as a meaningful principle of conduct in a New World characterized by religious, cultural, and linguistic pluralism as well as increasing violence? In some way, the "horrid" scenes and "Spectacle of Reproach" unfolding at the Pennsylvania frontier were familiar images for Mennonites raised on stories and illustrations collected in various martyrologies, most notably the magisterial *Martyrs' Mirror,* compiled by Thieleman van Braght in 1660 and republished in 1685 with 104 illustrations by Jan Luyken depicting the violent torture and death of hundreds of Anabaptists. About ten years before Denny's incriminating plea, the predominantly German-speaking Mennonites of the Franconia Conference had commissioned the "Brethren" of the Ephrata Seventh-Day Baptist community to translate and print the Dutch *Martyrs' Mirror* (1748–1749); the finished German translation was distributed to Pennsylvania Mennonite families in the early 1750s. When war arrived in 1755, Mennonites seemed resolved to follow the example of their blood witnesses and face the attacks of imperial invaders and the anger of their neighbors.[11]

Suffering Church in Anabaptism," *Mennonite Quarterly Review,* LIX (1985), 5–23; Alan F. Kreider, "'The Servant Is Not Greater Than His Master': The Anabaptists and the Suffering Church," ibid., LVIII (1984), 5–29.

11. Thieleman J. van Braght, *Het bloedigh Tooneel der Doops-Gesinde, en weereloose Christenen . . .* (Dordrecht, 1660); Van Braght and Jan Luyken, *Het bloedig Tooneel, of Martelaers Spiegel der Doops-Gesinde of weereloose Christenen . . .* (Amsterdam, 1685). For the most recent English-language edition, see *The Bloody Theater; or, Martyrs Mirror of the Defenseless Christians . . . Translated from the Original Dutch or Holland Language from the Edition of 1660 by Joseph F. Sohm,* 8th ed. (Scottdale, Pa., 1968). In my research on the Dutch *Martyrs' Mirror,* I have predominantly relied upon Sarah Covington, "Paratextual Stategies in Thieleman van Braght's *Martyr's Mirror,*" *Book History,* IX (2006), 1–29; James W. Lowry, *The "Martyrs' Mirror" Made Plain: A Study Guide and Further Studies* (Aylmer, Ont., 1997); Lowry, "*Martyrs' Mirror* Picture Albums and Abridgments: A Surprising Find," *Pennsylvania Mennonite Heritage,* XXV, no. 4 (October 2002), 2–8; John S. Oyer and Robert S. Kreider, *Mirror of the Martyrs: Stories of Courage, Inspiringly Retold, of 16th Century Anabaptists Who Gave Their Lives for Their Faith* (Intercourse, Pa., 2003); Gerald C. Studer, "A History of the Martyrs' Mirror," *Mennonite Quarterly Review,* XXII (1948), 163–179; A. Orley Swartzentruber, "The Piety and Theology of the Anabaptist Martyrs in Van Braght's *Martyrs' Mirror,*" ibid., XXVIII (1954), 5–26, 128–142. For the most recent work interpreting the Pennsylvania *Martyrs' Mirror* as a means for German peace sects to forge a common identity and resist the militarization of Pennsylvania's Indian policies, see Jan Stievermann, "A 'Plain, Rejected Little Flock': The Politics of Martyrological Self-Fashioning among Pennsylvania's German Peace Churches, 1739–65," *WMQ,* 3d Ser., LXII (2009), 287–324.

See also T[hieleman] J. [van] Braght, *Der blutige Schau-Platz oder Martyrer-Spiegel der Tauffs Gesinnten oder wehrlosen-Christen . . . ,* [trans. Johann Peter Miller] (Ephrata, Pa., 1748–1749). Pennsylvania German historians have a shared a long-standing fascination with the Ephrata *Martyrs' Mirror,* yet most accounts only repeat early findings (including certain errors and erroneous judgments)

In translating, printing, and disseminating the *Martyrs' Mirror,* Pennsylvania Mennonites again took up recurring questions about the translation of spiritual concepts and beliefs across time, cultures, continents, and languages: How could they prepare themselves for persecution and bridge the distance from the co-religionists who had actually experienced martyrdom? Could a book—especially a translation—achieve such a task among a generation of Mennonites who had become accustomed to peace and religious toleration? Renewed threats of war, the possibility of mandatory armed service, and thus the erosion of Pennsylvania's freedom of conscience all required church leaders to create more than a theoretical awareness of theology, beliefs, and church discipline; the peculiar identity of the Mennonites as a suffering church once again had to become a lived faith borne from experience or at least from a palpable sense of its spirit. In order to continue as nonresistant Christians, Mennonites had to translate their time-honored principles of martyrdom and suffering to the New World. The task of translators, printers, and readers would be this: to create and receive the Pennsylvania *Martyrs' Mirror* not merely as a faithful linguistic translation of Van Braght's 1660 compilation but also as a spiritual and physical manifestation of martyrdom.

FOR ANABAPTISTS IN early modern Europe, suffering and martyrdom sanctioned the existence and formation of religious community. Paraphrasing a quotation from the ancient Christian writer Tertullian, the *Martyrs' Mirror* stated, "The blood of martyrs is the seed of the church." In turn, the stories of sacrificed believers or blood witnesses became sacred texts. Just as the martyrs followed Christ's sacrifice, martyr texts continued the tradition of the scriptures in chronicling a history of persecution. The goal of the earliest martyrologies was "to show how snugly present persecution fit its scriptural template." Van Braght made the coherence between biblical martyrdom and

by Samuel Pennypacker and Julius Friedrich Sachse. See Daniel R. Heatwole, *The Ephrata Martyrs' Mirror: Past and Present* (Scottdale, Pa., [n.d.]); Samuel W. Pennypacker, "A Noteworthy Book," *PMHB,* V (1881), 276–289; Julius Friedrich Sachse, *The German Sectarians of Pennsylvania, 1708–1742: A Critical and Legendary History of the Ephrata Cloister and the Dunkers,* I (1899) (New York, 1971); Sachse, *The German Sectarians of Pennsylvania, 1742–1800: A Critical and Legendary History of the Ephrata Cloister and the Dunkers,* II (1900) (New York, 1971). The reader of Sachse's work should always be aware that the "legendary" far outweighs the "critical" in his scholarship. New findings and more innovative interpretations include Julia Kasdorf, "'Work and Hope': Tradition and Translation of an Anabaptist Adam," *Mennonite Quarterly Review,* LXIX (1995), 178–204; David Luthy, "The Ephrata Martyrs' Mirror: Shot From Patriots' Muskets," *Pennsylvania Mennonite Heritage,* IX, no. 1 (January 1986), 2–5.

Anabaptist persecution and suffering even more explicit by adding an entire volume of accounts chronicling martyrdom from Christ through the time of the apostles, the persecution of early Christians, and up to the Anabaptist movement. The blood shed by those who followed Christ would metaphorically and spiritually be poured onto the pages of the martyr books, infusing them with the spirit of martyrdom.[12]

Translating the spirit of martyrdom onto the printed page became more difficult as certain Mennonite communities were no longer persecuted. In the early seventeenth century, Dutch Mennonites began to enjoy toleration and prosperity, thus lacking a continual infusion of martyr spirit. Doctrinal disputes and regional differences, moreover, seemed to call for the articulation of a unifying tradition of martyr histories. In response, martyrologies expanded their geographical reach to encompass a variety of Anabaptist traditions. In 1615, the Dutch Mennonite Hans de Ries published the largest martyr book yet, *History of the Martyrs or Genuine Witnesses of Jesus Christ*, and his 1631 expanded edition for the first time carried the title *Martyrs' Mirror*. De Ries also introduced the use of elaborate title pages featuring

---

12. Quoted in Lowry, *"Martyrs' Mirror" Made Plain*, 9; Brad S. Gregory, *Salvation at Stake: Christian Martyrdom in Early Modern Europe* (Cambridge, Mass., 1999), 227-228. This chapter expands and complicates the scholarly emphasis on Christian martyr books as a textual means of harnessing the memory of past suffering to produce communal and spiritual identification among religious groups such as the Anabaptists in continental Europe and the Quakers in England. For instance, Friedericke Pannewick's collection *Martyrdom in Literature: Visions of Death and Meaningful Suffering in Europe and the Middle East from Antiquity to Modernity* (Wiesbaden, 2004) generally argues that "the shared remembrance inscribed in literary texts creates amongst the audience / readers a community of suffering, forming a sense of identity and shaping a perception of past and future in equal measure" (9). The material features and presence of martyr books still play a surprisingly small role in this scholarship, as does the translation of martyrologies into other languages. Early modern English discourses and traditions of martyrdom have received the most scholarly attention, including Thomas S. Freeman and Thomas F. Mayer, *Martyrs and Martyrdom in England, c. 1400-1700* (Woodbridge, Eng., 2007); Susannah Brietz Monta, *Martyrdom and Literature in Early Modern England* (Cambridge, 2005); and John R. Knott, *Discourses of Martyrdom in English Literature, 1563-1694* (Cambridge, 1993). Gregory's seminal *Salvation at Stake* provides the most comprehensive overview of late medieval and early modern concepts of Christian martyrdom, and he gives a comparative context between British Protestant, Continental Anabaptist, and Catholic martyr traditions that is largely absent from other accounts. His chapter *"Nachfolge Christi*: Anabaptists and Martyrdom" (197-249) usefully traces the often neglected development of Anabaptist martyrologies up to the *Martyrs' Mirror*. An equally magisterial work for the German-language sphere in the early modern period is Peter Burschel, *Sterben und Unsterblichkeit: Zur Kultur des Martyriums in der frühen Neuzeit* (München, 2004). On martyrdom in antiquity, see Elizabeth A. Castelli, *Martyrdom and Memory: Early Christian Culture Making* (New York, 2004); and Jan Willem van Henten and Friedrich Avemarie, eds., *Martyrdom and Noble Death: Selected Texts from Graeco-Roman, Jewish, and Christian Antiquity* (London, 2002).

execution scenes. For his 1660 *Martyrs' Mirror,* Van Braght collected and authenticated previously published or unpublished martyr stories from different regions and traditions, added a lengthy volume recounting martyr stories from Christ onward, and prefaced everything with an introduction that posited the martyr stories as evidence of the continuous unfolding of an eschatological battle that required a rigorous stance of discipleship.[13]

Once the Anabaptist faith had spread beyond its original homelands, Mennonites began to use translations of their "confessions" (statements of theology, social ethics, and church policy) to increase understanding of their beliefs among outsiders. For instance, the 1632 Dordrecht Confession of Faith was consecutively translated into German, French, and English. The first English translation, published in Amsterdam in 1712, was specifically designed for the use of co-religionists who had immigrated to Pennsylvania. In the preface, the publisher casts translation as a tool of interdenominational communication and exchange, allowing Mennonite immigrants to position themselves in a new culture and language:

> Therefore it hath been thought fit and needful to translate, at the desire of some of our Fellow-believers in Pensylvania *[sic]*, our Confession of Faith into English, so as for many years it hath been printed in the Dutch, German, and French languages: which Confession hath been well approved of both in the Low-Countries and in France, by severall eminent persons of the Reformed Religion; And therefore it hath been thought worth the while to turn it also into English, so that those of that Nation may become acquainted with it, and so mighe *[sic]* have a better opinion thereof and of its professors; and not only so, but also that every well-meaning soul might enquire and try all things, and keep that which is best.

Mennonite immigrants could now share the fundamental articles of their faith with their English-speaking neighbors. Yet the English translation not only fulfilled the purpose of outward justification; it also reminded Mennonites of their faith's theological and spiritual principles. In paraphrasing Paul's dictum, "Prove all things; hold fast that which is good" (I Thess. 5:21), the preface establishes a principle guiding the contact with other denominations and cultures in moments of religious and ethnic diversity *and*

---

13. Gregory, *Salvation at Stake,* 197–249; Burschel, *Sterben und Unsterblichkeit,* 159–196; Hans de Ries, *Historie der Martelaren . . .* (Haerlem, 1615); de Ries, *Martelaers Spiegel der werelosen Christen: t'zedert Ao. 1524* (Haerlem, 1631).

the process of translation itself. Repeated in the translation of the "Appendix" to the Dordrecht Confession published in Philadelphia in 1727, this motto asked Mennonites in the New World to "hold fast" to the most treasured ideals of their faith—such as nonresistance—while reaching out to other groups in order to establish points of spiritual contact and understanding.[14]

Nevertheless, Pennsylvania Mennonites soon began to question the resilience of the province's founding principle of "freedom of conscience" when rumors of war reminded them of the conditions they had left behind in Europe. Consequently, they assiduously supported Quakers in the Assembly, lobbied for quick naturalization, and wrote petitions against military service. Pennsylvania Mennonites also asked their wealthy co-religionists in Holland for support. A 1745 letter by the leaders of the Skippack congregation expressed the Mennonites' fear that their dearest religious principles might be curtailed. Mennonites anticipated that the governor would require military service in violation of their pacifist stance, thus undermining the freedom of conscience that had originally drawn them to "so distant a land." They therefore sought the spiritual weapons Anabaptists had traditionally wielded in their battle against the "wolves" of the world: martyr books. Their letter asked for assistance from the Dutch congregations in translating and publishing in German Van Braght's *Martyrs' Mirror* "so that our posterity may have before their eyes the traces of those loyal witnesses of the truth, who walked in the way of truth and have given their lives for it." Evidence of stalwartness in the face of persecution in the past would strengthen Pennsylvania Mennonites for the future. Yet the stakes for Pennsylvania Mennonites were even higher than they had been for Van Braght in 1660 and Luyken in 1685. The *Martyrs' Mirror* translation requested by the Skippack Mennonites needed to become far more than a symbolic device providing the youth with an understanding of their heritage; it had to continue the physical link between past, present, and future suffering. Pennsylvania Mennonites had to create a threefold translation: they desired a linguistically accurate translation from Dutch to German. Theological content needed to be transferred without distorting articles of faith. Most impor-

14. Beulah Stauffer Hostetler, "The Place of Confessions in the Mennonite Church (MC)," *Pennsylvania Mennonite Heritage*, no. 2, XII (April 1989), 2–6; *The Christian Confession of the Faith of the Harmless Christians, in the Netherlands Known by the Name of Mennonists* (Amsterdam, 1712); *An Appendix to the Confession of Faith of the Christians, Called, Mennonites* . . . (Philadelphia, 1727); *The Christian Confession of the Faith of the Harmless Christians, in the Netherlands, Known by the Name of Mennonists* (Amsterdam and Philadelphia, 1727).

tant, the translation and translators needed to carry the spiritual meanings *and* physical experience of suffering and martyrdom into a new edition, printed for readers in the New World.[15]

The problem of translation was thus foremost on the Mennonites' minds. Although the Skippack congregation had "greatly desired to have this work published for a number of years," they rejected offers from the German printer Christoph Saur, who had published the first American edition of the Mennonite hymnal *Ausbund* (1742). The letter to the Amsterdam congregation hinted at several reasons for not employing Saur:

> The establishment of a new German printing office has renewed the hopes, but the bad paper used here for printing has caused us to reconsider. Besides, up to this time, there has not appeared, either among ourselves or others, anyone who understands the languages well enough to make a faithful translation. We have for certain reasons not been able to entrust it to those who have volunteered and promised to do it, for however much we are concerned to have it translated, we are equally concerned that the truth remain unblemished by the translation.

Saur's paper might not have been particularly poor by colonial standards, but the Mennonites wanted to have the "sacred" text of their "blood witnesses" produced in the highest possible quality. Second, Saur clearly did not have the linguistic acumen to translate such a lengthy text from Dutch into German. Most important, the Mennonites feared that the spiritual "truth" embedded within the original martyr stories might be corrupted or changed through the translation. Saur was a radical Pietist with Dunker ties. German Baptists or Dunkers favored baptism by immersion, whereas Mennonites did not. Saur had also been criticized—especially by Lutheran and Reformed ministers—for inserting "apocryphal" texts favored by radical Pietists into the Lutheran translation of the Bible. The Mennonites' worries about translation, therefore, went deeper than a potential distrust of Saur's

15. MacMaster, Horst, and Ulle, *Conscience in Crisis*, 25–59 (quotation on 25). Ethelbert Stauffer describes the Anabaptist notion of discipleship and, thus, the lives of nonresistant Christians as "sheep among wolves" (Stauffer, "Anabaptist Theology," trans. and ed. Friedmann, *Mennonite Quarterly Review*, XIX [1945], 212). For Pennsylvania German political support for the Quakers, see Tully, "Englishmen and Germans," *Pennsylvania History*, XLV (1978), 237–256. Leaders of the Mennonite Congregations in Pennsylvania, "To All the Ministers and Elders of the Nonresistant Mennonite Congregations of God in Amsterdam and Haarlem, October 19, 1745," in MacMaster, Horst, and Ulle, *Conscience in Crisis*, 84–86.

skill, his paper, and his fidelity as a printer. Translation carried the charge to transmit the spiritual essence of radical discipleship, and the Mennonites wondered how such a translation could inspire a similar stance among their youth. Skippack Mennonites eventually contacted the German Seventh-Day Baptist community at Ephrata to aid with the translation and printing of the "sacred" martyrology. Here the Mennonites found an able translator in Peter Miller.[16]

In spite of certain differences between both communities highlighted in differing views about baptism (Ephrata practiced immersion, Mennonites did not), both Mennonites and Ephrata Brethren and Sisters similarly inscribed suffering and martyrdom in the physical objects and conduct of their lives. Similar to the plain dress and way of life of the Mennonites, the Ephrata cloister attempted to manifest a metaphysical ideal of suffering in a physical reality. Even before the *Martyrs' Mirror,* Mennonites and Ephrata Brethren had collaborated on printing Mennonite devotional books that included several martyr stories, thus initiating a transfer of theological content and spiritual symbolism. Indeed, the Ephrata-Mennonite collaboration ensured the "translation" of early modern martyr book culture to the New World through the confluence of similar traditions.[17]

Specifically, Conrad Beissel, longtime leader of the Ephrata cloister, championed translating and printing the *Martyrs' Mirror* as a means of purifying and perfecting the earthly selves of the Brethren. According to the *Chronicon Ephratense,* Beissel "was the instigator of this work, [and] never allowed a suspension of work or carnal rest in the Settlement, and therefore seized every opportunity to keep all those who were under his control in perpetual motion, so that no one might ever feel at home again in this life, and so forget the consolation from above, which purpose this Book

---

16. *Ausbund, das ist: Etliche schöne christliche Lieder* . . . (Germantown, Pa., 1742); MacMaster, Horst, and Ulle, *Conscience in Crisis,* 84–86 (quotations on 86); Milton Rubincam and Thomas R. Brendle, *William Rittenhouse and Moses Dissinger: Two Eminent Pennsylvania Germans* (Scottdale, Pa., 1959). On Christoph Saur and his son, Christoph II, see Donald F. Durnbaugh, "Christopher Sauer, Pennsylvania-German Printer: His Youth in Germany and Later Relationships with Europe," *PMHB,* LXXXII (1958), 316–340; Frasca, "'To Rescue the Germans out of Sauer's Hands,'" ibid., CXXXI (1997), 329–350; Stephen L. Longenecker, *The Christopher Sauers: Courageous Printers Who Defended Religious Freedom in Early America* (Elgin, Ill., 1981); Anna Kathryn Oller, "Christopher Saur, Colonial Printer: A Study of the Publications of the Press, 1738–1758" (Ph.D. diss., University of Michigan, 1963); MacMaster, Horst, and Ulle, *Conscience in Crisis,* 88; John C. Wenger, *History of the Mennonites of the Franconia Conference* (Telford, Pa., 1937), 319.

17. Harold S. Bender, *Two Centuries of American Mennonite Literature: A Bibliography of Mennonitica Americana, 1727–1928* (Goshen, Ind., 1929).

of Martyrs excellently served." The *Chronicon* thus describes this effort as a distillation process that infused the resulting volumes with a renewed spirit of suffering: "When this [work] is taken into consideration, as also the low price, and how far those who worked at it were removed from self-interest, the biographies of the holy martyrs, which the book contains, cannot fail to be a source of edification to all who read them." Granted, the continued insistence on the translation and publication of the *Martyrs' Mirror* as a work of physical and mental exhaustion could be interpreted as vanity or self-pity. Yet Miller and his associates genuinely sought to imitate the martyrs represented in the book to achieve a spiritual union with Christ, the ultimate martyr.[18]

The production costs and work hours must have been overwhelming by any standard. According to the *Chronicon,* fifteen Brethren worked on the project, "nine of whom had their work assigned in the printing department, namely, one corrector, who was at the same time the translator, four compositors and four pressmen; the rest had their work in the paper-mill. Three years were spent on this book, though not continuously, for there was often want of paper." According to Miller's testimony to the Swedish minister Israel Acrelius, seven hundred copies of the original printing of twelve hundred or thirteen hundred had been sold in 1754. The binding of the *Martyrs' Mirror* was apparently completed in stages or on demand. This assumption is also supported by the many variants of the Ephrata *Martyrs' Mirror* still in existence, especially with regard to the inclusion or exclusion of frontispieces and illustrations. In any case, the sheer size of the enterprise placed the Ephrata Brethren into a spirit of suffering and discipleship.[19]

In his new preface to the Ephrata *Martyrs' Mirror,* Miller cast the translation and printing of the book as a form of *imitatio;* accordingly, he emphasized that the Brethren did not regret the "pains, the work, the industry, and the diligence in this important and lengthy endeavor, especially as the

18. [Jacob Gast and Peter Miller], *Chronicon Ephratense; a History of the Community of Seventh Day Baptists at Ephrata, Lancaster County, Pennsylvania, by "Lamech and Agrippa,"* trans. J. Max Hark (Lancaster, Pa., 1889), 210, 214; [Gast and Miller], *Chronicon Ephratense; enthaltend den Lebens-Lauf des ehrwürdigen Vaters in Christo Friedsam Gottrecht, Weyland Stiffters und Vorstehers des geistl. Ordens der Einsamen in Ephrata in der Graffschaft Lancaster in Pennsylvania; zusammen getragen von Br. Lamech u. Agrippa* (Ephrata, Pa., 1786).

19. [Gast and Miller], *Chronicon Ephratense,* trans. Hark, 213. In the *Chronicon,* Miller stated that "the edition consisted of 1300 copies" (213), but he mentioned to the visiting Swedish minister Israel Acrelius that it was 1,200 copies; see Felix Reichmann and Eugene E. Doll, eds., *Ephrata as Seen by Contemporaries* (Allentown, Pa., 1952), 60.

memorial of the sacrificed confessors . . . always encouraged us to continue, so that we finally completed the work to the greatest enjoyment of others and ourselves." Linking them spiritually and physically to the subjects of the book, the translators and printers' own sacrifice made the translation of the *Martyrs' Mirror* a worthy representation of the original sacrifice of the martyrs. Here, translation allowed readers to partake in the spiritual drama revealed or "mirrored" in the *Martyrs' Mirror.* The preface explicitly exhorted the readers to gain—through the pain and suffering invested in the volume—a palpable sense of the original sufferings represented. Miller concluded:

> Attentive readers! Thus receive this work—for which we have spared neither trouble nor industry—and perceive in reading this book the same taste and awakening by the blessed blood witnesses which others have enjoyed in the translating and printing thereof; then will your life and death serve discipleship, which had been the aim of this [work]. [Signed:] The publisher of this book.

The preface imagined a reception of the text through both sensory ("taste") and spiritual ("awakening") experience, thus expanding communication to a supralinguistic dimension. The translation of martyrdom thus reached deep into a common language that ultimately transcended language itself: the imitation of the suffering of Christ and, in turn, the suffering of the saints who followed his example. The Ephrata *Martyrs' Mirror* created a community of martyrdom that extended both spiritually and physically from the "blood witnesses" in the book, to the translators and printers at Ephrata, and to the Mennonite readers.[20]

Mirroring Miller's preface, the Mennonites' endorsement of the translation and printing at the end of the volume resumes the theme of imitatio. The two Mennonite leaders in charge of inspecting the work, Tielmann (or Dielman) Kolb and Henrich (or Heinrich) Funck, expressed their belief that

> the Lord will kindle through his H. Spirit in the hearts of all men a desire and hunger for this book, so that they may not mind the little

---

20. [Van] Braght, *Martyrer-Spiegel,* [trans. Miller], 4: "So lasset dann, aufmercksame Leser, diese unsere Arbeit, daran wir keine Mühe und Fleiß gespart haben, bey euch eine Aufnahme finden, und empfindet im Durchlesen dieses Buchs denselben Geschmack und Erweckung von den seligen Blut-Zeugen, den Andere bey dem Übersetzen und Abdrucken hievon genossen haben, so wird euch ihr Leben und Hingang zur Nachfolge gereichen, als welches das Augmärck gewesen ist. Der Verleger dieses Buchs."

money, but purchase the same, take their time with it, and read it with devotion, so they may see and learn, how the faith in Christ must be built, and how one's life and conduct may serve to follow the defense-less lamb, and thus to inherit the eternal kingdom with Christ and his followers.

Kolb and Funck's afterword projected what the Mennonites valued most in the translation: preserving the spiritual meanings of the martyr stories. Yet the book is also a physical object that answers the "desire and hunger" Pennsylvania Mennonites had for the martyr stories and their palpable presence in their lives. It is both spiritual essence and emotional nourishment.[21]

The Mennonites' endorsement also echoed the Pauline principle, "Prove all things; hold fast that which is good," evoked in the earlier Mennonite confessions. In their afterword, Kolb and Funck thus judged the spiritual value and correctness of the translation:

> They [Funck and Kolb] have not found one point in the whole work that does not contain the same sense and foundation of faith, as it was conceived in Dutch. They have certainly found different words where they halted and which, they thought, might have been rendered more pleasantly in both the Dutch and the high-German. One should not be surprised that in such a large book a word here and there is not captured in the most precise manner, but no one should be accused in this regard, for we are all human beings who frequently err.

Just as the English edition of the Dordrecht Confession advised readers to shy away from a literalist judgment of both the translation and the faith itself, the inspectors of the *Martyrs' Mirror* emphasized that they expected a spiritually sound translation in which the spirit of the martyrs remains in-

21. Tielmann Kolb and Henrich Funck, "Kurtze Nachrede einiger Mitglieder der Gemeinde der Mennonisten, als welche die hochdeutsche Uebersetzung gegen der holländischen genau überlesen, und darauf die vor dem Register angeführte Druckfehler zur Bekanntmachung haben zugesandt" [A brief afterword by several members of the congregation of Mennonites, who have diligently read the High German translation from the Dutch and submitted the printing errors listed in the index for publication], in [Van] Braght, *Martyrer-Spiegel*, [trans. Miller], n.p.: "Ferner aber glauben wir, daß dieses noch das Beste zu diesem Werck seyn werde, daß nemlich der HErr durch seinen H. Geist die Herzen der Menschen sämtlich wolle anzünden mit einer Lust und Begierde zu diesem Buch, damit sie mögen ein wenig Geldes nicht ansehen, sondern sich dasselbe anschaffen, auch sich gute Zeit darzu nehmen, und mit Andacht fleisig darin zu lesen, damit sie sehen und erlernen, wie man müsse im Glauben an Christum bestellet seyn, und wie man sich im Leben und Wandel soll zubereiten, dem wehrlosen Lamm zu folgen, und also ein Erbe des ewigen Reichs mit Christo und seinen Nachfolgern zu werden."

tact, even while the precise wording might have been changed or even improved. They distinguished language as a realm subject to human fallacies from the realm of divine inspiration and meaning, which can be carried into another language (and even another continent) through the spirit of suffering and martyrdom.[22]

Finally, Kolb and Funck ensured that the chain of suffering continued by the Ephrata Brethren during the production of the *Martyrs' Mirror* would remain unbroken. Although styling themselves less self-consciously as martyrs than the Ephrata Brethren did, they nevertheless stressed their hard work—a key ingredient in the Mennonite ideology of discipleship—in checking the entire text: "Since Henrich Funck and Tielmann Kolb have a special love for this book, they have both—with the agreement of the community—dedicated the time and attention to comparing one sheet after another . . . with the Dutch book. During this work, they did not skip one verse." The linguistic and theological authentication is thus buttressed by the two readers' emotional attachment to the book, their own physical and mental exertions in proofreading such a large volume, and the communal sanction of their efforts.[23]

Many surviving copies of the Ephrata translation of the *Martyrs' Mirror* demonstrate that Mennonite readers in mid-eighteenth-century Pennsylvania came to share Kolb's and Funck's special love for this book. With the help of the German translation, Pennsylvania Mennonites—as well as other German peace sects—participated in an emotionally, even sensually charged veneration of martyrdom and the martyr books encapsulating this spirit. Readers personalized individual copies of the *Martyrs' Mirror* and treated the book as their most prized treasure. For instance, elaborately wrought Fraktur writings placed the reader—represented by the owners' names written in colorful lettering—spiritually and physically in the midst of the spiritual drama unfolding inside the book (Figure 15). A hand-drawn

---

22. Kolb and Funck, "Kurtze Nachrede," in [Van] Braght, *Martyrer-Spiegel*, [trans. Miller], n.p.: "Sie haben aber in der gantzen Arbeit nicht einen Puncten gefunden, der nicht demselben Glaubens-Grund und Sinn in sich hält, wie in dem Holländischen begriffen ist. Sie haben zwar unterschiedliche Wörter gefunden, daran sie seynd angestanden und gedachten, es hatte solches beydes im Holländischen und Hochteutschen lieblicher können gegeben werden: man darf sich aber nicht verwundern, wann in einem solchen grosen Buch ein Wort hie oder da nicht zum feinsten getroffen wird; doch darf man darum niemand beschuldigen, weil wir auch Menschen seynd, die oft fehlen."

23. Ibid.: "Weil aber Henrich Funck und Tielmann Kolb eine besondere Liebe zu diesem Buch haben, so haben sie beyde mit Gemeinschäfftlicher Bewilligung die Zeit und Ruhe daran gewandt, und haben einen Bogen nach dem andern, . . . mit dem Holländischen Buch vergleichen, in welcher Arbeit sie nicht einen Vers übergangen haben."

*Figure 15. Fraktur Inscription by Anna Barbara Bach, Written in 1758. From
T[hieleman] J. [van] Braght,* Der blutige Schau-Platz oder Martyrer-Spiegel der taufs
gesinnten oder wehrlosen-Christen . . . , *[trans. Johann Peter Miller] (Ephrata, Pa.,
1748–1749). By permission of The Historical Society of Pennsylvania (HSP)*

image in a *Martyrs' Mirror* copy owned by an Ephrata Brother known as "Amos" not only reflects his contemplation of the mystery of Christ's suffering and atonement but also his active involvement in it. The depiction of the apostles and Mary mourning under the cross—especially their dress and demeanor—closely resembles similar images of Ephrata Brethren and Sisters elsewhere in the cloister's manuscript illuminations (Figure 16). The Ephrata Brethren thus attempted not just to disseminate the *Martyr's Mirror* but also to continue writing it. Translation, printing, and manuscript illustration, in other words, created a spiritual community extending from Christ, to the apostles, to the martyrs of the Protestant Reformation (especially the Anabaptists), and, finally, to the Ephrata Brothers and Sisters.[24]

In spite of such appreciation by Pennsylvania Mennonites, a sizable portion of the 1748-1749 Ephrata edition remained unbound and unsold at Ephrata; ultimately, the Continental Congress authorized confiscation of the books to produce cartridge wadding for the Revolutionary army in 1776. At this juncture, the Ephrata *Martyrs' Mirror* turned from a book representing suffering and martyrdom into a martyred or suffering book. Coinciding with a vehement backlash against loyalists and pacifists suspected of being loyalists, the confiscation of the *Martyrs' Mirror* demonstrated to Mennonites and other German peace sects symbolically and physically the need to withdraw from a society that had promised complete liberty of conscience but now abridged this civil right for the sake of attaining political freedom. The *Chronicon Ephratense* argued that the confiscation "gave great offence in the country, and many thought that the war would not end favorably for the country, because the memorials of the holy martyrs had been maltreated." In other words, the books containing the stories of the martyrs had become martyrs themselves.[25]

A flyleaf inscription in a *Martyrs' Mirror* copy owned by a Mennonite named Joseph von Gundy condemns the confiscation vehemently and provides a useful account of the purchase of the remaining copies by Mennonites after the Revolution:

This book was printed in [Ephrata] in Lancaster County. . . . It was *seized* by Congress in 1776 and *taken unbound* to Philadelphia. Approximately 150 or a few more were made into cartridges and shot

24. Don Yoder, "A Fraktur Primer," American Folklife Center at the Library of Congress, *Folklife Annual* (1988-1989), 100-111.

25. [Gast and Miller], *Chronicon Ephratense,* trans. Hark, 213-214 n. 2.

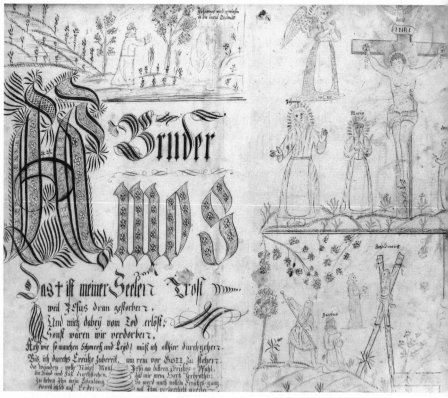

*Figure 16. Manuscript Illustrations in Ephrata Brother Amos's Copy of
T[hieleman] J. [van] Braght,* Der blutige Schau-Platz oder Martyrer-Spiegel der
Tauffs Gesinnten oder wehrlosen-Christen . . . , *[trans: Johann Peter Miller] (Ephrata,
Pa., 1748–1749). By permission of the Schwenkfelder Library, Pennsburg, Pa.*

against their [former] [English] brothers, making a murder book out
of it until their own conscience told them it had not been printed for
such a purpose. Then the government made a pronouncement to the
lovers of this volume that if they would repay them their money and
the cartage, they could have back the remaining books. This we did,
sending them payment in 1786 when Congress money was worth so
little that this book unbound did not cost me over four shillings and
six pence or half a dollar and ten pence. Thus, 175 books were returned, many of which were no longer complete and also damaged
which I myself saw. But I was lucky that this copy is not lacking a
single page. As it is here, it cost me $1.60.

Crucially, Gundy describes the fate of the books as martyrdom or captivity. Just as the Anabaptist martyrs of old resisted and died for their convictions, the unbound copies of the Ephrata *Martyrs' Mirror* were quite literally killed by being shot from muskets; in a sardonic irony, the testimony of pacifists aided the taking of life, thus making it a "murder book." Just as the Franconia conference Mennonites had feared conscription into military service above any threats to their physical lives, Gundy regarded the spiritual perversion of the book as a worse offense than its physical destruction.[26]

The remaining copies of the Ephrata *Martyrs' Mirror* literally and spiritually became the equivalents of the suffering bodies of the ancient and Anabaptist martyrs, and Gundy's flyleaf inscription becomes the very last account of an Anabaptist martyr — the book itself. Gundy's prose, therefore, describes the confiscated copies like the bodies of martyrs. First, they are "seized and taken." In German, the combination of the past participles *genommen* and *geführt* makes the metaphor of "book as martyred body" even stronger; *geführt* (past participle of the word *führen*, to lead) is not usually paired with an impersonal object, such as the books, but rather with a person or animal. For the writer, the taking of copies of the *Martyrs' Mirror* resembles the arrest and imprisonment usually experienced by the martyrs represented within the book. Gundy makes this analogy even more explicit. The adverb *ungebunden* (unbound) seems to contradict the notion of captivity (the books are not bound). Of course, *unbound* refers to the pages of the volumes; they are not yet bound into individual books; they are loose assemblies of Mennonite martyr stories. One can understand the implications for the Mennonite sensibility only by visualizing what a *bound* copy of the Ephrata *Martyrs' Mirror* looks like. Luthy describes the book as "bound between oak boards covered with leather, the book weighed thirteen pounds. It was the largest book printed in colonial America." The specimens of the *Martyrs' Mirror* I have seen are all dressed in a type of ironclad lockbox worthy of the Mennonites' most treasured spiritual possession. For the copies of the *Martyrs' Mirror* to be taken unbound to Philadelphia thus means that they are as unprotected and defenseless as the actual martyrs

26. Transcription of the handwritten flyleaf in the Von Gundy 1748–1749 *Martyrer-Spiegel*, in David Luthy, "The Ephrata Martyrs' Mirror: Short from Patriots' Muskets," *Pennsylvania Mennonite Heritage*, IX, no. 1 (January 1986), 2–5 (quotation on 5; emphasis added), translation by Luthy. Luthy concluded his article by stating that 1986 marks the three hundredth anniversary of "the book's return in 1786 from its Philadelphia captivity" (5).

were when they were "seized . . . and taken" by the respective authorities. Like captives being redeemed, the confiscated volumes of the *Martyrs' Mirror* only return because the Mennonite admirers of the book pay a ransom to secure their release. This analogy also provides an uncanny echo of the captivity and release (or death) of many European frontier inhabitants among the Indians, giving the suffering of the books both a European and an American context.[27]

The metaphorical and physical connection between the text as body and the book as martyr therefore climaxes at the moment of return, not the moment of confiscation. Like the martyrs within the book (who were tortured, dismembered, and executed), the books themselves return mutilated and dismembered. Of the copies purchased back by Mennonites, Gundy explains, "many . . . were no longer complete and also damaged *which I myself saw.*" Gundy here becomes a witness to the martyrdom of these volumes in the same way that the disciples became witnesses of the sacrifice of Christ through the observation of his wounds. At the same time, Gundy describes the copy in which he inscribed this account as miraculously intact: "I was lucky that this copy is not lacking a single page." His good fortune is that, besides having a complete copy, he owns an even more precious relic: the book that survived in spite of its captivity. The completeness of Gundy's copy, of course, also makes it free from the spiritual stain of having been actively used for musket wadding. His copy is one of the few that has survived with an unburdened conscience.[28]

Removed in time and space from the immediacy of blood sacrifice, American Mennonites also had to negotiate the exigencies of translation. For the translators, readers, and owners of the Ephrata *Martyrs' Mirror,* suffering not only became the subject to be represented and translated; it was also the key or language that made such a crossing possible. In translating and transmitting the Mennonite *Martyrs' Mirror,* suffering and martyrdom were both signifier and signified, simultaneously the subject to be represented and the language representing it. The *Martyrs' Mirror* was a book of suffering as well as a suffering book. The Ephrata *Martyrs' Mirror* became a fitting representation and manifestation of the martyrs' suffering and sacrifice because at all stages of its production and reception it established both physical and spiritual connections: the translator and printers suffered

27. Luthy, "Ephrata Martyrs' Mirror," *Pennsylvania Mennonite Heritage,* IX, no. 1 (January 1986), 3.

28. Ibid., 5 (emphasis added).

for its completion in emulation of the martyrs; the readers who checked the translation completed an equal labor of love and sacrifice; owners and readers adorned individual copies with elaborate Fraktur writings or drawings that positioned the self in the midst of the spiritual drama unfolding inside and outside the book; and, finally, the book itself participated in the continuation of "defenseless" resistance to persecution and violence by literally being torn apart by war. During the eighteenth-century wars for empire (including the Revolutionary War), America became a "Bloody Theater" not unlike the scenario described in the texts and illustrations of the *Martyrs' Mirror.*

"Fellows in Sufferings": The Friendly Association and the English Quaker–German Sectarian Cooperation for Peace

On the heels of the publication and dissemination of the Ephrata *Martyrs' Mirror,* the reformist Quaker minister John Churchman wrote in his journal, recording the turbulent events of the French and Indian War in 1756:

> The Indians having burnt several houses on the frontiers of this Province, also at Gnadenhutten in Northampton County, and murdered and scalped some of the inhabitants; at the time of this meeting two or three of the dead bodies were brought to Philadelphia in a waggon, with an intent as was supposed to animate the people to unite in preparations of war to take vengeance on the Indians, and destroy them: They were carried along several of the streets, many people following, cursing the Indians, also the Quakers because they would not join in war for destruction of the Indians. The sight of the dead bodies and the outcry of the people, were very afflicting and shocking to me: Standing at the door of a friend's house as they passed along, my mind was humbled and turned much inward when I was made secretly to cry; *What will become of Pennsylvania?*

Churchman bewailed not only the immediate loss of human life but also the disappearance of a vision of the province as a haven of peacefulness. The trials and persecution of nonresistant Christians ensued as the mob in the streets called for the formation of a mandatory militia and blamed pacifist members of the Assembly for the lack of defense. As the Mennonites confirmed the traditional foundation of their faith in the stories of suffering and persecution collected in the *Martyrs' Mirror,* Churchman—as well as other reform-minded Friends—reemphasized the spiritual principles of the Quaker religion, as his "mind was humbled and turned much inward." For Quakers, Mennonites, and other German peace churches such as the Schwenkfelders, the demise of a peaceful Pennsylvania returned them to the historical roots of their denominations—the religious conflicts of late-sixteenth- and seventeenth-century Europe and the suffering of the nonresistant faiths for their testimony. While frontier warfare heightened tensions and exacerbated differences among political and religious factions such as the Proprietary and Quaker parties, it brought members of various nonresistant sects—both English and German—closer together. They found a common spiritual ground in the language of suffering for peace.[29]

Quaker responses to war in the mid- and late eighteenth century galvanized a reform movement that advocated and in many ways affected a reorientation of Pennsylvania Friends to a testimony of simplicity, a commitment to pacifism, and an active labor in matters of social justice. Historical scholarship, however, explains the Quaker reform movement almost exclusively as a change emerging from within, propagated by so-called religious or reformist Quakers such as John Woolman, John Churchman, and Anthony Benezet. The religious and spiritual life of the Pennsylvania

29. John Churchman, *An Account of the Gospel Labours, and Christian Experiences of a Faithful Minister of Christ* (Philadelphia, 1779), 175. Schwenkfelders were the followers of Caspar Schwenckfeld von Ossig (1489–1561), a Silesian nobleman who became a Protestant reformer and spiritualist. Importantly, his teachings and beliefs bear many resemblances to Quakerism. In 1518 or 1519, Schwenckfeld experienced an awakening that he called a "visitation of God." In 1525, he came to a spiritual interpretation of the Lord's Supper and began to teach that the true believer ate the spiritual body of Christ. He emphasized that, to become a true Christian, one must not change only outwardly but also inwardly. Schwenckfeld also rejected infant baptism and the outer forms and rites of the church. For more than 150 years, Schwenkfeld's followers existed in a precarious world of Lutheran and Roman Catholic persecution, while practicing, secretly, their spiritual life. In 1719, when the Jesuits sent missionaries to "convert" them, the Schwenkfelders sent emissaries to Vienna to plead to the emperor of the Holy Roman Empire for toleration, but none came. Finally, in 1726 they fled to what would be a temporary refuge in Saxony, to the estate of Count Nikolaus Ludwig von Zinzendorf. Yet, when the elector of Saxony died in 1733, the Jesuits sought to have the Schwenkfelders return to Silesia. Instead of returning, a sizable portion of the Schwenkfelders decided to flee and seek refuge in Pennsylvania, while a majority remained in Silesia, many of them eventually being converted by the Jesuits. The largest migration landed in Philadelphia in September 1734. There were six migrations in all, from 1731 to 1737, and the entire group (for the most part) settled in what is today Montgomery County, just north of Philadelphia. See Horst Weigelt, "The Emigration of the Schwenkfelders from Silesia to America," in Peter C. Erb, ed., *Schwenkfelders in America: Papers Presented at the Colloquium on Schwenckfeld and the Schwenkfelders, Pennsburg, Pa., September 17–22, 1984* (Pennsburg, Pa., 1987), 5–19; Hunt Schenkel, "Caspar Schwenckfeld, the Schwenkfelders, the Schwenkfelder Library" (paper presented at the sixth Society of Early Americanists Biennial Conference, Hamilton, Bermuda, March 4–7, 2009).

Quakers seems shielded from the influence of those like-minded German denominations that apparently played a key role in upholding the *political* dominance of Quaker politicians throughout much of the colonial period. The only sustained work on German-Quaker cooperation in peace activism has received little attention from political and cultural historians.[30]

Reformist Quakers were encouraged in their stance against war and insistence on freedom of conscience by the culture of pacifism practiced among German sectarians. In the writings exchanged and read by German and English pacifists, the language of spiritual congeniality formed the foundation for any political cooperation, such as the Friendly Association for Regaining and Preserving Peace with the Indians by Pacific Measures. The translation and exchange of a broad range of religious literature between English Quakers and German Pietists and sectarians, moreover, established a wider cultural foundation in which a discourse of suffering and pacifism could take root. The exchange of spiritual classics among Quakers and Schwenkfelders brought closer together than ever before not just the leaders of both groups—such as Israel Pemberton, Anthony Benezet, and Christopher Schultz—but also larger circles within their respective communities. In highlighting rather than eclipsing the role of the translator and of translation, publications read by English Quakers and German sectarians and Pietists proved that spiritual community could be established and fostered across linguistic divisions. Translation helped transcend linguistic and cultural differences and create a common spiritual language—even or especially in times of conflict. German peace sects concretely supported the Quaker Friendly Association, which resulted in a joint activism for peace and the pursuit of a common language of suffering for peace through the personal and communal exchange of letters, manuscripts, and books in translation.

DURING THE EIGHTEENTH CENTURY, the common stereotype used to designate Mennonite and Amish people—"the quiet in the land"—was

30. Richard Baumann, *For the Reputation of Truth: Politics, Religion, and Conflict among the Pennsylvania Quakers, 1750–1800* (Baltimore, 1971); Jack D. Marietta, *The Reformation of American Quakerism, 1748–1783* (Philadelphia, 1984); Hermann Wellenreuther, *Glaube und Politik in Pennsylvania, 1681–1776: Die Wandlungen der Obrigkeitsdoktrin und des Peace Testimony der Quäker* (Cologne, 1972); "The Political Dilemma of the Quakers in Pennsylvania, 1681–1748," *PMHB*, XCIV (1970), 135–172; "The Quest for Harmony in a Turbulent World: The Principle of 'Love and Unity' in Colonial Pennsylvania Politics," ibid., CVII (1983), 537–576. Also see Peter Silver, *Our Savage Neighbors: How Indian War Transformed Early America* (New York, 2008), esp. chap. 4, 95–123; Stieverman, "A 'Plain, Rejected Little Flock,'" *WMQ*, 3d Ser., LXVI (2009), 287–324.

a misnomer. Mennonites, Schwenkfelders, and other German peace sects publicly explained and defended their stance through petitions, "remonstrances," and printed broadsides. Next to their effort in having the *Martyrs' Mirror* translated and printed, Mennonites made active use of petitions to the Pennsylvania Assembly. For example, a petition of the Lancaster Mennonites to the Pennsylvania Assembly dated May 15, 1755 — briefly before the first Indian attacks struck the frontier — explicates the Mennonites' spiritual objections to the text of the Naturalization Oath: they were afraid that their pledge to defend the king meant taking up arms in times of war. Generally, they agreed that scriptures commanded them to serve a secular government in keeping with Christ's injunction to "render to Cesar, the things that are Cesar's." When this service violated their "Peace of Conscience," however, the Mennonites were ready to suffer. They anticipated allegations of disloyalty and the criticism that they "would endeavor to Screen [themselves] from lending [their] Assistance against the Invader." Finally, the Mennonite petition evoked William Penn's *Charter of Privileges* as the political anchor with which nonresistant sects hoped to fasten their conscientious objections: "Your Petitioners therefore requests that the Honourable House may allow us the Priviledge Granted in William Penn's Charter for this Province, that all the Inhabitants (behaving themselves Honestly), that their Consciences be by no means molested."[31]

Quakers such as John Woolman and John Churchman followed the Mennonite example in the 1750s and again championed suffering. In an epistle from the General Spring Meeting of Ministers and Elders for Pennsylvania and New-Jersey, held at Philadelphia, the speaker explains: "And if, for the further Promoting His most gracious Purposes in the Earth, He should give us to taste of that bitter Cup which His faithful Ones have often partook of, O that we may be rightly prepared to receive it!" Those Quakers who were prepared to suffer for their testimony of peacefulness had a dual battle to fight. On the one hand, such epistles to Quakers across North America served to renew other Friends' commitment to this basic tenet of their faith and discourage any further accommodations to worldly demands for contributions to military expenditures. In the Pennsylvania Assembly, then, these Friends had to bypass Quaker politicians who continued to grant money that indirectly supported the war effort. In an "Address of Some of the

31. Lancaster County Mennonites, "To the Honourable the House of Representatives for the Province of Pennsylvania in General Assembly Conven'd in Philadelphia May the 15th 1755," quoted in MacMaster, Horst, and Ulle, *Conscience in Crisis*, 92–93.

People Called *Quakers* in the Said Province, on Behalf of Themselves and Others" that was delivered to the Assembly on November 7, 1755 (recorded in John Churchman's *Account of the Gospel Labours*), a group of Friends publicly rejected the practice of allotting money for the "King's use" and admonished their co-religionists sitting in that Assembly to bear the consequences of their faith's insistence on peacefulness.[32]

The address by the religious Quakers resembled the Mennonite petition in several fundamental points. They also reminded the Assembly and their co-religionists of the inconsistency between any contributions toward military expenditures and the provisions of the Pennsylvania Charter. Thus, they joined discourses of religious and civil liberty; any provisions violating the Charter essentially subverted both. Like the Mennonites, they signaled their resolve to the secular authorities by reminding them (and themselves) of their willingness to accept suffering over any compromise of their consciences.

Instead of granting funds to government committees that would ultimately channel them into the war effort, reformist Quakers as well as several German peace sects advocated "raising money to cultivate our friendship with our Indian neighbours, and to support such of our fellow subjects, who are or may be in distress, and for such other like benevolent purposes." Such proposals directly contributed to the founding of the Friendly Association for Regaining and Preserving Peace with the Indians by Pacific Measures in 1756, which "involved Quakers, Mennonites, and Schwenkfelders in a common effort." When Governor Robert Hunter Morris and the Council declared war on the Delaware Indians in April 1756, a group of influential Quakers headed by Israel Pemberton organized several meetings in Philadelphia with Indian delegations as well as the province's Indian negotiators Conrad Weiser and Andrew Montour. The Quakers pitched the Friendly Association as a mediating body between the provincial government and the Indians, representing themselves as descendants of the peaceful proprietor William Penn.[33]

Pemberton clearly knew about the consistency between Quaker and German sectarians' attitudes toward war and their ideas about affecting peace with the Indians. Within a short time, both Mennonite and Schwenkfelder

32. *An Epistle from Our General Spring Meeting of Ministers and Elders for Pennsylvania and New-Jersey, Held at Philadelphia, from the 29th of the Third Month, to the 1st of the Fourth Month, Inclusive, 1755; to Friends on the Continent of America* ([Philadelphia], 1755), 3; Churchman, *Account of the Gospel Labours*, 170.

33. Churchman, *Account of the Gospel Labours*, 171; MacMaster, Horst, and Ulle, *Conscience in Crisis*, 134; Theodore Thayer, "The Friendly Association," *PMHB*, LXVII (1943), 356–376.

congregations raised considerable sums toward the budget of the Friendly Association, designed to appease Indians with payments and gifts, thus hoping to restore the original peaceful relationship instituted by the Quaker founders and the Delawares. The German sectarian response to the Quaker solicitations for funds reveals a deep sense of reciprocity between both groups. Schwenkfelder leader Christopher Schultz, for instance, reviewed his denomination's involvement in the Friendly Association in the historical sketches ("Historische Anmerkungen") he prepared for his people. In explaining the Schwenkfelder cooperation, Schultz first cited the shared objections and scruples against war among several religious groups in the province. He particularly emphasized that their actions were based on a thorough understanding of the reasons for the war—the maltreatment of the Indians and the waging of war for unholy purposes. Then, he continued, all the groups holding similar spiritual notions and the same assessment of the political situation joined in an organization to restore peace with the Indians. For the sake of conscience and in order to oppose the mistreatment of the Indians, Schultz wrote, pacifist groups had "united in a plan, and [decided] to let others who are of the same conviction know and invite them to participate, in order to attempt the utmost to restore the peace with the Indians and forthwith preserve it more thoroughly." Crucially, Schultz represented the entire endeavor, not as the brainchild of individual Quakers such as Israel Pemberton (a common criticism among opponents of the Friendly Association), but rather as a joint resolve of various groups sharing religious values and political opinions.[34]

The Quaker representatives of the Friendly Association also strove to prove that the organization joined several denominations across Pennsylvania. In a published letter to Governor William Denny, the officers of the Association specifically mentioned having garnered support from other *"religious Societies,"* such as the Mennonites and Schwenkfelders. In evoking the unity among religious groups, Quakers harked back to a common understanding of Pennsylvania history and the—real or perceived—peaceful coexistence with the Indians. The kind of interdenominational cooperation that William Penn had solicited in the founding of the province could, if

34. Christopher Schultz, "Historische Anmerkungen was sich von Anno 1750 an folgentlich biß 1775 mit den Schenkfeldern, merkliches Verlauffen," Schwenkfelder Collection, Pennsburg, Pa., n.p. (annual entries): ". . . so haben erstgemeldte sich zu einem Plan vereiniget, und es andere dergln. Gesinntheiten wissen lassen und si[e] mit dazu angewohnen, um das äusserste zu versuchen, daß Friede mit den Indianern wieder hergestellet und fernerhin besser mögte erhalten werden. . . ."

revived, restore an ideal situation that had been squandered by the governor and other warmongering individuals.[35]

German support for the Quaker Friendly Association came from several sides. Saur not only used his newspaper, *Pennsylvanische Berichte,* to support the cause of restoring peace with the Delaware Indians and finding ways to prevent general armament, but he wrote a personal letter of encouragement to Israel Pemberton. Saur particularly offered consolation and support for Quakers who were being used as scapegoats for the Indian attacks and the lack of defense: "As many ignorant as well as ill-minded people are enreached [enraged] towards friends, ascribing to them all mischief done by the Indians without any sound reason, I should be very glad and willing to assist in what manner I can." Judging from the opening of the letter ("I am glad to hear . . ."), Pemberton had approached Saur about the efforts of the Friendly Association. After responding to Pemberton, Saur simultaneously publicized the matter in his newspapers and sent correspondence along his personal network of friends, probably contacting key leaders among German sectarian groups, such as Christopher Schultz among the Schwenkfelders as well as Andrew Ziegler and Benjamin Hershey among the Mennonites.[36]

Schwenkfelders and Mennonites responded quickly, and before the end of 1756 both groups had organized subscribers, corresponded and met per-

35. Friendly Association for Regaining and Preserving Peace with the Indians by Pacific Measures, *To William Denny, Esquire Lieutenant Governor and Commander in Cheif* [sic] *of the Province of Pennsylvania, etc.; the Address of the Trustees and Treasurer of the Friendly Association for Regaining and Preserving Peace with the Indians by Pacific Measures* [Philadelphia, 1757], 4 (emphasis in original).

36. All letters connected to the Friendly Association are here cited with their original dating styles intact, demonstrating that even non-Quakers, like Christoph Saur, sometimes abided by Quaker dating styles in their correspondence with Quaker members of the Friendly Association. Quakers objected to the pagan names for the months from January to August, instead substituting numbers ("1st month" or "4 mo.," for example); they sometimes maintained the names for the months from September to December, since they merely derived from Roman numerals. Until the calendar reform took effect in Great Britain and its colonies in 1752, the year began in March and ended in February. In Quaker dating practices before 1752, March was the first month, April the second, and so forth. With the adoption of the Gregorian calendar, Quakers consistently numbered all months, beginning with January as the first month. For further information, see Mark M. Smith, "Culture, Commerce, and Calendar Reform in Colonial America," *WMQ,* 3d Ser., LV (1998), 557–584.

Christoph Saur, "Friend Pemberton, [G]ermantown 4 mo. 25th 1756," Papers of the Friendly Association, Quaker Collection, Haverford College, Haverford, Pa., quoted in McMaster, Horst, and Ulle, *Conscience in Crisis,* 136. Numerous issues of *Pennsylvanische Berichte* represent the pacifist, German sectarian, and Quaker points of view on war, Indian negotiations, and liberty of conscience (see, for instance, Aug. 16, 1756).

sonally with Pemberton in Philadelphia, and, by 1758, raised fifteen hundred pounds.[37] A Schwenkfelder subscription list is particularly conclusive about the group's motivations for joining the Friendly Association:

It is the will of the within subscribers, that it may be known that they are a few families of dispersed people in Silesia, who have always, under God's blessing, maintained themselves by the labors of their hands only, and have been forced to leave their estates behind in Silesia, on account of their confession, and who have already here, partly suffered by the incursions of the Indians, in relieving their poor distressed neighbors. Therefore, they hope that their contributions, small as it is, will not be contempted, for it may well be compared with the two mites which the poor widow *in Evangelio* cast in, for they have cast in their living. Nevertheless, they do it with cheerfulness and delight, to be assisting in the intended salutary endeavors, as also they are ready to satisfy their true loyalty to the King's government to which they have submitted.

Most important, the subscription list started with a public declaration ("that it may be known") of the origin and history of the Schwenkfelders;

37. Among the extensive Papers of the Friendly Association in the Quaker Collection at Haverford College, letters and documents trace the cooperation between the Friendly Association, Pemberton, the Mennonites, and Schwenkfelders. My focus here lies primarily in tracing justifications for the cooperation in similar ideas of pacifism and concepts of suffering. For documents on the Mennonite involvement in the Friendly Association (all in Papers of the Friendly Association, Quaker Collection), see Israel Pemberton, "To Benjamin Hersey and others the Menonists in Lancaster Co. Philadelphia the 14th 1 mo 1761," "To M. Ziegler and others of the Menonists near Skippack. Phila. the 8th 4 mo. 1757"; Isaac Whitelock, "Esteemed Friend Israel Pemberton. Lancaster the 11th of 7 mo 1757," "Esteemed ffrd. [Israel Pemberton]. Lancaster 24th 8th mo 1758," "Esteemed ffrd. [Israel Pemberton]. Lancaster 24th 2nd 1759," "Esteemed Friend [Israel Pemberton]. 6/6/1760"; Andrew Ziegler, "friend Is: Pemberton. 10/14/1756." The Lancaster Quaker Isaac Whitelock frequently served as an intermediary or messenger between the Lancaster Mennonites and the Friendly Association, particularly Israel Pemberton. For the more extensive communication between the Schwenkfelders and the Friendly Association, see Israel Pemberton to Christopher Schultz, July 9, 1757, Pemberton Letters, Schwenkfelder Library, Pennsburg, Pa.; Pemberton to Schultz, Aug. 15, 1760, in "Wars Revolutionary" [103.102], Schwenkfelder Library; Pemberton to Schultz, July 15, 1765, MS Voc P2, Wesley K. Schultz Collection, Schwenkfelder Library; "Received from Caspar Kriebel and Christopher Schultz the sum of One hundred and five pounds twelve Shillings . . . 6/7/1757," I, 354, Schultz, "Beloved Friend [Pemberton]. Hereford Decr. 1, 1760," IV, 59, Schultz and Caspar Kriebel, "Dear Friend Isr. Pemberton. Towamenson May 23 1757," "To the Friendly Association. [Confusion about Subscription]. 12/2/1756," I, 243, all in Papers of the Friendly Association, Quaker Collection. Schultz and Pemberton led a lively correspondence for several years after the Friendly Association concluded its activities in 1763.

as refugees from religious persecution in Silesia, Germany, they had suffered for their faith and will not make any declaration involving their faith and conscience lightly. Rhetorically, they set themselves apart from other groups because they had suffered for their faith within that same generation, retained a lively memory of persecution, and continued to base their religious and civic principles on this experience.[38]

More than the historical reference among Quaker reformers to suffering as the reason the Friends came to Pennsylvania from England, the Schwenkfelders served as a living community of people who had fled persecution. Thus, the Schwenkfelder subscribers linked past and present in a narrative of suffering that was designed to satisfy spiritual and secular demands. By referencing the Gospels, the subscribers stated that they are doing their duty toward God and fellow man. Further, they argue that this monetary contribution to refugee relief and Indian diplomacy should be ample tribute to the king's claim to their loyalty. In this subtle interweaving of civil and religious duties and demands, the Schwenkfelders tried to anticipate claims of disloyalty, impositions of war taxes, and, finally, mandatory military service. Their subscription to the Friendly Association was both religious testimony and political activism.

The need to defend their stance in the public forum without losing sight of the religious principles that had been guaranteed by Pennsylvania's Charter became particularly pressing during the Paxton Boys massacre of December 1763 and the ensuing pamphlet war. During the Seven Years' War, actual border warfare and Indian incursions into seemingly safe areas of Pennsylvania had placed the incessant call for Quakers and other pacifists to abandon their religious principles into the context of actual human suffering and a fever pitch of emotions. Even though hostilities had ceased for a while, a coalition of English, Scots-Irish, and German settlers from the area around the Paxton Township butchered a friendly and defenseless group of Conestoga Indians. Then the Paxton mob marched toward Philadelphia, threatening to take and kill the Christian Indians from the Wyalusing area who had been evacuated to the city in order to protect them from

---

38. Schwenkfelder Subscription to the Friendly Association, Nov. 13, 1756, quoted in MacMaster, Horst, and Ulle, *Conscience in Crisis*, 140–141. The list includes the names of forty-two individual contributors. With the exception of Maria Yeakle, all subscribers mentioned are male, reflecting the patriarchal nature of German immigrant society. The forty-two subscribers thus represented more or less forty-two families, which represented a sizable portion of the overall Schwenkfelder population. For instance, the largest migration of Schwenkfelders arriving in 1734 included forty families or 180 persons (Weigelt, "The Emigration," in Erb, ed., *Schwenkfelders in America*, 11).

armed frontiersmen. An attack against the city was averted when Benjamin Franklin and others negotiated with the men at Germantown, yet the aftermath of the affair brought on a pamphlet war abounding in tirades that blamed pacifists inside and outside the Assembly for any shortcomings in public safety. As Pemberton surmised, the Paxton massacre and the march of the Paxton Boys could in no way be excused as the desperate actions of embattled frontiersmen trying to defend their homes. Rather, Pennsylvania was witnessing an assault on the underlying premise that the civic life of the province was guided by religious principles. The Paxton Boys and their defenders seemed to create a society in which violence against racial, ethnic, or religious difference was justified through majority rule or brute force.[39]

How far the Paxton Boys incidents had brought Pennsylvania's civic and political culture from the ideas of peaceful coexistence between whites and Indians as well as among ethnically and denominationally different European groups becomes clear in the maneuvering preceding elections after the massacre. Trying to keep the solid German-Quaker block from voting, an adviser for the Proprietary party, Samuel Purviance, wrote to James Burd in Lancaster:

As soon as your ticket is agreed on let it be Spread through the County that all your party intend to come *well armed* to the Election and that you intend if there's the least partiality in either Sheriff Inspectors or Managers of the Election that you will *thrash the Sheriff every Inspector Quaker and Menonist to Jelly* and further I would report it that not

---

39. Israel Pemberton wrote to John Fothergill: "Great pains has been taken to extenuate the Crime, and to represent the Rioters to be men of Reputation, drove to this extremity by the severity of their distresses; others who have made it their business to inquire, insist on the contrary, that few among them have suffer'd by the Indians, and that they consisted chiefly of Idle Fellows, many of whom have been Soldiers in the province Service, who for want of Employment have been hired on this occasion" ("To Doctor Jno. Fothergill, London. Philada 3 mo 7th [day] 1764," Pemberton Papers, Historical Society of Pennsylvania, Philadelphia). For a collection of the pamphlets debating the meaning of the Paxton riots, see John R. Dunbar, *The Paxton Papers* (The Hague, 1957). For historiographic interpretations of the riots, see Krista Camenzind, "From the Holy Experiment to the Paxton Boys: Violence, Manhood, and Race in Pennsylvania during the Seven Years' War" (Ph.D. diss., University of California, San Diego, 2002); Alison Olson, "The Pamphlet War over the Paxton Boys," *PMHB*, CXXIII (1999), 31–55; David Sloan, "'A Time of Sifting and Winnowing': The Paxton Riots and Quaker Non-Violence in Pennsylvania," *Quaker History*, LXVI (1977), 3–22; Robert F. Ulle, "Pacifists, Paxton, and Politics: Colonial Pennsylvania, 1763–1768," *Pennsylvania Mennonite Heritage*, I, no. 4 (1978), 18–21; Alden T. Vaughan, "Frontier Banditti and the Indians: The Paxton Boys' Legacy, 1763–1777," *Pennsylvania History*, LI (1984), 1–29; Vaughan, "Philadelphia under Siege," *American History*, XXXIII, no. 6 (February 1999), 26–32.

a Menonist nor German should be admitted to give in a Ticket without being Sworn that he is naturalized and worth £50 and that he has not voted already and further that if you discovered any person attempting to give in a Vote without being Naturalized or Voting twice you would that Moment *deliver him up to the Mob to Chastize him.*

The suffering of German and English pacifists for their faith was no longer a looming fear but had become a very real possibility. Liberty of conscience ceased to exist when the basic civic participation to ensure this privilege—voting—could be curtailed by mob intimidation. The letter stands out through its very specific instructions for spreading the fear of violence, particularly targeting Quakers, Mennonites, and Germans in general. The threats are calibrated to antagonize pacifists: *"well armed"* highlights the Mennonites' and Quakers' refusal to bear arms; *"thrash the Sheriff every Inspector Quaker and Menonist to Jelly"* makes clear that the Mennonites' and Quakers' peace testimony should specifically engender a violent response from their opponents and that violence should target entire groups indiscriminately; and, finally, *"deliver him up to the Mob to Chastize him"* rouses the specter of what would later be known in American culture as a "lynching," extralegal "justice" performed by a mob incensed by racial or ethnic prejudice. When supporters of the American Revolution later tarred and feathered conscientious objectors (including Mennonites), such mob violence could be labeled "patriotism."[40]

A number of politicians and leaders—including Benjamin Franklin, Joseph Galloway, and even Israel Pemberton—believed that a change from Proprietary to royal government was the only way to maintain good order in the province while curbing the power of the growing Presbyterian faction. Many Quakers as well as most German sectarians opposed the movement for royal government, fearing that repealing the *Charter of Privileges* would practically end freedom of conscience and other liberties enjoyed by Pennsylvanians and bring an Episcopal bishop to Philadelphia invested with the full powers of the Church of England. While affirming his people's lasting allegiance and friendship, Schwenkfelder leader Christopher Schultz sent Pemberton a strongly worded letter "encouraging" him and the Quakers to remain firm in the principles established by the Quaker founders. Schultz began by couching the hostilities Quakers experienced from all sides in both spiritual and civic terms: "I have been hindered by several circum-

40. Samuel Purviance, Jr., to James Burd, September 20, 1765, Shippen Papers, HSP.

stances to see Philadelphia (this last winter) and pay Thee a visit to inform myself how Friends bear up with the Care, Insurrections, and Diffamations from an unruly and wicked People in the Country who neither know nor understand what they do or say, acting in both parts against the Rules of God and man." The "unruly and wicked People" resembled any Old or New Testament people violating both spiritual and civic laws (like the Israelites during the forty years in the desert). Similar to the interpretation of worldly persecution as a sign of the apocalypse in the Mennonite theology of martyrdom, Schultz read the Quakers' duress as part of a larger spiritual battle.[41]

The rest of the letter moved directly to the specific struggles in which—as Schultz emphasizes at the end—Quakers and Schwenkfelders (and other German peace sects) must demonstrate solidarity. If the *Charter of Privileges* was indeed repealed, "it would be very hard and striking to the heart." Such suffering would particularly apply to those nonorthodox denominations who were not protected by Acts of Parliament: "It is true Quakers and Unitas Fratrum [Moravians] are protected in their Religions by Laws of the Realm of Great Britain, but what should be our Case and other Societies of the like Principles who have so far trusted themselves under the Wings of this Government erected and constituted for the best time by Quakers?'" In other words, for groups like the Schwenkfelders, Mennonites, and Dunkers, only the Quaker government and its protection of religious liberty would stand between them and spiritual, if not physical, martyrdom. Schultz reminded the Quakers of the purpose of their forefathers and the promises they had extended to groups like the Schwenkfelders. The letter, here, turned from sympathy to exhortation:

> Therefore we earnestly desire and admonish you in brotherly love to use all possible means to prevent the Destruction and depriving of religious Liberty in any respect so laudably planned by your Fathers, for the Benefit of all settlers whose worthy Followers we hope you will approve yourselves in taking care that their Intention be not violated and what alterations should be made or agreed to it may be with Safety of Conscience for every Individual in this Province. And since you are the people who made the first agreement for the Settlement of this Province your Consent or non-consent to any alteration must consequently be of very great weight. And though we trust your best

41. Schultz to Pemberton, Apr. 4, 1764, MS Voc S9, Schwenkfelder Library.

endevours in these critical circumstances will not be wanting nevertheless we thought to encourage you a little with these few Words, the freedom of which you will indulge from your Fellows in Sufferings.

Crucially, Schultz set up an ideal for the Quakers and for Pemberton to emulate: the forefathers who settled the province and established religious liberty. By repeating references to "your Fathers" and "the people who made the first agreement for the Settlement," Schultz rhetorically redirected the spiritual identification heralded in "Fellows in Sufferings" from the *current* Quakers to the *original* Quakers. It is precisely the idea of suffering that tied both groups together; if Pemberton and other Quakers took the route of least resistance, they would sever this bond and betray the promises proffered to the German sects.[42]

Schultz knew exactly the self-pitying state of mind his friend Pemberton and other Quakers were in after the Paxton riots and the concomitant backlash against the Quakers. In a letter to Samuel Fothergill, Pemberton complained that "the minds of the people have been kept in such a ferment till lately that there did not appear any oppo[rtunity] of a fairer hearing which together with the *weakness that attends us* has prevented anything being as yet published in reply to their malevolent aspersions, as well as the occasion requires; whether there will be found *strength enough among us* I must leave until our next meeting for sufferings." Probably recognizing the Quakers' plaintive state of mind, Schultz had to reeducate Pemberton in the true meaning of taking up the cross, suffering, and martyrdom. Thus, Schultz's letter again emphasized that Schwenkfelder families had just recently "transported themselves with their Families hither, in hopes for a full and free Enjoyment of the celebrated Privileges of the said Charter." Pemberton needed a lesson in suffering, and Schultz was happy to deliver it.[43]

With the outside encouragement of their German allies and the insistence of reformist Friends such as John Woolman, John Churchman, and Anthony Benezet, the official position of the Pennsylvania Quakers turned against the royal government petition, with the "Meeting for Sufferings" of the Philadelphia Yearly Meetings actually discouraging Friends from supporting it. Eventually, the entire plan, along with its staunchest de-

---

42. Ibid.

43. Ibid.; Israel Pemberton, "[To Samuel Fothergill]. Philadelphia the 13th 6 mo 1764," Pemberton Papers, HSP.

fenders—Franklin and Galloway—were defeated. Yet that the Charter re-mained intact until 1776 did not mean that the right not to bear arms and other crucial principles was untouched. The rise of the colonial struggle against Great Britain in the 1770s also increased the pressure on pacifists to abandon their stance and join the cause of liberty. Quakers as well as German peace sects quickly recognized and publicly complained that the de-fense of this new liberty through armed resistance simultaneously negated the freedom of conscience promised by the Pennsylvania Charter. What seemed like an overthrow of despotism to the patriots was merely another form of tyranny to the nonresistant sects. When the Pennsylvania Assembly passed a tax for non-associators on November 24, 1775, it practically can-celled the Charter's provision that "no Person or Persons inhabiting in the Province or Territories who shall confess and acknowledge one Almighty God, the Creator, Upholder and Ruler of the World, and profess him or themselves obliged to live quietly under the civil Government, shall be in any Case molested or prejudiced in his or their Person or Estate." While more and higher fines punished nonresistants, threats of violence as well as punishments like being tarred and feathered pushed pacifist groups into the margin of society, treating them as disloyal to the cause, even traitors. On March 17, 1777, a military draft law required all able-bodied men to en-roll in the militia, pay a heavy fine, or find a substitute. When militia cap-tains in York County tried to recruit men by labeling anyone who refused as tories, a young Mennonite man criticized the effort and was promptly sentenced to being tarred and feathered, though no person was ultimately found to execute the punishment. Quakers suspected of collaborating with the British—including Israel Pemberton—were arrested and shipped to Virginia for detainment.[44]

Again becoming "Fellows in Sufferings," Quakers and German sectari-ans moved closer together. As the frequent translation of both Quaker and German pacifist tracts into English or German demonstrates, the core sup-porters of pacifist principles tried to speak with a unified voice against this unprecedented abridgment of their liberties. As Pemberton wrote to John Fothergill in London, a testimony given by the Meeting for Sufferings was "translated into German and dispersed among that people, the thoughtful

44. MacMaster, Horst, and Ulle, *Conscience in Crisis*, 172; *The Charter of Privileges Granted by the Honourable William Penn, Esq; to the Freeholders and Inhabitants of Pennsylvania, October 28, 1701* (Philadelphia, 1725), 3; John Landis Ruth, *The Earth Is the Lord's: A Narrative History of the Lan-caster Mennonite Conference* (Scottdale, Pa., 2001), 321-322, 329.

part of whom have been solicitous to have the advice of ffrds [Friends] that the Menonists sent down special deputation of three of th[ei]r preachers to the mo[nthly] meeting of Gwynnedd for this purpose." Published in German by Christopher Saur, the testimony advised against the use of violence to settle differences with Great Britain, trying to restore "peace and harmony of civil society." Linking past and present suffering, the Quakers explicitly condemned the activities of the patriots as violating Pennsylvania's original liberty of conscience. Anticipating persecution, the text ended in a prayer of hope that "through [God's] assistance and favour, to be enabled to maintain our testimony against any requisitions which may be made of us, inconsistent with our religious principles." A longer defense of the Quakers' pacifist stance, *The Ancient Testimony and Principles of the People Called Quakers*, was published by the same Meeting for Sufferings in 1776 and also translated and printed in German.[45]

By far the most effective argument against mandatory military service appeared in a "Remonstrance" sent by the Schwenkfelders (and written by Christopher Schultz) to the Committee of the County of Berks. Similar to previous protests against any form of imposed military service and the encroachment upon religious liberty, the Schwenkfelders first appealed to the "Province Charter, unalterable by any People or Body of People whatsoever." Turning a civic law into a religious doctrine, the "Remonstrance" further called liberty of conscience a "Sacred Right and Property to every Person inhabiting in this Province. . . . Therefore to wrest the Enjoyment of the Same from any Body must be Sacrilege [and e]xite divine Vengeance, and must be void in Effect." In evoking religious liberty as a "Sacred Right," the Schwenkfelders self-consciously joined the rights discourse of the American Revolution but applied it to the side opposing the violent overthrow of British rule:

45. Israel Pemberton, "To John Fothergill. Philada. 2 mo. 15 1775," Pemberton Papers, HSP; *The Testimony of the People Called Quakers, Given Forth by a Meeting of the Representatives of Said People, in Pennsylvania and New-Jersey, Held at Philadelphia the Twenty-Fourth Day of the First Month, 1775* ([Philadelphia, 1775]), 1 (translated in German as *Ein Erklärungs-Zeugniss der sogenannten Quäker, aufgesetzt in einer Versammlung der Vorsteher besagter Gemeinen in Pennsylvanien und Neu-Jersey, welche zu Philadelphia gehalten worden den 24sten Tag des ersten Monats, 1775* [Germantown, Pa., 1775]); *The Ancient Testimony and Principles of the People Called Quakers, Renewed, with respect to the King and Government; and Touching the Commotions Now Prevailing in These and Other Parts of America, Addressed to the People in General* ([Philadelphia, 1776]) (translated and published in German as *Das alte Zeugniss und die Grund-Sätze des Volks so man Quäker nennet, erneuert, in Ansehung des Königs und der Regierung; und wegen den nunmehr herrschenden Unruhen in diesem und andern Theilen America; and das Volk überhaupt gerichtet* [Germantown, Pa., 1776]).

And your Remonstrants impulsed by dire Necessity beg Leave further to Say, and declare, that they find themselves as in Duty bound to their Country, themselves, and their Posterity to protest against the said Resolves of the sd. Last Convention, and that we are unwilling and cannot Submit to the same, as being unconstitutional and Subversive of our most dearest Rights of civil and religious Priviledges, *tearing* our Charters, *taking* our Property from us without our Consent, *subjugating* us under a military Despotick, arbitrary yea military Government Execution, *depriving* us of the choisest most precious Pearl of a free People, the Trial by Juries and of the protection of the civil Law.

By turning Revolutionary rhetoric against itself, the "Remonstrance" laid bare the inconsistencies between demands of liberty toward Great Britain and infractions against freedom of conscience at home. On a syntactical level, the document even went as far as imitating the staccato movement of the famous list of grievances against George III in the Declaration of Independence. Whereas the patriots supposedly suffered under such crimes perpetrated by the king, conscientious objectors had to endure them from their fellow Americans. Christopher Schultz continued to write petitions against a mandatory enforcement of militia service or fines for conscientious objectors throughout the Revolutionary War; in order to reveal to a larger community how Quakers and Schwenkfelders spoke a common language of suffering and nonresistance, Schultz, Kriebel, and other leaders copied the manuscript and distributed Quaker epistles on the peace testimony.[46]

True to their nonresistant, peaceful stance, the Pennsylvania Mennonites

46. [Christopher Schultz], "To the Committee of the County of Berks, the Remonstrance of Several Inhabitants of the Said County [Draft of a Petition. 1777]," MS VS-15-2, Schwenkfelder Library (the strike-through sections are in the original; emphasis added); Schultz, "An die Ehrwürdigen Abgeordneten von den Freyen Leuten von dem Staat Pennsylvanien in der General Assembly versammelt, die Bittschrift der Glieder von der Gemeinschaft genant [sic] Schwenkfelder, einwohner in den Counties Philadelphia, Berks und Northampton," MS VS-15-2, Schwenkfelder Library; "Aufrichtige Erklärung einiger sogenannter Schwenkfelder, wegen gegenwärtiger Militz u. Affairen. May 1. 1777," MS VS-15-2, Schwenkfelder Library; "Copy or draft of an agreement re: military service. Goshehoppe, 2. Maj 1777," MS VS-15-2, Schwenkfelder Library; "Meinung über die sogenanten Quäcker die sich des Continentalgeldes weigern," MS VS-15-2, Schwenkfelder Library. Abraham Yeakle (Jäckel) transcribed minutes of Quaker meetings in German script for Schwenkfelder readers. See, for instance, Abraham Yeakle [Abraham Jäckel], trans., "Der Bericht von dem Volck das Quackers genennet werden, gegeben beÿ einer Versammlung von den Vorstellungen von dem nähmlichen Volck in Pensylvania und Neujersey, gehalten zu Philadelphia den vierten Tag des ersten Monats, 1775," MS VS-15-2, Schwenkfelder Library.

and Dunkers published a *Declaration* that undermined the entire political propaganda of dividing people into "us" and "them." True faith, accordingly, should overcome such divisions as God surely rules over the British and the Americans, patriots and loyalists, militiamen and conscientious objectors. Addressing themselves to "all friends and inhabitants of this country . . . be they English or Germans," the Mennonites and Dunkers wrote:

> We have dedicated ourselves to serve all men in every Thing that can be helpful to the Preservation of Men's Lives, but we find no Freedom in giving, or doing, or assisting in any Thing by which Men's Lives are destroyed or hurt. . . . This Testimony we lay down before our worthy Assembly, and all other Persons in Government, letting them know, that we are thankful as above-mentioned, and that we are not at Liberty in Conscience to take up Arms to conquer our Enemies, but rather to pray to God, who has Power in Heaven and on Earth, for us and them. . . . We heartily pray that God would govern all Hearts of our Rulers, be they high or low, to meditate those good Things which will pertain to our and their Happiness.

The emphasis on addressing people across linguistic and ethnic divisions anticipates the universalizing tone the Mennonite writers take in trying to justify their own stance while overcoming barriers and animosities. Even under the dual pressure of backlashes from other Pennsylvanians and an impending war with Great Britain, the German peace sects emphasized what they perceived to be the center of their religion and the founding principle of the province. The words "We . . . crave the Patience of all the Inhabitants of this Country,—what they think to see clearer in the Doctrine of the blessed Jesus Christ, we will leave to them and God" echoed the exact phrasing of the first paragraph of the *Martyrs' Mirror*. Indeed, the chronicle of the Anabaptist martyrs seemed to have fulfilled the purpose the Pennsylvania Mennonites imagined when they had asked their Dutch brethren for assistance, to "arm ourselves . . . with patience and endurance, and to make every preparation for the steadfast constancy in our faith."[47]

47. *A Short and Sincere Declaration, to Our Honorable Assembly, and All Others in High and Low Station of Administration, and to All Friends and Inhabitants of This Country, to Whose Sight This May Come, Be They English or Germans* (Philadelphia, 1775), 1 (published in German as *Eine kurze und aufrichtige Erklärung, an unsere wohlmeinende Assembly, und alle andere . . .* [Philadelphia, 1775]). Also see Ruth, *The Earth Is the Lord's*, 325; Leaders of the Mennonite Congregations in Pennsylvania, "To All the Ministers and Elders," in MacMaster, Horst, and Ulle, *Conscience in Crisis*, 85.

QUAKERS, MENNONITES, AND Schwenkfelders thus cooperated during several periods of armed conflict and resisted a communal ethics that linked loyalty to military service and thereby curtailed the promise of religious freedom originally extended by Penn's *Charter of Privileges*. This political cooperation was supported by the development of a more submerged but at once broad and effective network of translation and exchange of spiritual writings between both groups. Quakers and Schwenkfelders, in particular, exchanged and translated materials relating to Indian treaties and negotiations as well as specific testimonies of native Americans proving the successes of the pacific measures taken by the Friendly Association and its supporters. Narratives or testimonies by Christian Indians revealed that a renewed friendship with the Indians could be built on the type of spiritual congeniality already enjoyed by Quakers and Schwenkfelders. Secondly, prominent Quakers such as Israel Pemberton and Anthony Benezet and Schwenkfelders such as Christopher Schultz passed back and forth translations, manuscript transcriptions, and publications of the core writings and ideas of one another's tradition and faith.

These exchanges were designed for and created a larger spiritual community beyond Pemberton and Schultz, who knew English perfectly and hardly needed any German translations. Instead, Pemberton frequently asked Schultz either to translate English materials into German or to proofread and correct other people's translations. In arranging to have German translations disseminated in manuscript form or printed, the English Quaker Pemberton thus acted as a clearinghouse or go-between for both English and German members and supporters of the Friendly Association. Materials championing amicable resolutions to conflicts with Indians were in particular demand on both sides. Soon after the establishment of the Friendly Association in 1756, Pemberton wrote to Schultz on July 9, 1757:

> Loving friend, I have just recd. [received] thy Letter with the Translation of Hopkin's Address; I am told Christ. Sour has gott it translated and printed already, but have not seen any of them, intend to write to him ab. [about] it. The Abridgment of Sergeant's Memoirs is in the Press and which I expect be printed next week, when it is done I purpose to send thee some of them.

Referring to an already lively industry of translating accounts and having them published, Pemberton passes English texts on to Schultz, receives his translations in return, has them published by Saur and other German printers, and finally disseminates the printed results back among the

Schwenkfelders, Mennonites, and so forth. The books Pemberton is referring to reflect precisely the ideals Quaker and Schwenkfelder supporters of the Friendly Association subscribed to: Samuel Hopkins's *Address to the People of New-England; Representing the Very Great Importance of Attaching the Indians to Their Interest; Not Only By Treating Them Justly and Kindly; but by Using Proper Endeavours to Settle Christianity among Them* (published in Boston in 1753 and reprinted by Franklin and Hall in 1757), which included *An Account of the Methods Used for the Propagation of the Gospel among the Said Indians, by the Late Reverend Mr. John Sergeant.* Crucially, such textual exchange between Pemberton and Schultz and their respective communities was cemented by actual encounters at some of the most significant events relating to Indian policy; Pemberton concludes the same letter: "Several of us intend to sett out for Easton next fourth Day—how long the Business will keep us there is uncertain but I think not less than two or three weeks. I shall be glad to see thee there." Translation and textual exchange here went hand in hand with actual interaction in the political arena.[48]

Quakers and German sectarians particularly valued evidence of Indians inclined toward Christianity or at least displaying an amicable spiritual disposition, which could then be used as a foundation for restoring peace. On August 15, 1760, Pemberton wrote to Schultz of "a visit from some Indians who are settled on the Susquehannagh *[sic]* and appear to be a sober people and to have alively *[sic]* Sense of Religion and their good Conduct rendred *[sic]* their visit very Acceptable to us." Crucially, Pemberton immediately promised a report of this visit that could then, in return, broadcast this encouraging sign to a wider readership: "When any of thy Neighbours come to town in aweek or two, if they will call on me I will Endeavor to furnish thee with amore particular Account of the In. [Indians] and of their Religious Sentiments." Schultz promptly responded to Pemberton on August 29, 1760, confirming that he would indeed "desire now such an Account," which "would be acceptable to several."[49]

One of the Indians living at the Susquehanna—nicknamed "Quaker Indians"—was Papunhank, also known as Munsee John, a Christian convert who had begun preaching in 1752 and moved to Wyalusing on

48. Pemberton to Schultz, July 9, 1757, Pemberton Letters, Schwenkfelder Library.

49. Pemberton to Schultz, Aug. 15, 1760, in "Wars Revolutionary" [103.102], Schwenkfelder Library; Christopher Schultz, "Worthy Friend Israel. Hereford Aug. 29. 1760," IV, 11, Papers of the Friendly Association, Quaker Collection.

the Susquehanna in 1760. In addition to the visit mentioned by Pemberton, John Woolman visited the Christian Indians in 1763. Nevertheless, Papunhank was baptized by the Moravian missionary David Zeisberger as "Johannes" and moved to the Friedenshütten mission community in 1765. Besides being a preacher who was influential among his people, Papunhank became particularly attractive to the cause of the Friendly Association because he was — unlike nativist preachers — opposed to war. Any transcriptions and translations of Papunhank's testimonials, therefore, played a particularly prominent role in the Schwenkfelder-Quaker transmission and translation network. Pemberton sent Schultz a manuscript relating to Papunhank, and Schultz had it translated from English into German. On December 1, 1760, Schultz wrote to Pemberton:

> With these Presents [money Schwenkfelders had donated to the Friendly Association] I do return the Remarks on the Behaviour of Pawpunahoak having copied and translated the same into High Dutch; it hath been very acceptable to several of my friends, who rejoice in perceiving the hand of Grace to operate so strongly on the poor Heathen. I thank [thee] for the communication of that Relation as well as for the Inquiry presented to me. If a high dutch Copy of the said Remarks should be of Service to thee, to shew them to some Friend, I would upon notice willingly furnish thee with one.

The translation of materials focusing on an Indian representing a propensity for peace and Christian spirituality thus built community between Quakers and Schwenkfelders in both directions. Pemberton reached out to Schultz by providing the "Remarks" originally penned in English, but he also profited by potentially receiving a German translation that he could have, in turn, passed on to other German pacifists like the Mennonites or Dunkers. Schultz's work as a translator thus created a sense of spiritual community with English Quakers, but he was also able to confirm the trust in a peaceful outcome of the war among his own people, who "rejoice in perceiving the hand of Grace to operate so strongly on" Papunhank. Although both Schwenkfelders and Quakers approached Papunhank and native American people in general with Christian paternalism, Pemberton's report and Schultz's translation countered contemporary stereotypes of the spiritual barrenness of native American souls. Translation was a tool for spreading a common message across linguistic divisions; but—beyond sheer instrumentality—translation was also the linguistic embodiment of the belief that members of different ethnic, cultural, and religious groups shared fundamental spiritual qualities. Rather than being pushed to the margins of this textual exchange, Papunhank became the spiritual center around which revolved Quaker and Schwenkfelder religious visions and activism for peace. Schwenkfelder translators and copyists evidently turned out large quantities of manuscript transcriptions and translations of such materials, as demonstrated by several (and almost identical) manuscript copies, in German, of a tract entitled "Erzehlung von Papunhoal dem Indianer." Though probably not identical with the "Remarks" mentioned in Schultz's letter, the manuscript fulfilled the same purpose of signifying to pacifists that Indians like Papunhank supported peaceful means of ending the war, and, more important, it demonstrated an attempt to incorporate other native Americans—through treaties, gift giving, and missionary activities—into an enlarged, transcultural concept of spiritual community. Although Papunhank gained membership in such a community only insofar as he catered to Christian ethics and spirituality, the translingual representation of his character, behavior, and beliefs became a powerful instrument in tying Quaker and Schwenkfelder pacifists ever closer together in imagining a communal ideal comprising European and native American members alike.[50]

Although the common cause of restoring amicable relations with Pennsylvania Indians and gaining evidence of their congenial spiritual disposition served to crystallize the politically most relevant contact point between Quakers and Schwenkfelders, the exchange and translation of one another's core writings bound both groups together on a more fundamental level. Since the exchange of such materials was not directly related to the concrete political goal of engendering support for the Friendly Association, it was less a means to an end than a textual and spiritual practice that created a mode of understanding community—a notion of a public sphere based, not on linguistic, cultural, or imperial conflict, but rather on a common vision transcending doctrinal and linguistic differences.

A letter Schultz wrote to Pemberton on April 15, 1768, encapsulates the broad interest of the Quakers in understanding not only the history and religion of the Schwenkfelder's but also the broader tradition of German

50. Carola Wessel, *Delaware-Indianer und Herrnhuter Missionare im Upper Ohio Valley, 1772–1781* (Tübingen, 1999), 313; Gregory Evans Dowd, *A Spirited Resistance: The North American Indian Struggle for Unity, 1745–1815* (Baltimore, 1992), 31–32; Edmund de Schweinitz, *The Life and Times of David Zeisberger: The Western Pioneer and Apostle of the Indians* (New York, 1971), 267–273; Silver, *Our Savage Neighbors*, 103–106; Christopher Schultz, "Beloved Friend [Israel Pemberton]. Hereford Decr. 1, 1760," IV, 59, Papers of the Friendly Association, Quaker Collection; [Christopher Schultz, trans.], "Erzehlung von Papunhoal dem Indianer," Schwenkfelder Library.

spiritualism and radical Protestantism. Schultz refers to an earlier letter in which he had provided Pemberton with an overview of a classic text of mystical Pietism, Gottfried Arnold's *Unparteyische Kirchen und Ketzerhistorie* (1699–1700), and he specifically refers Pemberton to the sections in the book dealing with Caspar Schwenkfeld. The letter furthermore reveals how the exchange of books, references, and translations created a continuously expanding sphere of common interest and spiritual inquiry. Schultz mentions having sent Anthony Benezet, his second-most active correspondent among the Quakers, "some short Account of the Historie of C. S. and his Followers, which if thou pleases I hope he will let thee see." And, finally, Schultz tells Pemberton that he included a "Book of Caspar Schw. [enkfeld]s Works, to be send to London if you can think proper." Indeed, a report of the activities of the American Schwenkfelders that Schultz sent to a remaining co-religionist in Silesia mentions that, through Pemberton, Benezet, and two prominent Quaker merchants in London (Jacob Hagen and John Hunt), Schultz was able to awaken an interest in Schwenkfeld at the royal court in London. The account of Caspar Schwenkfeld Schultz sent to Benezet is preserved in an English-language draft as well as a German translation dated three days later, April 16, 1768. The account presents in a nutshell the formative impact of the Schwenkfelders' suffering from absolutist church and state persecution in the Holy Roman Empire on their testimony for peace and toleration in Pennsylvania. Schultz describes the Schwenkfelders' deliberations on how to protect their faith permanently: "Considering, that the Princes of Such States are Souvereigns of an arbitrary Power, such Toleration might be only during Pleasure or of One Man's Life, and hearing of the full Freedom of Conscience established in Pennsylvania by the Quackers, Founders of that Province, under the Sanction of the British Crown and Constitution, and the mild Government of the House of Hannover they resolved to go to that Place." In their new home, the Schwenkfelders' main wish is "that Christ and his Kingdom may be revealed in the Hearts of Us and of all Men." When during times of war the mutual Quaker-Schwenkfelder peace testimony was imperiled by widespread armament, fines for objectors, and, most important, public and communal ostracism, both groups moved ever closer together in finding spiritual correspondences.[51]

51. Christopher Schultz, "Dear Friend Israel. Hereford April 15th 1768," XX, 16, Pemberton Papers, HSP; Schultz to Carl Ehrenfried Heintze, Feb. 3, 1769, Schwenkfelder Library; Schultz to Anthony Benezet, Apr. 13, 1768, MS VS 1-4[10], Schwenkfelder Library.

A letter from Anthony Benezet to Schultz demonstrates how far the translation and exchange of spiritual classics among both groups created a spiritual map of community that highlighted avenues of mutual understanding over doctrinal differences. In referring to a German translation of a letter by the American Quaker Elizabeth Webb to the British Court chaplain Anton Wilhelm Boehm that Schultz had been proofreading, Benezet wrote:

> I am strong in the belief that this book will be of service in giving the reader a prospect of the simplicity and plainness of Christianity and tends to remove that partial orthodoxy and proud conceit in favour of the particular opinions and practices so prevelant [sic] amongst the sects, which annex a holiness to opinions, even such as are right in themselves rather than those pious practices which change the heart.

The continual encounter with different yet similar spiritual concepts in the writings from the Schwenkfelder and Quaker traditions, therefore, allowed members of Christian sects — who, especially in Pennsylvania, were notorious for quarreling over arcane doctrinal differences — to focus their vision on core ideals common to all. The "pious practices" that remained constant were, for example, the practical activities of Quaker and Schwenkfelder supporters of peace and an equitable Indian policy.[52]

Granted, one could read Benezet's comments as a condescending lecture to Schultz on the dangers of sectarian narrowness and disagreement. Yet Quakers like Benezet and Pemberton also realized that they profited from learning about Schwenkfelder (as well as Mennonite, Moravian, and Dunker) spirituality as much as they did from that of the Society of Friends. Benezet clearly promoted among his co-religionists a greater awareness of the religious principles, traditions, and history of related religious groups such as the Schwenkfelders. While advising the Jersey Quaker Samuel

---

52. Benezet to Schultz, July 15, 1783, MS Voc B¹, Schwenkfelder Library. The printed version of the German translation appeared as J. M. Jorck, trans., *Einige Glaubens-Bekentnisse und göttliche Erfahrungs-Proben, in einem Send-Schreiben von Elisabetha Webb an Anton Wilhelm Böhm, Capellan zum Prinzen Georg von Dänemark, im Jahr 1712; aus der englischen Sprache übersetzt von J. M. Jorck, im Jahr 1783* (Philadelphia, 1783). The English printing of Webb's letter first occurred in 1781: *A Letter from Elizabeth Webb to Anthony William Boehm, with His Answer* (Philadelphia, 1781). Benezet also mentions Webb's letter and its translation into German in a letter to his Quaker friend George Dillwyn; see Benezet, "To George Dillwyn, [1783]," MSS 852, Anthony Benezet Papers, Quaker Collection, Haverford College. The popularity of Webb's letter in both German and English is demonstrated by the second printing in Philadelphia of the German edition in 1798 and the publication of three English editions in 1781, 1783, and 1798.

Smith on compiling his comprehensive "History of Pennsylvania," Benezet wrote to Smith:

> I would just remark, least I should hereafter forget it. That in making mention of our Testimony against war, as it so momentous a Subject is will be well in a particular Manner to enforce on the Mind of the Reader. That from the beginning and promulgation of the Gospel, some in all ages have bore that testimony; but particularly since the reformation not only the Quakers but the Menonists, a great People in Germany, perhaps no less than an hundred Thousand. Who have I believe in the province 50 places of Worship, have since Luther's time bore that testimony, and many, very many of them, lay'd down their lives in the fire for the support of it. The followers of Caspar Swenkfeld have also from the same time, in great Numbers and much simplicity and Truth bore the same testimony in Selecia and Moravia.

Importantly, Benezet not only attempted to instill in Smith a greater awareness of the historical codependency of Quaker and German sectarian testimonies for peace, but also, in mentioning their presence in Pennsylvania in his own day, he linked past to present and ultimately confirmed the sense of a living and vital spiritual community among members of these religious groups. In transferring the ideal of mutual exchange to Smith's historiographic treatment of Pennsylvania, Benezet tried to ensure the proper remembrance and interpretation of this relationship in the political or public sphere as well as for future readers.[53]

Benezet continued this conversation with other Quakers, appraising the contributions of German peace sects to nonviolent resistance. In his lengthy correspondence with Quaker George Dillwyn, he recommended works of seventeenth-century European Pietism and Quietism, including those of Madame Guyon (1648–1717) (whose *Plain Path to Christian Perfection* he had translated), Miguel de Molinos's *Spiritual Guide,* Anton Wilhelm Boehm's *Collected Works,* and the recurrent bestseller of the Pietist tradition, Johann Arndt's *True Christianity.* By the same token, Benezet noted the translation of Elizabeth Webb's letter into German as an important Quaker contribution to this common pool of spiritualist writings that not only found a readership among various English and German denomina-

---

53. Don Yoder, "The Schwenkfelder-Quaker Connection: Two Centuries of Interdenominational Friendship," in Erb, ed., *Schwenkfelders in America,* 127; Anthony Benezet, "To Samuel Smith. Philadelphia the 17th. 1st [?] mon: 1765," MSS 852, Benezet Papers, Quaker Collection.

tions but also continued to shape their reciprocal interaction in communal affairs. Continuing, like Schultz and Pemberton, the exchange of evidence for a higher spiritual acumen among native Americans, Benezet recommended to Dillwyn his own English translation of Conrad Weiser's account of his travels with Indians, originally published in Saur's newspaper, thus completing the transfer of a common spiritual language through various instances of cultural and linguistic crossing (from Weiser's conversation with Iroquois Indians, his original manuscript account in German, the German printing, and Benezet's English translation). Benezet took a keen interest in the missions Moravians set up among the Delaware Indians (his sister Susan was married to Moravian missionary Johann Christoph Pyrlaeus) and praised Moravians for being far more active than Quakers in propagating Christianity among the Indians. He also vehemently protested the Gnadenhütten massacre (in the Ohio territory) perpetrated against peaceful Moravian Indians on March 8, 1782, as "an inconsiderate barbarity, scarce to be paralelled [sic] in history," while praising the Indians' peace testimony. Their death was an instance of martyrdom in the New World that both English Quakers and German sectarians could revere.[54]

Yet Benezet's admiration for and propagation of German spiritual works and the testimony of German peace sects in America went far beyond a seemingly elite sphere of correspondence and manuscript exchange. Manuscript exchange and print discourse went hand in hand in establishing a common spiritual language between various religious groups and engendering activist causes, such as pacifism and abolitionism. Archival holdings in the Schwenkfelder Library, for instance, demonstrate the spread of Benezet's writings; an autographed copy of an important compilation Benezet produced to advocate peace is found there alongside an English-language copy of seventeenth-century English spiritualist John Everard autographed

54. See the following letters in MSS 852, Benezet Papers, Quaker Collection: Anthony Benezet, "To George Dillwyn. 2 mo. 15, 1774," "To George Dillwyn. 9 mo: 15. 1779," "To George Dillwyn. [1779]," "To George Dillwyn. 7 mo. 1783," "To George Dillwyn. 4 mo. 1780," "To George Dillwyn. 17th 8th mo: 1783," "To Caspar Wister. 25th. 4th mo: 1784." See also Conrad Weiser, *Translation of a German Letter, Wrote by Conrad Weiser, Esq; Interpreter, on Indian Affairs, for the Province of Pennsylvania* [Philadelphia, 1757]; [Weiser], "A Letter from Conrad Wieser [sic] the Indian Interpreter for the Province of Pennsylvania. To Christopher Sower Printer in Germantown," MS Jonah Thompson Collection, II, 155, HSP. On Benezet's support of the Moravian Indian missions and his use of the peace testimony of the Moravian Indians as an example for the Quakers, also see in MSS 852, Benezet Papers: Benezet "To George Dillwyn. 7 mo. 1783," "To George Dillwyn. 9 Mo: 14: 1783," "To George Dillwyn. 17th 8th mo: 1783." On the massacre, see C. A. Weslager, *The Delaware Indians: A History* (New Brunswick, N.J., 1972), 315-317.

by Benezet and Schultz, including a handwritten table of contents by the latter. That Schultz was not the only German reader interested in such classics of English spiritualism is demonstrated by Christoph Saur's translation of Everard's *Some Gospel Treasures; or, The Holiest of All Unvailing* in 1757, also found in the Schwenkfelder archives.[55]

The joint interest of English Quakers and German sectarians in the writings of John Everard points at a phenomenon that brings us full circle to the translingual and transdenominational spread of mystical writings—especially theories of language and religious reform—in England and Germany in the mid-seventeenth century. Although the *Theologia Germanica* ascribed to late medieval German mystic Johannes Tauler had gained renewed currency among radical Protestants in Interregnum England and among radical Pietists in Germany, Tauler's ideal of Christian perfection again circulated among readers in mid- to late-eighteenth-century Pennsylvania. Working from a French translation of the German original of Tauler's *Plain Path to Christian Perfection*, Benezet highlighted in his preface the transmission and translation history in which he participated:

The treatise of which the following is an extract, was written in the German language, about two hundred and fifty years ago, and since translated into the French. — Tho' the reader is not to expect elegancy of language, in writings of that age; yet, it is thought, the plainness of honest simplicity of the author, who had solely the amendment of the hearts of his readers in view; and the divine unction which attends his writings, will make it acceptable and profitable to the awakened, unprejudiced inquirers, of every religious denomination.

Similar to the repeated injunctions against valuing the formal aspects of language over the spiritual content found in Mennonite translations, Benezet clarifies yet again what translation and a common spiritual language meant to radical Protestant readers in colonial Pennsylvania. Across time (250

55. Anthony Benezet, comp., *The Plainness and Innocent Simplicity of the Christian Religion; with Its Salutary Effects, Compared to the Corrupting Nature and Dreadful Effects of War; with Some Account of the Blessing Which Attends on a Spirit Influenced by Divine Love, Producing Peace and Good-Will to Men* (Philadelphia, 1782), VN42-17, Schwenkfelder Library; John Everard, *Some Gospel Treasures* . . . (Germantown, Pa., 1757); Everard, *The Gospel Treasury Opened; or, The Holiest of All Unvailing; the Second Part; Militia Coelestis; or, The Heavenly Host: Two Sermons upon Psal. 68, 17* (n.p., n.d.), VN 13-3, Schwenkfelder Library (copy autographed by Anthony Benezet and Christopher Schultz).

years) and three languages (German, French, and English), the spiritual meanings underlying all languages and found particularly in the expressions of those writers (like Boehme or Beissel) who claimed direct inspiration—"the divine unction which attends [Tauler's] writings"—ensure the establishment of a common spiritual language for readers "of every religious denomination." As in the seventeenth century, English and German spiritualists once more drank from a common pool of mysticism and subscribed to the ideal that, amid the confusion of religious, linguistic, and political diversity in Pennsylvania, those in pursuit of truth would speak a common spiritual language. Of course, events like the Paxton Boys and Gnadenhütten massacres seemed to herald the demise of utopian, Philadelphian, and other esoteric ideals of community in America. Yet the ideal of translingual and interdenominational reconciliation through a common spiritual language remained intact among a variety of groups and individuals; after all, such concepts had been borne from the spiritual confusion, the religious wars, and the martyrdom of religious dissidents in early modern Europe and thus gained new fuel from the warfare and religious factionalism characterizing late colonial and early national Pennsylvania. If Indian, imperial, and Revolutionary War allowed European pacifists and their native American converts to take up the cross of martyrdom once more, it also urged them to pursue the dream of a common language in the New World.[56]

One of the most widespread yet scarcely acknowledged phenomena in colonial Pennsylvania, therefore, is the publication of a variety of texts in translation—especially of anything relating to spirituality and religion. Franklin's fear that the spread of German-language printing houses and the importation of German books into the colony was destroying the English culture and language in the province clearly did not match the reading interests of his contemporaries—both English and German. Whereas English readers clearly read a variety of religious works translated from the German and created a large market for such materials, German printers like Christoph Saur, Anton and Gotthard Armbrüster, and Henry Miller filled a strong demand among German readers for translations of English spiritual works. Although translation was more the norm than the exception in

---

56. [Johannes Tauler], *The Plain Path to Christian Perfection, Shewing That We Are to Seek for Reconciliation and Union with God, Solely by Renouncing Ourselves, Denying the World, and Following our Blessed Saviour, in the Regeneration* . . . [trans. Anthony Benezet] (Philadelphia, 1772), preface [iii]. A second edition was published in 1780.

all fields of interest, religious and spiritual works (including tracts on moral and social causes such as abolitionism, pacifism, and temperance) held the greatest translingual and transdenominational appeal.

In the context of this study, one of the most significant translated works published in the mid-eighteenth century is Johannes Kelpius's *Kurtzer Begriff oder leichtes Mittel zu beten, oder mit GOtt zu reden* (translated as *A Short, Easy, and Comprehensive Method of Prayer*). Kelpius apparently wrote this book in the first decade of the 1700s as a digest of at least two significant European contributions to a spiritualist notion of inward prayer by August Hermann Francke and the Quietist French mystic Madame Guyon. Although one printed edition of Kelpius's work might have been published before his death in 1708 by the Philadelphia printer Reynier Jansen, the first extant edition appeared in German in 1756, at a time when war and internal pressure on pacifist sects to abandon their testimony mounted. The German edition was quickly followed by two English editions published by the two competing German printers Henry Miller (1761) and Christoph Saur, Jr. (1763). According to an English inscription in an extant copy of the Miller printing, Kelpius's German original was translated by Christopher Witt, who also produced the English translations of Kelpius's hymn texts. Although an exact readership would be difficult to determine, the German and English printings as well as the English inscription point toward a translingual audience for a book that appealed to several spiritual ideals championed by nonresistant, pacifist groups such as the Quakers, Mennonites, Schwenkfelders, Dunkers, and a variety of sectarian, radical Pietist Protestants.[57]

---

57. August Hermann Francke, *Schrifftmäßige Anweisung recht und Gott wolgefällig zu beten: Nebst hinzugefügten Morgen- u. Abend-Gebetlein und einem kielischen Responso, die Gewißheit und Versicherung der Erhörung des Gebets betreffend* (Halle, 1695). Julius Friedrich Sachse assumes that Daniel Falckner could have brought copies of this book back from Halle upon his return to Pennsylvania in 1700 (*The German Pietists of Provincial Pennsylvania, 1694–1708* [1895; rpt. New York, 1970], 102–104). And see Madame Guyon [Jeanne Marie Bouvier de la Mothe], *Moyen court et très facile de faire oraison* (Grenoble, 1685). Kelpius might have used the following German translation of Madam Guyon's book: *Kurzes und sehr leichtes Mittel zu Beten: Welches alle gar leicht in Uebung bringen können um dadurch in kurzer Zeit zu hoher Vollkommenheit zu gelangen* (Altona, [circa 1700]). Altona (a suburb of Hamburg) was a center of Pietist activity and reform in the late seventeenth and early eighteenth centuries, and Kelpius's group stopped there on their way to Pennsylvania. Although Kelpius left Germany in 1693, his contacts in Altona might have sent the book to him in Pennsylvania. The three extant printings are 1) [Johannes Kelpius], *Kurtzer Begriff oder leichtes Mittel zu beten, oder mit GOtt zu reden* ([Philadelphia 1756, or Germantown, Pa., 1756]), 2) [Kelpius], *A Short, Easy, and Comprehensive Method of Prayer; Translated from the German; and Published for a Farther Promotion, Knowledge, and Benefit of Inward Prayer, by a Lover of Internal Devotion* (Philadelphia, 1761);

Kelpius followed the mystical ideal of the *via negativa,* that is, the belief that, to achieve perfect mystical union with God and thus a state of Christian perfection, individual believers must not actively pursue knowledge of God; specifically, one must not make concrete images of God in one's mind. He reminded readers "how necessary it is not to suffer any Thoughts to enter into the Mind, neither good nor bad, and to be free from all Figures and Images, in order to perform the inward prayer." In prayer, therefore, the believer must strive for the

> Union with and Conformity to the Will of God: so that by the Resignation to, the Union with and the Change of our Wills into the Will of God, after many Vicissitudes, Trials and Purifyings in and after this Life, we shall find ourselves so settled and stablished [sic], that we shall not find any more Self-love in us; but that we only will what God wills, and the Will of God is become wholy [sic] our Will.

Like a state of spiritual martyrdom, inward prayer must result in a complete abandoning of all self-will and a perfect submission to God. The soul, according to Kelpius, in this state reaches a "State of inward Silence" in its abandonment to the three Christian virtues "Faith, Hope and Love." For Kelpius, the true language of the soul was one of complete silence, that is, a freedom from the vain human pursuit of making imperfect signifiers to capture the perfect essence and nature of God. Pure language and pure love were equally free from human will and filled entirely with the presence of God. Kelpius's ideal of prayer sought to attain a perfect union with God by abandoning human language and the human desire to know God. The beginning of a perfect language was the end of language itself. If prayer became a "losing or sinking of our Wills into the Will of God," human language could be absolved from its desire to build a tower as an expression of its futile attempt to be like God.[58]

Radical Pietists like Kelpius and Beissel, as well as "religious" Quakers like Churchman and Benezet, thus considered suffering, martyrdom, and physical death as the spiritual liberation of the human soul and of its origi-

---

3) [Kelpius], *A Short, Easy, and Comprehensive Method of Prayer; Translated from the German; and Published for a Farther Promotion, Knowledge, and Benefit of Inward Prayer; by a Lover of Internal Devotion . . .* , 2d ed. (Germantown, Pa., 1763). A facsimile of the inscription is produced in Julius Friedrich Sachse, ed., *The Diarium of Magister Johannes Kelpius* (Lancaster, Pa., 1917), 98–99.

58. [Kelpius], *A Short, Easy, and Comprehensive Method of Prayer* (1761), 3–4, 18; Peter Miller to Benjamin Franklin, in Labaree et al., eds., *Papers of Benjamin Franklin,* XVIII (New Haven, Conn., 1974), 131. See Chapter 2, note 9, above, for a definition of *via negativa* and *via positiva* in mysticism.

nal, divinely inspired language. It is at the moment of dying, therefore, that Churchman would break forth into a veritable hymnody uttered by his soul without voluntary human mediation. His biography described this moment as a stunning transformation of outward human language into an approximation of an inner language of the soul, expressed in song:

> In the two last weeks of his time it appeared that his desire and hope, mentioned in the forepart of his illness, for light again to appear was fully answered by the fresh influence thereof, so that altho' his pain was often great he would many times in a day *break forth into a kind of melody with his voice, without uttering words, which as he sometimes intimated was an involuntary aspiration of his soul* in praise to the Lord who had again been pleased to shine forth in brightness after many days of poverty and deep baptism, which tho' painful had proved beneficial to him, being a means of further purifying from the dregs of nature, saying he was at times afraid to discover that melody in the hearing of some that visited him, lest they could not comprehend its meaning, and might therefore misconstrue it.

After a period of deep disconsolation and suffering ("poverty and deep baptism"), Churchman has reached the moment of greatest physical pain and bodily death. At the lowest human point, then, Churchman is visited by an illumination revealing his spiritual fulfillment. His spiritual body, in other words, is filled when his physical or human body has been emptied of all power, ambition, and strength. The outward evidence of his inward, spiritual transformation is a loss of human language in favor of song, breaking forth spontaneously and without words. The text casts this utterance as a language of a different order—the "aspiration of his soul in praise to the Lord" or, in other words, the inner language of the soul that Augustine had theorized as most closely related to the divine tongue. In dying, Churchman spiritually and linguistically returns to the state of Adam before the fall, speaking—or rather singing—a language once again reverberating with the divine meanings or light of the universe. Similar to Peter Miller's assumption that singing had been unaffected by the confusion of languages, this description of Churchman's dying moments envisions God reversing the effects of Babel by allowing the individual to utter, once more, a spiritually fulfilled language. Just as death in the assurance of Christ's atonement and saving grace was reversing Adam's fall into sin, it was also undoing the disjunction between the human word and the divine Word of God; in dying, Churchman would once more gain a heavenly body and a heavenly language.[59]

I am not suggesting that Kelpius's via negativa and mystical concept of inward prayer were a direct influence on Churchman's belief that his (almost) empty shell of a body was best equipped to speak or sing a perfect, divine language that left behind words altogether. Nevertheless, both texts were part of a long arch of esoteric and mystical visions of a fundamental renovation of human spirituality and language, reaching across two centuries from Boehme's language mysticism in the early seventeenth century to the revival of mystical concepts of language and community in late colonial, Revolutionary, and early national America. As in seventeenth-century Europe, radical Protestants in colonial Pennsylvania circulated common ideas through textual exchange, especially in translation. The ideal of a common spiritual language mediated a concrete activism for peace in the public sphere. Although speculations of linguistic and religious reform in Europe provided the underlying vision that informed the founding of Pennsylvania as a Philadelphian experiment, they now forged both spiritually and politically efficacious relationships between a variety of groups, such as Quakers, Schwenkfelders, Mennonites, Moravians, and radical Pietists. Individuals and groups who participated in the construction of such a common language recognized the linguistic and religious multiplicity of Pennsylvania, not as a restaging of Babel, but rather as a society where an emphasis on congruencies created a harmony of the spirits.

59. Churchman, *Account of the Gospel Labours*, 246–247.

Confusio Linguarum Redux

MORAVIAN MISSIONS, MULTILINGUALISM, AND THE
SEARCH FOR A SPIRITUAL LANGUAGE

riting at the end of the eighteenth century, Bernhard Adam Grube (1715–1808), a Moravian missionary among the Delaware or Lenni Lenape people, displayed a mystical desire for linguistic and spiritual union with his prospective Indian proselytes. Written in parallel columns in the Delaware language on the left and English or German on the right, one of his manuscript volumes listed easy phrases designed to initiate conversations with the Indians about the Christian faith (Figure 17): "Friends / I will tell you something / I wish, you could understand me / I come for Love's sake to you. (or) because I love you. / I wish you the Peace of god and his goodness / I wish with all my heart that I could talk you[r] Language / I would tell you very sweet Words / I think you would be very glad of it." While reflecting the Augustinian quest for a union between many peoples and languages within the Christian church, Grube also continued the Pennsylvanian ideal of spiritual community founded on mutual affection. Although scholars have chronicled the historical development of Moravian missions in America, few have analyzed the linguistic works of missionaries such as Grube, David Zeisberger, John Heckewelder, and Johann Christoph Pyrlaeus in light of the intense early modern occupation with the *confusio linguarum* and the search for a perfect or universal language. The "sweet Words" Grube wanted to tell the North American Indians were part of a larger effort to forge a common spiritual language from the many tongues Moravians encountered across the globe. For Moravian missionaries, linguistic multiplicity was certainly a practical obstacle to communication, but it was also an opportunity to participate in the history of salvation by helping to repair the linguistic and spiritual breach inflicted at Babel.[1]

---

1. Bernhard Adam Grube, "Einige dellawarische Redensarten und Worte," Bethlehem, Oct. 12, 1800, MS Am 767 (13), Houghton Library, Harvard University. For contemporary accounts of Mora-

Delanggoomauchtook!	Friends
kôcu ktelaaptonalohummo odrn quontamolokhümmo aaptonagan.	I will tell you something.
Jukketeek(ch) pentawijeek(uch) wentschi paja eli ahooleek(uch) odrn wentschi paja titte ktaholohümmo	I wish, you could understand me I come for Loves 'sake to you. (or) because I love you.
Jukkella langsoome laak(uch) gischellemelank woak wullanettowoagan	I with you the Peace of God and his goodness
Jukketeek(ch) nhittawi alliechsija eliechsijeek	I wish with all my heart that I could take you Language
Kehellan taam güwinggi lehenneewo winggangil aaptonewoagannall gischet lemelangunk wentschijeijük güch)	I would tell you very sweet Words
Ntelitheha ktelli aa wulelentammenneewo	I think ye would be very glad of it.

Figure 17. "Einige kleine Anreden an die Indianer." From Bernhard Adam Grube, "Einige Dellawarische Redensarten und Worte," Bethlehem, Oct. 12, 1800, MS Am 767 (13), Houghton Library, Harvard University. Courtesy, Houghton Library, Harvard University

Specifically, Zeisberger and other missionaries applied early modern theories of language and spiritual community to the hymnals, grammars, dictionaries, and translations prepared for other missionaries and for the Indians of late-eighteenth-century Pennsylvania and Ohio. The Moravians' pervasive efforts in translating German and English hymns and compiling a comprehensive lexicon and grammar in the Delaware language rested on the continued purchase of seventeenth-century language philosophies—in particular, Neoplatonic linguistics—among Pietist Protestant groups in eighteenth-century Europe and North America. Influenced by Jacob Boehme and Jan Amos Comenius, the Moravian leader Count Nikolas Ludwig von Zinzendorf had coined the notion of a *Natursprache* (natural language) or *Centralsprache* (central language), facilitated by the spiritual convergence of the many ethnic, linguistic, and cultural constituencies of the Moravian faith. Fundamentally, the mystical, Paracelsian notion that all human languages carried vestiges or signatures of the divine meanings of the world motivated and structured the Moravian missionaries' encounter with linguistic difference. Multilingual hymn singing, in particular, seemed to restore a mystical harmony between language and the divine spirit, while

---

vian missionary activities, see David Crantz, *The History of Greenland: Including an Account of the Mission Carried on by the United Brethren in That Country*, 2 vols. (London, 1820); John Heckewelder, *A Narrative of the Mission of the United Brethren among the Delaware and Mohegan Indians, from Its Commencement, in the Year 1740, to the Close of the Year 1808 . . .* (Philadelphia, 1820); Johann Jakob Bossard, ed., *C. G. A. Oldendorp's History of the Mission of the Evangelical Brethren on the Caribbean Islands of St. Thomas, St. Croix, and St. John*, trans. Arnold R. Highfield and Vladimir Barac (Ann Arbor, Mich., 1987); August Gottlieb Spangenberg, *An Account of the Manner in Which the Protestant Church of the Unitas Fratrum, or United Brethren, Preach the Gospel, and Carry on Their Missions among the Heathen* (London, 1788). For scholarly accounts of the Moravian missions in North America, see Stefan Hertrampf, *"Unsere Indianer-Geschwister waren lichte und vergnügt": Die Herrnhuter als Missionare bei den Indianern Pennsylvanias, 1745–1765* (Frankfurt am Main, 1997); Jane T. Merritt, "Dreaming of the Savior's Blood: Moravians and the Indian Great Awakening in Pennsylvania," *William and Mary Quarterly*, 3d Ser., LIV (1997), 723–746; Merritt, *At the Crossroads: Indians and Empires on a Mid-Atlantic Frontier, 1700–1763* (Chapel Hill, N.C., 2003); Corinna Dally-Starna and William A. Starna, "American Indians and Moravians in Southern New England," in Colin G. Calloway, Gerd Gemünden, and Susanne Zantop, eds., *Germans and Indians: Fantasies, Encounters, Projections* (Lincoln, Nebr., 2002), 83–96; Hermann Wellenreuther, "Introduction," in Wellenreuther and Carola Wessel, eds., *The Moravian Mission Diaries of David Zeisberger, 1772–1781*, trans. Julie Tomberlin Weber (University Park, Pa., 2005), 1–87; Carola Wessel, *Delaware-Indianer und herrnhuter Missionare im Upper Ohio Valley, 1772–1781* (Tübingen, 1999). On the intersections between Moravian missions, linguistics, and early national Indian policy, see Sean Harvey's excellent dissertation, "American Languages: Indians, Ethnology, and the Empire for Liberty" (Ph.D. diss., College of William and Mary, 2009), esp. chap. 1, "Language and the Affinity of Nations" (22–76).

uniting singers — across linguistic divisions — in a common spiritual language.[2]

Such emblematic and visionary spiritual harmony among a multiplicity of voices notwithstanding, multilingual missionaries such as David Zeisberger and Johann Christoph Pyrlaeus encountered native American peoples whose language, culture, and religion stretched even the Moravian capacity for discerning underlying correspondences. Missionary work was often conceived as a transformation of native American souls from a lower to a higher state, resembling the alchemical process of purification. The history of the Moravian missions written by August Gottlieb Spangenberg — Zinzendorf's representative in North America and bishop in charge of the Indian missions — later described the missionary endeavor as a transformation or conversion accompanied by a spiritual fire. Focusing their preaching on Jesus Christ,

> the brethren began to translate some parts of the gospel, especially what relates to the sufferings and death of Jesus, and read that to the heathen. This gave an opportunity to speak with them farther on that head. Then God opened their hearts, that they attended to the word, and it proved to them also the power of God. They became desirous of hearing more about it, and the *fire*, which had been kindled in them by the Holy Ghost, spread farther and farther. And thus many were *converted* to God.

The encounter with often hostile and seemingly savage peoples in the mission field as well as a multiplicity of languages bearing little or no resemblance to any European tongue, however, challenged the missionaries' faith in the transforming power of the gospel and such tools as multilingual preaching and singing. Spangenberg, in particular, believed that the North American Indians stood — culturally and spiritually — on the bot-

2. The encounter between European missionaries and native Americans has received important critical attention from literary scholars and historians whose common concern is the recovery of Indian perceptions of this encounter and the negotiation between indigenous beliefs and Christianity. I exclusively focus on the Moravian side without denying the importance of trying to evaluate the repercussions of this encounter on the missionized peoples. I examine the mental, philosophical, theological, and linguistic maps Moravian missionaries brought with them to America. See Kristina Bross, *Dry Bones and Indian Sermons: Praying Indians in Colonial America* (Ithaca, N.Y., 2004); David J. Silverman, "Indians, Missionaries, and Religious Translation: Creating Wampanoag Christianity," *WMQ*, 3d Ser., LXVII (2005), 141–174; Laura M. Stevens, *The Poor Indians: British Missionaries, Native Americans, and Colonial Sensibility* (Philadelphia, 2004); Hilary E. Wyss, *Writing Indians: Literacy, Christianity, and Native Community in Early America* (Amherst, Mass., 2000).

tom rung of the ladder toward earthly sanctification. Quite contrary to the kindling of a holy fire, therefore, missionaries had to do the grunt work of extinguishing what was most objectionable in Indian culture: "For the things that a heathen has heard, seen, thought, spoken, and done from his youth onward are evil, and have to be eradicated." Many missionaries became disheartened by what they regarded as demonic practices and egregious vices among the Indians. The missionaries' belief in universal atonement often conflicted with their perception of native American culture and customs. Zinzendorf's injunction for greater cultural and spiritual latitude among Moravian missionaries—"Do not measure souls with a *Herrnhut* yard-stick"—could not or would not always be heeded; missionaries often instituted rules to structure practical life in the missions along the example of Herrnhut, the original and prototypical Moravian communal settlement.[3]

Ultimately, the goal of transforming Indian people and their souls along an alchemical trajectory (from lower to higher form) cannot exclusively explain Moravian persistence in their missionary endeavors, particularly the missionaries' monumental pursuit of translating scriptures, hymns, and other devotional materials into several Indian languages and of recording their grammar and lexicon. In facing a multiplicity of peoples and languages among the American Indians, these missionaries were, once again, confronted with the central early modern concern of reconciling both religious and linguistic differences. Although practical concerns for creating more effective missionary tools certainly spurred their tireless efforts in translating hymns and assembling vocabularies, missionaries such as David Zeisberger and John Heckewelder also understood their work as participating in a larger, eschatological and utopian effort—along the lines of Comenius's *Pansophia* and *Panglottia*—to study the underlying linguistic and spiritual relationships among the diversity of human languages and faiths and to wield this knowledge for the restoration of a common spiritual language and community. While saving as many Indian souls as possible, Moravian missionaries understood their language work as a great treasure bearing a mystical significance. Moravian missionaries-linguists hoped to gain access to the underlying spiritual and linguistic structures of American Indian cul-

3. Spangenberg, *Account*, 61 (emphasis added). Hertrampf describes Spangenberg's negative view of native Americans in detail. For Spangenberg, missions thus primarily became a means to fight the forces of evil in the world (92–95). See Spangenberg quoted in Hertrampf, *"Unsere Indianer-Geschwister,"* 94: "Denn die Dinge, die ein Heide von Jugend an gehört, gesehen, gedacht, geredet und getrieben hat, sind böse, und müssen ausgereutet werden"; Zinzendorf quoted in Wessel, *Delaware-Indianer,* 78–79: "Messet die Seelen nicht mit der Herrnhuter Elle."

tures and, through translation work, link native Americans to the Moravian faith in Christ's suffering body, sacrificial love, and universal atonement. Thus, they once again returned to Augustinian and early modern mystical beliefs in deep and underlying correspondences. The challenge of facing Babel among the many tongues of the American Indians also became the opportunity for overcoming Babel by finding a common spiritual language.

Within the Moravians' overall linguistic work among native Americans — especially the Delaware or Lenni Lenape — one can discern three related but distinct avenues. Contemporary Moravian missionaries and commentators already pointed out the two most obvious ways in which they could build a common spiritual language with their Indian converts. In the first place stood the complete and utter focus on Christ — particularly the central mystery of his suffering and sacrifice. As other scholars have shown, the Moravian imagery and language of torture and heroism was received well among Indian audiences, even if the missionaries did not consciously exploit spiritual and cultural similarities. Secondly, Moravian missionaries closely observed their converts' emotional responses — including crying and other expressions of grief — and interpreted them as part of a universal language shared all around the Moravian mission system. By circulating accounts of a particular mission's social, spiritual, and emotional life in the form of mission diaries and letters, the Moravians established a semiotics of supralinguistic communication within a global Christian community. While the textual presentation in letters and diaries mediated such nonverbal communication, signs of religious emotion and conversion nevertheless bridged the gap between members of different ethnic groups and, more abstractly, between internal and external speech. Similar to Comenius's *Orbis Pictus Sensualium*, sensory perception alleviated the anxiety about the putative arbitrariness between thought and sign or inner and outer speech, which was particularly strong for missionaries trying to judge a "heathen's" spiritual state.[4]

The perplexing relationship between language and being was the third and most consequential dimension of the missionaries' encounter with native American languages. What, the missionaries asked, do Indian languages tell us about their speakers' spiritual framework, their "internalized action" — in short, their heart and soul? If certain religious concepts or expressions — for example, the metaphor of the Lamb for the sacrificial re-

4. See, in particular, Rachel M. Wheeler, *To Live upon Hope: Mohicans and Missionaries in the Eighteenth-Century Northeast* (Ithaca, N.Y., 2008).

deemer—did not exist in a certain Indian language, did this mean that its speakers were incapable of entertaining the corresponding thought? Could missionaries cultivate or forge a spiritual community between German and English Moravians on the one hand and Indian Moravians on the other hand? If, as Zeisberger said in his "Grammaticalischer Aufsatz von der Delawar Indianer Sprache" (later translated and published as "A Grammar of the Language of the Lenni Lenape or Delaware Indians"), Indian and European languages did not resemble one another structurally, could the translator-linguist-missionary still accomplish a horizontal, spiritual integration between the souls or spirits expressed with more or less immediacy by those languages?[5]

The spiritual significance of the vocabularies, grammars, spelling books, and hymnals Zeisberger and other missionaries produced went beyond their practical applications in the mission field. Read in light of the meaning that Neoplatonist theologians attached to the Christian church's multilingualism, its global missions, and its search for a unified spiritual language, the Moravian missionaries' linguistic works pursued the transcendence of Babel as a pivotal contribution to a universal, chiliastic vision. The linguistic works produced during different stages of the Moravians' encounter with native Americans follow a trajectory from practical linguistic primers to mystical "keys" unlocking the gates of human languages. This development is particularly evident in materials ranging from the manuscript lexicon of the Mohawk language by Johann Christoph Pyrlaeus, to David Zeisberger's manuscript works, to his printed vocabulary and hymnal, and, finally, to John Heckewelder's defense of Indian language and culture in his *Account of the History, Manners, and Customs of the Indian Nations Who Once Inhabited Pennsylvania and the Neighbouring States*, first published in 1819. The practical recording of Indian words and phrases successively gave way to studies of grammatical structures and comparative linguistics and, finally, a metaphysical argument for the complexity, effability, and nobility of Indian languages.[6]

5. David Zeisberger, "Grammaticalischer Aufsatz von der Delawar Indianer Sprache" [Grammar of the Delaware Indian language], [n.p., n.d.], MS Am 767 (6), Houghton Library, Harvard University; Zeisberger, "A Grammar of the Language of the Lenni Lenape or Delaware Indians; Translated from the German Manuscript of the Late Rev. David Zeisberger, for the American Philosophical Society, by Peter Stephen Duponceau," American Philosophical Society, *Transactions*, n.s., III (Philadelphia, 1830), 65–251.

6. John Heckewelder, *History, Manners, and Customs of the Indian Nations Who Once Inhabited Pennsylvania and the Neighbouring States*, rev. ed., ed. William C. Reichel (Philadelphia, 1876). "Ef-

THE LIFE AND WORK OF Johann Christoph Pyrlaeus (1713-1785)—author of a 554-page manuscript lexicon of the Mohawk language—remain largely unknown. Pyrlaeus was one of the few Moravian missionaries who had enjoyed a university education. After studying Lutheran theology at the University of Leipzig, he joined the Moravians in 1739 and arrived in Bethlehem in 1741. In Pennsylvania, he married Susanna Benezet, the sister of the famous Philadelphia Quaker Anthony Benezet. In 1743, Pyrlaeus and his wife moved to Tulpehocken, where he taught in the local school and studied the Mohawk language under the tutelage of Conrad Weiser. From July to September 1743, the couple lived at Canajoharie to study the Mohawk language and customs firsthand. From 1744 to 1746, Pyrlaeus conducted a school in Bethlehem, teaching Mohawk language and culture to Zeisberger and other prospective missionaries. Simultaneously, Pyrlaeus became the first musical instructor of the famed Collegium Musicum at Bethlehem. In 1751, Pyrlaeus and his wife moved to England, where he served as a Moravian minister, and finally to Germany, where he died at Herrnhut in 1785.[7]

In some ways, Pyrlaeus was an atypical Moravian missionary, as he spent comparatively little time among native Americans and was university educated. Yet, by combining intensive linguistic study with teaching and musical instruction, Pyrlaeus also set a standard for his students and followers. In particular, he understood multilingualism not merely as a necessity of missionary work but also as a means to celebrate the union of peoples and languages within the Moravian Church. For instance, he actively participated in translating hymns for the practice of polyglot singing that became a special means to celebrate missionary occasions in Bethlehem and other communal settlements around the world during the 1740s. Pyrlaeus's com-

fability" is a neologism used as an obvious antonym to "ineffability," that is, the capability of a system of signs, specifically a language, to express all possible thoughts or ideas.

7. My sketch of Pyrlaeus's life and missionary activities is based on Joseph Mortimer Levering, *A History of Bethlehem, Pennsylvania, 1741-1892, with Some Account of Its Founders and Their Early Activity in America* (Bethlehem, Pa., 1903), 69-70; William N. Schwarze and Samuel H. Gapp, trans., *A History of the Beginning of Moravian Work in America, Being a Translation of Georg Neisser's Manuscripts: "Kurzgefasster Aufsatz von der mährischen u. böhmischen Brüder anfänglicher Ausbreitung in den nord-americanischen Colonien u. Missionen vom Jahr 1732 bis 1741"; "Angemerkte Vorkommenheiten bey den Brüdern in den Forks of Delaware um die Zeit des Anbaues von Bethlehem, in dem Jahr 1741"; "Kurzgefasste Berichte von den Vorgängen der ersten Hälfte des Jahres 1742"* (Bethlehem, Pa., 1955), 149-150; Wellenreuther and Wessel, eds., *Mission Diaries of Zeisberger*, trans. Weber, 65-66, 72, 605; Wessel, *Delaware-Indianer*, 79-80. Pyrlaeus apparently knew Mahican as well, but it is unclear where or how he learned that language. According to Levering, *History of Bethlehem*, 205, the Indian language school was transferred to Gnadenhütten in 1747, where it operated until the attack in 1755 that killed several Moravian missionaries.

bined work as linguist, translator, and music instructor represented a triad on which the Moravian missionary approach came to rest. Both Pyrlaeus and Zeisberger deployed musical harmony to create a single spiritual language among the polyglot constituents of the Moravian Church. The Moravian world mission became a linguistic mission.

Pyrlaeus's voluminous "Lexicon der macquaischen Sprachen" (A dictionary of the Mohawk language) is the product of one of the Moravians' early linguistic encounters with an Indian language and represents the practical effort to record as much of that language as possible. The "Lexicon" was clearly produced and added to over years of study in the Mohawk language. The largest section of the manuscript book consists of unordered vocabulary entries in Mohawk and German. There are no columns separating the languages, which are sometimes side by side, sometimes interlinear. Most likely, this portion of the book reflected Pyrlaeus's own study and experiences at Canajoharie; much of this material is indeed concrete and practical, including section titles such as "Weather," "Vermin," "Animals," and so forth. Pyrlaeus later added an alphabetical index of German words as they appear in the "Lexicon" in order to increase the usability for the school or the missions. The second half of the book consists largely of meditations on Christ, including English section titles such as "Concerning Christ's Death" and "Of Christ's Resurrection." The text of these pieces is written in Mohawk only, although it contains marginalia and interlinear comments in both English and German. Such texts could not have been of much use to novices and probably served the missionary for recording a specific religious conversation with groups or individuals. Another remarkable feature is a set of historical or ethnographic accounts about European relationships with the Mohawks or the political organization of the Five Nations.[8]

Although not enough is known about Pyrlaeus and his work, the sheer extent of the manuscript volume demonstrates how seriously he took his work and how well he must have known the Mohawk language. The interesting mix of German and English for both translations and annotations addresses an important trend among Moravian missionaries in North America: they increasingly came to use both languages almost interchangeably. As the change from German to English—or vice versa—often does not appear

8. John Christopher [Johann Christoph] Pyrlaeus, "Lexicon der macquaischen Sprachen," MS 497.33 P99, American Philosophical Society, Philadelphia: "Witterung," "Ungeziefer," "Thiere." For instance, one such historical narrative is entitled "Narratio historica facto a Principe Indiano [signature given] dicto per Praeceptorem C. W. [Conrad Weiser] die 29. April. 1743" (213).

purposeful, it can only be deduced that the translator-writer considered one or the other language more opportune to express a specific point. Following Zinzendorf's dictum of a Natursprache, Moravian missionaries seemed to use whatever word or phrase fit the meaning of an idea best. Finally, the "Lexicon" did not appear to fulfill any representative, argumentative, or symbolic value; it rather situates language within the concrete, experiential world of the Mohawks and places the missions within the arena of Indian-European diplomacy.

David Zeisberger (1721–1808) was probably the most important Moravian missionary, and he is certainly the most well known today. Zeisberger was born in Moravia, from where he fled with his parents to Zinzendorf's estate in Saxony. His parents went with the first group of Moravian missionaries to Georgia in 1736, and Zeisberger himself came to America in 1740. He was one of the first students in Pyrlaeus's school for Indian missionaries. During frequent travels to the Iroquois, Zeisberger was officially adopted by the Onondagas, and he became fluent in their language. He led the Moravian mission among the Delawares on the Muskingum River in Ohio from 1772 to 1781. After the dissolution and expulsion of that mission community, he moved with a group of Christian Indians to Ontario. Zeisberger returned to the Ohio region in 1798 and died in Goshen on November 13, 1808.[9]

The extent of linguistic works written by Zeisberger, ascribed to him, or produced by him in collaboration with other missionaries is overwhelming. I have surveyed and studied the manuscript works held by the American Philosophical Society and the Houghton Library at Harvard University, which form the largest body of Zeisberger's linguistic materials, including his numerous translations. Relatively few of Zeisberger's linguistic works and translations have been printed; all of them are in some way based on previous manuscript materials. Surprisingly, these linguistic works have played a relatively minor role in the renewed scholarly attention on Zeisberger. The few historical treatments that comment on language issues in the mission settlements rarely inspect or analyze the linguistic works themselves. Rather than providing a chronological overview of Zeisberger's work, I present his linguistic treatises and translations in three different groups—hymn translations, vocabularies, and grammars. Specifically, I

9. Earl P. Olmstead, *Blackcoats among the Delaware: David Zeisberger on the Ohio Frontier* (Kent, Ohio, 1991); Olmstead, *David Zeisberger: A Life among the Indians* (Kent, Ohio, 1997); Wellenreuther, "Introduction," in Wellenreuther and Wessel, eds., *Mission Diaries of Zeisberger*, trans. Weber, 72–74; Wessel, *Delaware-Indianer*, 79–80.

find that Zeisberger's occupation with Indian languages—first Onondaga and then Delaware—increasingly focused on the ontological relationship between language and being. While his hymn translations functioned as yet another key to unlocking the "gates" to the hearts of his Indian brethren and sisters, his occupation with the vocabulary and particularly the grammar of the Delaware language demonstrates his attempt to penetrate into the inner, metaphysical structures of that language and its speakers.[10]

Zeisberger's translations of hymns from the German and English Moravian hymnals probably constitute his largest output of writing in the Delaware language. The importance of hymn translation and their use in the mission settlements is reflected materially and textually by the extant manuscript volumes that resulted in Zeisberger's *Collection of Hymns*, published in 1803. Hymn translation was a continuing and daily effort for Zeisberger, including multiple stages of production from drafts, to revisions, to collection in manuscript volumes, and, ultimately, to publication. Some preliminary drafts can be found in small, scantily bound booklets and even envelopes of letters sent to Zeisberger, still containing the sealing wax of

10. The American Philosophical Society owns the following Zeisberger manuscripts: "Onondago-German Vocabulary," MS 497.33 Z30; "On the Prepositions of the Onondago Language," MS 497.3 Z30. The Houghton Library at Harvard University owns the following Zeisberger manuscripts: "The Church Litany [of the Moravian Church, in the Delaware Language]," MS Am 767 (8); "A Collection of Hymns for the Use of the Christian Indians of the Mission of the United Brethren in North America," MS Am 767 (7); Delaware-German and Delaware-English Vocabularies and Phrases, MS Am 767 (5); Dictionary in English, German, Onondaga, and Delaware [part may be in the hand of Abraham Luckenbach], MS Am 767 (1); German-Delaware Dictionary, MS Am 767 (4); "Grammaticalischer Aufsatz von der Delawar Indianer Sprache" [Grammar of the Delaware Indian language], MS Am 767 (6); Hymns in the Delaware Language, MS Am 767 (9); Hymns in the Delaware Language [fragments], MS Am 767 (18); Indian Grammar and Vocabulary [fragments] [mostly Delaware, but including "A Small Vocabulary of a Cherokee Words"], MS Am 767 (19); Sermons in the Delaware Language [includes a translation of a work by August Gottlieb Spangenberg on the forgiveness of sin], MS Am 767 (11); "Sermons to Children," MS Am 767 (12); Short Biblical Narratives in German and Delaware, MS Am 767 (14); Vocabularies in German, Onondaga, Delaware, and Mohican [two separate vocabularies bound together], MS Am 767 (3).

See also David Zeisberger, *A Collection of Hymns, for the Use of the Christian Indians of the Missions of the United Brethren, in North America* (Philadelphia, 1803); *Essay of a Delaware-Indian and English Spelling-book, for the Use of the Schools of the Christian Indians on Muskingum River . . .* (Philadelphia, 1776); Zeisberger, "Grammar of the Language of the Lenni Lenape," APS, *Transactions*, n.s., III (1830), 65–251; *Vocabularies By Zeisberger; from the Collection of Manuscripts Presented by Judge Lane to Harvard University, Nos. 1 and 2* (Cambridge, Mass., 1887). The most extensive discussion in more recent historical scholarship about language and the linguistic works of Zeisberger and the Moravian missions is in Wessel, *Delaware-Indianer*, chap. 5, 166–181. Wessel mentions linguistic works at the Moravian Archives in Bethlehem, but she did not mention or inspect the extensive collection at the Houghton Library, Harvard University.

the sender. Full of revisions, deletions, and additions, these hymn drafts were part of an important element in the translation process. Hymns were worthy of continuous revision because at stake was the transfer of religious concepts and thus the creation of a common spiritual language.[11]

Zeisberger and his Indian "helpers" collaborated in order to make the hymn translations the product of a joining of hearts and minds. A conference at the beginning of the Muskingum mission stipulated collaboration with bilingual Indian assistants: "Not one verse shall be introduced that has not first been revised by the Brothers set to this task, i.e. David, Rothe, Anton, Nathanael and Jo Pepi, Samuel, Wilhelm, Shebosch, Abraham, Johannes and the other white Brothers who are present." In his diaries, Zeisberger recorded the same practice of collaborative translation and revision: "With the help of the [Indian] Brothers, we revised some of the hymns which have been translated into the Indian language." In reflecting the communal experience of faith within the mission settlements, the Delaware hymn translation furthered the approximation of spoken and inward language.[12]

Echoing John Gambold's prefatory remarks in the 1754 Moravian *London Hymnal* (see Chapter 5), Zeisberger's preface to the printed version of the Delaware hymnal also reveals that the translation process subordinated linguistic felicity, aesthetics, and literal correspondence to the faithful transfer of spiritual concepts: "The chief care in translating has been, to preserve the true sense of the originals, which has caused, in some instances, an alteration of the tune or metre, or a necessity of extending one verse into two." Zeisberger's largest manuscript hymnal and the printed hymnal also share a feature of linguistic and spiritual convergence anticipated by Zinzendorf. By giving English section titles, the hymnals hint at the increased importance of English in the colonies and particularly the Moravian mission settlements. Hymn titles, except for those taken from the English hymnal, however, are still provided in German as well as in Delaware. In both the manuscript and the printed hymnal, references to the melodies—no

---

11. See, in particular, Zeisberger, Hymns in the Delaware Language [fragments], MS Am 767 (18), Houghton Library, Harvard University.

12. Conferenz-Protokoll Langundo-Utenünk, Aug. 17, 1772, Moravian Archives, Bethlehem, box 315, folder 2, item 4, quoted in Wessel, *Delaware-Indianer,* 176: from "Es soll kein vers introducirt werden, ohne daß er erst von denen dazu gesetzten Brüdern revidirt worden. David, Rothe, Anton, Nathanael, und Jo Pepi, Samuel, Wilhelm, Shebosh, Abraham, Johannes und die anderen weißen Brüder die da sind"; Entry for Jan. 31, 1773, in, Wellenreuther and Wessel, eds., *Mission Diaries of Zeisberger,* trans. Weber, 128.

score is given in any of these hymnals—are usually in German. Even the printed version, therefore, is still very much tied to communal singing, with tunes intonated by the missionaries and learned by heart by their Indian congregations.[13]

Within the mission communities, hymnody found the same applications Gambold had outlined in his preface—the moving of the affections and the memorization of essential Christian beliefs. Zeisberger wrote in the preface to his Delaware hymnal:

> As the singing of psalms and spiritual songs has always formed a prin-
> cipal part of the divine service of our Church, even in congregations
> gathered from among the heathen, it has been for many years my
> ardent wish, to furnish, for the use of the Christian Indians, a regu-
> lar and suitable hymnbook, wherein the grand subjects of our faith
> should be recorded and set forth in verse, which is so easily imprinted
> in the memories, particularly of young people. All our converts find
> much pleasure in learning verses with their tunes by heart, and fre-
> quently sing and meditate on them at home and abroad.

All of the hymns collected in the Delaware hymnal have an end rhyme, even though the Delaware language did not seem to share the use of this literary device with European languages. Most of the time, the syllables given in a specific line of a Delaware translation correspond to the meter of the original hymn tune. Zeisberger, in other words, shaped the target language of his translations beyond the initial task of finding a transliteration of an oral language. It remains unclear whether this imposition of European artistic standards aided memorization; according to an Indian visitor, the mission-aries' gesture of singing in the Indian language did promote a sense of ap-preciation and connection: "Afterward he told our Indian Brothers . . . that he was surprised he could understand me so well, since he could not under-stand anything from the Indians' sermons or make any sense out of them. He could even understand some when we sang, although not all of it, and he was happy to hear that we sing in his language." The hymns also formed an important educational tool in the mission schools, where they were used to teach both Christian beliefs and the Delaware language. They were further-more the center of the evening "Singstunden" (singing hours)—one of

13. Zeisberger, *Collection of Hymns*, vi. Zeisberger's printed hymnal is very closely based on his manuscript hymnal "A Collection of Hymns for the Use of the Christian Indians of the Mission of the United Brethren in North America," MS Am 767 (7), Houghton Library, Harvard University.

the most popular and most widely implemented daily rituals in all mission settlements. The commentaries of the Indian visitors as well as Zeisberger's testimony in his missionary diaries are relatively vague about the precise response of the Indian converts to singing. Since most of the hymns collected in the Delaware hymnals touched in some way on Christ's life, suffering, and sacrifice, how exactly the hymns promoted the inculcation of specific doctrines among the Indian singers is also unclear. More likely is that the combination of the Delaware language with the harmonies of the Moravian hymns promoted a vague sense of happiness or spiritual well-being.[14]

One should clearly doubt whether the 530 hymns collected in the printed Delaware hymnal were indeed memorized and used among Delaware converts. The completion and the completeness of the hymnal, it seems, must have been much more relevant to Zeisberger than to his congregation. In his preface, Zeisberger distinguished that "some of these hymns contained in this collection have been for many years in blessed use among us; these have been carefully revised and amended; others have been in later years translated by myself." The extent and intensity of Zeisberger's occupation with the hymn translations as well as his other linguistic work thus seemed to exceed the practical and communal function of the hymns within the missions. The final lines of Zeisberger's preface to the printed hymnal injected the hymn translations into a larger, eschatological struggle:

> May God our Saviour, who is the Saviour also of the heathen, grant his blessing to this work, that a people who formerly did not know him, but now, through the power of his saving name, has been turned from darkness to light, and from the power of Satan unto God . . . may be the more excited to bring Him praise, honor and adoration for the grace and mercy which He has conferred upon them!

Even though this may seem like a standard reflection of a missionary's goal of saving souls for Christ, Zeisberger positioned his linguistic work within

---

14. Zeisberger, *Collection of Hymns*, [v]. This claim is not based on any knowledge of the Delaware language. I did a cross-sampling of hymn tunes that I am familiar with and tried to follow the Delaware text given by Zeisberger by reading phonetically. In most cases, the phrasing of the original tunes indeed agrees with the number of syllables given in a particular line of Delaware. See entry of May 18, 1772, in Wellenreuther and Wessel, eds., *Mission Diaries of Zeisberger*, 96. Zeisberger's diaries abound in references to the use of singing at the schools as well as references to the singing hours. See, for example, Sept. 2, 1774: "We began singing instruction with the children to teach them some new verses" (227); Jan. 12, 1778: "We resumed holding school for the children and Singing Services in the evenings. Both were pleasant for the children and adults" (430).

the enduring Moravian endeavor—begun by Comenius—to harness multi-lingualism and the spiritual correspondences between languages as a tool for ushering in a new age.[15]

Zeisberger's vocabularies and especially his grammars demonstrate an increasing occupation with abstract, spiritual concepts as well as the structural, metaphysical elements of language. In his early "Onondaga-German Vocabulary," he already moved beyond the almost random recording of words and phrases—requiring a later index—found in Pyrlaeus's "Lexicon." Similar to Comenius's *nomenclator* principle, Zeisberger ordered vocabulary and phrases according to subject areas. Words for commonplace objects or actions are often inserted into a larger spiritual context. Moreover, this vocabulary already reveals many features properly found in a grammar, such as conjugations of verbs within commonly used phrases. On the first page of the vocabulary, for instance, Zeisberger began with one of the main subjects of missionary preaching: "Gott der Allmächtige" (God the Almighty / All Powerful). The rest of the page, then, lifts out a key concept from this phrase—power—and inserts it in different semantic and grammatical contexts: "Ich bin mächtig" ("I am powerful"), "Es ist in meiner Macht" ("It is in my power"), "Es steht in deiner Macht" ("It is in your power"), and so forth. Although much of the vocabulary is occupied with practical matters such as hunting, cooking, or sleeping, spiritual associations are never far away. Visually, Zeisberger introduced the parallel arrangement in separate columns, which became a regular feature of comparative linguistics among missionaries.[16]

Once Zeisberger added other languages—particularly Delaware—to his treasury of native American tongues, he began to assemble comparative vocabularies, such as a quadrilingual dictionary in English, German, Onondaga, and Delaware, with English and German combined in the first column (Figure 18). The words in this dictionary are ordered alphabetically following the English. Zeisberger's vocabulary list is primarily concerned with verbs, particularly abstract ones such as "to abase" and "to abate." As there is no interruption in the alphabetical order and hardly any changes or revisions, this dictionary was the final product in a process of collecting and ordering.[17]

Order, therefore, is the underlying principle of this collection—not

15. Zeisberger, *Collection of Hymns*, vi–vii.

16. Zeisberger, "Onondago-German Vocabulary," MS 497.33 Z30, APS.

17. Zeisberger, Dictionary in English, German, Onondaga, and Delaware [part may be in the hand of Abraham Luckenbach], MS Am 767 (1), Houghton Library, Harvard University.

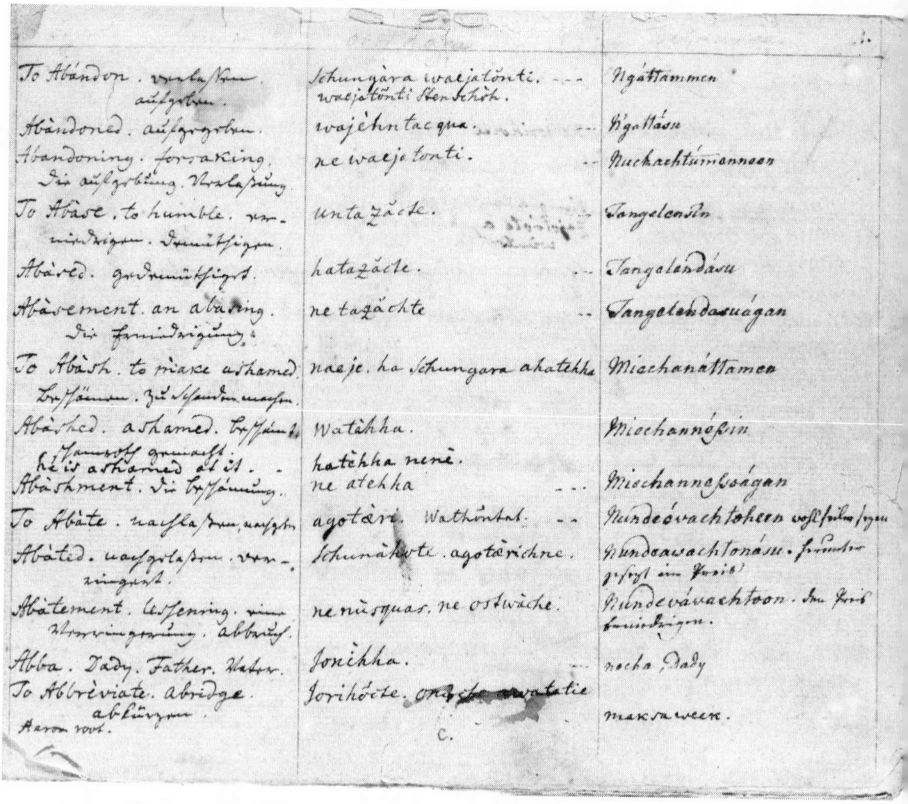

Figure 18: *Page from David Zeisberger, Dictionary in English, German, Onondaga, and Delaware, MS Am 767 (1), Houghton Library, Harvard University. Courtesy, Houghton Library, Harvard University*

practical usability in the mission field. The selection of Onondaga and Delaware as the Indian languages that stand side by side with English and German also reflected a larger spiritual vision more than an actual communal reality. Although Mahican and Delaware were common languages within many of the Moravian mission settlements, the well-known tensions between Iroquois and Delawares in the eighteenth century made a mixing of their people and their languages in Moravian missions unlikely. Above all, Zeisberger had selected for this vocabulary the four languages that *he* knew best, and their parallel arrangement on each page of this dictionary serves as a linguistic map of Zeisberger's mind. If the respective peoples did not necessarily live together in political harmony, Zeisberger could nevertheless make their languages stand in the most orderly and harmonious relationship to one another.

As Comenius tried to harness multiple languages—and, ultimately, reveal a universal language—to promote peace among the peoples of seventeenth-century Europe, Zeisberger attempted a similarly utopian project for the languages and peoples of late-eighteenth-century America. That those peoples and nations did not inhabit a stable middle ground only heightens the *spiritual* significance of the neat stability of their textual co-existence on the pages of Zeisberger's vocabulary. Rather than mere tools of missionary activity, Zeisberger's linguistic works appear more and more as symbolic statements about the spiritual significance of linguistic difference, linguistic unity, and the study of all underlying similarities. In the role of linguist, therefore, the missionary Zeisberger penetrated historical or geo-graphical differences to discover universal or even mystical similarities. In his "Grammaticalischer Aufsatz von der Delawar Sprache" (Essay on the grammar of the Delaware language), Zeisberger declared—in a decidedly seventeenth-century gesture—that the Delaware language "is an oriental language and comes closest to the Hebrew." Throughout the early modern period, scholars, theologians, and mystics had speculated on the status of Hebrew as the original tongue spoken in Eden. In addition, Gambold, in the preface to the *London Hymnal*, had mysteriously declared that German had preserved a "good deal of the old Oriental Genius." For both Gam-bold and Zeisberger, the comparative linguistic search for common roots is trumped by a pseudomystical assumption that certain languages—possibly German or Delaware—retained hidden spiritual links between human lan-guage and the divine logos. Anticipating Heckewelder's later move to turn Delaware into the *Ursprache* of North America, Zeisberger, in his *History of the North American Indians,* found that, notwithstanding geographical differences, "the speech of each of these peoples is but a dialect of one and the same language."[18]

Study of the deep grammatical structures of the Delaware language thus provided access to the people's internal and spiritual composition—and

18. Zeisberger, "Grammaticalischer Aufsatz," MS Am 767 (6), 1, Houghton Library, Harvard Uni-versity: ". . . es ist eine Orientalische Sprache u. kommt der Hebräischen am nächsten"; Archer Butler Hulbert and William Nathaniel Schwarze, eds., *David Zeisberger's History of the Northern American Indians* (Columbus, Ohio, 1910), 141; [John Gambold], "Preface," *A Collection of Hymns of the Chil-dren of God in All Ages, from the Beginning till Now; in Two Parts; Designed Chiefly for the Use of the Congregations in Union with the Brethren's Church* (London, 1754). For the best account of the cre-ation and ultimate breakdown of a cultural and communal middle ground among English, Germans, and native Americans—including Delaware and Iroquois peoples—on the Pennsylvania and Ohio frontier, see Merritt, *At the Crossroads.*

vice versa. Someone, like Zeisberger, who understood the Indians' mind and soul would also gain the fullest comprehension of their complex linguistic system. In the short preface to Zeisberger's "Grammaticalischer Aufsatz," he declares epigrammatically that "whoever wants to speak Indian, first has to learn how to think Indian." Reflecting Comenius's (and before him Augustine's) concept of thought as "internalized action," Zeisberger laid the focus of his grammar on verbs:

> The most important part of learning a language in order to express oneself in orally are the verbs, especially the personal forms, or, as I call it, to familiarize oneself with the *modum personale*. This provides insight and understanding into the language, and if one has only made a beginning and learned a few of those verbs, one can easily inflect the others. It would be too cumbersome and would only confound the mind to provide rules. It is better to learn this in conversation with the Indians *than from a book;* thus, one also learns the pronunciation, which one cannot learn from a book.

What Zeisberger means by the *modum personale* is at length demonstrated throughout most of his grammar. Peculiar to Delaware, the combination of the personal verb form ("ich sage" / "I tell") with an indirect object ("ich sage dir" / "I tell you") is expressed in a single word. The grammatical complexity of single words expressing—simultaneously—the agent, the action, and the recipient confounded Zeisberger's attempt to regularize the language in a grammatical system. Especially for speakers of the English language—which has successively lost most of its inflections and thus requires greater circumlocution to express grammatical relationships—this feature of the Delaware language might seem like an obstacle for effective communication.[19]

In Zeisberger's Neoplatonist linguistics, however, the opposite is the case. In his *History*, Zeisberger wrote: "[The Indians] are able to express themselves with great clearness and precision, and so concisely that much circumlocution is required to convey the full meaning of their expressions in an European language." Precision, in a naturalist, Neoplatonist understanding of language, rests on the direct, unmediated relationship between word and referent. The more words it takes, therefore, to refer to an object or express a specific idea, the more imprecise a language becomes. Zeis-

---

19. Zeisberger, "Grammaticalischer Aufsatz," MS Am 767 (6), 1, 14, Houghton Library, Harvard University.

berger's emphasis on the precise or exact words the Delaware language uses to express specific natural objects or their properties harked back to the biblical act of naming:

They, in many cases, have several names for one and the same thing under different circumstances. They have ten different names for a bear, according to its age and sex. They have one word for fishing with a rod, another for fishing with a net, another for fishing with a spear or harpoon. Such words do not in the least resemble one another.

Apparently, Delaware words retained a closer connection to their natural referents. For Zeisberger, communication among the Indians was thus less prone to empty rhetoric, conforming to a general radical Protestant rejection of learned, doctrinal disputes and to their suspicions toward higher education. He said about the relationship between language and manners:

Indians usually treat one another with kindness and civility and in their bearing toward one another are modest. They are communicative but thoughtful. Of empty compliments they know nothing. . . . Greetings are expressed in all sincerity. If sentiments do not correspond to words or forms, the latter are dispensed with.

Here, then, may be the ultimate reason for Zeisberger's fascination and life-long study of Indian languages. He had found a language that seemed less prone to the obfuscation of the links between words and spiritual ideas than any European language. Could Babel be undone through an intense occupation with Indian languages? Ironically, this idealized perception clashed with Zeisberger's impression that those languages were simultaneously lacking in spiritual knowledge: "In spiritual things, of which they are totally ignorant, there was utter lack of expressions. But since the gospel has been preached among them, their language has gained much in this respect." The key figure in this dilemma became the missionary-translator. Having a true appreciation of the Indian languages, he could mend their deficit in spiritual knowledge by introducing the principles of the Christian faith.[20]

Zeisberger's longtime co-worker and literary executor John Hecke-welder made this spiritual and even eschatological significance of the study of Indian languages more explicit. In his *History, Manners, and Customs of the Indian Nations*, Heckewelder not only valorized Indian languages—particularly the Delaware or Lenni Lenape—but he also justified the Mora-

20. Hulbert and Schwarze, eds., *Zeisberger's History*, 115, 143, 144.

vian project of trying to learn and convert Indian peoples in their respective languages. For this purpose, Heckewelder first established Delaware—the most important tongue for Zeisberger, himself, and other Moravian missionaries—as the "universal language" of North America: "There can be no doubt, therefore, that this universal language, so much admired and so generally spoken by the Indian nations, is that of the Lenni Lenape, and is improperly named the Chippeway by Carver, and the Algonquin by La Hontan." Along with the idea of Lenni Lenape as the Ursprache of North America came aesthetic and spiritual validation. Going beyond Zeisberger, Heckewelder called Delaware a "beautiful language."[21]

Sensing that beauty did not suffice to hold Delaware up against the languages of European civilization, Heckewelder based his strongest argument on the notion of effability. He countered Western prejudices against Indian languages by claiming and trying to prove that they were in fact capable of expressing any complex or spiritually elevated thought. First, he deflated the common assumption that Indians used signs and motions so frequently because they had to make up for a lack of words in their language. According to Heckewelder, people listening to speakers of a foreign language they do not understand usually pay more attention to gestures than words and thus overestimate the role of the former. More important, the Indians who had become multilingual within the Moravian mission system provided the greatest proof for the effability of Indian languages:

> I have frequently questioned Indians who had been educated at our schools, and could understand, read, write, and speak both English and German, whether they could express their ideas better in either of those languages than in their own, and they have always and uniformly answered that they could express themselves with far the greatest ease in their own Indian, and that they never were at a loss for words or phrases in which to clothe every idea that occurred to them, without being in any case obliged to gesticulate or make motions with their hands or otherwise. From the knowledge which I have acquired of their language, I have reason to be satisfied that it is so.

Following Augustine's distinction between inner and outer speech, Heckewelder assumed a priori that Indians hold the same wealth of spiritual notions as Europeans. He argued that the Indian language was equally capable of expressing those ideas. Heckewelder's epistemological frame-

21. Heckewelder, *History*, 124.

work was replete with references to translingual or multilingual abilities. The knowledge of a shared understanding of spiritual things and a shared ability to express those things in either language could only emerge through the testimony of bilingual or multilingual individuals. Linguistic facility, on both sides, had advanced so far that individuals could judge for themselves which language served them better in expressing spiritual notions. Whereas Zinzendorf still found this ability lodged firmly within the community (contributing to a unified Natursprache), Heckewelder saw individuals capable of such judgment.[22]

Ultimately, the effability of both Indian and European languages—combined with the skill of self-conscious reflection on the ties between actual and spiritual language—broke down any remaining barriers, linguistic or spiritual, between the different constituencies of the Moravian faith. Heckewelder's final verdict on the compatibility of European and Indian minds as well as languages, therefore, rang in the end of the confusio linguarum:

It is true, that ideas are not always expressed in those languages in the same words, or under the same grammatical forms as in our own; where we [they?] would use one part of speech, we are obliged to employ another, and one single word with them will not seldom serve a purpose for which we would have to employ several; but still, *the ideas are communicated, and pass with clearness and precision from mind to mind.*

For Heckewelder, linguistic multiplicity no longer presented an obstacle to spiritual unity. In an ultimate feat of communication, the Moravian missionaries and their Indian converts speak from "mind to mind" in a spiritualized, supralinguistic moment of harmony. Heckewelder's treatise came full circle to the Neoplatonist philosophers of the seventeenth century in defining the Lenni Lenape language as a type of Ursprache or original tongue of Eastern North America. Heckewelder lionized the Delaware language in order to turn the Moravian missionaries' multilingualism and linguistic study into a soteriological milestone in the struggle against the spiritual confusion wrought at Babel.[23]

As his former missionary apprentice, Heckewelder also functioned as Zeisberger's executor. Zeisberger's "Last Will and Testament" emphatically explained the larger value of his translations and linguistic work as a

22. Ibid., 128–129.
23. Ibid., 129–130 (emphasis added).

great treasure reminiscent of Christian Rosenkreuz's mysterious gift and the Rosicrucian Society's secretive effort of spreading his knowledge to deserving individuals:

And I will, that my said Executor, shall carefully put up into a close Box or Trunk, all Manuscripts and Papers, containing my Labours of Translations into the Delaware Language, and shall not lend out nor dispose of any part thereof otherwise than by the direction of the President, or Directors of the Heathen Society, unto whom my said Executor shall make known the contents of a Conversation we had on this Subject, whereby the principle Object was, that nothing belonging to the same be lost—nor put into any hands incapable of making the proper Use of, and compleating the same.

Zeisberger feared that the improper use of his translations could waste the treasure he had accumulated. Although the details of Zeisberger's conversation with his executor remain unknown, comments by Heckewelder himself as well as other Moravian missionaries in the field using Zeisberger's translations revealed the nature of this treasure. As detailed in the preface, Heckewelder and other Moravian missionaries credited Zeisberger with nothing less than the creation of a spiritual language.[24]

Zeisberger's and Heckewelder's ideal of spiritual communication between European and Indian peoples in North America, of course, was no less utopian than Comenius's proposal for a universal language or *Panglottia* following the turmoil of the Thirty Years' War. Heckewelder's vindication of native American languages and cultures—specifically the Delaware—came at a moment when colonial and postcolonial politics, land grabbing, and racial bias silenced and expelled native people and native voices. Able to accomplish little of practical consequence, Heckewelder nevertheless wanted to set the historical record straight:

If I should . . . be thought to have shewn some partiality for the Delawares and their connexions, with respect to the affairs between them and the Six Nations, I have only to reply, that we have been attentive to all the Six Nations told us of these people, until we got possession of their whole country; and now, having what we wanted, we ought not to turn them off with this *story on their backs,* but rather, out of

24. David Zeisberger, "Last Will and Testament. July 8, 1805," box 227, folder 18, Moravian Archives, Bethlehem.

gratitude and compassion, *give them also a hearing,* and acquit them honourably, if we find them deserving of it.

Writing in 1819, Heckewelder became involved in a contest about the historical representation of the colonial and Revolutionary past in the public discourse of the new nation. At this critical juncture, which he compared metaphorically to a public hearing or trial, Heckewelder pled for an equitable treatment of the Delawares' story—their political and economic dispossession already being a fait accompli. Casting himself in the role of attorney, he assigned his readers the responsibility of jury. His role in this trial was to uncover the distortion of evidence performed by previous witnesses in the case who had themselves been victims of linguistic deception: "Ignorant of the language, or being but superficially acquainted with it, they have relied on ignorant or careless interpreters, by whom they have been most frequently led astray; in what manner, this little work will abundantly shew." Heckewelder here described the true curse of Babel: it is not the existence of linguistic multiplicity; rather, it is the formation of prejudices based on misinformation and deception. The heritage of the Moravian missions was a method of gaining access to the innermost workings—the spiritual language—of another people in spite of linguistic differences.[25]

Heckewelder also sensed that in the new nation the occupation with the confusio linguarum changed from the problem of spiritual dispersion to a political and cultural backlash against linguistic multiplicity. Anticipated by Benjamin Franklin's injunction against English-German bilingualism in colonial Pennsylvania, the cultural and linguistic ideology of the early Republic conflated national unity with English monolingualism. In the postcolonial moment of early-nineteenth-century America, European languages other than English went down a path of political and cultural obsolescence similar to that of native American tongues. Yet Heckewelder's plea for the Delaware language once again holds the key to a door still offering a way out of Babel. The recurring tragedy of human conflict, dispersion, and struggle for domination, Heckewelder says, can be disrupted if we stop to give an equal and fair hearing to all peoples and listen to the "story on their backs." The common idiom of humanity is the story of human suffering.

25. Heckewelder, *History,* xvii, xviii.

Index

89–91; and accounts of Delaware Indians, 104–116; and Ockanickon's "dying words," 116–126; and friendship, 159–180; and Quaker-German Protestant cooperation, 286–299

Lloyd, Thomas: and Keithian controversy, 130–132; and friendship with Francis Daniel Pastorius, 143, 146, 160, 163–169; and his daughters' correspondence with Pastorius, 163, 169–175

London Hymnal. See Gambold, John

Lyra Davidica, 216–217

Manuscript exchange: and spiritual community, 11–12, 148, 159–162, 166, 173–174, 182–192, 240–246, 271, 286–293; and promotional literature, 66–67, 74, 89, 91; and multilingualism, 144–145, 147–148; and hymnody, 210–218; and Fraktur writing, 224–228, 265

Marshall, Christopher, 195, 201

Martyrdom, 12; and Ephrata, 221; spiritual, 224; and Martyrs' Mirror, 245, 253–255, 257–269; and Anabaptists, 245, 254–255; and Benjamin Franklin's Association, 250; and translation, 254–255, 258–263; and martyrologies, 255–258; and Quaker-German Protestant cooperation, 280–281, 293–298

Martyrs' Mirror, 20, 253; translation of, 197, 224, 245–246, 254, 256–257; and Anabaptist theology of martyrdom, 254–255; and early martyr books, 255–256; and Pennsylvania Mennonites, 257–259; and Peter Miller, 259; and Ephrata, 259–260; production of, 260; and suffering, 260–261; and inspection of the translation, 261–265; and Fraktur writing, 265; and Revolutionary War, 265–269

Mennonites: and German peace sects, 12; and William Penn, 67, 108; and Mar-

tyrs' Mirror, 245, 253, 257–269; and pacifism, 245–246, 272, 288, 296; and Christoph Saur, 249; and war, 252, 270; and translation, 254, 256–257; and martyrdom, 254–256; and Quaker cooperation, 273–285, 299

Miller, Henry (Heinrich), 295–296

Miller, Peter, 56, 193; and singing at Ephrata, 195–202, 222, 226, 298; and Martyrs' Mirror, 259–265

Model, Georg Leonhard, 112–115

Modum personale, 318

Moravians: and translation, 1–6; and German immigration, 12; and communication networks, 13; and Jan Amos Comenius, 23, 52; and Count Zinzendorf's language theory, 50–54, 228–230; and Delaware Indian spirituality, 110–111, 288; and global church, 193, 207; and hymnody, 196, 200–201, 205, 217, 230; and London Hymnal, 230–236; and polyglot singing, 236–241, 243; and pacifism, 245, 280; and Quakers, 291, 293, 299; and native American linguistics, 301–323. See also Heckewelder, John; Zeisberger, David; Zinzendorf, Count Nicholas Ludwig von

Multilingualism: and translation, 8–9, 208; and singing, 11, 193, 201, 209–215, 230, 236–241, 243, 303; and Francis Daniel Pastorius's poetics, 12, 56–57, 59, 140, 144–157, 159; and Rosicrucian Manifestos, 24–25; and promotion of Pennsylvania, 27, 63, 89; and spiritual language, 41; and Moravians, 53–54, 230, 236–241, 304, 307–308, 315, 320–321; and community in Pennsylvania, 128–130, 197, 206; and Peter Miller, 200; and Johannes Kelpius, 201, 208, 215, 220

Music. See Hymnody

Watts, Isaac, 232–233
Webb, Elizabeth, 291–292
Witt, Christopher, 56; and Johannes Kelpius, 201, 208; as translator, 210–214; and *Kurtzer Begriff,* 296
Woolman, John, 270, 272, 281, 288

Zachary, Lloyd, 181–182, 185
Zeisberger, David: and spiritual language, 1; as translator, 1; and John Heckewelder, 1, 193; hymn translations by, 4–6, 205, 236; and Neoplatonist language theory, 56; and Johannes Papunhank, 288; and native American missions, 301; and study of Indian languages, 303–308, 310–311; life of,

310; *Collection of Hymns,* 311–314; and Indian vocabularies, 314–316; and Delaware grammar, 317–318; and *modum personale,* 318; *History of the North American Indians,* 318–319; last will and testament of, 321–322
Ziegler, Andrew, 275
Zimmermann, Johann Jakob, 100, 206
Zinzendorf, Count Nikolaus Ludwig von: and Neoplatonism, 50; childhood of, 51; influences on, 51–52; and Renewed Unitas Fratrum, 52; and theory of language and community, 52–55, 228–230, 239, 310, 312; and mysticism, 201; and hymnody, 217, 236–238, 303; and mission theology, 305